EXETER MEDIEVAL ENGLISH TEXTS AND STUDIES
General Editors: Marion Glassc—

MIDDLE ENGLISH VERSE ROMANCES

EDITED BY DONALD B. SANDS

UNIVERSITY OF EXETER

First Published by Holt, Rinehart and Winston, Inc., 1966

This edition, University of Exeter, 1986

© S.M. Sands & E.S. Ryll, 1986

ACKNOWLEDGMENT is gratefully made for permissions granted by the following publishers and individuals for the use of their materials: to Professors Robert W. Ackerman and Auvo Kurvinen for permission to use their respective texts of *Sir Gawain and the Carl of Carlisle*; to the Early English Text Society, Oxford, England, for use of the text of G. H. McKnight's *Floris and Blauncheflur*; to the English Department of Smith College, Northampton, Mass., for the text of Laura Sumner's *The Wedding of Sir Gawain and Dame Ragnell* and the text of Margaret Wattie's *Lai le Freine*; to Ginn and Company, Boston, for William Edward Mead's *The Squyr of Lowe Degre*; and for use of the texts of *King Horn, Havelok, Athelson, Gamelyn, Sir Orfeo, Sir Launfal,* and *The Tournament of Tottenham* to Walter Hoyte French and Charles Brockway Hale, editors, *Middle English Metrical Romances* (© 1930). Reprinted by permission of Prentice-Hall, Inc., Englewood Cliffs, New Jersey.

ISBN 0 85989 228 X

Printed in Great Britain by Short Run Press Ltd., Exeter

Contents

Preface

E NCOMPASSED here are twelve Middle English metrical romances, all of them, in their own way, very genuine and delightful. In recent years they have suffered neglect. To be sure, all have at one time or another been given individual editions, but these have usually been diplomatic editions intended to establish texts and provide material for philological investigation; few have attempted to present the romances as examples of imaginative literature. The result has generally been that they hindered Middle English metrical romances from being read as literature. For the most part, indeed, the metrical romances seem to be read very little, if at all. They are overshadowed by Chaucer, Langland, and the Pearl Poet and are perhaps penalized because they are not the supreme products of an age. But the neglect to which they have been subjected is unjust. They are first attempts at secular fiction and hence deserve a place in literary history. They were intended originally to entertain and they can entertain today.

The present collection is not inclusive. Out of the extant metrical romances in Middle English far less than a quarter are represented. The very low-grade pieces—and there are a few—were not considered nor were those verging on the chronicle or the pious legend. With some reluctance, very long romances of good quality were omitted simply because, if included, they would have had to be presented in fragmentary form, and snippets always leave a reader with a feeling of being cheated. Pieces by Chaucer were excluded because they are available in editions for both the scholar and the intelligent nonspecialist, pieces in Middle Scots because they belong to a relatively late and different literature, and romance of profound difficulty like *Sir Gawain and the Green Knight* because they would overtax editorial technique.

Yet sufficient romances are here, competent, certainly, to represent the distinctive phases of the genre in Middle English. There are four which belong to the "Matter of England," three fall into the category Breton *lai*, two present a composite of sentiment and chivalry, and three show the late tendency toward grotesquerie and burlesque. In part, the collection gives an idea of what the Middle English audience wanted in its fiction. In part, it also provides insight into secular taste largely unburdened by the religiosity of the time, relatively free of the pretenses of courtly love, and uncommitted to a show of historical accuracy. But most of all, here, unabashed and naïve, is the medieval delight in storytelling, its *Lust zu fabulieren*, which is the essence of imaginative literature regardless of whatever else it may say along the way about the church, the subconscious, and society.

The texts themselves have been subject to editorial procedures which allow almost anyone to read them with reasonable ease. Graphemically, they have been modernized; their spelling has been regularized. The treatment hopefully may not offend the specialist even though it is designed primarily for the literary reader. To be sure, such treatment has been tried out on Middle English texts only recently, but it is by no means novel to Medieval Latin, Old Icelandic, and Middle High German. Graphemic and mechanical modernization in no way dilute the literary and linguistic integrity of a Middle English text. Dialect criteria remain; prosodic cruces survive untouched. In short, if these modernized pages do not look like diplomatically edited ones, the fact does not indicate at all that they are less genuine. But a few details may be welcome.

First of all, each text is capitalized and punctuated according to modern practice. Next, each text is typographically modern. No type faces not current today are used; hence, the yogh (ȝ) and the thorn (þ) and edh (ð) are changed to g/gh and th. Logograms and abbreviations are rendered into Middle English without note being taken of them, although the few textual emendations made are usually signaled by note. Further, each text, in so far as possible, has been orthographically regularized. Within a hundred lines of a particular text it is possible to find the word for "night" spelled *niȝt/niȝht/niȝght*, all of which would be pronounced [nɪçt] and all of which would here be given the form nearest to Chaucer's: *night*. Instances arise, however, where complete regularization is impossible—for example, those where meter would suffer if variants were reduced to a single form. It would be ideal, of course, if all texts could be rendered into a standard Middle English *koiné*—say, Chaucer's "London English" of 1375 to 1400; but *Horn* and *Havelok* are just too archaic to be re-formed according to the norms of Chaucer's language; a piece in Western or Northern dialect would lose some of its individuality if "Londonized."

Editorial apparatus is designed to give a quality of immediacy to textual elucidation. The twelve romances are no more difficult than the *Canterbury Tales*. In most cases they are easier since their creators possessed neither the intellect nor the erudition of Chaucer. In their present form their appearance is no stranger than that of a long poem by Byron. Inevitably, however, difficulties arise. If a single word needs clarification, a modern synonym is provided in the outside margin. If a whole line is difficult, a translation of it is given in footnote position. Translations are not signaled by superscript numbers. Presumably, a reader stopped by a difficult line will instinctively look below for clarification. There are only a few exigitical asides. I have assumed it sensible to comment occasionally on such items as place and personal names, but footnote remarks on feudal convention and folklore are kept to a minimum.

The prose introductions discuss the individuality of a piece, its sources and tradition, and finally its language and prosody. Their purpose is, first, to summarize relevant facts and, second, to give the reader an idea of what to expect so that he will neither be disappointed nor puzzled by what he actually reads. Larger literary histories do not do a particularly good job on the romance. Arthurian pieces from Spencer to Tennyson tend to obscure the nature of the metrical romance of Middle English times. It is true that some vagueness often exists as to what *Horn, Havelok,* and *Launfal* really are and the introductions may help to bring their general nature into focus. The references at the end of each introduction indicate where the mass of bibliographic material may be found for a given romance. They lead to standard lists—to Wells, the *Cambridge Bibliography,* and Brown and Robbins—and do not usually give individual titles. Occasionally, however, full titles of articles and critical editions do appear, but I have had to assume that an interested reader will turn first to standard lists for older titles and then to the annual bibliographic supplements of the *MLA* for more recent ones.

The initial general Introduction which describes the genre (it does not—directly, at least—evaluate it) may suffer from overcondensation, but even so it will probably be useful to someone not well acquainted with Middle English. To obviate some language difficulties, I have appended to the end of the Introduction a few comments on pronunciation and prosody. The terminal Glossary lists Middle English words of high frequency—those in particular, that look like Modern English but differ markedly in meaning and those that have no apparent Modern English counterparts at all.

Many people—in particular, my wife—have been helpful and encouraging during the process of preparing the twelve texts. I am grateful to my colleagues at Boston College, Edward L. Hirsh, Maurice J. Quinlan, John L. Mahoney, and Charles L. Regan. Their comments were always honest and useful and I am indebted to their patience and good sense.

Ann Arbor, Michigan   *D.B.S.*
January, 1966

Introduction

E STIMATES as to the number of surviving Middle English romances vary—roughly from forty to sixty—and the uncertainty which is responsible for the variation is not surprising. No really pat and satisfying delimitation of the genre can be made. For example, we could say, and come fairly near the mark, that the romance appeared in England after the Conquest and fell into disrepute toward the end of the fifteenth century. But prior to Senlac there was translated into Old English the romance *Appolonious of Tyre* and after the Renaissance had gotten under way in England a long poem—*The Fairy Queen*—was written which satisfies certain concepts of the medieval romance better than does just about any extant romance in Middle English. Perhaps it is sensible to begin in such a manner, for what follows presupposes the idea that, however perceptive an observation may be, there is always lurking behind it, like an unexorcised ghost, the inevitable and disconcerting exception.

Even if we restrict the romance to the Middle English period, we can look in vain for a truly representative piece, for such does not really exist. There is great variety and no one romance is like the next even in its own particular group. Very generally, one can say that the Middle English romance is usually metrical, and the most favored prosodic convention is the iambic tetrameter couplet. The narrative concerns a series of incidents often very loosely strung together—and even with this said one has probably said too much. The Breton *lais* contain excellent plots and *Havelock*, the longest romance in this collection, has a well-patterned plot where hero and heroine start from afar, cross paths, join courses, and lead us to an altogether satisfactory conclusion. Subject matter and personae may be evenly aristocratic, but whether the audience itself was such is very much open to question. Not lords, knights, and franklins, but coopers, brewers, and tavern keepers heard Havelock shout defiance at the false regent Godard. The purpose of the romance was to entertain despite a minstrel's occasional assertion that moral edification is his intent. So far the definition of the genre lacks concision and starting off in another direction may be helpful.

1

It is usual to segment the great corpus of surviving romances of the medieval period into *matters*. The term indicates a general body of narrative material usually centered about legendary or quasi-historical figures associated with a geographical area. Jehan Bodel, a thirteenth-century French poet in his *Chanson des Saisnes*, says that there are three basic "matters" and modern literary historians generally use his classification.

There is, first in order of antiquity, the "Matter of Rome the Great." Here one would naturally think of Homer in Latin, of medieval versions and retellings of the *Aeneid*. Many episodes of the Trojan story were embellished and popularized in England. There is, to be sure, Caxton's *Eneydos*, which can be accounted as very late Middle English, but no real translation or adaptation of Virgil into English until Douglas's, which was completed about 1512 and printed in 1553. There is in Middle English *The Geste Historial of the Destruction of Troy*, adapted from Guido delle Colonne, and Lydgate's enormous *Troy Book*, also adapted from Guido's Latin prose. The story of ancient Thebes, taken in medieval times chiefly from the *Thebiad* of Statius, is represented by Lydgate's *Siege of Thebes* and less directly by Chaucer's tale of Palamon and Arcite told by the Knight in the *Canterbury Tales*. Alexander the Great also became medieval romance material and Middle English possesses several romances concerning him, although Alexander by the thirteenth century became more of a legendary than a strictly historical figure.

The "Matter of France," which here consists of pedestrian translations into Middle English of better French romances, encompasses the Carolingian stories, those connected either explicitly or tenuously with Charlemagne. Middle English does know a fragmentary *Song of Roland*, a late fourteenth-century translation of the great French *Chanson de Roland*. Other romances in Middle English concerning Charlemagne do not really rise above the quality of the English *Roland*. There is *The Sowdone of Babylone* (which tells of a Saracen attack on Rome thwarted by Charles and his paladins), a *Sir Firumbras* (which duplicates roughly the latter half of *The Sowdone*), and Caxton's prose *Charles the Grete* (which sketches the whole legendary life of Charlemagne). The peripheral heroes of Charlemagne's court appear in *Roland and Vernagu*, *The Sege of Melayne*, *Otuel*, and *Duke Rowlande and Sir Ottuell of Spayne*—all of which usually remain mere titles in literary histories since their literary qualities are not arresting. One startlingly well-done romance concerning Charlemagne does exist in Middle Scots, *The Taill of Rauf Coilyear*, probably composed in the last quarter of the fifteenth century and printed in 1572. It seems to be an original poem; no French original exists. Rauf, the hero, a purveyor of charcoal, puts Charlemagne up for a night and treats him as an equal; later in court, Rauf recognizes his guest and, although abashed by the magnificence of court, retains his manly dignity and independence.

Bodel's "Matter of Britain" covers the Arthurian material, by far the most widespread and pervasive of romance categories. Here, as with the "Matter of France," there is the paradox that the figure who gives the material its inception has in most of the romances slipped into second place. Both Arthur and Charlemagne have been called "masters of ceremony," their royal dignity in late pieces often being completely absent, their reputation sunk to that of cuckold, dotard, or ineffectual oaf. Perhaps only one Middle English romance deals exclusively with Arthur; it is a strange piece, inserted in a Latin chronicle and composed perhaps in the mid-fifteenth century. In six hundred odd lines it does something which no other independent Middle English poem does: it gives us a summary of what a medieval Englishman would normally have been aware of about the life of Arthur—namely, his miraculous birth, his coronation, his establishment of the Round Table, his invasions of France, Rome, and other areas, his betrayal by Modred, and his death after a final great battle. The poem (usually called the Marquis of Bath's "Arthur") may have served as a pedagogic device to make young people aware of a legendary figure. If any other Middle English romance can be said to concentrate on Arthur, it is the alliterative *Morte Arthure*, a Northern poem of great competence written before 1400, which tells primarily of Modred's treason and Arthur's death, and does so more in the manner of the factual chronicler than in that of the usual romance writer.

It was, however, with Arthur's knights—Gawain, in particular, and to a lesser degree with Lancelot, Perceval, and Tristram—that Middle English romancers were concerned. Gawain is the hero of the finest of all English romances, *Sir Gawain and the Green Knight,* usually ascribed to the northwest Midland poet who wrote the *Pearl,* a contemporary of Chaucer and a master craftsman. Gawain, in fact, seems to have been the most popular of Arthur's knights in medieval England; he is the hero of more independent romances than any other Arthurian figure. Even though in Tennyson he is a moral reprobate, he was to Middle English audiences the very paragon of courtesy. (Only in Malory and in the stanzaic romance *Le Morte d'Arthur*—the latter dealing with the love of Lancelot and Guinevere and the destruction it ultimately causes—does Gawain show both facets of his late literary personality, duplicity and chivalry.) Two romances printed in this collection, *Sir Gawain and the Carl of Carlyle* and *The Wedding of Sir Gawain and Dame Ragnell,* are relatively late in Middle English literature; but both, despite their buffoonery, allow Gawain his proper dignity. Lancelot, who ultimately displaces Gawain in both French and English literature in popularity, is represented in medieval English romance only by a Lowland Scottish *Lancelot of the Laik,* Perceval only in a late fourteenth-century *Sir Percyvelle of Galles,* and Tristram only in a Northern poem *Sir Tristrem,* written in the early fourteenth century and of little literary appeal.

Bodel's classification, popular though it still may be, leaves many romances quite outside its categories. Modern literary historians add at least four—and even these do not quite suffice. The most necessary addition in some ways is that of the "Matter of Breton," the category covering the Breton *lais*. Literary excellence and not the number of romances involved creates the category. The problem of what poems can be admitted into the "Matter of Breton" and what poems may not is delicate. An Anglo-Norman woman Marie de France in the mid-twelfth century wrote fifteen narrative poems adapted reputedly from Celtic originals once current in Brittany. None of the Celtic originals survive, but literary historians generally accept the derivation. Two Middle English versions of Marie's *lais* written in Anglo-Norman are contained in this collection, *Lai le Fresne* and *Sir Launfal*. Perhaps Marie started a literary fiction; Middle English poets with excellent tales to tell could attribute their works to ancient Celtic tales of Breton or Brittany. Indirectly and, it may be, unconsciously, Chaucer pays tribute to Marie by making two of the finest narratives in his *Canterbury Tales* appear, by inference at least, as Breton *lais*. They are "The Wife of Bath's Tale" (here present in its analogue *The Wedding of Sir Gawain and Dame Ragnell*) and "The Franklin's Tale."

An additional category which Bodel does not mention is of great importance to English literature—the "Matter of England," the name associated with such romances as *King Horn, Havelok the Dane, Athelston,* and *Gamelyn*, romances which treat with native material. Three other pieces, each much longer than any of the four just named, are sometimes added to the list. One is *William of Palerne*, which treats of a prince of Spain who has been turned into a werewolf by a wicked stepmother. The werewolf befriends the son of the King of Apulia. The fact that a werewolf figures prominently in the tale has somehow caused the romance to be classed among the English pieces, werewolves being presumably Germanic in origin. Another romance, much different in theme and content from the four English romances present in this collection, is *Sir Bevis of Hampton*. Here we find a wife who plots the murder of her husband Guy, Earl of Southampton, and who thereafter marries the man who commits the murder. Her son Bevis is sold into slavery and reaches the court of King Hermin of Armenia, where he performs deeds of bravery and ultimately marries a princess. The piece is formless, although it does end with the wicked stepfather getting his just deserts. *Bevis* is better known than it might be if its plot did not bear certain resemblance to the plot of *Hamlet* and if Drayton had not bothered to recount the tale in his *Poly-Olbion*. The third romance sometimes grouped here is the enormously popular *Guy of Warwick*: it is primarily English in its title, the bulk of its ten thousand odd lines dealing with conventional deeds of knight errantry all over the Christian and Saracen world.

But the four genuinely English romances that begin the collection are unified by several features. They are, unfortunately, all that exist of the native poems and one might wish them to be somewhat better—at least as good, for example, as the *Chanson de Roland* or the *Nibelungenlied*. Paradoxically, they gain much by being the products of a language and people lacking status; at least this is true of *Horn* and *Havelock*, which were composed at a time when English and the English people were socially and culturally subservient to a Norman French aristocracy. Neither of the two romances smacks of artistic affectation. They are awkward in language, forthright in their emotion, winningly naïve in characterization. Neither is marked by conventions of courtly love; neither presents jousts or tourneys; neither appears to place social precedence over human worth. *Gamelyn* displays similar features plus a total lack of interest in aristocratic convention. It is a tale of rough farm life and of rough-mannered men quarreling over an inheritance. *Athelston*, despite its faults and despite its concern with political power, impresses us today with its harsh honesty, its brutal meting out of just retribution. Perhaps only *Horn* stands a little outside the tight group of four. It does possess a balladlike quality and gropes for chivalric atmosphere. Yet *Horn* is as naïvely forthright in its human values as *Gamelyn* and as unaffectedly sincere in its emotions of loyalty and friendship as *Athelston* and *Havelok*.

Any categorization has to have its catch-all. Middle English romance varies in such a label from one literary history to the next. "Miscellaneous" is the weakest and probably the most stable designation; "Composite Romances" is fairly accurate; and "Romances of Chivalry and Sentiment," restrictive though it is, holds up remarkably well. At any event, those romances that do not cluster about the matters familiar to Bodel and do not generally localize themselves in theme or tradition belong here. *The Squire of Low Degree*, for example, is supposed to take place in Hungary, but its creator apparently knew nothing at all about Hungarian manners and customs; his "Hungary" could just as well have been Armenia or Damascus or Egypt. *Floris and Blancheflour* is localized somewhere in the Saracen world, despite its Christian sympathies. One wonders, however, just how much the poet knew or cared about the North African coast and the ancient cities of the Fertile Crescent. As in *The Squire*, the *mise en scène* of *Floris*, however, suggests one feature of these romances that cannot quite fit into any formal category: a goodly number of them derive by devious and now obscure means from Arabic tales. No one has really assessed the debt western European narrative art of the medieval period owes to the genius of the Arabic world, but in many romances its influence must be great, although so distant that perhaps no one now will ever be able to indicate its nature exactly and accurately.

Almost any genre which has run a course of maturing and fruition will in its decline possess pieces either of perverse virtuosity or grotesque distortion. Two selections here, *The Wedding of Sir Gawain and Dame*

Ragnell and *Sir Gawain and the Carl of Carlyle*, are romances in the usual sense, perhaps, but something is lost and something added. The façade of chivalry and knighthood may be present in both, but the focus of the narrative is on other things. In one, the slightly indecorous problem of what women desire most is treated with a gross vigor quite foreign to the chivalric tone of the early romances. In the other, the chivalric "courtesy" of Sir Gawain is tested, not by feats of arms or by courtly conduct, but by ludicrous trials, the final one being Gawain's submission to his host's request to sleep with the host's wife. A few other romances display similar traits, among them *The Awntyrs of Arthure at the Terne Watheleyne*, *The Jeaste of Syr Gawayne*, and *The Turk and Sir Gawaine*. Grotesque distortion of the earlier romance is seen in *The Tournament of Tottenham*, but this cannot be classed as an antiromance like Chaucer's "Tale of Sir Thopas" in the *Canterbury Tales*, which pillories forthrightly a defunct and effete literary mode. *The Tournament*, like some pieces in early Scottish and German literature, is more likely social satire than burlesque of a literary genre. With it the form and matter of romance are secondary to a desire to poke fun at social pretensions.

Middle English romance possesses, as noted previously, no homogeneous essence which would make possible a brief and valid description of the genre. A similar statement can be made about its style: all Middle English romances show to a greater or lesser degree *en bloc* descriptive techniques; tedious catalogues of trees, foods, clothes, weapons; frequent rhyme tags and expletive phrases; occasional enthusiastic obtrusion of the minstrel; numerous asseverations and elaborate curses. But all these are also common to other medieval genres—the saint's life, the chronicle, the pious legend, the versified exemplum. A rather curious way to show up the Middle English romance is to contrast it with the epic, classic and medieval. Admittedly, a definition of the epic is no easier than a definition of the romance and, it must be conceded, that any comparison between them lets the romance off as a very poor thing indeed.

The epic hero—Aeneas, Ulysses, Beowulf, Roland—can be a national or racial hero, one possessing a certain ethnic significance; the romance hero as often as not reflects no real racial or ethnic pride. Epic society has its classes, but no great rift exists between the aristocrat and the serf. Ulysses talks with his swine herd; Gawain would probably not even notice him. Romance, though often dealing in slaughter, is not tragic, as is the epic, where battle and death are recognized as both the highest test of human character and as the greatest human evil. Great geographic areas are often traversed by the romance hero, but his territories tend to be fabulous, ill-defined, and stagy. It is usually quite the opposite with the epic hero: Ulysses' adventures are unthinkable without a knowledge of the islands of the Aegean; the Burgundians of the *Nibelungenlied* take their grim journey up a real Rhine valley, through a real Austria, and down into a real Hungarian plain; Beowulf's youthful exploits in northern Denmark and final heroism in southern Sweden give us indirectly and accurately about the first reliable geographic data concerning the Scandinavian world. One final feature of the romance—and an almost damning one—deserves notice: most romance heroes and heroines tend to be "flat"—that is, they lack inner contradictions, ethical standards based on elements other than convention and lip service, true inner turmoil (despite their excessive displays of grief or devotion). Aristotle is often quoted as saying that character is all important in the epic. Exactly what he means is debated, although most commentators on Aristotle connect his idea of well-defined character with its ultimate creation of a dramatic conflict, a conflict of often tragic and supremely pathetic significance. Romance characters tend to be nonpareils: they are paragons of beauty, goodness, evil, saintliness; usually no humanizing and magnanimous inner weakness arises to give their perfection credibility and strength. It is just this feature of romance characterization that prevents the appearance of great scenes. One looks in vain in romance for a Hagen, a basically cruel and dismal figure, who suddenly emerges in the final stanzas of the *Nibelungenlied* as an utterly astonishing individual, spirited and heady in the shambles of Etzel's barracks as all his people are fighting hopelessly and foolishly against Kriemhild's warriors; one looks in vain also for a Roland, who suddenly and very movingly recognizes the foolishness of his pride and exonerates himself in our eyes by forgetting himself at the last and lost moment when he summons Charlemagne for help.

Like much medieval literature, the romances were not meant to be read in private to oneself. They were recited to an audience perhaps in the hall of a manor, more likely perhaps in the large room of a tavern. They are pieces to be listened to and we today do well if we can develop a manner of reading Middle English romances that suggests ease, involvement in the narrative, and a mastery of its frequently rough and irregular rhythms. The pieces in this collection do not show the polish and apparent metrical regularity of Chaucer's verse as it appears, for example, in the editions of the *Canterbury Tales* where extra and missing syllables are somehow straightened out by editorial dexterity. With *Horn* in particular and also with *Launfal, The Wedding of Sir Gawain and Dame Ragnell,* and others a "defective" line must be faced up to: no amount of emending can replace a whole verse foot that is missing in a line or can delete a whole verse foot that is one too many for the general metrical pattern.

Much of the difficulty in reading Middle English aloud is obviated by recognizing pronunciation differences between Middle English and Modern. Such differences can be summarized briefly here; their number is, in essentials, modest and they can be conveniently schematicized. Vocalic differences come first; they are the significant ones and the most obvious. First of all, the so-called short or lax vowels [ɪ] and [ɛ] of today are generally the same as they were during romance times. The vowels of *bit* and *bet* correspond in sound and spelling to Middle English short *i* and short *e*. The short *u* of today, as in *put* [ʊ], is far less common than the accented schwa, as in *but* [ʌ]. The latter did not presumably exist in Middle English; most words which show accented schwa today in Middle English times had the value of the short *u* of *put*. Consequently, all Middle English words like *cut*, *hut*, *nut* and *shut* should be given the vocalic value [ʊ]. The short *a* of today is a low front vowel [æ], the vowel usually heard in *that* and *hat*; but we have to assume that such a vowel did not exist in Middle English, rather a "Continental short *a*" [a] like the *a* in French *la* or in German *Mann*. (The sound can best be approximated by trying to pronounce *hat* with the vowel not quite as far back as the vowel [ɑ] in *father* and not quite so fronted as the vowel in *that*.) Modern English may not have a short "Germanic *o*"; yet it is likely that Middle English words containing an *o* followed by two or more consonants possessed a short vowel *o*—a vowel "short" in the manner in which Modern German *Post* and *Hostie* have short vowels. Unstressed *e*'s—especially pronounced final *e*'s—probably were equivalent to our unstressed schwa [ə] heard in the initial syllable of *about*.

One must assume that all long vowels in Middle English underwent a shift at the close of the Middle English period. One way of approaching the difference between Modern English and Middle English long vowels is to trace the current long vowels back to their earlier values. Of the front sequence, the modern diphthong [ai] as in *my* [mai] was in Middle English the simple [i] as in *me* [mi]; the modern monophthong [i] as in *me* was in Middle English the simple [e] as in *may* [me]. Finally, the modern front vowel [e], if now spelled with an *a* as in *name*, was in Middle English the back vowel [ɑ] as in *father*. Of the back sequence, the modern diphthong [au] as in *out* was in Middle English the simple [u] as in *boot*; the modern monophthong [u] as in *boot* was in Middle English the simple [o:] as in *boat*.

Diphthongs in Middle English have certain peculiarities. The Modern English diphthong [au] as in *out* appears in words of Romance origin in Middle English usually with the spelling *au* as in Middle English *cause*. It also appears in Middle English in words of native origin where the spelling is either *au* as in *saugh* 'saw' or *aw* as in *lawe* 'law.' The combinations in Middle English *ay/ai/ey/ei* are assumed to possess the so-called cockney pronunciation of *Daily Mail* [dæɪli mæɪl], a diphthong made up of the low front vowel [æ] and the high front vowel [ɪ]. Two additional diphthongs are very difficult unless etymological backgrounds of their words are known. They are the diphthongs [ɪu] and [ɛu]. The former was in Middle English usually written *ew* and appeared in such common words as *blew, knew, newe,* and *trewe.* The latter, usually written *ew* also, appeared in such words as *beauté, fewe, lewed,* and *shewen.*

Consonants offer few difficulties. Only the Middle English sound for the letters *gh* need cause concern. After a front vowel (*a*[a], *e, i*) *gh* was pronounced like *ch*[ç] in German *ich* and after back vowels (*a*[ɑ], *o, u*) like German *ch*[x] in *ach.* The combinations *ng/nk* as in Middle English *song/munk* were pronounced with the velar nasal [ŋ] heard in Modern English *song* followed by the velar stop of *g* as in *go* or *k* as in *king.* Initial *gn/kn* were pronounced as bipartite sounds; hence, *knight* would be [knɪçt] and *gnauen* [gnɑuən].

The problem of final *e* concerns prosody primarily. An adroit handling of it can regularize the scansion of an apparently difficult line and make the reading aloud of Middle English verse a wholly bearable experience. Any rules set up for final *e*'s are of the rule-of-thumb variety. Generally it is well to establish first whether the lines of a Middle English verse composition belong to the tetrameter or pentameter variety. Once the line length is known, then a reader can pattern his oral rendition of the lines accordingly. (Verse feet in the romances are predominantly iambic, but anapests and trochees that appear should often be taken as welcome prosodic variations.) It is usual to say that all final *e*'s are pronounced except those followed by a word beginning with a vowel or with *h,* or those followed by a word like *was* or *his* or some other monosyllabic word of high frequency. The final *e* at the end of a line (the *e* that creates the Middle English feminine rhyme) is presumably pronounced, although it can be elided effectively if the following line begins with a vowel.

The tetrameter line is the most common in this collection, and the one offering most difficulties. A comment or two on its peculiarities will not be amiss. In general, when reading romances aloud, one should be guided intuitively by normal English iambic rhythm. Yet anyone so guided can run into baffling situations where iambic patterns seem to break down entirely. It is quite possible to read certain lines of tetrameter verse on a trochaic pattern. It may indeed be that they were originally so read. There are, however, a few devices which can help sustain an iambic pattern. First of all, certain normally octosyllabic lines may lack one syllable which can be inserted indirectly by pausing in the middle of the line—in other words, allowing a caesura to make up for a missing unstressed or sometimes stressed syllable. Occasional lines of octosyllabic verse seem to begin with a trochee with the following three feet regular iambs; such lines read well. But instances occur where there are only seven syllables and where the first unstressed syllable of the first foot appears to be missing. Here a reader can decide whether the first or final foot is catalectic—that is, lacking an unstressed syllable. In either case, a pause at the beginning of the verse or at the end can make such a line read passably. Anapests, especially initial anapests, sometimes seem to produce a ten-syllable line if the rhyme is feminine. Syllabic reduction can be brought about in several ways, as by the zeroing of any final e or by the syncopating of a medial e either in an inflectional suffix, as in the word *cometh*, or in a trisyllabic word like *Engelond*, where the first syllable bears primary stress and the last secondary. On the other hand, little apparent break in rhythm occurs if many anapests in initial or any other position are read as anapests, even if they create lines of ten syllables. Ultimately, one encounters a verse of five feet that cannot be reduced to four; even if the preceding and the following verses are of four feet, such a line can be made to seem by a person reading aloud to be a perfectly harmless prosodic variation.

The following lines (they introduce the Harleyian manuscript version of *Sir Orfeo*) may be instructive. Pronounced unstressed e's are overdotted, silent ones underdotted; caesural pauses which make up for an apparently missing syllable are indicated by a double bar; stressed syllables are marked by a grave and unstressed by a breve. .

> We redyn ofte and fynde ywryte,
>
> As clerkes don || us to wyte,
>
> The layes that ben || of harpyng
>
> || Ben yfounde of frely thing.
>
> 5 Sum ben of wele and sum of wo,
>
> And sum of ioy and merthe also;
>
> Sum of trechery and sum of gyle
>
> And sum of happes that fallen by whyle;
>
> Sum of bourdys and sum of rybaudry
>
> 10 And sum ther ben of the feyre.
>
> Of alle thing that men may se
>
> || Moost oloue forsothe they be.

Admittedly, the notation here is done to taste. Lines three and four could be altered so that each would have eight and not seven syllables; but the caesural pause in line three and the slight pause before the stressed *ben* of line four seem rhetorically effective. The initial anapests of lines seven and nine could, with certain emendation, be regularized into iambs; but the four-foot iambic line can become quite tedious without such variations as anapests. Whatever pattern is followed, however, a reader's voice should suggest ease, intimacy, and involvement, for such can evoke a charm from even the roughest page of tetrameter lines.

Bibliographic Abbreviations

Billings. Anna H. Billings. *A Guide to the Middle English Metrical Romances*. Dealing with English and Germanic legends and with the cycles of Charlemagne and of Arthur. New York, 1901.

Brown and Robbins. Carleton Brown and Rossell Hope Robbins. *The Index of Middle English Verse*. New York, 1943.

CBEL. F. W. Bateson, ed. *The Cambridge Bibliography of English Literature*. Volume I: 600–1660. New York, 1941. Also Volume V: Supplement A.D. 600–1900, George Watson, ed., Cambridge, 1957.

French and Hale. Walter H. French and Charles B. Hale, eds. *Middle English Metrical Romances*. Englewood Cliffs, N. J., 1930.

Hibbard. Laura A. Hibbard. *Mediaeval Romance in England*. A study of the sources and analogues of the noncyclic metrical romances. New York, 1924.

Kane. George Kane. *Middle English Literature*. A critical study of the romances, the religious lyrics, *Piers Plowman*. London, 1951.

MED. Hans Kurath and Sherman M. Kuhn, eds. *Middle English Dictionary*. Ann Arbor, Mich., 1952–date.

OED. James A. H. Murray, *et al.*, eds. *The Oxford English Dictionary*. Oxford, 1933.

Wells. John E. Wells. *A Manual of the Writings in Middle English 1050–1400*. New Haven, 1916. Also Supplements 1919, 1923, 1926, 1929, 1932, 1935, 1938, 1941, 1951.

PART 1

The Matter of England

King Horn

ITH the tale of Horn and the fair Rymenhild we have the earliest extant English romance. This distinction it can claim; other distinctions, especially technical and esthetic, are hard to come by. Yet *Horn* possesses considerably more interest than a good number of more competent pieces: it can be viewed as the prototypic Middle English romance, it can be taken as the most instructive example of the shift of Middle English prosody from the old accentual norm to the French-inspired syllabic norm, and it can serve as a veritable catalog of traditional romance motifs. There are three manuscripts: Harleian 2253 in the British Museum, London; Laud, Misc., 108 in the Bodleian Library, Oxford; and MS Gg. 4.27.2 in the University Library, Cambridge—the last named being the oldest (*c.* 1250) and generally considered the best. Just where the poem was originally composed is conjectural, since none of the manuscripts is the original, but all, in varying degree, show a predominance of Southern dialect features intermixed with Midland. The poet is believed to have written at the end of the first quarter of the thirteenth century, because linguistically he would belong somewhere around 1225 and because the postulated descent of manuscripts from a lost original would place him some twenty-five years prior to the suggested date when the oldest extant manuscript, the Cambridge, was copied. But so bare and formulaic in language and narrative technique is *Horn* that we are hard put to say just what sort of a man the poet was. Certain it is that he lacks chivalric ideas, that he does not, beyond conventional lip service, show deference to churchly matters, that he intends to entertain a rough and naïve group of people who could be townsmen or soldiers or farmers. He lacks the national consciousness of the *Havelok* poet, the outright anti-clericalism of the *Gamelyn* poet, and the delicacy and sentiment often apparent in pieces composed in the century to follow. There is, in fact, a distinct facelessness about *Horn*; it is as if all archetypic-romance motifs were gathered in and compressed to their barest essentials, united by the most rudimentary transitions, and let stand without more ado. It seems especially futile in the case of *Horn* to speculate about the historicity of

its action and characters and about the referents of its geographical names. Horn, Murry, Mody, and the rest do not correspond to or suggest any actual historical pattern. Nor do the Saracens, who never landed in force on the English coast, although the Scandinavians did (in several great waves beginning in the eighth century) and it is probably they who conditioned the minds of both minstrel and audience to the savagery of deep-sea raiders. It has been occasionally suggested that Suddene is the Isle of Wight and Westernesse the Wirral in Cheshire; but one wonders whether a thirteenth-century audience would have felt itself constrained to identify either locale. Only Ireland (Yrlonde) seems to be a name which might readily have been associated with a known geographical area; yet even here the name may have suggested more some vague distant land rather than that particular island just west of St. George's Channel.

Prosodically *Horn* is a transitional piece. It contains the rhymed couplet introduced from the French, but does not lengthen the two- and three-stress lines taken over from the Old English half-line into the usual tetrameter line of later romances. It hovers between the older trochaic rhythm and the coming iambic and never really favors one over the other, a feature perhaps which prompts Kane to remark that the prosody "sometimes looks and possibly is incompetent." Two schools have grown up around it: one—that of W. H. French—assumes the basic line to be iambic trimeter with numerous "standard variations"; the other—that of Joseph Hall—assumes the basic line to be trochaic trimeter with numerous anacrusic syllables—that is, syllables which occasionally introduce a line, but which are not to be counted as part of its basic prosodic pattern. Approached without presuppositions, however, the three manuscripts (admittedly they may be in varying degree "corrupt") show a three-stress line with numerous two- and four-stress lines intermixed and with feminine rhymes far outnumbering the masculine. In reading *Horn* aloud, one should, if only for practical purposes, give up the idea that the lines are or should be regularly trochaic or regularly iambic and concentrate on the stresses per line. One peculiarity must be noted—the high number of lines with two stresses following one upon the other, as in "Horn tok his leve" and " 'Knight,' quath heo, 'trewe' "; but here difficulty can usually be resolved if the reader inserts a caesural pause between the two stresses. For the rest, *Horn* reads aloud quite as well as many other Middle English narrative poems.

The language of *Horn* is here normalized and modernized somewhat more than that of the following pieces because of its difficulty. Double terminal consonants (as in *will/full/tall*) are present where the manuscripts often show a single consonant. Further, *wh-/ch-* are present where the manuscripts show these as well as variants of these. Usually, *-ai-* is shown where Modern English has *-ai-* (hence, *rain* for the original *rein*);

-ei- is similarly treated. Also, *-i/-ie* appear as *-y/-ye* where such substitution seems to enhance ease of reading. Finally, *c/k* and *v/u* appear in the positions Modern English orthography would have them appear. The combination *-eo-* (as in *heo* "she" and *beon* "be") is retained since it probably represents a distinctive [oe]; retained also is the *-u-* now usually represented by *-i-* (as in *furst* "first" and *dunt* "dint") since the *-u-* probably represents a distinctive [y]. It should be noted that among the verb forms, which are generally standard Middle English, the plural verbs, the past participle, and the infinitive usually lack *-n* and that the present participle ends in *-inde.* Pronouns show a wide variation, but here *ich/I* are shown for "I," *he/heo* for "he/she," and *hi/hem* for "they/them."

REFERENCES: Brown and Robbins, No. 166; Billings, p. 1; *CBEL*, I:147; Hibbard, p. 81; Kane, pp. 48–49; Wells, pp. 8–10.—The classic edition, with all three texts printed diplomatically, is Joseph Hall, *King Horn* (Oxford, 1901); a provocative introduction to the problems besetting all phases of *Horn* scholarship is Walter H. French, *Essays on King Horn* (Ithaca, N. Y., 1940).

Alle beon hi blithe	
That to my song lithe!	*listen*
A song ich shall you singe	
Of Murry the Kinge.	
5 King he was biweste	*in the West*
So longe so hit laste.	
Godhild het his quen;	*was called*
Faire ne mighte non ben.	*fairer*
He hadde a sone that het Horn;	
10 Fairer ne mighte non beo born,	
Ne no rain upon birine,	*rain upon*
Ne sunne upon bishine.	*shine*
Fairer nis non thane he was:	
He was bright so the glas;	
15 He was whit so the flur;	*flower*
Rose-red was his colur.	
He was fair and eke bold	*also*
And of fiftene winter old.	
In none kingeriche	*kingdom*
20 Nas non his iliche.	*equal*
Twelf feren he hadde	*comrades*
That he alle with him ladde,	*kept*
Alle riche mannes sones	

6 "As long as he lived."

And alle hi were faire gomes   *youths*
25 With him for to pleye.
And mest he luvede tweye:
That on him het Athulf child
And that other Fikenhild.
Athuld was the beste
30 And Fikenhilde the werste.

Hit was upon a someres day,
Also ich you telle may,   *of which*
Murry, the gode king,
Rod on his pleying
35 By the see side,
Ase he was woned ride.   *accustomed to*
With him riden bute two—
All too fewe ware tho!   *those*
He fond by the stronde   *shore*
40 Arived on his londe
Shipes fiftene
With Sarazins kene.
He axede what hi soghte   *asked*
Other to londe broghte.   *or*
45 A payn hit ofherde   *pagan/heard*
And him well sone answarede:
"Thy lond folk we shulle slon   *slay*
And alle that Christ luveth upon   *believes in*
And thee selve right anon.
50 Ne shaltu today henne gon!   *shall you/hence*
The king alighte off his stede,
For tho he havede nede,   *then*
And his gode knightes two.
All too fewe he hadde tho!
55 Swerd hi gunne gripe
And togadere smite.
Hi smiten under shelde
That sume hit y-felde.   *felt*
The King hadde all too fewe
60 Togenes so fele shrewe.   *against/many /rogues*

So fele mighten ythe   *easily*
Bringe hem three to dithe.   *death*

The payns come to londe
And neme hit in here honde.   *took*
65 That folk hi gunne quelle   *kill*
And churchen for to felle.   *destroy*
Ther ne moste libbe   *live*
The fremde ne the sibbe.   *strangers/kin*

Bute hi here lawe asoke   *religion/forsook*
70 And to here toke.   *theirs*
   Of alle wimmanne
   Wurst was Godhild thanne.
   For Murry heo weop sore   *wept/bitterly*
   And for Horn yute more.
75 Heo wente ut of halle
   Fram hire maidenes alle.
   Under a roche of stone
   Ther heo livede alone.
   Ther heo servede Gode
80 Agenes the paynes forbode.   *contrary to*
                                   /interdict

   Ther heo servede Christ
   That no payn hit ne wiste.   *in such a way*
                                   that/knew

   Evre heo bad for Horn child   *prayed*
   That Jesu Christ him beo mild.   *merciful*
85 Horn was in paynes honde
   With his feren of the londe.   *comrades*
   Muchel was his fairhede,
   For Jesu Christ him makede.
   Payns him wolde slen
90 Other all quik flen.   *or/alive/flay*
   Yef his fairnesse nere,
   The children alle aslawe were.
   Thanne spak an admirad   *amir*
   (Of wordes he was bald),
95 "Horn, thu art well kene
   And that is well y-sene.
   Thu art gret and strong,
   Fair and evene long.   *quite/tall*
   Thu shalt waxe more   *bigger*
100 By fulle seve yere.   *seven*
   Yef thu mote to live go   *were to/alive*
   And thine feren also–
   Yef hit so bifalle–
   Ye sholde slen us alle.
105 Tharfore thu most to stere,
   Thu and thine y-fere;
   To shupe shulle ye funde   *ship/hasten*
   And sinke to the grunde.   *bottom*
   The see you shall adrenche   *drown*
110 Ne shall hit us noght ofthinche.   *make sorry*

---

77   The "rock of stone" refers to a subterranean chamber such as hermits used.
91   "Were it not for his fine looks."
105   "Therefore you must [go] into a boat."

For if thu were alive,

With swerd other with knive   *by*

We sholden alle deye

And thy fader deth abeye."   *atone for*

115 The children hi broghte to stronde,

Wringinde here honde,

Into shupes borde   *aboard ship*

At the furste worde.   *immediately*

Ofte hadde Horn beo wo,

120 Ac nevre wurs than him was tho!   *but*

The see bigan to flowe   *rise*

And Horn child to rowe.

The see that shup so faste drof

The children dradde therof.   *were afraid*

125 Hi wenden to wisse   *expected/for sure*

Of here lif to misse   *lose*

All the day and all the night

Till hit sprang day-light–

Till Horn saw on the stronde   *shore*

130 Men gon in the londe.

"Feren," quath he, "yonge,

Ich telle you tithinge: *news*

Ich here foweles singe   *birds*

And that grass him springe.

135 Blithe beo we on live;

Ure shup is on rive."   *shore*

Off shup hi gunne funde   *hasten*

And setten fout to grunde.

By the see side

140 Hi leten that shup ride.

Thanne spak him child Horn

(In Suddene he was y-born),

"Shup by the see flode,

Dayes have thu gode.

145 Bi the see brinke,   *edge*

No water thee na drinke.   *take in*

Yef thu cume to Suddene,

Gret thu well of mine kenne,   *greet*

Gret thu well my moder,

150 Godhild, quen the gode,

And seye the payne king,   *tell*

Jesu Cristes withering,   *adversary*

That ich am hol and fer   *whole/sound*

On this lond arived her.

155 And seye that hi shall fonde   *experience*

---

134   "And [see] that the grass grows."
135   "Let us be happy we're alive."

The dent of mine honde."   *blow*
The children yede to tune
By dales and by dune.
Hi metten with Almair King–
160 Christ yeve him His blessing!–
King of Westernesse–
Christ yive him muchel blisse!
He him spak to Horn child
Wordes that were mild:
165 "Whannes beo ye, faire gumes,   *whence/youths*
That her to londe beoth y-cume,
Alle throttene,   *thirteen*
Of bodye swithe kene?   *very*
By God that me makede,
170 A swich fair ferade
Ne sauw ich in none stunde   *time*
By westene londe!
Seye me what ye seche."
Horn spak here speche;
175 He spak for hem alle,
For so hit moste bifalle:
He was the faireste
And of wit the beste.

"We beoth of Suddenne,
180 Y-come of gode kenne,   *kin*
Of Christene blode
And kinges swithe gode.   *exceedingly*
Payns ther gunne arive
And duden hem of live.
185 Hi slowen and todrowe   *tore apart*
Christene men y-nowe.
So Christ me mote rede,
Us hi dude lede
Into a galeye
190 With the see to pleye.
Day hit is y-gone and other
Withute sail and rother.   *rudder*
Ure ship bigan to swimme
To this londes brimme.   *edge*
195 Nu thu might us slen and binde,
Ure honde bihinde.

---

170   "Such a fine company."
184   "And put them to death."
187   "As Christ may be my guide."
190   "To sport upon the sea."
191   "One day has passed and a second."

Bute yef hit beo thy wille,
Helpe that we ne spille." *perish*

Thanne spak the gode king
200 (Y-wis he has no nithing) *villain*
"Seye me, child, what is thy name?
Ne shaltu have bute game."
The child him answerde
Sone so he hit herde:
205 "Horn ich am y-hote *called*
Y-comen ut of the bote
Fram the see side.
King, well mote thee tide."
Thanne him spak the gode king:
210 "Well bruk thu thy nevening!
Horn, thu go well shulle
By dales and by hulle!
Horn, thu lude sune *loud/shall sound*
By dales and by dune!
215 So shall thy name springe
Fram kinge to kinge
And thy fairnesse
Abute Westernesse,
The strengthe of thine honde
220 Into evrech londe.
Horn, thu art so swete *appealing*
Ne may ich thee forlete." *abandon*
Hom rod Aylmar the King
And Horn mid him, his fundling, *foundling*
225 And alle his y-fere,
That were him so dere.

The king com into halle
Among his knightes alle.
Forth he clupede Athelbrus, *called*
230 That was stiward of his hus.
"Stiward, tak nu here
My fundling for to lere *instruct*
Of thine mestere, *occupation*
Of wude and of rivere,
235 And tech him to harpe
With his nailes sharpe,

---

202 "You'll have nothing but pleasure."
208 "King, may you prosper well."
210 "May you enjoy your name well." The King here and in the following lines puns
     on Horn, the name, and horn, the instrument, equating the far-carrying sound of
     a horn with fame.
234 *Wude* "forest" and *rivere* "river land" refer to hunting with hounds and hawks.

Bifore me to cerve
And of the cupe serve.
Thu tech him of alle the liste   *knowledge*
240 That thu evre of wiste;
And his feren thu wise   *instruct*
Into othere servise.
Horn thu underfonge   *take charge of*
And tech him of harpe and songe."

245 Athelbrus gan lere
Horn and his y-fere.
Horn in herte laghte   *comprehended*
All that he him taghte.
In the curt and ute
250 And elles all abute   *elsewhere*
Luvede men Horn child,
And mest him luvede Rymenhild,
The kinges owene doghter.
He was mest in thoghte;
255 Heo luvede so Horn child
That negh heo gan wexe wild.
For heo ne mighte at borde   *table*
With him speke no worde
Ne noght in the halle
260 Among the knightes alle
Ne nowhar in non othere stede.   *place*
Of folk heo hadde drede;
By daye ne by nighte
With him speke ne mighte.
265 Hire sorewe ne hire pine   *anguish*
Ne mighte nevre fine.   *end*
In heorte heo hadde wo
And thus hire bithoghte tho: *decided/then*
Heo sende hire sonde   *would send*
                                 /messenger

270 Athelbrus to honde,
That he come hire to,
And also sholde Horn do,
All into bure,   *apartment*
For heo gan to lure;   *look melancholy*
275 And the sonde seide   *should say*
That sik lay that maide
And bad him come swithe
For heo nas nothing blithe.

---

254   "He was most in [her] thought."
264   The pronoun *heo* 'she' is omitted as occasionally pronouns are in *Horn*.
270   *To honde* here suggests "into the presence of."

The stiward was in herte wo,
280 For he nuste what to do.   *did not know*
    What Rymenhild hure thoghte
    Gret wunder him thughte,
    Abute Horn the yonge
    To bure for to bringe.
285 He thoghte upon his mode   *in his mind*
    Hit nas for none gode;
    He tok him another,
    Athulf, Hornes brother.   *comrade*

    "Athulfe," he sede, "right anon
290 Thu shalt with me to bure gon
    To speke with Rymenhild stille   *privily*
    And witen hure wille.   *learn*
    In Hornes y-like   *likeness*
    Thu shalt hure biswike.   *deceive*
295 Sore ich me ofdrede   *fear*
    Heo wolde Horn misrede."   *persuade toward*
                                                   ill

    Athelbrus gan Athulf lede
    And into bure with him yede.
    Anon upon Athulf child
300 Rymenhild gan wexe wild.
    Heo wende that Horn hit were
    That heo havede there.
    Heo sette him on bedde;
    With Athulf child heo wedde;
305 On hire armes tweie
    Athulf heo gan leie.   *embrace*
    "Horn," quath heo, "well longe
    Ich habbe thee luved stronge.
    Thu shalt thy trewthe plighte
310 On min hond her righte
    Me to spuse holde
    And ich thee lord to wolde."

    Athulf sede on hire ire   *ear*
    So stille se hit were,   *as softly as/could*
                                                   be

315 "Thy tale nu thu linne,   *cease*
    For Horn nis noght herinne.
    Ne beo we noght y-liche: *equal*

---

282   "Seemed very strange to him."
300   "Rymenhild became passionate."
304   "She showed her desire to child Athulf."
309–312   "You shall immediately plight your troth to me to have me as wife and I to possess you as lord."

Horn is fairer and riche,
Fairer by one ribbe   *rib*
320 Thane eny man that libbe.   *lives*
Thegh Horn were under molde–   *although/earth*
Other elles wher he wolde
Other henne a thusend mile–   *hence*
Ich nolde him ne thee bigile!"

325 Rymenhild hire biwente   *turned*
And Athelbrus fule heo shente.   *foully/abused.*
"Hennes thu go, thu fule theof,
Ne wurstu me nevre more leof!
Went ut of my bur   *go*
330 With muchel mesaventur!   *ill fortune*
Shame mote thu fonge   *grip*
And on highe rode anhonge!   *gallows/hang*
Ne spek ich noght with Horn–
Nis he noght so unorn!   *ugly*
335 Horn is fairer thane beo he!
With muchel shame mote thu deye."

Athelbrus in a stunde   *immediately*
Fell anon to grunde.
"Lefdy min owe,   *lady/own*
340 Lithe me a litel throwe!   *listen to/space*
Lust why ich wonde   *hear/hesitated*
Bringe thee Horn to honde.
For Horn is fair and riche;
Nis no whar his y-liche.   *equal*
345 Aylmar, the gode king,
Dude him on my loking.   *placed/care*
Yef Horn were hei abute,
Sore I me dute
With him ye wolden pleye
350 Bitwex you selve tweye.
Thanne sholde withuten othe   *doubt*
The king maken us wrothe.   *sorry*
Rymenhild, foryef me thy tene,   *displeasure*
Lefdy, my Quene,
355 And Horn ich shall thee fecche,
Wham so hit recche."

Rymenhild, yef heo cuthe,
Gan linne with hire muthe.

322 "Either wherever else he would [be]."
328 "You will no more be a favorite of mine."
348 "I would sorely suspect."
356 "Whoever may give a thought about it."
357–358 "Rymenhild, as well as she could, kept silent."

Heo makede hire wel blithe—
360 Well was hire that sithe.   *occasion*
"Go nu," quath heo, "sone,
And send him after none   *mid-day*
On a squieres wise.   *dress*
Whane the king arise
365 To wude for to pleye,
Nis non that him biwreye.   *shall betray*
He shall with me bileve   *remain*
Till hit beo nir eve   *near*
To haven of him my wille.
370 After ne recche ich what me telle."   *care/people/say*

Athelbrus wende hire fro.   *turned away*
                                                        /from

Horn in halle fond he tho
Bifore the king on benche
Win for to shenche.   *pour*
375 "Horn," quath he, "so hende,   *gracious*
To bure nu thu wende
After mete stille   *mealtime*
                                                        /quietly

With Rymenhild to dwelle.   *tarry*
Wordes swithe bolde
380 In herte thu hem holde.
Horn, beo me well trewe;
Ne shall hit thee nevre rewe."   *regret*
Horn in herte laide
All that he him saide.
385 He yede in well righte   *immediately*
To Rymenhild the brighte.
On knees he him sette
And sweteliche hire grette.   *sweetly*
Of his faire sighte   *appearance*
390 All the bur gan lighte.
He spake faire speche—
Ne dorte him no man teche.   *needed/instruct*
"Well thu sitte and softe,
Rymenhild the brighte,
395 With thine maidenes sixe
That thee sitteth nixte.   *beside*
Kinges stiward ure
Sende me into bure;
With thee speke ich sholde.
400 Seye me what thu woldest;

379–380 The sense seems to be "Restrain yourself from uttering presumptuous words."
393 "May you sit [i.e., live] well and comfortably."

Seye, and ich shall here
What thy wille were."

Rymenhild up gan stonde
And tok him by the honde.
405 Heo sette him on pelle   *coverlet*
Of win to drinke his full.
Heo makede him faire chere
And tok him abute the swere.   *neck*
Ofte heo him kuste
410 So well so hire luste.   *as much as*
                  /pleased

"Horn," heo sede, "withute strif,   *assuredly*
Thu shalt have me to thy wif.
Horn, have of me rewthe   *pity*
And plist me thy trewthe.   *pledge/troth*

415 Horn tho him bithoghte
What he speke mighte.
"Christ," quath he, "thee wisse,   *guide*
And give thee hevene blisse
Of thine husebonde,
420 Wher he beo in londe.   *wherever*
Ich am y-bore too lowe
Swich wimman to knowe.
Ich am y-come of thralle
And fundling bifalle.   *have become*
425 Ne feolle hit thee of kunde
To spuse beo me bunde;
Hit nere no fair wedding
Bitwexe a thrall and a king."

Tho gan Rymenhild mislike   *to show displeas-*
                   ure
430 And sore gan to sike.   *sigh*
Armes heo gan buwe;
Adun heo feol y-swowe.   *aswoon*

Horn in herte was full wo
And tok hire on his armes two.
435 He gan hire for to kesse
Well ofte mid y-wisse.   *certainly*
"Lemman," he sede "dere,   *darling*
Thin herte nu thu stere.   *control*

425–426 "Nor would it be natural for you to be bound to me as spouse."
431 "She bent her arms," perhaps suggesting a motion of despair like throwing up
  one's arms.

Help me to knighte
440 By all thine mighte,   *with*
To my lord the king
That he me yive dubbing;   *confers /knighthood*

Thanne is my thralhod
Y-went into knighthod   *turned*
445 And I shall wexe more
And do, lemman, thy lore."   *instruction*

Rymenhild, that swete thing,
Wakede of hire swowing.   *swoon*
"Horn," quath heo, "well sone
450 That shall beon y-done.
Thu shalt beo dubbed knight
Are come sevenight.
Have her this cuppe   *take*
And this ring theruppe   *in addition*
455 To Athelbrus the stiward,
And see he holde foreward.   *keep/agreement*
Seye ich him biseche,
With loveliche speche,   *ardent/words*
That he adun falle
460 Bifore the King in halle
And bidde the King arighte   *immediately*
Dubbe thee to knighte.
With selver and with golde
Hit wurth him well y-yolde.
465 Christ him lene spede   *grant/success*
Thin erende to bede."   *business/present*

Horn tok his leve,
For hit was negh eve.   *near*
Athelbrus he soghte
470 And yaf him that he broghte,
And tolde him full yare   *quickly*
Hu he hadde y-fare,   *progressed*
And sede him nis nede,
And bihet him his mede.   *promised/reward*

475 Athelbrus also swithe   *as soon as possible*

Wente to halle blive.   *quickly*
"King," he sede, "thu leste   *harken*

---

439 "Help me to [become] a knight."
445 "And I shall grow in stature."
464 "He [Athelbrus] shall be well rewarded."

A tale mid the beste.
Thu shalt bere crune
480 Tomorewe in this tune;
Tomorewe is thy feste–
Ther bihoveth geste.
Hit nere noght forloren   *lost*
For to knighty child Horn,
485 Thine armes for to welde:
God knight he shal yelde."   *prove*

The King sede sone,
"That is well y-done.
Horn me well y-quemeth;   *pleases*
490 God knight him bisemeth.   *seems*
He shall have my dubbing
And after wurth my derling.   *become/favorite*
And alle his feren twelf
He shall knighten himself;
495 Alle he shall hem knighte
Before me this nighte."
Till the light of day sprang
Aylmar him thughte lang.
The day bigan to springe;
500 Horn com bifore the Kinge,
Mid his twelf y-fere.
(Sume hi were luthere.)
Horn he dubbede to knighte
With swerd and spures brighte.
505 He sette him on a stede whit–
Ther nas no knight him y-lik.
He smot him a litel wight   *gentle/blow*
And bed him beon a god knight.

Athulf fell a-knees thar
510 Bifore the King Aylmar.
"King," he sede, "so kene,
Grante me a bene!   *boon*
Nu is knight Sire Horn
That in Suddene was y-boren;
515 Lord he is of londe
Over us that by him stonde;
Thin armes he hath and sheld
To fighte with upon the feld;
Lat him us alle knighte

---

482 Probably "Appropriate festivities are called for."
488 A line where 'that' is probably an error for 'he'; if so, the meaning is "He is indeed
   excellent."
502 "A certain one of them was wicked."

520 For that is ure righte."

Aylmar sede sone y-wis,
"Do nu that thy wille is."
Horn adun lighte
And makede hem alle knightes.
525 Murie was the feste
    All of faire gestes—   *games*
    Ac Rymenhild nas noght ther,
    And that hire thughte seve yer.
    After Horn heo sente
530 And he to bure wente.
    Nolde he noght go one;   *alone*
    Athulf was his mone.   *companion*
    Rymenhild on flore stod
    (Hornes come hire thughte god)   *arrival*
535 And sede, "Welcome, Sire Horn,
    And Athulf knight thee biforn.
    Knight, nu is thy time
    For to sitte by me.   *stay*
    Do nu that thu er of spake:
540 To thy wif thu me take.
    Ef thu art trewe of dedes,   *to your word*
    Do nu ase thu sedes.
    Nu thu hast wille thine
    Unbind me of my pine."   *release/anguish*

545 "Rymenhild," quath he, "beo stille!
    Ich wulle don all thy wille,
    Also hit mot bitide.
    Mid spere I shall furst ride
    And my knighthod proue,
550 Ar ich thee ginne to wowe.   *woo*
    We beth knightes yonge,
    Of o day all y-sprunge;   *one/arisen*
    And of ure mestere   *calling*
    So is the manere: *custom*
555 With sume othere knighte
    Well for his lemman fighte
    Or he eny wif take—
    Forthy me stondeth the more rape.   *therefore*
                               /pertains/haste

    Today, so Christ me blesse,
560 Ich wulle do pruesse   *deeds of valor*
    For thy luve in the felde

---

528   "And that [i.e., Horn's absence] seemed seven years to her."
547   "In such manner as it should occur."

Mid spere and mid shelde.
If ich come to live,   *return/alive*
Ich shall thee take to wive."

565 "Knight," quath heo, "trewe,
Ich wene ich may thee leve.   *believe*
Tak nu her this gold ring
(God him is the dubbing);
Ther is upon the ringe
570 Y-grave 'Rymenhild the yonge.'
Ther nis non betere anonder sunne
That eny man of telle cunne.
For my luve thu hit were
And on thy finger thu him bere.
575 The stones beoth of suche grace   *power*
That thu ne shalt in none place
Of none duntes beon ofdrad   *blows/afraid*
Ne on bataille beon amad   *crazed*
Ef thu loke theran
580 And thenke upon thy lemman.   *sweetheart*

And Sire Athulf, thy brother,
He shal have another.
Horn, ich thee biseche
With loveliche speche   *ardent*
585 Christ yeve god erndinge   *success*
Thee agen to bringe."
The knight hire gan kesse
And heo him to blesse.
Leve at hire he nam   *leave/took*
590 And into halle cam.
The knightes yeden to table
And Horne yede to stable.
Thar he tok his gode fole   *horse*
Also blak so eny cole.   *just as/coal*
595 The fole shok the brunye   *armor*
That al the curt gan denye.   *resound*
The fole bigan to springe
And Horn murye to singe.
Horn rod in a while
600 More than a mile.
He fond o shup stonde   *riding*
With hethene hunde.   *heathen/dogs*
He axede what hi soghte
Other to londe broghte.

568   "Good is its ornamentation"; but *dubbing* in this sense is unique.

605 An hund him gan bihelde
    That spak wordes belde: *arrogant*
    "This lond we wulles winne   *propose to*
                                                     /conquer
    And sle that ther is inne."   *those who*
    Horn gan his swerd gripe
610 And on his arme wipe.
    The Sarazins he smatte   *smote*
    That his blod hatte.
    At evreche dunte
    The heved off wente.   *head*
615 Tho gunne the hundes gone   *rush*
    Abute Horn alone.
    He lokede on the ringe
    And thoghte on Rymenhilde.
    He slogh ther on haste   *killed*
620 On hundred by the laste.   *at least*
    Ne mighte no man telle
    That folk that he gan quelle.   *slay*
    Of alle that were alive
    Ne mighte ther non thrive.
625 Horn tok the maisteres heved
    That he hadde him bireved   *cut off*
    And sette hit on his swerde
    Anouen at than orde.
    He ferde hom into halle   *traveled*
630 Among the knightes alle.
    "King," he sede, "well thu sitte
    And alle thine knightes mittel   *with you*
    Today, after my dubbing,
    So I rod on my pleing   *as/pleasure*
635 I fond o shup rowe   *floating*
    Mid watere al biflowe   *encompassed*
    All with Sarazines kin
    And none londisse men   *native*
    Today for to pine   *torment*
640 Thee and alle thine.
    Hi gonne me assaille.
    My swerd me nolde faille:
    I smot hem alle to grunde
    Other yaf hem dithes wunde.   *mortal/wounds*
645 That heved I thee bringe

---

612 "So that his [Horn's] blood grew hot."
624 *Thrive* "prosper" is understatement; the poet implies all were killed.
628 "Up above at the point."
631 " 'King,' he said, 'may you be well.' "

Of the maister-kinge.
Nu is thy wile y-yolde,
King, that thu me knighty woldest."

A morewe tho the day gan springe,   *when*
650 The King him rod an huntinge.
At hom lefte Fikenhild,
That was the wurste moder child.   *most evil*
                                                          /mother's child

Horn ferde into bure
To sen aventure.   *seek*
655 He saw Rymenhild sitte
Also heo were of witte.   *mad*
Heo sat on the sunne
With tieres all birunne.   *covered*
Horn sede, "Lef, thin ore!   *favor*
660 Why wepestu so sore?"
Heo sede, "Noght I ne wepe,
Bute ase I lay aslepe
To the see my net I caste
And hit nolde noght y-laste.   *remain intact*
665 A gret fish at the furste   *immediately*
My net he gan to berste.
Ich wene that ich shall leose
The fish that ich wolde cheose."

"Christ," quath Horn, "and Seint Stevene
670 Turne thine swevene!
Ne shall I thee biswike   *deceive*
Ne do that thee mislike.   *displease*
I shall me make thin owe
To holden and to knowe
675 For everech othere wighte
And tharto my treuthe I thee plighte."
Muchel was the ruthe   *sorrow*
That was at thare truthe,   *pledging*
For Rymenhild weop ille   *bitterly*
680 And Horn let the tires stille.
"Lemman," quath he, "dere,
Thu shalt more y-here.

647–648 "Now is the trouble you took, King, in wishing to knight me repaid."
657   "She sat at the window."
661–662 "She said, 'I weep for nothing except as I was lying asleep.' "
670   "Give a favorable turn to your dream."
675   Either "Despite every other person" or "In preference to every other person."
680   "And Horn stilled her tears."

Thy sweven shall wende
Other sum man shall us shende.   *harm*
685 The fish that brak the line–
Y-wis he doth us pine.   *shall torment*
That shall don us tene   *cause/anguish*
And wurth wel sone y-sene."   *shall be*

Aylmar rod by Sture
690 And Horn lay in bure.
Fikenhild hadde envye
And sede thes folie: *rash words*
"Aylmar, ich thee warne
Horn thee wule berne!   *destroy*
695 Ich herde whar he sede,
And his swerd forth leide,
To bringe thee of live
And take Rymenhild to wive.
He lith in bure
700 Under coverture   *sheets*
By Rymenhild thy doghter–
And so he doth well ofte.
And thider thu go all right,   *immediately*
Ther thu him finde might.
705 Thu do him ut of londe   *exile*
Other he doth thee shonde!"   *shall harm*

Aylmar agen gan turne
Well mody and well murne.   *angered/saddened*
He fond Horn in arme
710 On Rymenhilde barme.   *bosom*
"Awey ut," he sede, "fule theof,
Ne wurstu me nevremore leof!
Wend ut of my bure
With muchel messaventure.
715 Well sone, bute thu flitte,   *hasten away*
With swerde ich thee anhitte.   *shall strike*
Wend ut of my londe
Other thu shalt have shonde!"

Horn sadelede his stede
720 And his armes he gan sprede.
His brunye he gan lace

683–684 The lines are awkward, but seem to mean "Your dream shall turn [to good]
      or a certain man shall harm us."
714 "With all ill-fortune [to you]."
720 Apparently "And spread the [chain-mail] armor over him [the horse]."

So he sholde into place.
His swerd he gan fonge—   *grasp*
Nabod he noght too longe.   *nor tarried*
                                                 /overlong

725 He yede forth blive
    To Rymenhild his wive.
    He sede, "Lemman derling,
    Nu havestu thy swevening!
    The fish that thy net rente,
730 Fram thee he me sente.   *away from*
    Rymenhild, have well godne day.
    No leng abiden I ne may.   *longer*
    In to uncuthe londe   *foreign*
    Well more for to fonde;
735 I shall wune there   *dwell*
    Fulle seve yere.
    At seve yeres ende,
    Yef I ne come ne sende,
    Tak thee husebonde;
740 For me thu ne wonde.   *tarry further*
    In armes thu me fonge   *take*
    And kes me well longe."
    Heo kuste him well a stunde   *a space*
    And Rymenhild feol to grunde.
745 Horn tok his leve;
    Ne mighte he no leng bileve.   *longer/hesitate*
    He tok Athulf, his fere,
    All abute the swere   *neck*
    And sede, "Knight so trewe,
750 Kep well my luve newe.
    Thu nevre me ne forsoke;
    Rymenhild thu kep and loke."   *guard*
    His stede he gan bistride
    And forth he gan ride.
755 To the havene he ferde   *harbor*
    And a god shup he hurede,   *hired*
    That him sholde londe   *bring*
    In westene londe.
    Athulf weop with ighe   *eye*
760 And all that him y-sighe.

    The whyght him gan stonde   *breeze/arose*
    And drof till Irelonde.

---

722 "As if he were going to a tournament."
728 "Now your dream has come to pass."
734 "Indeed to seek further [adventure]."
738 "If I neither come nor send a [message]."

To lond he him sette   *disembarked*
And fot on stirop sette.
765 He fond by the weye
Kinges sones tweye–
That on him het Harild
And that other Berild.
Berild gan him preye
770 That he sholde him seye
What his name were
And what he wolde there.
"Cutberd," he sede, "ich hote,   *am called*
Y-comen ut of the bote,
775 Well feor fram biweste
To seche mine beste."   *fortune*
Berild gan him nier ride   *nearer*
And tok him by the bridel:
"Well beo thu, knight, y-founde;
780 With me thu lef a stunde.   *stay/a space*
Also mote I sterve,
The King thu shalt serve.
Ne saw I nevre my live   *in my life*
So fair knight arive!"
785 Cutberd he ladde into halle
And hi a kne gan falle;
He sette him a knewelyng   *kneeling*
And grette wel the gode King.
Thanne sede Berild sone,
790 "Sire King, of him thu hast to done;
Bitak him thy lond to werye;   *commit/guard*
Ne shall hit no man derye,   *harm*
For he is the faireste man
That evre yut on thy londe cam."
795 Than sede the King so dere,
"Welcome beo thu here!
Go nu, Berild, swithe,
And make him full blithe.
And whan thu farst to wowe,
800 Tak him thine glove:
Y-ment thu havest to wive,
Away he shal thee drive;

---

767   "One was called Harild."
779   The locution is essentially "Well met."
781   An asseveration similar to "As I live and breathe," although *sterven* means "die."
790   "Sir King, you have to do with him," implying "You should engage his services."
799–804   The passage is disputed; it could mean "When you [Berild] go a-wooing, entrust him [Horn] with your glove [i.e., as a symbol that he will not compete with you]; [but if] you intend to marry, he'll drive you away; because of Cutberd's handsomeness, assuredly you'll never succeed [in love]."

For Cutberdes fairhede
Ne shall thee nevre wel spede."

805 Hit was at Christesmasse,
Neither more ne lasse;
There cam in at none   *mid-day*
A geaunt swithe sone   *giant*
Y-armed fram paynime   *pagandom*
810 And seide thes rime: *words*
"Site stille, Sire King,
And herkne this tithing: *news*
Her buth payns arived;
Well mo thane five
815 Her beoth on the sonde,   *sand*
King, upon thy londe;
On of hem wile fighte
Agen three knightes.
Yef other three slen ure,
820 All this lond beo youre;
Yef ure on overcometh your threo,
All this lond shall ure beo.
Tomorewe be the fightinge,
Whane the light of daye springe."

825 Thanne sede the King Thurston,
"Cutberd shall beo that on;
Berild shall beo that other,   *second*
The thridde Harild, his brother;
For hi beoth the strengeste
830 And of armes the beste.
Bute what shall us to rede?
Ich wene we beth alle dede."

Cutberd sat at borde   *table*
And sede thes wordes:
835 "Sire King, hit nis no righte
On with three to fighte–
Agen one hunde
Thre Christen men to fonde.
Sire, "I shall alone
840 Withute more y-mone   *comrades*
With my swerd well ethe   *quite/easily*
Bringe hem three to dethe."

---

819   "If the other [your] three slay our [one]."
831   "But what shall be our counsel?"
837–838   "Three Christian men to take their chances against one [heathen] dog."

The King aros amorewe,
That hadde muchel sorwe;
845 And Cutberd ros off bedde–
With armes he him shredde.   *equipped*
Horn his brunye gan on caste   *corselet*
And lacede hit well faste
And cam to the Kinge
850 At his uprisinge.
"King," he sede, "cum to felde
For to bihelde
Hu we fighte shulle
And togare go wulle."   *together*
855 Right at prime tide
Hi gunnen ut ride
And funden on a grene
A geaunt swithe kene,
His feren him biside
860 Hore deth to abide.

The ilke bataille
Cutberd gan asaille.   *engage*
He yaf dentes y-nowe;
The knightes felle y-swowe.   *aswoon*
865 His dent he gan withdrawe,   *withhold*
For hi were negh aslawe;   *almost/slain*
And sede, "Knights, nu ye reste
One while ef you leste."   *a/while/desire*
Hi sede hi nevre nadde
870 Of knighte dentes so harde–
Bote of the King Murry,   *except/from*
That wes swithe sturdy.
He was of Hornes kunne,   *kin*
Y-born in Suddene.

875 Horn him gan to agrise   *shudder*
And his blod arise.
Bifor him saw he stonde
That driven him of londe   *he who*
And that his fader slow.
880 To him his swerd he drow.   *against/him*
He lokede on his ringe
And thoghte on Rymenhilde.
He smot him thuregh the herte
That sore him gan to smerte.
885 The payns, that er were so sturne,   *bold*
Hi gunne away urne.   *run*

---

855   The time is 6 A.M.

Horn and his compaynye
Gunne after hem well swithe hiye   *hasten*
And slowen alle the hundes
890 Er hi here shipes funde.   *reached*
To dethe he hem alle broghte:
His fader deth well dere hi boghte.   *atoned for*
Of alle the Kinges knightes
Ne scathede wer no wighte–   *harmed/man*
895 Bute his sones tweye
Bifore him he saw deye.
The King bigan to grete   *lament*
And teres for to lete.   *let fall*
Me laiden hem in bare   *men/bier*
900 And burden hem ful yare.   *buried/quickly*

The King com into halle
Among his knightes alle.
"Horn," he sede, "I seye thee,   *tell*
Do as I shall rede thee.
905 Aslawen beth mine heirs
And thu art knight of muchel pris   *value*
And of grete strengthe
And fair o bodie lengthe.
My rengne thu shalt welde   *realm/rule*
910 And to spuse helde   *receive*
Reynild, my doghter,
That sitteth on the lofte."   *upper room*

"O Sire King, with wronge   *wrongly*
Sholte ich hit underfonge–   *accept*
915 Thy doghter, that ye me bede,   *offer*
Over rengne for to lede.   *rule*
Well more ich shall thee serve,
Sir King, or thu sterve.   *die*
Thy sorwe shall wende   *turn*
920 Or seve yeres ende.
Whanne hit is wente,   *gone*
Sire King, yef me my rente.   *reward*
Whanne I thy doghter yerne,   *desire*
Ne shaltu me hire werne."   *refuse*
925 Cutberd wonede there   *dwelled*
Fulle seve yere
That to Rymenhild he ne sente
Ne him self ne wente.
Rymenhild was in Westernesse

---

917   *More* is ambiguous, but here context suggests "further."
927   "During which time he neither sent [a message] to Rymenhild."

930 With well muchel sorinesse.

A king ther gan arive
That wolde hire have to wive;
Aton he was with the King   *agreed*
Of that ilke wedding.
935 The dayes were shorte,   *few*
That Rymenhild ne dorste   *dared*
Leten in none wise.   *hesitate*
A writ heo dude devise;
Athulf hit dude write,
940 That Horn ne luvede noght lite.   *he who*
    /not a little

Heo sende hire sonde   *messenger*
To evereche londe
To seche Horn the knight
Ther me him finde mighte.   *there where/one*
945 Horn noght ther of ne herde
Till o day that he ferde
To wude for to shete.   *shoot*
A knave he gan y-mete.
Horn seden, "Leve fere,   *comrade*
950 What sechestu here?"   *seek you*
"Knight, if beo thy wille,
I may thee sone telle.
I seche fram biweste
Horn of Westernesse
955 For a maiden Rymenhild,   *on behalf of*
That for him gan wexe wild.
A king hire wile wedde
And bringe to his bedde,
King Mody of Reynes,
960 One of Hornes enemis.
Ich habbe walke wide   *far*
By the see side;
Nis he nowar y-funde.
Walaway the stunde!
965 Wailaway the while!
Nu wurth Rymenhild bigiled."   *shall be/lead*
    awry

Horn y-herde with his ires,
And spak with bidere tires,   *bitter*
"Knave, well thee bitide!   *good fortune*
970 Horn stondeth thee biside.
Agen to hure thu turne
And seye that heo nu murne   *should not sorrow*
For I shall beo ther bitime   *quickly*
A Soneday by prime."   *early morning*

975 The knave was well blithe
     And highede agen blive.   *hastened*
     The knave there gan adrinke–   *did/drown*
     Rymenhild hit mighte ofthinke!   *might well/regret*
     The see him con ded throwe   *did*
980 Under hire chambre wowe.   *wall*
     Rymenhild undude the dure-pin   *bolt*
     Of the hus ther heo was in
     To loke with hire ighe   *eye*
     If heo oght of Horn y-sighe.
985 Tho fond heo the knave adrent   *drowned*
     That heo hadde for Horn y-sent
     And that sholde Horn bringe.
     Hire fingres heo gan wringe.

     Horn cam to Thurston the King
990 And tolde him this tithing.   *report*
     Tho he was y-knowe   *informed*
     That Rymenhild was his owe;
     Of his gode kenne–   *kin*
     The King of Suddenne–
995 And hu he slow in felde
     That his fader quelde;   *he who/killed*
     And seide, "King the wise,
     Yeld me my servise!   *repay*
     Rymenhild help me winne!
1000 That thu noght ne linne!
     And I shall do to spuse
     Thy doghter well to huse.
     Heo shall to spuse have
     Athulf, my gode felawe,   *comrade*
1005 God knight mid the beste   *among*
     And the treweste."
     The King sede so stille,   *softly*
     "Horn have nu thy wille."   *desire*
     He dude writes sende   *writs*
1010 Into Irlonde
     After knightes lighte,   *agile*
     Irisse men to fighte.
     To Horn come y-nowe
     That to shupe drowe.   *ship/embarked*
1015 Horn dude him in the weye   *set out*
     On a god galeye.
     The wind him gan to blowe

983–984 "To see for herself whether she might espy anything of Horn."
993 "Horn told him" is understood.
1000 "May you not fail me!"
1001–1002 "And I shall cause your daughter to be well married."

In a litel throwe.   *time*
The see bigan to posse   *drive*
1020 Right into Westernesse
Hi strike sail and maste
And ankere gunne caste
Or eny day was sprunge
Other belle y-runge.
1025 The word bigan to springe
Of Rymenhilde weddinge.
Horn was in the watere—
Ne mighte he come no latere.
He let his shup stonde   *ride*
1030 And yede to londe.
His folk he dude abide   *caused to/wait*
Under wude side.
Horn him yede alone
Also he sprunge of stone.
1035 A palmere he thar mette
And faire hine grette:
"Palmere, thu shalt me telle
All of thine spelle."   *story*
He sede upon his tale,   *in the course of*
1040 "I come fram o brudale;   *bridal party*
Ich was at o wedding
Of a maide Rymenhild.
Ne mighte heo adrighe   *forbear*
That heo ne weop with ighe.
1045 Heo sede that heo nolde
Ben y-spused with golde.
Heo hadde on husbonde
Thegh he were ut of londe.
And in strong halle,
1050 Bithinne castel walle
Ther I was atte yate,   *gate*
Nolde hi me in late.
Mody y-hote hadde   *commanded*
To bure that me hire ladde.   *men/conduct*
1055 Away I gan glide—
That deol I nolde abide.   *sorrow/endure*
The bride wepeth sore
And that is muche deole!"

1027–1028   "Horn was in the water [? jumped into the water to wade ashore]—nor
         might he arrive any later." (i.e., he was just in the nick of time).
1032   "At the edge of a forest."
1034   "As if he sprang from stone," the allusion being to a pagan idea that man arose
         from an individual, hence solitary stone.
1046   "Be wedded with a gold [ring]."
1047   "She said that" is to be understood.

Quath Horn, "So Christ me rede,
1060 We shulle chaungy wede.   *exchange*
                                                /clothing

Have her clothes mine
And tak me thy sclavine,   *give/robe*
Today I shall ther drinke
That some hit shulle ofthinke."   *regret*
1065 His sclavin he dude dun legge
And tok hit on his rigge.   *put/back*
He tok Horn his clothes–
That nere him noght lothe.   *unpleasing*
Horn tok burdon and scrippe   *staff/wallet*
1070 And wrong his lippe.   *wrung*
He makede him a ful chere   *foul/countenance*
And all bicolmede his swere.   *dirtied/neck*
He makede him unbicomelich   *unappealing*
Hes he nas nevremore y-lich.   *as/never yet/like*

1075 He cam to the gateward,   *gate guard*
That him answerede hard.   *roughly*
Horn bad undo softe   *meekly*
Many time and ofte;
Ne mighte he awinne   *succeed*
1080 That he come therinne.
Horn gan to the yate turne   *gate*
And that wiket unspurne.
The boye hit sholde abugge.   *rogue/pay for it*
Horn threw him over the brigge   *drawbridge*
1085 That his ribbes hi tobrake   *cracked*
And suthe com in atte gate.   *thereafter*
He sette him well lowe   *sat down*
In beggeres rowe.
He lokede him abute
1090 With his colmie snute.   *dirty/nose*
He segh Rymenhild sitte
Ase heo were of witte,   *distraught*
Sore wepinge and yerne;   *sorely/deeply*
Ne mighte hure no man wurne.   *stop*
1095 He lokede in eche halke;   *corner*
Ne segh he nowhar walke
Athulf his felawe,
That he cuthe knowe.
Athulf was in the ture   *tower*
1100 Abute for to pure   *look*

1067   "He took from Horn his clothes."
1082   "And kicked open the wicket" (the small door within the gate itself).
1087   *Lowe* "low" implies "at the very foot of the table."
1098   "As far as he could perceive."

After his cominge,
Yef shup him wolde bringe.
He segh the see flowe   *sailing*
And Horn nowar rowe.
1105 He sede upon his songe
"Horn, nu thu ert well longe.
Rymenhild thu me toke   *entrusted*
That I sholde loke.
Ich habbe y-kept hure evre;   *constantly*
1110 Com nu other nevre–
I ne may no leng hure kepe.   *longer*
For sorewe nu I wepe."

Rymenhild ros off benche
Win for to shenche,   *pour*
1115 After mete in sale,   *hall*
Bothe win and ale.
On horn heo bar anhonde,   *drinking horn*
So lawe was in londe.   *custom*
Knightes and squier
1120 Alle dronken of the ber;   *beer*
Bute Horn alone   *only*
Nadde therof no mone.   *share*
Horn sat upon the grunde;
Him thughte he was y-bunde.
1125 He sede, "Quen so hende,   *gracious*
To meward thu wende;   *toward me*
Thu yef us with the furste;
The beggeres beoth ofthurste."   *very thirsty*

Hure horn heo laide adun
1130 And fulde him of a brun
His bolle of a galun;
For heo wende he were a glotoun.
Heo seide, "Have this cuppe
And this thing theruppe.
135 Ne saw ich nevre, so ich wene,
Beggere that were so kene."
Horn tok hit his y-fere   *gave/companion*
And sede, "Quen so dere,
Win nelle ich much ne lite   *desire*

1106   "Horn, now you are very slow [in coming]."
1108   "That I should take care [of her]."
1124   "He seemed overcome [with emotion]."
1127   "Pour for us among the first."
1129–1131   "She laid aside her horn [the one she had been using] and filled his bowl
      with a gallon from a brown [wooden bowl]."
1133–1134   "She said, 'Have this cup [your original one] and this thing [the brown
      bowl] too.'"

1140 But of cuppe white.
Thu wenest I beo a beggere,
And ich am a fishere
Well feor y-come by este   *in an easterly*
                                                        direction
1145 My net lith her by honde   *lies/at hand*
By a well fair stronde.
Hit hath y-lege there
Fulle seve yere.
Ich am y-come to loke
1150 Ef eny fish hit toke.
Ich am y-come to fishe:
Drink null I of dishe–
Drink to Horn of horne.
Feor ich am y-orne."   *far/traveled*
1155 Rymenhild him gan bihelde;   *look upon*
Hire heorte bigan to chelde.   *chill*
Ne knew heo noght his fishing,
Ne Horn himselve nothing.
Ac wunder hire gan thinke
1160 Why he bad to Horn drinke.
Heo fulde hire horn with win
And dronk to the pilegrim.
Heo sede, "Drink thy fulle
And suthe thu me telle   *then*
1165 If thu evre y-sighe   *saw*
Horn under wude lighe."   *lie*
Horn dronk of horn a stunde   *while*
And threw the ring to grunde.
He seyde, "Quen, now seche
1170 What is in thy drenche."   *drink*

The Quen yede to bure
With hire maidenes foure.
Tho fond heo what heo wolde,
A ring y-graven of golde
1175 That Horn of hure hadde: *received/from*
Sore hure dradde

1140 "Except from a white cup," the reference being to the white [? silver-mounted]
horn (l. 1117 and l. 1129) with which she had served the guests of rank and
from which Horn now wishes to be served.
1142 Horn tries here to make her think of her early foreboding dream.
1152–1153 "I do not wish to drink from a [humble] dish—[I desire to] drink to Horn
from the [white] horn."
1157–1158 "She did not understand his fishing nor [recognize] Horn himself."
1159 "But it seemed strange to her."
1168 "And threw the ring [which Rymenhild had given him] into the bottom [of the
drinking cup]."

That Horn y-sterve were,   *died*
For the ring was there.
Tho sente heo a damesele
1180 After the palmere.
"Palmere," quath heo, "trewe,
The ring that thu threwe,
Thu seye whar thu hit nome   *got*
And why thu hider come."
1185 He sede, "By Seint Gile,   *Gilles*
Ich habbe go many mile,
Well feor by yond weste
To seche my beste.   *fortune*
I fond Horn child stonde
1190 To shupeward in londe.
He sede he wolde agesse   *strive*
To arive in Westernesse.
The ship nam to the flode   *took/sea*
With me and Horn the gode.
1195 Horn was sik and deide
And faire he me preide,   *courteously*
'Go with the ringe
To Rymenhild the yinge.' "   *young*
Ofte he hit kuste–   *kissed*
1200 God yeve his saule reste!"

Rymenhild sede at the furste,   *thereupon*
"Herte, nu thu berste,
For Horn nastu namore,   *have you*
That thee hath pined so sore."
1205 Heo feol on hire bedde,
Ther heo knif hudde,   *hid*
To sle with king lothe
And hureselve bothe
In that ulke nighte,
1210 If Horn come ne mighte.
To herte knif heo sette,
Ac Horn anon hire kepte.   *caught up*
He wipede that blake of his swere   *dirt/off/neck*
And sede, "Quen so swete and dere,
1215 Ich am Horn thin owe.
Ne canstu me noght knowe?
Ich am Horn of Westernesse.
In armes thu me kusse!"
Hi kuste hem mid y-wisse   *each other/truly*

1189–1190 "I found in a land Horn about to go aboard ship."
1204   "Who has caused you so much anguish."
1207   "To slay the hateful king with."
1216   "Don't you know me?"

1220 And makeden muche blisse.

"Rymenhild," he sede, "I wende   *shall go*
Adun to the wudes ende;
Ther beth mine knightes
Redy to fighte;
1225 Y-armed under clothe,
Hi shulle make wrothe   *angry*
The King and his geste
That come to the feste.
Today I shall hem teche
1230 And sore hem areche."   *strike*

Horn sprong ut of halle
And let his sclavin falle.   *cloak*
The quen yede to bure
And fond Athulf in ture.
1235 "Athulf," heo sede, "be blithe
And to Horn thu go well swithe.
He is under wude bowe   *bough*
And with him knightes y-nowe."

Athulf bigan to springe
1240 For the tithinge.
After Horn he arnde anon   *ran*
Also that hors mighte gon.
He him overtok y-wis—
Hi makede swithe muchel blis.
1245 Horn tok his preye   *warriors*
And dude him in the weye.
He com in well sone
(The yates were undone)
Y-armed full thikke   *heavily*
1250 Fram fote to the nekke.
Alle that were therin
Bithute his twelf ferin   *except*
And the King Aylmare,
He dude hem alle to care   *made/sorry*
1255 That at the feste were;
Here lif hi lete there.
Horn ne dude no wunder
Of Fikenhildes false tunge.
Hi sworen othes holde

1225 The men carry concealed weapons.
1242 "As fast as [his] horse might go."
1246 "And put them on the march."
1257–1258 "Horn exacted no terrible vengeance on the false tongue of Fikenhild."
1259–1261 "They swore oaths of allegiance that [they] never should betray Horn."

1260 That nevre ne sholde
Horn nevre bitraye
Thegh he at dithe laye.   *near/death*
Hi runge the belle
The wedlak for to felle.   *carry out*
1265 Horn him yede with his   *his men*
To the kinges palais;
Ther was bridale swete
For riche men ther ete.
Telle ne mighte tunge
1270 That glee that ther was sunge.

Horn sat on chaere
And bad hem alle y-here.
"King," he sede, "thu luste   *listen to*
A tale mid the beste.
1275 I ne seye hit for no blame:
Horn is my name.
Thu me to knight hove   *elevated*
And knighthod have proved.
To thee, King, men seide
1280 That I thee bitrayde;
Thu makedest me fleme   *flee*
And thy lond to reme.   *leave*
Thu wendest that I wroghte
That I nevre ne thoghte,
1285 By Rymenhild for to ligge,
And that I withsegge.   *deny*
Ne shall ich hit biginne   *undertake*
Till I Suddene winne.
Thu kep hure a stunde   *for a time*
1290 The while that I funde   *fight to gain*
Into min heritage
And to my baronage.   *retainers*
That lond I shall ofreche   *obtain*
And do my fader wreche.
1295 I shall beo king of tune
And bere kinges crune.
Thanne shall Rymenhilde
Ligge by the king."

Horn gan to shupe drawe   *repair*
1300 With his Irisse falawes–
Athulf with him, his brother;
Nolde he non other.

1268 "Since noble men were feasting there."
1275 "I do not say [reveal] it for reproach [of you]."
1294 "And do vengeance on behalf of my father."

That shup bigan to crude;   *make way*
The wind him bleu lude.
1305 Bithinne dayes five
That shup gan arive
Abute middelnighte.
Horn him yede well righte;   *immediately*
He tok Athulf by honde
1310 And up he yede to londe.
Hi founde under shelde
A knight hende in felde.
O the shelde wes y-drawe   *on*
A crois of Jesu Christes lawe.   *faith*
1315 The knight him aslepe lay
All biside the way.
Horn him gan to take   *seize*
And sede, "Knight, awake!
Seye what thu kepest   *guard*
1320 And why thu her slepest?
Me thinkth by thine crois lighte
That thu longest to ure Drighte.   *belong/Lord*
Bute thu wule me shewe,
I shall thee tohewe."   *cut to pieces*
1325 The gode knight up aros;
Of the wordes him gros.
He sede, "Ich serve agenes my wille
Payns full ille.
Ich was Christene a while;   *once*
1330 Tho y-come to this ile   *isle*
Sarazins blake
That dude me forsake—
On Christ ich wolde bileve.
On him hi madede me reve
1335 To kepe this passage—
Fram Horn that is of age,
That wunieth biweste,
Knight with the beste.
Hi slowe with here honde
1340 The king of this londe
And with him fele hundred   *many*
And therof is wunder   *strange*
That he ne cometh to fighte.
God sende him the righte

1311–1312 "They found a knight with shield [fully armed] skilled in combat."
1323 "Unless you reveal [your duties] to me."
1326 "At the words he was terrified."
1332 "Who caused me to give [my religion] up."
1334–1335 "Against him [Horn] they made me prefect to stand guard in this pass."
1344 Either "May God send him immediately" or "May God grant [that] the right be his [on his side]."

1345 And wind him hider drive
    To bringe hem of live.   *slay*
    Hi slowen King Murry,
    Hornes fader, king hendy.   *courteous*
    Horn hi ut of londe sente;
1350 Twelf felawes with him wente,
    Among hem Athulf the gode,
    Min owene child, my leve fode.   *son*
    Ef Horn child is whol and sund   *healthy*
    And Athulf bithute wund   *without*
1355 (He luveth him so dere
    And is him so stere),
    Mighte I seon hem tweye,
    For joye I sholde deye."

    "Knight, beo thanne blithe
1360 Mest of alle sithe.
    Horn and Athulf his fere   *comrade*
    Bothe hi ben here."
    To Horn he gan gon
    And grette him anon.
1365 Muche joye hi makede there
    The while hi togadere were.
    "Childre," he sede, hu habbe ye fare?
    That ich you segh, hit is ful yare.   *long ago*
    Wulle ye this londe winne
1370 And sle that ther is inne?"   *whoever*
    He sede, "Leve Horn child,
    Yut liveth thy moder Godhild;
    Of joye heo miste
    If heo thee alive wiste."

1375 Horn sede on his rime,   *speech*
    "Y-blessed beo the time
    I com to Suddene
    With mine Irisse menne.
    We shulle the hundes teche
1380 To speken ure speche.
    Alle we hem shulle slee
    And all quik hem flee."
    Horn gan his horn to blowe;
    His folk hit gan y-knowe;   *recognize*

1355-1356   "He [Horn] loves him [Athulf] very dearly and is to him like a guardian."
1358   The conclusion of a conditional sentence containing two if-clauses (ll. 1353–
      1354 and l. 1357) separated by a parenthetic remark (ll. 1355–1356).
1360   "Most of all occasions."
1373-1374   "She might [have] joy if she knew you [to be] alive."
1380   That is, "To yield to us."

1385 Hi comen ut of stere
      Fram Hornes banere.
      Hi slowen and fughten
      The night and the ughten.   *early morning*
      The Sarazins kunde
1390 Ne lefde ther non in th'ende.
      Horn let wurche   *had/built*
      Chapeles and chirche;
      He let belles ringe
      And masses let singe.
1395 He com to his moder halle
      In a roche walle.
      Corn he let ferye
      And makede feste merye.
      Murye lif he wroghte–   *led*
1400 Rymenhild hit dere boghte.

      Fikenhild was prut on herte   *arrogant*
      And that him dude smerte.
      Yonge he yaf and elde
      Mid him for to helde.   *hold*
1405 Ston he dude lede
      Ther he hopede spede.   *to succeed*
      Strong castel he let sette,   *had built*
      Mid see him biflette;
      Ther ne mighte lighte   *alight*
1410 Bute fowel with flighte.
      Bute whanne the see withdrowe,
      Mighte come men y-nowe.
      Fikenhild gan wende   *intend*
      Rymenhild to shende.   *ravish*
1415 To wowe he gan hure yerne;   *ardently*
      The King ne dorste him werne.   *refuse*
      Rymenhild was full of mode;   *anxiety*
      Heo wep teres of blode.
      That night Horn gan swete   *sweat*
1420 And hevye for to mete   *dream*
      Of Rymenhild, his make,   *mate*
      Into shupe was y-take.
      The shup bigan to blenche;   *lurch*

1385–1386 Apparently, "They went over the stern [lit. 'rudder'] away from Horn's banner."
1389–1390 "There remained none of the Saracen race there in the end."
1397   "He had corn brought"; the original reads *serie*, which seems an error.
1400   "Rymenhild paid for it dearly," the implication being that Horn's absence allowed Fikenhild to plot against her.
1403   "He gave [money] to young and old."
1408   "[And] caused [it] to be moated about with sea water."
1422   "[Who] was taken aboard ship."

His lemman sholde adrenche.   *drown*
1425 Rymenhild with hire honde
Wolde up to londe;
Fikenhild agen hire pelte   *repulsed*
With his swerdes hilte.

Horn him wok of slape
1430 So a man that hadde rape.   *like/haste*
"Athulf," he sede, "felawe,
To shupe we mote drawe.   *go*
Fikenhild me hath y-don under   *betrayed*
And Rymenhild to do wunder.
1435 Christ, for his wundes five,
Tonight me thuder drive!"   *thither*
Horn gan to shupe ride,
His feren him biside.

Fikenhild, or the day gan springe,
1440 All right he ferde to the Kinge,   *straightway/went*
After Rymenhild the brighte,
To weden hire by nighte.
He ladde hure by the derke   *at night*
Into his niwe werke.   *fortress*
1445 The feste hi bigunne,   *festivities*
Er that ros the sunne.
Er thane Horn hit wiste,
Tofore the sunne upriste,
His shup stod under ture
1450 At Rymenhilde bure.
Rymenhild, litel weneth heo   *suspects*
That Horn thanne alive beo.
The castel they ne knewe
For he was so newe.
1455 Horn fond sittinde Arnoldin,
That was Athulfes cosin,
That ther was in that tide
Horn for t'abide.   *to await*
"Horn knight," he sede, "kinges sone,
1460 Well beo thu to londe y-come.
Today hath y-wedde Fikenhild
Thy swete lemman Rymenhild.
Ne shall I thee lye:
He hath giled thee twye.   *beguiled*
1465 This tur he let make
All for thine sake.

1425–1426 "Rymenhild wished to swim up to land."
1434 "And has caused Rymenhild distress."

Ne may ther come inne
No man with none ginne.   *device*
Horn, nu Christ thee wisse,   *guide*
1470 Of Rymenhild that thu ne misse."
Horn cuthe all the liste   *knew/cunning*
That eny man of wiste.
Harpe he gan shewe   *draw forth*
And tok felawes fewe,
1475 Of knightes swithe snelle   *agile*
That shrudde hem at wille.
Hi yeden by the gravel   *beach*
Toward the castel.
Hi gunne murye singe
1480 And makede here gleowinge.   *harping*

Rymenhild hit gan y-here
And axede what hi were.   *asked*
Hi sede hi weren harpurs
And sume were gigours.   *fiddlers*
1485 Heo dude Horn in late   *let*
Right at halle gate.
He sette him on the benche,
His harpe for to clenche.   *grasp*
He makede Rymenhilde lay—   *song*
1490 And heo makede walaway.   *lamentation*
Rymenhild feol y-swowe—   *a swoon*
Ne was ther non that louwe.   *laughed*
Hit smot to Hornes herte
So bitere that hit smerte.
1495 He lokede on the ringe
And thoghte on Rymenhilde
He yede up to borde
With gode swerdes orde.   *sword's/edge*
Fikenhildes crune   *top of the head*
1500 Ther y-fulde adune;   *thumbled*
And all his men arowe,   *in order*
He dude adun throwe.
Whanne hi weren aslawe   *slain*
Fikenhild he dude todrawe.   *tear apart*
1505 Horn makede Arnoldin thare
King after King Aylmare.
Of all Westernesse
For his meoknesse.
The King and his homage   *vassals*
1510 Yeven Arnoldin trewage.   *tribute*

1470   "So that you do not lose Rymenhild."
1476   "Who dressed themselves [disguised.themselves] as it pleased them."

Horn tok Rymenhild by the honde
And ladde hure to the stronde
And ladde with him Athelbrus,
The gode stiward of his hus.
1515 The see bigan to flowe   *rise*
And Horn gan to rowe.   *sail*
Hi gunne for arive
Ther King Mody was sire.   *lord*
Athelbrus he makede ther king
1520 For his gode teching.   *guardianship*
He yaf alle the knightes ore
For Horn knightes lore.
Horn gan for to ride;
The wind him blew well wide.   *afar*
1525 He arivede in Irlonde,
Ther he wo fonde;
Ther he dude Athulf child
Wedden maide Reynild.
Horn come to Suddenne
1530 Among all his kenne.   *kin*
Rymenhild he makede his quene,
So hit mighte well beon.
All folk hem mighte rewe
That loveden hem so trewe.
1535 Nu ben hi bothe dede—
Christ to hevene hem lede!
Her endeth the tale of Horn
That fair was and noght unorn.   *ugly*
Make we us glade evre among,
1540 For thus him endeth Hornes song.
Jesus, that is of hevene king,
Yeve us alle His swete blessing.

1521–1522 Perhaps, "He [Athelbrus] showed favor to all knights because of Knight
    Horn's counsel"; but the original seems unsatisfactory.
1526 A grammatically clumsy line (*fonde* should be *fondede*), which may mean
    "Where he experienced sorrow [because of his separation from Rymenhild]."
1532 "Just as it might well be."
1533 Perhaps, "Everyone might sympathize with them [because of their troubles]."
1539 "Let us ever be glad among ourselves."

Havelok the Dane

ORN and *Havelok the Dane* are usually printed together and discussed together, often as though they were of equal literary value. The fact is unfortunate because the latter is really a better piece all around. The two are indeed roughly contemporary, the composition of *Havelok* being dated only a half century later than that of *King Horn*; the audience for which the two were composed must have been of the same humble stamp. Even the exile-and-return motif is essential to both as is also the male-Cinderella motif, the eventual rise of an ill-starred youth to power and stature. Yet the similarities are less striking than the differences. The meter of *Havelok* is a genuine iambic tetrameter. Where the locale of *Horn* is a never-never land of sea-faring Saracen versus God-fearing Christian, the lands of *Havelok* are a real England and a real Denmark. Its Latin subtitle *Incipit vita Hauelok quondam rex anglie et denemarchie* must have matched some sort of popular realization that Englishmen of the North were in blood half-Scandinavian and that they just before the Conquest had actually been part of a dual kingdom of England and Denmark. The story itself may have had a significance to its original audience which is lost to the reader today. It would be wrong to impute a nationalistic ardor to *Havelok*, at least in the modern sense; but it is arresting to note that this most English of all Middle English romances recalls the initial lines of *Beowulf*:

> Hwæt, wē Gār-Dena   in gēardagum
> Þēodcyninga   þrym gefrūnon
> Hū þā æþelingas   ellen fremedon!

('Lo, we have heard of the glory of the kings of the people of the Spear-Danes in days of old, how the noble ones performed deeds of valor!')

Here, even in the eighth century, northern Englishmen were also attuned to hearing tales of their Danish cousins and in terms which almost associate them with the Danes—indeed, almost as though there were really no difference between them at all.

The long poem of Havelok and Goldborow is sometimes called the *bourgeois romance* of the Matter of England. The label is not derogatory, but it is a slippery one, since the majority of the sixty-odd extant Middle English metrical romances are *bourgeois* in that they are designed to satisfy a nonaristocratic palate. Where the label does apply concerns the point of view of the poet. He is *bourgeois* in the now almost unused good sense of the term. He is distressed over current inequities in law; unquestioningly he accepts, not birth and power, but work, virtue, and integrity as paramount; his deepest wisdom derives from plain, homely proverbial expression. Just when he composed the poem we have no definite knowledge; the dates usually given range from 1250 to 1300. Older scholarship placed the date at 1300 or somewhat later, although for historical reasons which now seem questionable. Evidence for dating the composition is hence thrown back on philological data. Final *e*, for example, is in *Havelok* as consistent and historical as it is in works written prior to 1300 and its use is very similar to that in works whch can be dated at or around 1275.

Four versions of the Havelok story deserve notice. The earliest is in Geoffry Gaimar's *Estorie des engles*, written about 1150 and hence over a hundred years before the Middle English poem. The next is also a twelfth century piece, the Old French *Lai d'havelok*. The third is that of the present English poem and the fourth a curious eighty-two line summary inserted in the translation of Peter Langtoft's *Chronicle* done by Robert Manning of Brunne (Bourne) in Lincolnshire. The four versions suggest various things. First, they attest the viability from the twelfth to the fourteenth century of the double plot of wronged prince and princess. Further, the *Lai* probably established a sort of appropriate dramatic sequence to the motifs of the Havelok legend and may indeed have been the source of the English poem, although not a direct one. Finally, the Robert Manning interpolation (it was written before 1338) indicates that in Lincoln and Grimsby the Havelok material enjoyed popular currency. There are indications that Grimsby possessed a popular tradition that a fisherman by the name of Grim founded the town and that he once befriended a castaway who turned out to be of royal blood. There is a town seal dating from the twelfth century bearing the names "Grym," "Habloc," and "Goldeburgh." People at one time pointed to a stone said to have been thrown by Havelok at his enemies and a chapel wherein Havelok and Goldborow were said to have been married. *Havelok*, in short, is one Middle English romance which rests firmly on popular local legend, although one which seems to have wandered first into a French cultural milieu for its narrative format and then back again to its native Lincolnshire for its ultimate artistic appeal.

The mass of scholarship treating the possible historicity of *Havelok* is formidable, but its evidence is thin, its reasonng fine, and its issue utterly frustrating. Here, as in similar studies of *Horn,* a very questionable technique is employed: recurrent types of personage or incident easily found within the range of medieval Northern European history are traced forward and attached to a romance figure or incident. As an illustration, the name *Havelok* is etymologically linked with the French name *Avelok*, which equates with the Old English *Anlaf*, a form of the Scandinavian *Olaf*; from this point, the Havelok of the poem can be traced to the historical Olaf Sictricson, who once bore the nickname *Cuaron*, a name of Celtic origin deriving from a word meaning "sandal" and a name, furthermore, which in the French versions of *Havelok* the hero himself at one time assumes. Scholarly reasoning can go further: Olaf Sictricson is known to have been confused by chroniclers with his cousin, Anlaf Guthfrithson, defeated in the Battle of Brunanburg in 937, and the careers of both Olaf and Anlaf show vicissitudes bearing some similarity to those suffered by the Havelok of romance. Other attempts to trace down the historicity of the Havelok legend—in particular, the historicity of Goldborow, Grim, and the two kings Birkabeyn and Aethelwold—are equally tenuous and, it must be admitted, equally unrewarding for the purposes of literary study.

Prosodically, *Havelok* is far more "competent" than *Horn*, although the widespread use of the little Oxford edition, wherein silent final *e*'s are underdotted, has made its verse appear in an unfairly favorable light. Yet irregularities are present; and it is helpful, when reading aloud, to insert a final *e* where it is deemed one might reasonably fit or obviate the need for one altogether by placing a caesural pause after the first of two consecutive accented syllables. But by and large *Havelok* does show—again in relation to *Horn*—a move toward a definite iambic rhythm, despite its possible dactyls and anapests and despite its undoubted and numerous trochees.

The one surviving manuscript (Laud Misc. 108 in the Bodleian, Oxford, dated *c*. 1300–1325) is not an autograph. It is the copy of another copy, itself probably descending from one or two other copies. Even though linguistically it belongs to the northeast Midlands, it contains Northern and Southern dialect features. The former can be explained by the fact that Lincolnshire, the probable home of the poet, is on the southern border of the Northern dialect area, the latter by the probability that a Southern scribe at one time copied the poem. It is, however, to an Anglo-Norman scribe that its orthographic eccentricities must be ascribed, particularly since the native [ç] and [x] are transcribed in the wildest variety and the native yogh is completely replaced by *y*. In fact, if *Havelok* is to be read with ease—read so that focus on its narrative is immediate—more adjustment of its text to norms of later ME are called for than with the text of *Horn*. Here, the graphemic irregularities of the Anglo-Norman scribe are removed: his *th*, *ct*, *cht*, *t*, and *c*, all of which can indicate the palatal and velar fricatives, are reduced to *gh*; his occasional *t* for *th*, *th* for *t*, *s* for *sh*, and *w* for *u* are similarly normalized. Modified also are other orthographic peculiarities of whatever origin: inorganic *h* (as in *hold* "old" and *hayse* "ease") is dropped and downright careless spellings (like *lon* for *lond* and *we* for *well*) are corrected. Inconsistent spellings of common words are regularized: for example, the ME forms of "out," "how," and "every" have been kept to *ut*, *hou*, and *everilk* except where rhyme might possibly suffer. The pairs *c/k*, *c/ch*, *i/j*, *l/ll*, and *u/v* are treated as they are in *Horn*. Generally, what was said of the inflections in *Horn* applies here, except that *he* stands for both "he" and "they." The present participle is in *-inde* (an incongruously southern form), the second person singular present in *-es* and sometimes *-t*, and the third person singular either in *-es* or *-eth*.

REFERENCES: Brown and Robbins, No. 114; Billings, pp. 15–24; CBEL, I:148–149; Hibbard, pp. 103–114; Kane, pp. 49–50; Wells, pp. 13–15. The most handy of all editions is that of W. W. Skeat, *The Lay of Havelok the Dane*, 2nd ed. (Oxford 1915, corrected reprint 1956), rev. by Kenneth Sisam, which contains a partially normalized text; an accessible diplomatic text is that in French and Hale, pp. 71–176.

Incipit Vita Hauelok Quondam Rex Anglie et Denemarchie

Herkneth to me, gode men,
Wives, maidnes, and alle men,
Of a tale that ich you wile telle,
5 Who-so it wile here and ther-to dwelle.
The tale is of Havelok y-maked;
Whil he was litel, he yede full naked. — *ill-clothed*
Havelok was a full good gome: — *fellow*
He was full good in every trome; — *troop*
He was the wighteste man at nede
10 That thurte riden on any stede. — *might*
That ye mowen nou y-here,
And the tale you mowen y-lere, — *learn*
At the beginning of ure tale,
Fill me a cuppe of full good ale;
15 And while I drinken, her I spelle, — *relate*
That Christ us shilde alle fro helle!
Christ late us evere so for to do
That we moten comen him to; — *may*
And, with-that it mote ben so,
20 Benedicamus Domino!
Here I schall biginnen a rim;

20 "May God bless us!"

Christ us yeve well god fin!
The rim is maked of Havelok,
A stalworthy man in a flok.   *company*
25 He was the wightest man at nede   *most courageous*
That may riden on any stede.

It was a king by are dawes,   *former*
That in his time were gode lawes
He dede maken and full well holden;
30 Him lovede yung, him lovede olde,
Erl and barun, dreng and thain,
Knight, bondeman, and swain,
Widwes, maidnes, prestes and clerkes,
And all for hise gode werkes.
35 He lovede God with all his might,
And holy kirke and soth and right.
Right-wise men he lovede alle,
And overall made hem forto calle.
Wreyeres and wrobberes made he falle   *traitors*
40 And hated hem so man doth galle;
Utlawes and theves made he binde,
Alle that he mighte finde,
And heye hengen on gallwe-tree;   *gallows*
For hem ne yede gold ne fee;
45 In that time a man that bore
Well fifty pund, I wot, or more,
Of red gold upon his back,
In a male whit or black,   *wallet*
Ne funde he non that him missaide,   *insulted*
50 Ne with ivele on hond layde.
Thanne mighte chapmen fare   *merchants*
Thurhut Englond with here ware
And baldelike beye and sellen,   *boldly*
Overall ther he willen dwellen,
55 In gode burwes, and ther-fram   *towns*
Ne funden he non that dede hem sham,
That he ne weren sone to sorwe brought,
And povere maked and broght to nought.
Thanne was Engelond at aise;   *ease*

---

28 "In whose time were good laws."
29 "[Which] he caused [to be] made and held very well."
31 A *dreng* in Northumbria at the time was a tenant with military obligations.
38 "And everywhere had them called [to preferment]."
44 "For them neither gold nor goods [i.e., as bribes] availed."
50 "Nor with evil [intent] laid hand [on him]."
54 "Anywhere they wished to remain."
57–58 "So that they [the merchants] were not brought suddenly to sorrow and made
       poor and reduced to nothing."

60 Michel was swich a king to praise
   That held so Englond in grith!   *peace*
   Christ of hevene was him with.
   He was Engelondes blome;   *flower*
   Was non so bold loverd to Rome
   That durste upon his menie bringe
65 Hunger ne othere wicke thinge.
   Whan he fellede hise fos,   *put to flight*
   He made hem lurken and crepen in wros: *hide/corners*
   They hidden hem alle and helden hem stille
70 And diden all his herte wille.
   Right he lovede of alle thinge;   *Justice/above*
   To wronge might him no man bringe,
   Ne for silver ne for gold–
   So was he his soule hold.
75 To the faderles was he rath;   *a help*
   Who-so dede hem wrong or lath,
   Were it clerk or were it knight,
   He dede hem sone to haven right;
   And who dide widwen wrong,
80 Were he nevre knight so strong,
   That he ne made him sone kesten
   In fetteres and full faste festen;
   And who-so dide maidne shame
   Of hire body or brought in blame,
85 Bute it were by hire wille,   *unless*
   He made him sone of limes spille.
   He was the beste knight at nede
   That evere mighte riden on stede
   Or wepne wagge or folk ut lede;
90 Of knight ne havede he nevere drede
   That he ne sprong forth so sparke of glede,
   And lete him knawe of hise hand-dede–
   Hu he couthe with wepne spede;
   And other he refte him hors or wede,   *either*
95 Or made him sone handes sprede

64–66 "[There] was no lord as far as Rome so bold that he dared bring hunger or other wicked things upon his people."
74 "So [greatly] was he observant of his soul's [good]."
76–78 "Whosoever did them [the fatherless] wrong or injury, were it clerk or were it knight, he caused them to have justice at once."
79–82 "And whoever did harm to widows, were he ever knight so strong, he caused him to be cast at once into fetters and bound very well."
86 "He had him castrated at once."
89 "Or bear weapons or lead men [in war]."
90–93 "He never had fear of [any] knight in that he did not jump forth like a spark from a coal and let him know the power [lit., deeds] of his hand—how he was able to prevail in arms."

And "Loverd, merci!" loude grede.   *cry*
He was large and no wight gnede.   *generous*
    /niggardly

Havede he non so god brede
Ne on his bord non so good shrede,
100 That he ne wolde thorwith fede
Povre that on fote yede–
Forto haven of Him the mede
That for us wolde on rode blede,
Christ, that all can wisse and rede
105 That evere woneth in any thede.

The king was hoten Athelwold.   *called*
Of word, of wepne he was bold;
In Engeland was nevre knight
That bettere held the lond to right.   *justly*
110 Of his body ne havede he eir   *heir*
Bute a maiden swithe fair,   *except*
That was so yung that sho ne couthe
Gon on fote ne speke with mouthe.
Than him tok an ivel strong   *seized/sickness*
115 That he well wiste and underfong   *perceived*
That his deth was comen him on
And saide, "Christ, what shall I don?
Loverd, what shall me to rede?
I wot full well ich have my mede: *reward*
120 Hu shall nou my doughter fare?
Of hire have ich michel care;
Sho is mikel in my thought: *much*
Of me self is me right nought.
No selcouth is though me be wo:
125 Sho ne can speke ne sho can go.   *walk*
Yif scho couthe on horse ride
And a thousande men by hire side,
And sho were comen intill elde   *of/age*
And Engelond sho couthe welde,   *govern*
130 And don of hem that hire were queme,
And hire body couthe yeme,
Ne wolde me nevere ivele like,
Ne though ich were in hevene-rike!"

98–105 "He never had such good roast meat nor such a good morsel of food on his
table that with it he wouldn't feed the poor who walked afoot—just to gain the
reward from Him, Christ, who desired to bleed for us upon the cross [and] who
is able to guide and advise all who ever dwell in any land."
118 "Lord, what shall be my help?"
124 "No wonder it is though I am anxious."
130–132 "And do with them what were pleasing to her and take care of her person,
I would not ever be displeased."

Whanne he havede this plainte maked,
135 Therafter stronglike he quaked.
He sende writes sone anon   *letters*
After his erles evereich on;
And after hise baruns, riche and povre,
Fro Rokesburw all into Dovere,   *Roxbury*
140 That he shulden comen swithe   *quickly*
Till him, that was full unblithe,   *sad*
To that stede ther he lay   *place*
In harde bondes night and day.
He was so faste with ivel fest   *sickness*
145 That he ne moughte haven no rest,
He ne moughte no mete ete   *food*
Ne he ne moughte no lithe gete;   *comfort*
Ne non of his ivel that couthe red;
Of him ne was nought buten ded.

150 Alle that the writes herden
Sorful and sorry till him ferden;   *journeyed*
He wrungen hondes and wepen sore
And yerne prayden Christes ore   *eagerly/grace*
That He wolde turnen him
155 Ut of that iuel that was so grim!
Thanne he weren comen alle
Bifor the king into the halle,
At Winchestre ther he lay,
"Welcome," he sayde, "be ye ay!
160 Full michel thank can I you
That ye aren comen to me now!"

Whanne he weren alle set,   *seated*
And the king haveden y-gret,   *greeted*
He greten and gouleden and goven hem ille,
165 And he bad hem alle been stille
And saide that greting helpeth nought,   *weeping*
"For all to dede am ich brought.
Bute now ye sen that I shall deye,
Now ich wille you alle praye
170 Of my doughter, that shall be
Yure levedy after me,
Who may yemen hire so longe,   *take care of*
Bothen hire and Engelonde,
Till that she woman be of elde   *age*
175 And that she mowe hit yemen and welde?"   *govern/wield*

148–149   "Nor no one knew help for his sickness; for him was [left] nothing except
      death."
160   "I thank you greatly."
164   "They mourned and lamented and grieved."

He answereden and saiden anon,
By Christ and by Saint Jon,
That th'erl Godrigh of Cornwayle
Was trewe man withuten faile;
180 Wis man of red, wis man of dede,   *counsel*
And men haveden of him mikel drede:
"He may hire alther best yeme,
Till that she mowe well been quene."

The king was payed of that rede;   *pleased/counsel*
185 A well fair cloth bringen he dede
And thercon laide the messebook,   *missal*
The caliz, and the pateyn ok,   *chalice/paten*
        /also

The corporaus, the messe-gere;   *corporal*
Ther-on he garte the erl swere   *made*
190 That he sholde yemen hire well,
Withuten lac, wituten tel   *fault/reproach*
Till that she were twelf winter old
And of speche were bold;
And that she couthe of curteysye
195 And speken of love-drurye;
And till that she loven moughte
Whom-so hire to gode thoughte;
And that he shulde hire yeve
The hexte man that mighte live–   *noblest*
200 The beste, faireste, the strangest ok;
That dede he him sweren on the book.
And thanne shulde he Engelond
All bitechen into hire hond.   *commit*

Whanne that was sworn on this wise,   *manner*
205 The king dede the maiden arise
And the erl hire bitaughte,   *committed*
And all the lond he evere awghte–   *owned*
Engelonde, every del–   *portion*
And prayde he shulde yeme hire well.

210 The king ne moughte don no more,
But yerne prayede Godes ore,   *grace*
And dede him hoslen well and shrive
I wot fif hundred sithes and five;   *times*
And ofte dede him sore swinge   *scourge*

---

182 "He will be able to take care of her best of all."
194–195 "And might know about courteous deportment and could speak of love-making."
197 "Whosoever seemed good to her."
212–213 "And had the sacrament properly given to him and [had himself] shrived."

215 And with hondes smerte dinge
    So that the blod ran off his fleis,   *flesh*
    That tendre was and swithe neis.   *soft*
    He made his quiste swithe well
    And sone gaf it evereilk del.
220 Whan it was goven, ne mighte men finde
    So mikel men mighte him in winde,
    Of his in arke ne in chiste,
    In Engelond, that noman wiste;
    For all was yoven, faire and well,
225 That him was leved no catel.   *possessions*

    Thanne he havede been ofte swungen,   *scourged*
    Ofte shriven and ofte dungen,   *beaten*
    "In manus tuas, loverde," he saide,
    Er that he the speche laide;
230 To Jesu Christ bigan to calle
    And deyede biforn his heymen alle.   *died/nobles*
    Than he was ded, there mighte men see
    The meste sorrwe that mighte be.
    Ther was sobbing, siking, and sor,   *sighing/grief*
235 Handes wringing and drawing by hor   *tearing/hair*
    Alle greten swithe sore,   *wept*
    Riche and povre that there wore;
    And mikel sorrwe haveden alle,
    Levedyes in boure, knightes in halle.

240 Whan that sorrwe was somdel laten   *abated*
    And he haveden longe graten,   *wept*
    Belles deden he sone ringen,
    Monkes and prestes messe singen;
    And sauteres deden he manye reden   *psalters*
245 That God self shulde his soule leden
    Into hevene biforn his Sone
    And ther withuten ende wone.
    Than he was to the erthe brought,
    The riche erl ne foryat nought
250 That he ne dede all Engelond
    Sone sayse intill his hond;

218–219 "He made his will quite appropriately and carried it out at once in all respects."
220–223 "When it [the will] was executed, one might not find in England so much [as a sheet] one might wind him in of his [possessions] that anyone knew of, neither in coffer nor in chest."
228 "Into thy hands [I commend my spirit]," from Luke 23:46.
229 "Before he lost [power of] speech."
245–247 "So that God himself should lead his soul into heaven before his Son and [should cause it] to dwell there without end."
249–251 "The powerful earl did not forget to have all England committed to his control at once."

And in the castels let he do	*had/placed*
The knightes he mighte tristen to;	*trust*
And alle the Englis dede he swere	*made/swear*
255 That he shulden him good fey beren;	*faith*
He yaf alle men that good him thoughte	
Liven and deyen till that he moughte,	
Till that the kinges doughter wore	
Twenty winter old and more.	
260 Thanne he havede taken this oth	
Of erles, baruns, lef and loth,	*dear/hostile*
Of knightes, cherles, free and thewe,	*thrall*
Justises dede he maken newe	
All Engelond to faren thorw	
265 Fro Dovere into Rokesborw.	
Schireves he sette, bedels, and greives,	*sheriffs/beadles /graves*
Grith-sergeans with longe gleives,	
To yemen wilde wodes and pathes	*govern*
Fro wicke men, that wolde don scathes,	*harm*
270 And forto haven alle at his cry,	
At his wille, at hise mercy,	
That non durste been him again,	*against*
Erl ne barun, knight ne swain.	*peasant*
Wislike, for soth, was him well	
275 Of folk, of wepne, of catel.	*weapons/goods*
Sothlike, in a lite thrawe,	*truly/space*
All Engelond of him stood awe;	
All Engelond was of him adrad	*afraid*
So is the beste fro the gad.	
280 The kinges doughter bigan thrive	
And wex the fairest wuman on live.	*grew/alive*
Of alle thewes was she wis	
That gode weren and of pris.	*value*
The maiden Goldeboru was hoten;	*called*
285 For hire was many a ter y-groten.	
Whanne the Erl Godrich him herde	
Of that maiden – hu well she ferde,	

256–257 "He gave men whatever seemed fitting to him for as long as they lived [literally, until they might live and die]."
267   "Peace-keepers with long lances."
274   "In truth, he had plenty indeed."
279   "[Just] as is the beast [afraid] of the goad."
282   "She understood all [matters of] precedence."
285   "For her [sake] was many a tear shed," a suggestion both of coming hardship and of the idea that beauty involves tragedy and sorrow.
286   *Him*, a reflexive, occurs in ME with verbs which in ModE often need no reflexive.

Hu wis sho was, hu chaste, hu fair,
And that sho was the righte eir   *heir*
290 Of Engelond, of all the rike–   *kingdom*
Tho bigan Godrich to sike,   *sigh*
And saide, "Whether she sholde be
Queen and levedy over me?
Whether sho sholde all Engelond
295 And me and mine haven in hire hond?
Datheit who it hire thave!
Shall sho it nevere more have.
Sholde ich yeve a fool, a therne,   *serving girl*
Engelond, thou sho it yerne?   *though/desire*
300 Datheit who it hire yeve   *cursed/gives*
Evere-more whil I live!
She is waxen all to prud   *grown/proud*
For gode metes and noble shrud,   *food/clothes*
That ich have yoven hire too ofte;
305 Ich have yemed hire too softe.   *cared for*
     /leniently

Shall it nought been als sho thenkes:
Hope maketh fool man ofte blenkes.
Ich have a sone, a full fair knave;
He shall Engelond all have!
310 He shall king, he shall been sire,
So brouke I evere my blake swire!"
Whan this traison was all thought,

Of his oth ne was him nought.
He let his oth all overga;
315 Therof ne yaf he nought a stra;   *straw*
But sone dede hire fete,   *fetch*
Er he wolde eten any mete,
Fro Winchestre, ther sho was,   *where*
Also a wicke traitur Judas,   *like*
320 And dede leden hire to Dovre,
That standeth on the seis-ovre;   *seashore*
And therinne dede hire fede
Povrelike in feeble wede.
The castel dede he yemen so   *guard*
325 That non ne mighte comen hire to

292–293   "And said, 'Should she be queen and lady over me?' " *Whether* is an interrogative particle.
296   "Cursed [be he] who endures it [of] her!"
307   "Hope often deceives a foolish man."
311   "If ever I may use my white neck!" The asseveration uses the ME *blake* from OE *blāk* 'white.'
314   "He let his oath (go) utterly neglected."
322   "And there did care for her wretchedly in humble garments."

Of hire frend, with hir to speken,
That evere mighte hire bale wreken.

Of Goldeboru shull we nou laten,   *ceases/weep*
That nought ne blinneth forto graten
330 Ther sho liggeth in prisoun:
Jesu Christ, that Lazarun
To live broughte fro dede bondes,
He lese hire with hise hondes!
And leve sho mote him y-see
335 Heye hangen on gallwe-tree,
That hire haved in sorrwe brought
So as sho ne misdede nought!   *although*

Say we nou forth in ure spelle!   *tale*
In that time, so it bifelle,
340 Was in the lond of Denemark
A riche king and swithe stark.   *very/strong*
The name of him was Birkabein;
He havede many knight and swain;
He was fair man and wight,   *bold*
345 Of body he was the beste knight
That evere mighte leden ut here   *command/army*
Or stede onne ride or handlen spere.
Three children he havede by his wif;
He hem lovede so his lif.   *as*
350 He havede a sone and doughtres two,
Swithe faire, as fell it so.   *befell*
He that wille non forbere,
Riche ne povre, king ne kaisere,
Deth him took than he best wolde   *when*
355 Liven—but hyse dayes were fulde—   *numbered*
That he ne moughte no more live,
For gold ne siluer, ne for no give.   *gift*

Whan he that wiste, rathe he sende   *quickly*
After prestes fer and hende,   *near*
360 Chanounes gode and monkes bethe   *both*
Him for to wisse and to rede;   *guide/advise*
Him for to hoslen and forto shrive,

---

327 "Who might ever avenge her of [her] evil."
328 "We shall now turn from Goldborow."
333 "[May] he release her from her bonds."
334-337 "And allow she might see him hanged high on the gallows who brought her
         into sorrow even though she did nothing wrong."
342 The name in its ON form means "[wearer of] birch bark leggings."
352 *He* finds its referent in *deth* of l. 354.
362 "To give him the sacrament and shrive [him]."

Whil his body were on live.   *alive*

Whan he was hosled and shriven,
365 His quiste maked and for him given,   *will/executed*
His knightes dede he alle site;
For thoru hem he wolde wite   *through/know*
Who mighte yeme hise children yunge   *govern*
Till that he couthen speken with tunge;
370 Speken and gangen, on horse riden,   *walk*
Knightes and swaines by here siden.
He spoken ther-offe and chosen sone
A riche man that, under mone,   *moon*
Was the trewest, as he wende,   *thought*
375 Godard, the kinges oune frende;
And saiden he moughe hem best loke,
Yif that he hem undertoke,
Till hise sone moughte bere
Helm on heved and leden ut here,
380 In his hand a spere stark,
And king been maked of Denemark.
He well trowede that he saide,
And on Godard handes laide;
And saide, "Here biteche I thee   *commit*
385 Mine children alle three,
All Denemark and all my fee,   *property*
Till that my sone of elde be;   *age*
But that ich wille that thou swere
On auter and on messe-gere,   *altar/vestment*
390 On the belles that men ringes,
On messe-book the prest on singes,
That thou mine children shalt well yeme,   *govern*
That hire kin be full well queme,
Till my sone mowe been knight;
395 Thanne biteche him tho his right,   *commit/due*
Denemark, and that thertill longes,   *belongs*
Casteles and tunes, wodes and wonges."   *fields*

Godard stirt up and swor all that
The king him bad, and sithen sat   *afterwards*
400 By the knightes that ther ware,
That wepen alle swithe sare   *very/bitterly*

---

366 "He had all his knights sit down."
375 *Friend* can be either "friend" or "relative."
376–377 "And [they] said [that] he would best be able to look after them if he would take charge of them."
388 "Except [only] that I desire that you swear."
393 Either "[So] that their relatives will be quite pleased" or, if *kin* is an error for *kind*, "[So] that it indeed quite befits their rank."

For the king, that deide sone.   *moon*
Jesu Christ, that makede mone   *moon*
On the mirke night to shine,
405 Wite his soule fro helle pine;   *guard/pain*
And leve that it mote wone   *permit/dwell*
In hevene-riche with Godes Sone!   *heavenly kingdom*

Whan Birkabeyn was laid in grave,
The erl dede sone take the knave,   *boy*
410 Havelok, that was the brother,
Swanborow, his sister, Helfled, the tother,   *other*
And in the castel dede he hem do,   *had/placed*
Ther non ne mighte hem comen to
Of here kyn, ther they sperd were.
415 Ther he greten ofte sore,   *wept*
Both for hunger and for cold,
Or he weren three winter old.   *before*
Feblelike he gaf hem clothes;   *unwillingly*
He ne yaf a note of his othes;
420 He hem clothede right ne fedde,
Ne hem dede richelike bedde.
Thanne Godard was sikerlike   *for/certainly*
Under God the moste swike   *greatest/traitor*
That evre in erthe shaped was,   *created*
425 Withuten on, the wike Judas.   *excepting*
                                             /wicked

Have he the malisun to-day
Of alle that evre speken may!
Of patriark and of pope,
And of prest with loken cope,   *fasted/cloak*
430 Of monekes and hermites bothe,
And of the leve holy rode   *dear/cross*
That God himselve ran on blode!
Christ warye him with his mouth!   *curse*
Waried wurthe he of north and suth!   *accursed/be*
435 Offe alle men that speken cunne,
Of Christ, that made mone and sunne!   *moon*
Thanne he havede of all the lond   *for*
All the folk tilled intill his hond,   *drawn*
And alle haveden sworen him oth,   *oaths*

---

410   The MS reads "the eir," which does not rhyme; the emendation 'the brother' is
      used by French and Hale, following Holthausen's edition of 1928.
411   *The tother* 'the second' is a product of false division (or metanalysis) and comes
      from *thet other*.
414   "Of their relatives, there where they were sequestered."
419   "He did not give a nut for his protestations."
426   "May he have today the curse."
432   "On which God himself bled."

440 Riche and povre, lef and loth,   *dear/hostile*
    That he sholden hise wille freme,   *perform*
    And that he shulden him nought greme,   *gainsay*
    He thoughte a full strong trechery,
    A traison and a felony,
445 Of the children forto make;
    The devel of helle him sone take!

    Whan that was thought, anon he ferde   *went*
    To the tour ther he woren sperde,   *tower/kept*
    Ther he greten for hunger and cold.   *wept*
450 The knave, that was sumdel bold,   *somewhat*
    Cam him again, on knees him sette,   *toward*
    And Godard full faire he ther grette.   *greeted*
    And Godard saide, "What is yow?
    Why grete ye and goulen nou?"   *cry/weep*
455 "For us hungreth swithe sore,"
    Saiden he, "We wolden more!
    We ne have to ete, ne we ne have
    Herinne neither knight ne knave
    That yeveth us drinke–ne no mete,
460 Halvendel that we moun ete!
    Wo is us that we weren born!
    Weilawi! nis it no corn   *wheat*
    That men mighte maken of bred?   *of which*
    Us hungreth! we aren ney ded!"   *near/dead*

465 Godard herde here wa,   *woe*
    Ther-offe yaf he nought a stra,   *gave/straw*
    But took the maidnes bothe samen–   *together*
    Also it were up-on his gamen,   *as if/sport*
    Also he wolde with hem leike–   *play*
470 That weren for hunger grene and bleike.   *pale*
    Of bothen he carf on two here throtes,   *in two*
    And sithen hem all to grotes.
    Ther was sorrwe, who-so it sawe,
    Whan the children by the wawe   *wall*
475 Layen and sprauleden in the blood.
    Havelok it saw and ther-by stood.
    Full sorry was that sely knave;   *innocent/boy*
    Mikel dred he moughte have,   *great/fear*
    For at hise herte he saw a knif

---

443   "He devised an utterly flagrant plot."
445   "To carry out on the children."
453   "And Godard said, 'What is the matter with you?' "
459–460   "Who [will] give us [anything] to drink—nor [do we have] any food, [even]
      half of what we [would] like to eat."
472   "And afterwards [cut] them utterly to pieces."

480 For to reven him hise lif.   *rob*
    But the knave, that litel was,
    He knelede bifor that Judas
    And saide, "Loverd, mercy nou!
    Manrede, loverd, biddi you!   *fealty/I offer*
485 All Denemark I wille you yeve,   *give*
    To that forward thu late me live;
    Here I wille on boke swere
    That nevre more ne shall I bere
    Again thee, loverd, sheld ne spere,
490 Ne other wepne that may you dere.   *harm*
    Loverd, haue mercy of me!
    To-day I wille fro Denemark flee,
    Ne nevere more comen again!   *back*
    Sweren I wole that Birkabein
495 Nevere yete me ne gat!"   *begot*
    Whan the devel herde that,
    Sumdel bigan him forto rewe;   *soften*
    Withdrow the knif, that was lewe   *warm*
    of the sely children blood.   *innocent*
500 Ther was miracle fair and good
    That he the knave nought ne slou,
    But for rewnesse him withdrow.   *pity/it*
    Of Havelok rewede him ful sore
    And thoughte he wolde that he ded wore,
505 But-on that he nought with his hend
    Ne drepe him nought, that fule fend!
    Thoughte he, als he him bistood,
    Starinde als he were wood: *crazed*
    "Yif I late him lives go,   *alive*
510 He mighte me wirchen michel wo.   *cause*
    Grith ne get I nevere mo;   *peace*
    He may me waiten for to slo;   *lie in wait/slay*
    And if he were brought off live,
    And mine children wolden thrive,
515 Loverdinges after me   *lords*
    Of all Denemark mighten he be.   *they*
    God it wite, he shall ben ded–
    Wille I taken non other red!   *counsel*
    I shall do casten him in the see,   *have/cast*
520 Ther I wille that he drenched be;   *drowned*
    Abouten his hals an anker good   *neck*

---

486 "On the condition [that] you let me live."
503–506 "He was very deeply touched with pity for Havelok but [literally, and] he
      thought he would that he were dead except that he did not at all wish to kill
      him with his [own] hand, the foul fiend!"
513 "And if he were killed."
517 "May God know it—he shall be dead."

That he ne flete in the flood."   *float*
Ther anon he dede sende
After a fishere, that he wende   *fisherman*
525 That wolde all his wille do;   */thought*
And sone anon he saide him to,
"Grim, thou wost thu art my thrall;   *know*
Will thu don my wille all
That I wille bidden thee,
530 To-morwen shall I maken thee free
And aughte thee yeven and riche make, *property*
With-than thu willt this child take   *provided*
And leden him with thee to-night,
Than thou seest the mone-light,   *when*
535 Into the see and don him ther-inne. *put*
All wille I taken on me the sinne!"
Grim took the child and bond him faste,
Whil the bondes mighte laste,
That weren of full strong line.   *cord*
540 Tho was Havelok in full strong pine! *pain*
Wiste he nevere er what was wo.
Jesu Christ, that makede go
The halte and the doumbe speke,
Havelok, thee of Godard wreke!

545 Whan Grim him havede faste bounden
And sithen in an old cloth wounden, *afterwards/old*
[He thriste in his mouth well faste]
A kevel of clutes, full unwraste,   *gag/rags/filthy*
That he moughte speke ne fnaste,   *sneeze*
Where he wolde him bere or lede.   *wheresoever*
550 Whan he havede don that dede,
What the swike him bad, he yede   *rogue/went*
That he shulde him forth lede
And him drenchen in the see—
That forwarde makeden he.
555 In a poke, ful and blak,   *bag/foul*
Sone he caste him on his bak,
And bar him hom to hise cleve,   *cottage*
And bitaughte him Dame Leve   *committed*
And saide, "Wite thou this knaue,   *guard*

---

538 "While the ropes would last," a line which appears again (1. 2437) and which
   here probably implies that Grim bound Havelok with all the rope he had.
542–544 "May Jesus Christ, who made the halt walk and the dumb speak, avenge you,
   Havelok, on Godard!"
547 The line is supplied from the "Cambridge Fragment" of *Havelok* (see introduction to the Skeat-Sisam edition noted in the *References.*)
550–554 The sentence changes its construction midway (temporal clause to 1. 553,
   then a clause—"That agreement they made"—which does not follow syntacti-
   cally); but instances of such a construction (anacoluthon) are rare in *Havelok*.

560 Also thou wilt my lif nou save!
   I shall drenchen him in the see;   *drown*
   For him shole we been maked free,
   Gold haven y-nou and other fee—   *property*
   That haveth my loverd bihoten me."   *promised*

565 Whan Dame Leve herde that,
   Up she stirte and nought ne sat
   And caste the knave so harde adoune
   That he crakede ther his croune
   Again a gret ston, ther it lay.
570 Tho Hauelok mighte say, "Weylawey,   *then*
   That evere was I kinges bern!   *son*
   That him ne havede grip or ern,
   Leoun or wulf, wulvine or bere
   Or other best, that wole him dere!"
575 So lay that child to middel night,
   That Grim bad Leve bringen light,   *until*
   For to don on him his clothes:
   "Ne thenkestu nought of mine othes
   That ich have my loverd sworen?
580 Ne wille I nought be forloren.
   I shall beren him to the se—
   Thou wost that so hoves me—
   And I shall drenchen him ther-inne;   *drown*
   Ris up swithe and go thu binne,   *within*
585 And blow the fir and light a candel."
   Als she shulde hise clothes handel   *when/had to*
   On for to don and blowe the fir,
   She saw ther-inne a light full shir,   *bright*
   Also bright so it were day,   *just as /as*
590 Aboute the knave ther he lay.   *boy*
   Of hise mouth it stood a stem
   Als it were a sunnebem;
   Also light was it ther-inne   *just as*
   So ther brenden cerges inne.   *as if/candles*
595 "Jesu Christ!" qwath Dame Leve,
   "What is that light in ure cleve?   *cottage*
   Ris up, Grim, and loke what it menes!   *means*
   What is the light, as thou wenes?"

---

560   " 'As if you wished to save my life.' " The present reading is an emendation (see
      Skeat-Sisam edition noted in *References*.)
572–574   " [Oh], that griffin or eagle, lion or wolf, she-wolf or bear, or other beast
      that would harm him [Goddard], has not gotten him!' "
578–579   " 'Aren't you thinking of my oaths which I have sworn my lord?' "
582   " 'You know that such I must do.' "
591–592   "From his mouth there rose a ray of light as if it were a sunbeam."
598   " 'What is the light, according to what you think.' "

He stirten bothe up to the knave   *jumped*
600 (For man shall god wille have),
    Unkeveleden him and swithe unbounden,   *ungagged*
    And sone anon upon him funden,
    Als he tirveden off his serk,   *drew off/shirt*
    On his right shuldre a kine-merk,
605 A swithe bright, a swithe fair.
    "Goddot!" qwath Grim, "this ure eir   *God knows*
    That shall been loverd of Denemark!
    He shall been king, strong and stark;
    He shall haven in his hand
610 All Denemark and Engeland;
    He shall do Godard full wo;
    He shall him hangen or quik flo;   *flay*
    Or he shall him all quick grave.   *alive/bury*
    Of him shall he no mercy have."
615 Thus saide Grim and sore gret,   *wept*
    And sone fell him to the feet
    And saide, "Loverd, have mercy
    Of me and Leve, that is me by!
    Loverd, we aren bothe thine,
620 Thine cherles, thine hine.   *thralls/servants*
    Loverd, we sholen thee well fede   *feed*
    Till that thu cone riden on stede,   *are able to*
    Till that thu cone full well bere
    Helm on heved, sheld, and spere.
625 He ne shall nevere, sikerlike,   *certainly*
    Wite, Godard, that fule swike.   *know/foul/rogue*
    Thoru other man, loverd, than thoru thee
    Shal I nevere freeman be.
    Thou shalt me, loverd, free maken,
630 For I shall yemen thee and waken;   *care for/watch*
    Thoru thee wile I freedom have."   *over*
    Tho was Havelok a blithe knave;
    He sat him up and cravede bred   *asked for/bread*
    And saide, "Ich am ney ded,   *nigh*
635 What for hunger, what for bondes
    That thou laidest on min hondes,
    And for the kevel at the laste,   *gag*
    That in my mouth was thrist faste.   *thrust*
    I was ther-with so harde prangled   *pinched*
640 That I was ther-with ney strangled."   *almost*
    "Well is me that thou maght ete!   *may*
    Goddoth!" quath Leve, "I shall thee fete

---

604 The MS reads *kynemerk*, meaning here "birth mark indicative of royalty."
616 "And immediately fell at his feet."
641 "I am glad that you can eat!"
642 "God knows!," said Leve, "I shall fetch for you."

Bred and chese, buttere and milk,
Pastees and flaunes; all with swilk
645 Shole we sone thee well fede,
Loverd, in this mikel nede;
Sooth it is, that men saith and swereth:
Ther God wile helpen, nought ne dereth."

Thanne sho havede brought the mete,   *when/food*
650 Havelok anon bigan to ete
Grundlike and was full blithe;   *heartily*
Couthe he nought his hunger mithe.   *hide*
A lof he et, I wot, and more,   *loaf/know*
For him hungrede swithe sore.
655 Three dayes ther-biforn, I wene,
Et he no mete, that was well sene,   *seen*
Whan he havede eten and was fed,
Grim dede maken a full fair bed,
Unclothede him and dede him ther-inne   *put*
660 And saide, "Slep, sone, with michel winne!   *joy*
Sleep well faste and dred thee nought;
Fro sorrwe to joye art thou brought."
Sone so it was light of day,   *as soon as*
Grim it undertok, the way
665 To the wicke traitour Godard,   *wicked*
That was in Denemark a stiward,
And saide, "Loverd, don ich have
That thou me bede of the knave;
He is drenched in the flood,   *drowned*
670 Abouten his hals an anker good;   *neck*
He is witerlike ded;   *surely*
Eteth he nevre more bred;
He lith drenched in the see.   *lies*
Yif me gold and other fee,   *give/property*
675 That I mowe riche be;
And with thy chartre make me free,
For thou full well bihetet me
Thanne I last spak with thee."   *when*
Godard stood and lokede on him
680 Thorough-like, with eyne grim,   *searchingly*
And saide, "Wiltu been erl?
Go hom swithe, fule drit-cherl;   *foul/dirt-thrall*

644–645 "Pasties [that is, meat cakes] and flaunes [that is, either custard or cheese
        pies]; with all such shall we feed you well right away."
648   "There where God wishes to help, nothing works injury."
664   *It* is a proleptic pronoun whose postcedent is the noun *way.*
668   "That which you asked me to do with the boy."
677–678 "For you very well promised it me when I last spoke with you," *bihetet* is a
        cratic form of "bihete it."

Go hethen and be everemore   *hence*
Thrall and cherl, als thou er wore.
685 Shaltu have non other mede;   *reward*
For litel shall I do thee lede
To the gallwes, so God me rede!
For thou haves don a wicke dede.   *wicked*
Thou maght stonden her too longe,
690 But thou swithe hethen gonge!"   *unless/quickly*

Grim thoughte too late that he ran   */hence*
Fro that traitour, that wicke man;
And thoughte, "What shall me to rede?   *for me/plan*
Wite he him onlive, he wile us bethe
695 Heye hangen on gallwe-tree;
Betere us is of londe to flee,
And berwen bothen ure lives,   *save*
And mine children and mine wives."
Grim solde sone all his corn,
700 Sheep with wolle, net with horn,   *cattle*
Hors, and swin, and geet with berd,   *goats*
The gees, the hennes of the yerd;
All he solde that ought doughte,
That he evre selle moughte;
705 And all he to the penny drough.
Hise ship he greithede well y-now;   *equipped*
He dede it tere and full well pike   *tar/pitch*
That it ne doutede sond ne krike;
Ther-inne dide a full good mast,   *placed*
710 Stronge cables and full fast,
Ores gode and full good sail;   *oars*
Ther-inne wantede nought a nail,   *lacked*
That evere he sholde therinne do.   *put*
Whan he havedet greithed so,
715 Havelok the yunge he dede ther-inne,
Him and his wif, hise sones thrinne,   *three*
And hise two doughtres, that faire wore;

686–687 "May God counsel me! I've half a mind to have [literally, for little I shall have] you lead to the gallows."

691 "It seemed to Grim too long until he ran."

694–695 "If he knows him [Havelok] [to be] alive, he will hang both of us high on the gallows."

696 "It's better for us to flee from the country."

703 "He sold all which was worth anything."

705 "And he turned everything to cash."

708 "So that it [should] fear neither sound nor inlet;" *sond* can also be 'sand' with the extended meaning 'shoal water,' but 'sound' seems more appropriate and is quite possible orthographically

714 "Whan he had equipped it [the boat] thus"; the neuter pronoun is affixed to *hevedet.*

And sone dede he lain in an ore
And drow him to the heve see,
720 There he might altherbeste flee.
Fro londe woren he bote a mile—
Ne were it nevere but ane while—
That it ne bigan a wind to rise
Out of the north (men calleth "bise")
725 And drof hem intill Engelond,
That all was sithen in his hond,
His, that Hauelok was the name;
But or, he havede michel shame,   *before*
Michel sorrwe and michel tene,   *grief*
730 And yete he gat it all bidene;   *anon*
Als ye shulen nou forthward lere,   *learn*
Yf that ye wilen thereto here.

In Humber Grim bigan to lende,   *land*
In Lindeseye, right at the north ende.
735 Ther sat his ship upon the sond,   *sand*
But Grim it drow up to the lond;
And there he made a litel cote   *cottage*
To him and to hise flote.   *household*
Bigan he there for to erde,   *dwell*
740 A litel hus to maken of erthe,
So that he well thore were
Of here herboru herborwed there;
And for that Grim that place aughte, *owned*
The stede of Grim the name laughte,
745 So that Grimesby calleth alle
That ther-offe speken alle;
And so shulen men callen it ay,
Bitwene this and domesday.

Grim was fishere swithe good,   *fisherman*
750 And mikel couthe on the flood;
Many good fish ther-inne he took,
Bothe with net and with hook.
He took the sturgiun and the qual   *whale*
And the turbut and lax withal;   *turbot/salmon*
755 He took the sele and ek the eel;
He spedde ofte swithe well.   *prospered*

---

718 "And quickly had an oar put in [place]."
719 "And made for the open sea."
724 *Bise* here is coguate to modern French *bise* "north wind."
742 "So that they were there in their shelter well protected there"; *thore* may be a
   scribal slip for *yore* "for a long time."
744 "The place took from Grim its name."
750 "And knew much about the sea."

Keling he took and tumberel, — *cod/porpoise*
Heering and the makerel,
The butte, the schulle, the thornebake. — *flat fish/plaice*
— */skate*
760 Gode paniers dede he make, — *baskets*
On till him and other thrinne
Till hise sones to beren fish inne — *for*
Up o-londe to selle and fonge;
Forbar he neither tun ne gronge
765 That he ne to yede with his ware;
Cam he nevere hom hand-bare — *bare handed*
That he ne broughte bred and sowel — *relish*
In his shirte or in his cowel; — *hood*
In his poke benes and corn—
770 Hise swink ne havede he noght forlorn.
And whan he took the grete lamprey,
Full well he couthe the righte way — *knew*
To Lincolne, the gode boru; — *town*
Ofte he yede it thoru and thoru,
775 Till he havede all well sold
And therfore the pennies told. — *counted*
Thanne he com thenne, he were blithe, — *when/thence*
For hom he broughte fele sithe — *many/times*
Wastels, simenels with the horn,
780 His pokes fulle of mele and corn,
Netes flesh, shepes, and swines; — *cattle/meat*
And hemp to maken of gode lines
And stronge ropes to hise netes,
That in the see he ofte setes.

785 Thus-gate Grim him faire ledde;
Him and his genge well he fedde — *household*
Well twelf winter other more.
Havelok was war that Grim swank sore — *aware/toiled*
For his mete, and he lay at hom: — *food/if*
790 He thoughte, "Ich am nou no grom; — *boy*
Ich am well waxen and well may eten
More than evere Grim may geten. — *obtain*
Ich ete more, by God on live, — *alive*
Than Grim and hise children five!
795 It ne may nought been thus longe:

---

761 "One for himself and three others."
763 "Up on land to sell and got [money for]."
764–765 "He neglected neither town nor farm which he might go to with his wares."
769–770 "In his bag [were] beans and wheat—his work he had not lost."
779 "Cakes, horn-shaped loaves of bread."
785 "In this manner Grim managed his affairs well."
795 "It cannot go on this way for long."

Goddot! I wile with hem gange,
For to leren sum good to gete; *learn how*
Swinken ich wolde for my mete. *work*
It is no shame forto swinken;
800 The man that may well eten and drinken
Thar nought ne have but on swink long;
To liggen at hom it is full strong. *shameful*
God yelde him, ther I ne may, *repay/since*
That haveth me fed to this day!
805 Gladlike I wile the paniers bere; *baskets*
Ich wot, ne shall it me nought dere, *know/harm*
They ther be inne a birthene gret *although/burden*
All so hevy als a net. *just as/ox*
Shall ich nevere lengere dwelle; *tarry*
810 To-morwen shall ich forth pelle." *hasten*

On the morwen, whan it was day,
He stirt up sone and nought ne lay;
And cast a panier on his back, *basket*
With fish giveled als a stack; *heaped*
815 Also michel he bar him one *himself/alone*
So he foure, by mine mone!
Well he it bar and solde it well;
The silver he broughte hom ilk del,
All that he ther-fore took;
820 Withheld he nought a ferthinges nok.
So yede he forth ilke day,
That he nevere at home lay. *tarried*
So wolde he his mester lere.
Bifel it so, a strong dere *dire/famine*
825 Bigan to rise of corn of bred,
That Grim ne couthe no good red, *knew/counsel*
How he sholde his meine fede; *family*
Of Havelok havede he michel drede,
For he was strong and well moughte ete
830 More thanne evere moughte he gete; *earn*
Ne he ne moughte on the see take
Neither lenge ne thornbake, *ling/skate*
Ne non other fish that doughte
His meiné feden with he moughte.
835 Of Havelok he havede care,

---

801   "Ought not to have [it] except as the result of labor;" the emendation of the MS
      that "that" to *Thar* "ought" was suggested by Skeat.
816   "As four of them, in my opinion."
820   "He kept back not the corner [that is, the least bit] of a farthing."
823   "Thus he would learn his calling."
833–834   "Nor any other fish that was worth anything with [which] he could feed his
      family."

Whilkgat that he mighte fare.   *in what manner*
Of his children was him nought;   */act*
On Havelok was all hise thought,
And saide, "Havelok, dere sone,
840 I wene that we deye mone   *die/may*
For hunger, this dere is so strong   *famine/dire*
And ure mete is uten long.   *exhausted/long*
                                                              ago

Betere is that thu henne gonge   *hence*
Than thou here dwelle longe;
845 Hethen thou maght gangen too late: *hence*
Thou canst full well the righte gate   *road*
To Lincolne, the gode boru—   *town*
Thou havest it gon full ofte thoru;
Of me, ne is me noght a slo.
850 Betere is that thu thider go,
For ther is many good man inne;
Ther thou mayt thy mete winne.
But wo is me! thou art so naked,   *ill clothed*
Of my sail I wolde thee were maked
855 A cloth, thou mightest inne gongen,   *garment*
Sone, no cold that thu ne fonge."

He took the sheres off the nail
And made him a covel of the sail,   *cloak*
And Havelok dide it sone on.   *put/quickly*
860 Havede he neither hosen ne shon,   *hose/shoes*
Ne none kines other wede;   *kind/clothes*
To Lincolne barfoot he yede.   *walked*
Whan he cam ther, he was full will: *perplexed*
Ne havede he no frend to gangen till;
865 Two dayes ther fastinde he yede,   *fasting*
That non for his werk wolde him fede;   *in that/no one*
The thridde day herde he calle: *third*
"Bermen, bermen, hider forth alle!"   *porters*
Povre that on fote yede   *poor people*
870 Sprongen forth so sparke of glede,   *as/live coal*
Havelok shof dune nine or ten   *shoved*
Right amidewarde the fen,   *mud*
And stirte forth to the cook,
Ther the erles mete he took   *there where*
875 That he boughte at the bridge:
The bermen let he alle lidge,   *lie*
And bar the mete to the castel,

---

849 "As for me, it's not a sloe-berry to me," perhaps implying "I can't do anything
     one way or the other."
856 "Son, so that you catch no cold."

And gat him there a ferthing wastel. *farthing/cake*

Thet other day kepte he ok *second /kept watch for /also*

880 Swithe yerne the erles cook, *eagerly*
Till that he say him on the bridge, *saw*
And by him many fishes lidge. *lying*
The erles mete havede he bought
Of Cornwaile and calde oft,
885 "Bermen, bermen, hider swithe!" *quickly*
Havelok it herde and was full blithe
That he herde "bermen" calle;
Alle made he hem dun falle
That in his gate yeden and stode, *way/walked*
890 Well sixtene laddes gode.
Als he lep the cook till, *when/leapt*
He shof hem alle upon an hill;
Astirte till him with his rippe *hastened/basket*
And bigan the fish to kippe. *snatch up*
895 He bar up well a carte-lode
Of sedges, laxes, of plaices brode, *cuttle-fish /salmon*

Of grete laumprees, and of eles;
Sparede he neither tos ne heles
Till that he to the castel cam,
900 That men fro him his birthene nam. *burden/took*
Than men haveden holpen him doun *when*
With the birthene of his croun,
The cook stood and on him low, *smiled*
And thoughte him stalworthe man y-now, *enough*
905 And saide, "Wiltu been with me?
Gladlike wile ich feden thee:
Well is set the mete thou etes,
And the hire that thou getes." *wages/earn*

"Goddot!" quod he, "leve sire, *God knows*
910 Bidde ich you non other hire,
But yeveth me y-now to ete!
Fir and water I wile you fete, *fetch*
The fir blowe and full wele maken;
Stickes can ich breken and craken,
915 And kindlen full well a fir,

883–884 "He [the cook] had bought the Earl of Cornwall's food and called repeatedly."
892 "He shoved them all [down] in a heap."
898 "He spared neither toes nor heels" [that is, he hurried].
907 "Well is invested the food you eat."
910–911 "I ask of you no other pay than [that you] give me enough to eat."

And maken it to brennen shir;   *bright*
Full well can ich cleven shides,   *split/sticks*
Eles to-turven of here hides;
Full well can ich dishes swilen,   *wash*
920 And done all that ye evere wilen."
Quoth the cook, "Wile I no more;
Go thou yunder and sit thore,   *there*
And I shall yeve thee full fair bred
And made the broys in the led.   *broth/kettle*
925 Sit now doun and et full yerne;   *eagerly*
Datheit who thee mete werne!"

Havelok sette him dun anon
Also stille als a ston,   *just as/as*
Till he havede full well eten;
930 Tho havede Havelok faire geten.
Whan he havede eten y-now,   *enough*
He cam to the wele, water updrow,   *went*
And filde ther a michel so;   *filled/tub*
Bad he non again him go;
935 But bitwen his hondes he bar it in,
All him one, to the kichin.   *by himself*
Bad he non him water to fete,
Ne fro bridge to bere the mete.
He bar the turves, he bar the star,
940 The wode fro the bridge he bar;
All that evere shulden he nitte,   *use*
All he drow and all he citte;   *hauled/cut*
Wolde he nevere haven rest
More than he were a best.
945 Of alle men was he mest meke,   *most/meek*
Lauhwinde ay and blithe of speke;   *smiling/ever*
                                                                     /speech

Evere he was glad and blithe:
His sorrwe he couthe full well mithe.   *could/hide*
It ne was non so litel knave,
950 For to leiken ne forto plawe,
That he ne wolde with him pleye;
The children that yeden in the weye   *ran/across*
Of him, he deden all here wille,   *desire*

---

918   "Skin off the hides of eels."
926   "Cursed [be he] who denies you food."
930   "Then had Havelok made out well."
934   "He asked no one to come [to help] him."
937–938   "He asked no one to fetch water for him nor bear the food from the bridge."
939   "He carried the peat, he carried the star-grass" [that is, grass used as kindling].
943–944   "He would never want rest [any] more than [if] he were a beast."
949–951   "There was no child however little that [desired] to sport and play with
        whom he would not spend time."

And with him leikeden here fille.   *sported*
955 Him loveden alle, stille and bolde,   *shy/forward*
Knightes, children, yunge and olde;
Alle him loveden that him sowen,   *saw*
Bothen heye men and lowe.
Of him full wide the word sprong,
960 Hu he was mikel, hu he was strong,   *big*
Hu fair man God him havede maked,
But-on that he was almest naked: *except*
For he ne havede nought to shride   *wear*
But a covel full unride,   *cloak/rough*
965 That was ful and swithe wicke;   *foul/wretched*
Was it nought worth a fir-sticke.   *faggot*
The cook bigan of him to rewe
And boughte him clothes, all spannewe;   *brand-new*
He boughte him bothe hosen and shon,   *hose/shoes*
970 And sone dide him dones on.
Whan he was clothed, hosed, and shod,
Was non so fair under God,
That evere yete in erthe were,
Non that evere moder bere;
975 It was nevere man that yemede
In kinneriche, that so well semede
King or cayser forto be,
Than he was shrid, so semede he;
For thanne he weren alle samen   *when/together*
980 At Lincolne, at the gamen,   *games*
And the erles men woren all thore,
Than was Havelok by the shuldren more   *taller*
Than the meste that ther cam: *tallest*
In armes him noman nam   *took*
985 That he doune sone ne caste.
Havelok stood over hem als a mast;   *like*
Als he was heye, als he was long,
He was bothe stark and strong;
In Engelond was non hise per   *equal*
990 Of strengthe that evere cam him ner.   *in*
Als he was strong, so was he softe;   *gentle*
They a man him misdede ofte,   *although*
                                                                               /mistreat

Nevere more he him missayde,
Ne hond on him with yvele layde.

---

961   "How handsome a man God had made him."
970   "And quickly made him put them on"; the *-es* of *dones* is a pronoun "them."
975–978   "There was never man who governed in [a] realm who seemed so well
       [befitted] to be king or emperor as he seemed when he was clad."
993–994   "Not at all did he insult him nor with evil [intent] lay hand on him."

995 Of body was he maiden-clene;   *pure*
     Nevere yete in game, ne in grene,   *sport*
                                                     /sexual desire

     With hore ne wolde he leike ne lie,   *harlot/play*
     No more than it were a strie.   *witch*
     In that time all Engelond
1000 Therl Godrich havede in his hond,
     And he gart comen into the tun   *caused to*
     Many erl and many barun;
     And alle that lives were   *alive*
     In Englond thanne wer there   *then*
1005 That they haveden after sent
     To been ther at the parlement.
     With hem com many champioun,
     Many wight ladde, blac and brown;   *active/lads*
     And fell it so that yunge men,
1010 Well abouten nine or ten,
     Bigunnen there for to laike;   *wrestle*
     Thider comen bothe stronge and waike: *weak*
     Thider comen lesse and more   *low/high*
     That in the boru thanne weren thore;
1015 Chaumpiouns and starke laddes,
     Bondemen with here gaddes,   *goads*
     Als he comen fro the plow;
     There was sembling y-now!
     For it ne was non horse-knave,   *there/stable boy*
1020 Though they sholden in honde have,
     That he ne cam thider, the leik to see;   *sport*
     Biforn here feet thanne lay a tree,
     And putten with a mikel ston
     The starke laddes, full good won.
1025 The ston was mikel and ek gret,
     And all so hevy so a net;
     Grund-stalwyrthe man he sholde be   *very strong*
     That moughte liften it to his knee;
     Was ther neither clerk ne prest,
1030 That mighte liften it to his brest.
     Therwith putten the chaumpiouns
     That thider comen with the barouns;
     Who-so mighte putten thore   *there*

1000 "The Earl Godrich ruled."
1008 "Black and brown," an inclusive formula, may mean "everyone" or, specifically,
        "people of low rank [*blac*] and high [*brown*]."
1018 "There was a tremendous crowd!"
1020 "Though they had a job to do."
1022–1024 "In front of their feet then lay a beam [that is, as a foul line], and the
        strong fellows heaved with great force a large stone."
1026 "And just as heavy as an ox."

Biforn another an inch or more,
035 Wore he yung, wore he old,
He was for a kempe told.   *master athlete*
/held

Al-so they stoden and ofte stareden,   *thus*
The chaumpiouns and ek the ladden,   *lads*
And he maden mikel strout
040 Abouten the altherbeste bout,
Havelok stood and lokede ther-till;
And of puttingge he was full will,
For nevere yete ne saw he or   *before*
Putten the ston, or thanne thor.   *ere/there*
045 Hise maister bad him gon ther-to,
Als he couthe ther-with do.
Tho hise maister it him bad,   *when*
He was of him sore adrad;
Therto he stirte sone anon,
050 And kipte up that hevy ston   *caught up*
That he sholde putten withe;
He putte, at the firste sithe,   *try*
Over alle that ther wore
Twelve fote and sumdel more.
055 The chaumpiouns that put sowen;   *saw*
Shuldreden he ilk other and lowen;
Wolden he no more to putting gange,   *go*
But seide, "We dwellen her too longe!"   *tarry*
This selcouth mighte nought been hid;
060 Full sone it was full loude kid   *quickly*
/made known

Of Havelok, hu he warp the ston   *threw*
Over the laddes everilkon;   *beyond/each one*
Hu he was fair, hu he was long,   *tall*
Hu he was wight, hu he was strong;   *bold*
065 Thorught England yede the speche,   *went/rumor*
Hu he was strong and ek meke;   *gentle*
In the castel, up in the halle,
The knightes speken therof alle,
So that Godrich it herde well:
1070 They speken of Havelok, every del.
Hu he was strong man and hey,
Hu he was strong, and ek full sley,   *skillful*
And thoughte Godrich, "Thoru this knave

1039–1040   "And they made fierce contention over the most masterly throw."
1042   "And of putting the shot he was quite ignorant."
1046   "[To see] how he might do at it."
1056   "They nudged each other and laughed."
1059   "This feat might not be hidden."
1070   "They talked about Havelok in every way."

Shall ich Engelond all have,
1075 And my sone after me;
For so I wile that it be. *desire*
The king Athelwald me dide swere
Upon all the messe-gere *implements for*
mass

That I shulde his doughter yeve *give*
1080 The hexte man that mighte live,
The beste, the fairest, the strangest ok;
That gart he me sweren on the book. *made*
Where mighte I finden any so hey,
So Havelok is, or so sley? *skillful*
1085 Thou I soughte hethen into Inde, *from here/India*
So fair, so strong, ne mighte I finde.
Havelok is that ilke knave
That shall Goldeboru have!"
This thoughte he with trechery,
1090 With traisoun, and with felony;
For he wende that Havelok wore
Sum cherles sone, and no more;
Ne shulde he haven of Engellond
Onlepy forru in his hond
1095 With hire that was therof eir,
That bothe was good and swithe fair.
He wende that Havelok wer a thrall;
Therthoru he wende haven all *by this*
/expected to

In Engelond, that hire right was— *due*
1100 He was werse than Sathanas *worse/Satan*
That Jesu Christ in erthe stoc! *buried*
Hanged worthe he on an ok!

After Goldeboru sone he sende, *quickly*
That was bothe fair and hende, *gracious*
1105 And dide hire to Lincolne bringe;
Belles dede he again hire ringen,
And joye he made hire swithe mikel;
But netheless he was full swiken. *treacherous*
He saide that he sholde hire yeve *give*
1110 The faireste man that mighte live.
She answerede and saide anon,
By Christ and by Saint Johan,

1080 *Hexte* "highest," although Godrich here and in l. 1083, plays on the dual mean-
      ing of *hey,* "noble" and "tall."
1094 "Possession of a single furrow."
1101 The MS reads *shop* "created"; French and Hale suggest *stoc,* which makes sense.
1102 "Might he be hanged upon an oak."
1106 "He had bells rung for her [arrival]."

That hire sholde noman wedde,
Ne noman bringen hire to bedde,
115 But he were king or kinges eir,   *unless*
Were he nevere man so fair.

Godrich the erl was swithe wroth   *angry*
That she swor swilk an oth,   *oath*
And saide, "Whether thou wilt be
120 Queen and levedy over me?
Thou shalt haven a gadeling–   *rogue*
Ne shalt thou haven non other king!
Thee shall spusen my cokes knave: *marry*
Shalt thou non other lovered have!   *lord*
125 Datheit that thee other yeve
Everemore whil I live!
To-morwe sholen ye been weddeth,
And, maugré thin, togidere beddeth.   *in spite of/you*
Goldeboru gret and yaf hire ille;
130 She wolde been ded by hire wille.
On the morwen whan day was sprungen,
And day-belle at kirke rungen,
After Havelok sente that Judas,
That werse was thanne Sathanas,
135 And saide, "Maister, wilte wif?"   *do you want*
"Nay," quoth Havelok, "by my lif!
What sholde ich with wif do?
I ne may hire fede ne clothe ne sho.
Whider sholde ich wimman bringe?   *whither*
140 I ne have none kines thinge.
I ne have hus, I ne have cote,   *cottage*
I ne have sticke, I ne have sprote,   *twig*
I ne have neither bred ne sowel,   *relish*
Ne cloth, but of an old whit covel.
145 This clothes that ich onne have   *these*
Aren the cokes, and ich his knave."
Godrich stirt up and on him dong   *struck*
With dintes swithe hard and strong,   *blows*
And saide, "But thou hire take
150 That I wole yeven thee to make,   *mate*
I shall hangen thee full heye,   *high*
Or I shall thristen ut thin eye."   *thrust*
Havelok was one and was adrad,   *alone/afraid*
And grauntede him all that he bad.

1119–1120 "Do you wish to be queen and lady over me?"
1125 "Cursed [be he] who gives you [any] other."
1129 "Goldeboru wept and appeared wretched."
1140 "I have no things of any kind."
1144 "Nor cloth except for an old white cloak."

1155 Tho sende he after hire sone,   *quickly*
  The fairest wimman under mone; *moon*
  And saide till hire, fals and slike, *treacherous*
  That wicke thrall, that foule swike: *traitor*
  "But thu this man understonde, *accept*
1160 I shall flemen thee of londe; *exile*
  Or thou shalt to the galwes renne,
  And ther thou shalt in a fir brenne."
  Sho was adrad for he so thrette, *threatened*
  And durste nought the spusing lette; *marriage/hinder*
1165 But they hire likede swithe ille,
  Sho thoughte it was Godes wille:
  God, that makes to growen the corn,
  Formede hire wimman to be born.
  Whan he havede don him, for drede,
1170 That he sholde hire spusen and fede,
  And that she sholde till him holde,
  Ther weren pennies thicke tolde,
  Mikel plenté, upon the book:
  He is hire yaf, and she is took.
1175 He weren spused faire and well,
  The messe he dede—everydel
  That fell to spusing–a good clerk,
  The erchebishop ut of Yerk,
  That cam to the parlement,
1180 Als God him havede thider sent. *as if*

  Whan he weren togidere in Godes lawe,
  That the folk full well it sawe, *so that*
  He ne wisten what he moughten,
  Ne he ne wisten what hem doughte:
1185 Ther to dwellen, or thenne to gonge. *thence*
  Ther ne wolden he dwellen longe,
  For he wisten and full well sawe
  That Godrich hem hatede, the devel him hawe! *have*
  And if he dwelleden ther ought *at all*
1190 (That fell Havelok full well on thought), *occurred*
  Men sholde don his leman shame, *beloved*
  Or elles bringen in wicke blame,
  That were him levere to been ded.

1165 "But although it pleased her ill indeed."
1169–1170 "When he [Godrich] had caused him [Havelok] out of fear to wed and
   support her."
1172–1174 "There were in great number pennies counted out, [a] great quantity, upon
   the book. He gave her his, and she took his."
1183–84 "They did not know what they might [do], nor did they know what would
   be best."
1192–93 "Or else bring [her] in ill repute, [something] which he would rather be dead
   [than experience]."

Forthy he token another red: *therefore/course*
195 That they sholden thenne flee   *thence*
     Till Grim and till hise sones three;
     Ther wenden he altherbest to spede,   *expected/prosper*
     Hem forto clothe and for to fede.
     The lond he token under fote—
200 Ne wisten he non other bote–   *remedy*
     And helden ay the righte sty   *ever/road*
     Till he comen to Grimesby.
     Thanne he comen there, thanne was Grim ded: *when/then*
     Of him ne haveden he no red;   *from/advice*
205 But hise children, alle five,
     Alle weren yet on live,   *alive*
     That full faire ayen hem neme
     Whan he wisten that he ceme,
     And maden joye swithe mikel   *very/much*
210 Ne weren he nevere ayen hem fikel.   *treacherous*
     On knees full faire he hem setten
     And Havelok swithe faire gretten,   *greeted*
     And saiden, "Welcome, lovered dere!
     And welcome be thy faire fere!   *companion*
215 Blessed be that ilke thrawe   *very/time*
     That thou hire toke in Godes lawe!
     Well is us we seen thee on live.
     Thou maght us bothe selle and yeve;
     Thou maght us bothe yeve and selle,
220 Withthat thou wilt here dwelle.   *if*
     We haven, loverd, alle gode,   *good things*
     Hors and net, and ship on flode,   *oxen*
     Gold and silver and michel aughte,   *possessions*
     That Grim ure fader us bitaughte.   *committed*
225 Gold and silver and other fee   *property*
     Bad he us bitaken thee.   *commit to*
     We haven sheep, we haven swin;
     Bileve her, loverd, and all be thin!   *remain*
     Thou shalt been loverd, thou shalt been sire,
230 And we sholen serven thee and hire;
     And ure sistres sholen do
     All that evere biddes sho: *she*
     He sholen hire clothes washen and wringen,
     And to hondes water bringen;
235 He sholen bedden hire and thee,   *provide beds for*

1199   "They took to their heels."
1207   "Who graceously went forth [to greet] them."
1217   "We are glad to see you alive."
1218   "You could both sell and give us [away]," presumably into slavery; but the phrase
       is mere declaration of loyalty to Havelok.
1234   "And bring water to her."

For levedy wile we that she be."
Whan he this joye haveden maked,
Sithen stikes broken and cracked,   *afterwards*
And the fir brought on brenne;   *made/to burn*
1240 Ne was ther spared goos ne henne,
Ne the ende ne the drake: *duck*
Mete he deden plenté make;
Ne wantede there no good mete,
Win and ale deden he fete,   *fetch*
1245 And hem made glade and blithe;
Wessail ledden he fele sithe.

On the night, als Goldeboru lay,
Sorry and sorrowful was she ay,   *ever*
For she wende she were biswike,   *thought/deceived*
1250 That she were yeven un-kindelike.
O night saw she ther-inne a light,   *at*
A swithe fair, a swithe bright,
All so bright, all so shir   *brilliant*
So it were a blase of fir.   *as if/blaze*
1255 She lokede north and ek south,   *also*
And saw it comen ut of his mouth
That lay by hire in the bed.
No ferlike thou she were adred!
Thoughte she, "What may this bimene?   *signify*
1260 He beth hayman yet, als I wene:
He beth heyman er he be ded!"
On hise shuldre, of gold red
She saw a swithe noble croiz;   *cross*
Of an angel she herde a voiz: *from*

1265 "Goldeboru, lat thy sorrwe be;
For Havelok, that haveth spuset thee,   *married*
Is kinges sone and kinges eir;
That bikenneth that croiz so fair.   *betokens*
It bikenneth more: that he shall
1270 Denemark haven and Englond all;
He shall been king, strong and stark,
Of Engelond and Denemark:
That shall thou with thin eyne seen,
And thou shalt queen and levedy been!"

1236 "Because we desire that she be [our] lady."
1246 "They drank healths many a time."
1250 "In that she were given [in marriage] beneath her rank."
1257-58 "[Of him] who lay by her in the bed. No wonder [it was] that she was ter-
    rified."
1260 "He shall be a man of high rank yet, I suspect."

1275 Thanne she havede herd the stevene   *when/voice*
      Of the angel ut of hevene,
      She was so fele sithes blithe
      That she ne mighte hire joye mithe;
      But Havelok sone anon she kiste,
1280 And he slep and nought ne wiste.
      Whan that aungel havede said,   *spoken*
      Of his slep anon he braid,   *from/started*
      And seide, "Lemman, slepes thou?   *dear one*
      A selkuth drem dremede me nou.

1285 Herkne nou what me haveth met!   *dreamed*
      Me thoughte I was in Denmark set,
      But on on the moste hill
      That evere yete cam I till.
      It was so hey, that I well moughte
1290 All the werd see, als me thoughte.   *world/seemed*
      Als I sat upon that lowe,   *hill*
      I bigan Denmark for to awe,   *possess*
      The borwes and the castles stronge;   *towns*
      And mine armes weren so longe
1295 That I fadmede all at ones,   *embraced/once*
      Denmark, with mine longe bones;   *limbs*
      And thanne I wolde mine armes drawe   *when*
      Till me, and hem for to haue,
      All that evere in Denmark liveden
1300 On mine armes faste cliveden;   *clung*
      And the stronge castles alle
      On knees bigunnen for to falle;
      The keyes fellen at mine feet.
      Another drem dremede me ek: *also*
1305 That ich fley over the salte se   *flew*
      Till Engeland, and all with me
      That evere was in Denmark lives   *alive*
      But bondemen and here wives;   *except*
      And that ich com till Engelond,   *arrived/in*
1310 All closede it intill min hond,
      And, Goldeboru, I gaf it thee.
      Deus! lemman, what may this be?"   *dear one*
      Sho answerede and saide sone:
      "Jeus Christ, that made mone,   *moon*
1315 Thine dremes turne to joye, . . .

1277–78   "She was so very much glad that she could not hide her joy."
1284   "I dreamed [just] now a strange dream."
1287   "But on one [of] the greatest hills."
1315   Two lines which perhaps should follow (one to rhyme with *joye*, another with
        trone) are lost.

That wite thou that sittes in trone!
Ne non strong, king ne caisere,
So thou shalt be, for thou shalt bere
In Engelond corune yet.
1320 Denemark shall knele to thy feet: *at*
Alle the castles that aren ther-inne
Shaltou, lemman, full well winne.   *obtain*
I wot, so well so ich it sowe,   *saw*
To thee shole comen heye and lowe,
1325 And alle that in Denemark wone,   *dwell*
Em and brother, fader and sone,   *uncle*
Erl and baroun, dreng and thain,   *vassal/thane*
Knightes and burgeys and swain,   *citizen/peasant*
And mad king heyelike and well.
1330 Denemark shall be thin evere-ilk del: *every/part*
Have thou nought theroffe doute,   *fear*
Nought the worth of one noute;
Theroffe withinne the firste yer
Shalt thou been king, withouten were. *doubt*
1335 But do nou als I wile rathe: *counsel*
Nimen wit to Denemark bathe,
And do thou nought on frest this fare;
Lith and selthe felawes are.
For shall ich nevere blithe be
1340 Till I with eyen Denemark see;
For ich wot that all the lond
Shalt thou haven in thin hond.   *possess*
Pray Grimes sones, alle three,
That he wenden forth with thee;   *go*
1345 I wot he wilen thee nought werne;   *refuse*
With thee wende shulen he yerne,   *eagerly*
For he loven thee hertelike.
Thou maght telle he aren quike,   *ready*
Whore-so he o worde aren;
1350 There ship thou do hem swithe yaren, *quickly/ready*
And loke that thou dwelle nought: *tarry*
Dwelling haveth ofte scathe wrought." *harm*

1316   "May You [that is, the Deity] who sits upon the thrown know that."
1317-18 "Nor [will there be] anyone so powerful as you will be, [neither] king nor emperor."
1329   "Any [you will be] made king solemnly and well."
1332   "Not the worth of one nut" [that is, not at all].
1336   "Let us two both go to Denmark"; the dual pronoun *wit* emends the *will* of the MS.
1337   "And do not put off this journey."
1338   Apparently a proverb, but the meaning of *lith* is uncertain; the sense may be something like "Speed and prosperity are fellows" [that is, go hand in hand].
1349   "Wheresoever they are in [the] world."

Whan Havelok herde that she radde, *counseled*
Sone it was day, sone he him cladde, *so soon as*
                      /*dressed*
1355 And sone to the kirke yede *church/went*
  Or he dide any other dede; *before*
  And bifor the rode bigan falle, *cross/did*
  Croiz and Christ bigan to calle, *address*
  And saide, "Loverd, that all weldes, *rules*
1360 Wind and water, wodes and feldes,
  For the holy milce of you, *mercy*
  Have mercy of me, loverd, nou,
  And wreke me yet on my fo, *avenge/foe*
  That ich saw biforn min eyne slo
1365 Mine sistres with a knif,
  And sithen wolde me my lif *afterwards*
  Have reft, for in the se *bereft*
  Bad he Grim have drenched me. *drowned*
  He hath my lond with mikel unright, *possesses*
                      /*injustice*
1370 With michel wrong, with mikel plight, *harm*
  For I ne misdede him nevere nought,
  And haveth me to sorrwe brought.
  He haveth me do my mete to thidge, *caused/beg for*
  And ofte in sorrwe and pine lidge. *lie*
1375 Loverd, have mercy of me,
  And late me well passe the se–
  Though ich have theroffe doute and care– *fear/anxiety*
  With-uten stormes overfare, *pass over*
  That I ne drenched be therine,
1380 Ne forfaren for no sinne; *be lost/because of*
                      /*any*
  And bringe me well to the lond
  That Godard haldes in his hond,
  That is my right, every del: *part*
  Jesu Christ, thou wost it well!" *know*

1385 Thanne he havede his bede said, *when/prayer*
  His offrende on the auter laid, *altar*
  His leve at Jesu Christ he took,
  And at his swete moder ok,
  And at the croiz that he biforn lay;
1390 Sithen yede sore grotinde away. *weeping*

  Whan he com hom, he wore yare, *they/ready*
  Grimes sones, forto fare *sail*

1371–72 "For I never did him an injustice ever and [he] has brought me to sorrow."

Into the se, fishes to gete,   *catch*
That Havelok mighte well of ete.
1395 But Havelok thoughte all another.   *quite/differently*
First he calde the eldeste brother,
Roberd the Rede, by his name,
William Wendut and Huwe Raven,
Grimes, sones alle three,
1400 And saide, "Lithes nou alle to me;   *listen*
Loverdinges, ich wile you shewe   *comrades/show*
A thing of me that ye well knewe.
My fader was king of Denshe lond;
Denemark was all in his hond
1405 The day that he was quick and ded;   *alive*
But thanne havede he wicke red,   *counsel*
That he me and Denemark all   *in that*
And mine sistres bitaughte a thrall;   *committed*
A develes lime he us bitaughte,
1410 And all his lond and all hise aughte,   *possessions*
For I saw that fule fend   *foul/fiend*
Mine sistres slo with hise hend;   *hands*
First he shar a-two here throtes,   *cut*
And sithen hem all to grotes,
1415 And sithen bad he in the se
Grim, youre fader, drenchen me.   *drown*
Deplike dede he him swere   *solemnly caused*
On book, that he sholde me bere
Unto the se, and drenchen ine,
1420 And he wolde taken on him the sinne.
But Grim was wis and swithe hende;   *skillful*
Wolde he nought his soule shende;   *harm*
Levere was him to be forsworen   *perjured*
Than drenchen me, and been forlorn;   *drown*
                                                         /utterly lost

1425 But sone bigan he forto flee
Fro Denemark, forto berwen me.   *protect*
For yif ich havede ther been funden,
Havede he been slain or harde bunden,
And heye been hanged on a tree–
1430 Havede gon for him gold ne fee.
For-thy fro Denemark hider he fledde,   *therefore/hither*
And me full faire and full well fedde,   *reared*
So that un-to this day
Have ich been fed and fostred ay.
1435 But nou ich am up to that elde   *age*

1409 "He committed us to a devil's limb" [that is, to a rogue].
1414 "And then [cut] them completely to pieces."
1430 "[Neither] gold nor property would have availed him."

Cumen, that ich may wepne welde,   *weapons/wield*
And I may grete dintes yeve,   *blows*
Shall I nevere whil ich live
Been glad, till that ich Denemark see;
1440 I praye you that ye wende with me,   *go*
And ich may mak you riche men;
Ilk of you shall have castles ten,   *each*
And the lond that thortil longes,   *thereto/belongs*
Borwes, tunes, wodes, and wonges.   *boroughs/fields*

. . . .

1625 . . . "With swilk als ich byen shall: *such/buy*
Thereof biseche ich you nou leve;   *permission*
Wile ich speke with non other reve,   *magistrate*
But with thee, that justise are,
That I mighte sellen my ware
1630 In gode borwes up and doun,   *towns*
And faren ich wile fro tun to tun."
A gold ring drow he forth anon
An hundred pund was worth the ston
And yaf it Ubbe for to spede.
1635 He was full wis that first yaf mede;
And so was Havelok full wis here:
He sold his gold ring full dere–
Was neuere non so dere sold
Fro chapmen, neither yung ne old: *merchants*
1640 That sholen ye forthward full well **heren,** *later*
Yif that ye wile the storie heren.

Whan Ubbe havede the gold ring,
Havede he yovenet for no thing,
Nought for the boru evere-ilk del.
1645 Havelok biheld he swithe well,   *examined*
Hu he was well of bones maked,
Brod in the sholdres, full well shaped,
Thicke in the brest, of body long;
He semede well to been well strong.
1650 "Deus!" quath Ubbe, "why ne were he knight?
I wot that he is swithe wight!   *know/bold*

1444 An estimated 180 lines have been lost. The gist of the missing portion probably
   was that the three sons agree to follow Havelok; and all the men, together with
   Goldeboru, sail for Denmark. Ashore, Havelok, William, and Roberd, disguised
   as peddlers, meet the Danish earl Ubbe and ask permission to sell their wares.
   Line 1625 opens in the middle of Havelok's plea.
1634 "And gave it to Ubbe [in hope] to succeed."
1635 Apparently a proverb: "He was quite wise who first gave a gift," although *mede*
   can have connotations approaching "bribe."
1643–44 "He would have given it up for nothing, not [even] for every bit of the
   town."
1650 "Deus!" said Ubbe, "why might he not be [a] knight?"

Betere semede him to bere
Helm on heved, sheld and spere,   *head*
Thanne to beye and selle ware,
1655 Allas, that he shall therwith fare!
Goddot! wile he trowe me,
Chaffare shall he late be."   *selling/abandon*
Netheles he saide sone,
"Havelok, have thy bone,   *request*
1660 And I full well rede thee   *advise*
That thou come and ete with me
To-day, thou and thy faire wif,
That thou lovest also thy lif.   *just as*
And have thou of hire no drede;   *fear*
665 Shall hire no man shame bede.   *offer*
By the fey that I owe to thee,   *faith*
Thereof shall I myself boru be."   *pledge*

Havelok herde that he bad,
And thou was he full sore adrad   *yet*
1670 With him to ete, for hise wif;   *because of*
For him wore levere that his lif
Him wore reft, than she in blame
Felle, or laughte any shame.   *encountered*
Whanne he havede his wille yat,
1675 The stede that he onne sat
Smot Ubbe with spures faste,
And forth away, but at the laste,
Or he fro him ferde,   *before/parted*
Saide he, that his folk herde: *so that*
1680 "Loke that ye comen bethe,   *both*
For ich it wile and ich it rede."   *desire/advise*

Havelok ne durste, they he were adrad,   *dare/although*
Nought withsitten that Ubbe bad.   *gainsay*
                                                   /that which

His wif he dide with him lede;
1685 Un-to the heye curt he yede.   *high/court/went*
Roberd hire ledde, that was red,   *who/red*
That havede tholed for hire the ded
Or any havede hire misseyd,
Or hand with ivele onne laid.

1652   "It would be more proper for him to bear."
1656   "By God, if he wishes to trust in me."
1674   "When he [Havelok] had agreed to his [Ubbe's] wish"; the MS reads *quath*,
        which is a bad rhyme; use of *yat* 'granted' (from OE *gēatan*) improves both
        sense and rhyme.
1687–88 "Who would have suffered death for her before anyone might have in-
        sulted her."

1690 William Wendut was that other
     That hire ledde, Roberdes brother,
     That was wight at alle nedes–   *courageous*
     "Well is him that good man fedes!"
     Than he weren comen to the halle,   *when*
1695 Biforen Ubbe and hise men alle,
     Ubbe stirte hem again   *went/toward*
     And many a knight and many a swain,
     Hem for to see and for to shewe.   *look upon*
     Tho stood Havelok als a lowe   *hill*
1700 Aboven tho that ther-inne wore,
     Right all by the heved more   *greater*
     Thanne any that ther-inne stood.
     Tho was Ubbe blithe of mood,
     That he saw him so fair and hende.   *courteous*
1705 Fro him ne mighte his herte wende–   *turn*
     Ne fro him ne fro his wif.
     He lovede hem sone so his lif.   *straightway/like*
     Weren non in Denemark, that him thoughte, *to him/seemed*
     That he so mikel love moughte.
1710 More he lovede Havelok one   *alone*
     Than all Denemark, by mine wone!   *opinion*
     Loke nou, hou God helpen can
     O many wise wif and man.   *in/way*

     Whan it was comen time to ete,
1715 Hise wif dede Ubbe sone in fete   *fetch*
     And till hire saide, all on gamen,   *sport*
     "Dame, thou and Havelok shulen ete samen, *together*
     And Goldeboru shall ete with me,
     That is so fair so flour on tree.   *who/as*
1720 In all Denemark is wimman non
     So fair so she, by saint Johan!
     Thanne he were set and bord laid   *table/set*
     And the beneisun was said,   *blessing*
     Biforn hem com the beste mete   *food*
1725 That king or caiser wolde ete:
     Cranes, swannes, veneisun,
     Lax, lampreys, and good sturgiun,   *salmon*
     Pyment to drinke and good claré,
     Win whit and red, full good plenté.
1730 Was ther-inne no page so lite   *little*
     That evere wolde ale bite.

1693   The gist of the proverb is that it is well for a man to feed [that is, maintain] a good retainer since good retainers are precious.

1728   Pyment is a spiced wine and claré a mixture of wine and honey, also spiced.

1731   "Who ever would request ale," here a drink below the dignity of Ubbe's household.

Of the mete forto telle
Ne of the win bidde I nought dwelle;
That is the storie for to lenge;   *prolong*
1735 It wolde anuie this faire genge.   *annoy/company*
But whan he haveden ilk thing deiled   *each/shared*
And fele sithe haveden wossailed,   *many/times*
    /drunk healths

With gode drinkes seten longe,
And it was time for to gonge,   *go*
1740 Ilk man to ther he cam fro,   *there where*
Thoughte Ubbe, "If I late hem go,
Thus one foure, with-uten mo,
So mote ich brouke finger or to,
For this wimman bes mikel wo!
1745 For hire shall men hire loverd slo."   *lord/slay*
He took sone knightes ten   *straightway*
And well sixty other men,
With gode bowes and with gleives,
And sende hem unto the greives,   *town official's*
1750 The beste man of all the toun,
That was named Bernard Brun;
And bad him, als he lovede his lif,
Havelok well yemen, and his wif,   *guard*
And well do waiten all the night   *watch*
1755 Till the other day, that it were light.   *next/when*
Bernard was trewe and swithe wight,   *very/bold*
In all the boru ne was no knight   *town*
That betere couthe on stede riden,
Helm on heved, ne swerd by side.   *head*
1760 Havelok he gladlike understood   *received*
With mikel love and herte good
And dide greithe a super riche   *prepare*
(Also he was no wight chiche)   *niggardly*
To his bihove ever-ilk del,   *need*
1765 That he mighte soupe swithe well.   *eat*

Also he seten and sholde soupe,   *as*
So comes a ladde in a joupe   *jacket*
And with him sixty other stronge
With swerdes drawen and knives longe,
1770 Ilkan in hande a full good gleive,   *each*
And saide, "Undo, Bernard the greive!

1733   "Nor need I not tarry over the wine."
1742–44   "Thus four alone, without more, as I may use [my] finger or toe, because
    of this woman [there] will be much harm."
1749   A gleive is usually a spear, but in *Havelok* it seems to mean sword.
1770· See note to line 1748.
1771   See gloss to line 1749.

Undo swithe and lat us in,
Or thu art ded, by saint Austin!"
Bernard stirt up, that was full big,   *jumped*
1775 And caste a brinie upon his rig,   *mail coat/back*
And grop an ax, that was full good,   *seized*
Lep to the dore, so he wore wood.   *leapt/mad*
And saide, "What are ye, that are ther-oute,
That thus biginnen forto stroute?
1780 Goth henne swithe, fule theves,   *hence/quickly*
                                                            /foul

For, by the Loverd, that mon on leves,   *believes*
Sholl ich casten the dore open,
Summe of you shall ich drepen!   *kill*
And the othre shall ich kesten   *others/cast*
1785 In feteres and full faste festen!
"What have ye said?" quoth a laddė,
"Wenestu that we been adradde?   *think you/afraid*
We sholen at this dore gonge   *go*
Maugré thin, carl, or ought longe."
1790 He gripen sone a bulder-ston   *boulder*
And let it fleye, full good won,   *forcefully*
Again the dore, that it to-rof.   *burst asunder*
Havelok it saw and thider drof   *ran*
And the barre sone ut-drow,
1795 That was unride and gret y-now,   *huge/enough*
And caste the dore open wide
And saide, "Her shall I now abide!
Comes swithe unto me!   *quickly*
Datheit who you henne flee!"   *cursed/hence*
1800 "No," quod on, "that shaltou coupe;"
And bigan till him to loupe,   *run*
In his hond his swerd ut-drawe,
Havelok he wende thore have slawe;   *intended/to have*
                                                            /slain

And with him comen other two
1805 That him wolde of live have do.
Havelok lifte up the dore-tree   *door-bar*
And at a dint he slow hem three.   *blow/killed*
Was non of hem that hise hernes   *brains*
Ne lay ther-ute again the sternes.
1810 The ferthe that he sithen mette   *fourth/next*
With the barre so he him grette   *met*
Bifor the heved that the right eye   *upon*

1779   "Who thus begin to raise a rumpus."
1789   "For all of you, fellow, before long."
1800   "No," said one, "that you'll pay for."
1805   "Who would take his life."
1809   "Did not lay out exposed to the stars."

Ut of the hole made he fleye	*fly*
And sithe clapte him on the crune	*then/struck*
1815 So that he stan-ded fell thor dune.	*stone dead*
The fifte that he overtook	
Gaf he a full sor dint ok,	*bitter/blow/also*
Bitween the sholdres ther he stood,	
That he spende his herte blood.	*shed*
1820 The sixte wende for to flee	*intended*
And he clape him with the tree	
Right in the fule necke so	*foul*
That he smot hise necke on to.	
Thanne the sixe weren doune feld,	*when/felled*
1825 The seventhe braid ut his swerd	*whipped*
And wolde Havelok right in the eye;	
And Havelok let the barre fleye	*fly*
And smot him sone again the brest	*against*
That havede he nevere shrifte of prest;	
1830 For he was ded on lesse while	
Than men moughte renne a mile.	*might*
Alle the othere weren full kene;	*very/tough*
A red they taken hem bitwene	*plan/made*
That he sholden him bihalve,	*surround*
1835 And brisen so that with no salve	*lay on*
Ne sholde him helen leche non.	*doctor*
They drowen ut swerdes, full good won,	*aplenty*
And shoten on him, so don on bere	*rushed/as/bears*
Dogges that wolden him to-tere,	*tear to pieces*
1840 Thanne men doth the bere beite.	*when/bait*
The laddes were kaske and teite	*vigorous/eager*
And umbiyeden him ilkon.	*surrounded /each one*
Sum smot with tree and sum with ston;	*cudgel*
Summe putten with gleive in back and side	*thrust/sword*
1845 And yeven wundes longe and wide	
In twenty stedes and well mo	*places*
Fro the croune till the to.	
Whan he saw that, he was wood	*crazed*
And was it ferlik hu he stood;	
1850 For the blood ran off his sides	
So water that fro the welle glides.	*like*
But thanne bigan he for to mowe	*mow*
With the barre and let hem shewe	*see*
Hu he couthe sore smite;	*bitterly*
1855 For was ther non, long ne lite,	*tall/little*

1826 "And would [strike] Havelok in the eye."
1829 "So that he never had shrift from a priest."
1849 "And it was a wonder how he stood"—his wounds being so severe.

That he moughte overtake,   *whom*
That he ne garte his croune cracke;   *made*
So that on a litel stund,   *in/while*
Felde he twenty to the grund.   *felled*

1860 Tho bigan gret dine to rise,   *din*
     For the laddes on ilke wise   *every/way*
     Assaileden him with grete dintes,
     Full fer he stoden, and with flintes   *far/they/stones*
     And gleives shoten him fro ferne,   *spears/afar*
1865 For drepen him he wolden yerne.   *to kill/gladly*
     But dursten he nehwen him no more   *draw near*
     Thanne he bore or leun wore.

     Huwe Raven that dine herde
     And thoughte well that men misferde   *attacked*
1870 With his loverd for his wif   *because of*
     And grop an ore and a long knif   *seized/oar*
     And thider drof also an hert   *ran/stag*
     And cam ther on a litel stert   *got/while*
     And saw how that the laddes wode   *maddened*
1875 Havelok his loverd umbistode   *surrounded*
     And beten on him so doth the smith
     With the hamer on the stith.   *anvil*

     "Allas!" quath Huwe, "that I was boren!
     That evere et ich bred of coren!   *wheat*
1880 That ich here this sorrwe see!
     Roberd! William! whare ar ye?
     Gripeth either uncer a good tree   *both of/you two*
                              /cudgel

     And late we nought thise dogges flee
     Till ure loverd wreke be.   *avenged*
1885 Cometh swithe and follwes me!
     Ich have in honde a full good ore.
     Datheit who ne smite sore!"   *cursed*
     "Ya! leve, ya!" quod Roberd sone,   *comrade*
     "We haven full good light of the mone."   *moon*
1890 Roberd a staf grop, strong and gret,   *seized*
     That moughte full well bere a net,
     And William Wendut grop a tree   *seized/cudgel*
     Mikel grettere than his the,   *thigh*
     And Bernard held his ax full faste
1895 (I saye was he nought the laste)
     And lopen forth so he weren wode   *leapt/crazed*

1867   "Than if he were a bear or lion."
1891   "Which an ox would do well to bear."

To the laddes ther he stode   *there where*
And yaf hem wundes swithe grete.
Ther mighte men well see boyes bete
1900 And ribbes in here sides broke   *broken*
And Havelok on hem well be wreke.   *avenged*
He broken armes, he broken knes,
He broken shankes, he broken thes.   *legs/thighs*
He dide the blode there renne dune   *caused*
1905 To the feet right fro the crune;
For was ther spared heved non.   *head*
He laiden on hevedes, full good won,   *vehemently*
And made crounes breke and crake
Of the broune and of the blake.
1910 He maden here backes also bloute   *pulpy*
Als here wombes and made hem route   *like/stomachs*
                                                                      /roar
Als he weren cradelbarnes–   *babies*
So dos the child that moder tharnes.

Datheit who recke! for he it servede.
1915 What dide he thore? He weren werewed.   *mauled*
So longe haveden he but and bet   *butted/beaten*
With neves under hernes set
That of tho sixty men and on   *those/one*
Ne wente away ther lives non.   *alive/not one*

1920 On the morwen when it was day,
Ilk on other wirwed lay   *each/strangled*
Als it were dogges that weren henged;   *wretches*
And summe laye in dikes slenget   *ditches/slung*
And summe in gripes by the her   *trenches/hair*
1925 Drawen ware and laten ther.   *left*
Sket cam tiding intill Ubbe   *quickly*
That Havelok havede with a clubbe
Of hise slawen sixty and on
Sergaunz, the beste that mihten gon.
1930 "Deus," quoth Ubbe, "What may this be?
Betere is I nime myself and see   *go*
What this baret oweth on wold
Thanne I sende yunge or old.
For yif I sende him unto,

1909   "Of the brown and of the fair," meaning all concerned; *black* is from OE
      blāc 'white.'
1913   "As does the child who loses [his] mother."
1914   "Cursed [be] who cares! for they deserved it."
1917   "With fists set under brains"; editors question the reading.
1932   "What this rumpus means."
1933   "Than [if] I [were to] send a young or old [man]."

1935 I wene men sholde him shame do–
And that ne wolde ich for no thing.
I love him well, by Hevene King!
Me wore levere I wore lame
Thanne men dide him any shame
1940 Or took or onne handes laide
Unornelike or shame saide."   *roughly*
He lep up on a stede light   *leapt*
And with him many a noble knight
And ferde forth unto the tun   *went*
1945 And dide calle Bernard Brun
Ut of his hus whan he ther cam.
And Bernard sone again him nam,   *toward/went*
All to-tused and all to-torn,   *cut up*
                                           /torn to pieces

Ner also naked so he was born   *almost/as*
1950 And all to-brised, back and the.   *utterly bruised*
                                           /thigh

Quoth Ubbe, "Bernard, what is thee?
Who haves thee thus ille maked,
Thus to-riven and all mad naked?"   *torn to pieces*

"Loverd, mercy," quoth he sone,   *quickly*
1955 "Tonight, also rose the mone,   *as/moon*
Comen her mo than sixty theves,   *more*
With lokene copes and wide sleves,
Me forto robben and to pine   *torment*
And for to drepe me and mine.   *murder*
1960 My dore he broken up full sket   *very/quickly*
And wolde me binden hond and feet.
Whan the godemen that sawe,
Havelok and he that by the wowe   *they/wall*
Laye, he stirten up sone anon   *immediately*
965 And summe grop tree and sum grop ston   *seized/cudgels*
And drive hem ut, they he weren crus,   *to drive/although*
                                           /fierce

So dogges ut of milne-hous.
Havelok grop the dore-tree
And at a dint he slow hem three.
970 He is the beste man at nede
That everemar shall ride on stede!
Als helpe God, by mine wone,   *opinion*
A thousand men is he worth one!   *alone*

1951   "Said Ubbe, 'Bernard, what is wrong with you?' "
1957   "With fastened cloaks and wide sleeves"; the exact—and sinister—meaning
        is now lost.
1967   "As dogs [are driven] out of a mill."

Yif he ne were, ich were nou ded,
1975 So have ich don my soule red!   *harm*
But it is of him mikel sinne;   *they/such/three*
He maden him swilke woundes thrinne   *very least*
That of the altherleste wounde   *steed/laid/low*
Were a stede brought to grunde.
1980 He haves a wunde in the side
With a gleive full unride.   *extremely/huge*
And he haves on thoru his arum   *one/arm*
Therof is full mikel harum.
And he haves on thoru his the,   *thigh*
1985 The unrideste that men may see;   *greatest*
And othere wundes haves he stronge,   *severe*
Mo than twenty, swithe longe.   *more*
But sithen he havede laught the sor   *since/felt/smart*
Of the wundes was nevere bor   *boar*
1990 That so faught so he faught thanne;
Was non that havede the herne-panne   *brain pan*
So hard that he ne dede alto-crushe
And also-shivere and alto-frushe.
He follwede hem so hund dos hare–   *hound/does*
1995 Datheit on he wolde spare!–
That he ne made hem everilk on
Lidge stille so doth the ston;
And ther nis he nought to frye
For other sholde he make hem lye   *either*
2000 Ded, or they him havede slawen,   *slain*
Or alto-hewen or alto-drawen.

Loverd, havi no more plight
That ich was greithed thus tonight.
Thus wolde the theves me have reft;   *robbed*
2005 God thank, he havenet sure keft!
But it is of him mikel scathe–   *great/pity*
I wot that he bes ded full rathe.   *know/will be*
                                             /soon

Quoth Ubbe, "Bernard, saist thou sooth?"
"Ya, sire, that I ne leye o tooth!

1975   "[As surely] as I have followed the dictates of my soul!"
1992–93   "So hard that he did not crush [it] to pieces and completely shiver and smash [it]."
1995   "A curse on [him who] he [Havelok] would spare."
1998   "And there is he [Havelok] not to be blamed."
2001   "Or cut or drawn to pieces."
2002–03   "Lord, I have no more harm [than] that I was thus roughly handled tonight."
2005   "God be thanked, they have surely paid for it!"
2009   "Yea, sir, [of] that I do not lie in my teeth" (a reading from Skeat-Sisam which makes sense, whereas the MS's *Ya, sire, that I ne lepe oth* does not).

2010 Yif I, loverd, a word leye,   *high*
    Tomorwen do me hengen heye."
    The burgeis that therin stode thore   *burgesses/there*
    Grundlike and grete othes swore,   *solemn*
    Litle and mikle, yunge and olde,
2015 That was sooth that Bernard tolde.
    Sooth was that he wolden him binde
    And trusse all that he mighten finde   *carry off*
    Of hise, in arke or in kiste   *coffer/chest*
    That he moughte in seckes thriste.   *sacks/thrust*
2020 "Loverd, away he haveden all born
    His thing and himself also-torn,
    But als God self barw him well,   *except/preserved*
    That he ne tinte no catel.   *lost/property*
    Who mighte so many stonde again   *stand up/against*
2025 By nighter-tale, knight or swain?   *night time*
    He weren by tale sixty and ten,   *count*
    Starke laddes, stalworthy men,
    And on, the maister of hem alle,   *one*
    That was the name Griffin Galle.
2030 Who moughte again so many stonde,
    But als this man of ferne londe   *except/distant*
    Haveth hem slawen with a tree?   *slain/cudgel*
    Mikel joye have he!   *much*
    God yeve him mikel good to welde,   *wealth/control*
2035 Bothe in tun and ek in felde!
    Well is set the mete he etes."
    Quoth Ubbe, "Gos him swithe fetes   *go/quickly/fetch*
    That I moughte his woundes see,
    If that he moughten holed be.   *made whole*
2040 For if he moughte covere yet   *recover*
    And gangen well upon hise feet,   *walk*
    Myself shall dubben him to knight,
    Forthy that he is so wight.   *since/courageous*
    And yif he livede, tho foule theves,   *those*
2045 That weren of Caimes kin and Eves,   *Cain's*
    He sholden hange by the necke.   *they*
    Of here ded datheit who recke,   *death/cursed be*
                                        /cares*

    When he yeden thus on nightes   *since/of/nights*
    To binde bothe burgmen and knightes!   *burgesses*

2020–21 "Lord, they would have carried off all his things and torn him [Havelok]
      to pieces."
2036 "Well is spent the food he eats"; a proverbial expression similar to that of
     line 907; the MS reads *We is set he etes mete;* both Skeat-Sisam and French
     and Hale emend as above and change the *fete* (l.2037) of the MS to *fetes.*

2050 For binderes love ich nevere mo, *outlaws/not at all*
    Of hem ne yeve ich nought a slo."

    Havelok was to Ubbe brought,
    That havede for him full mikel thought *anxiety*
    And mikel sorwe in his herte
2055 For hise wundes, that were so smerte.

    But whan his wundes weren shewed *seen*
    And a leche havede knawed *doctor/found out*
    That he hem moughte full well hele, *heal*
    Well make him gange and full well mele, *walk/talk*
2060 And well a palefrey bistride,
    And well upon a stede ride,
    Tho let Ubbe all his care
    And all his sorwe overfare; *pass*
    And saide, "Cum now forth with me,
2065 And Goldeboru, thy wif, with thee,
    And thine sergaunz alle three, *retainers*
    For nou wile I youre warrant be; *surety*
    Wile I that non of here frend *desire/friends*
    That thou slowe with thin hend
2070 Moughte waite thee to slo *as*
    Also thou gange to and fro.
    I shall lene thee a bour *loan/room*
    That is up in the heye tour,
    Till thou mowe full well go *walk*
2075 And well been hol of all thy wo. *cured*
    It ne shall no thing been bitwene
    Thy bour and min, also I wene, *as/intend*
    But a fair firrene wowe.
    Speke I loude or spek I lowe,
2080 Thou shalt full well heren me
    And than thu wilt, thou shalt me see. *when*
    A roof shall hile us bothe o night *cover/at*
    That none of mine, clerk ne knight,
    No sholen thy wif no shame bede *proffer*
2085 No more than min, so God me rede!"

    He did unto the boru bring *town*
    Sone anon, all with joyinge, *rejoicing*
    His wif and ek his sergaunz three, *retainers*
    The beste men that moughte be.
2090 The firste night he lay therinne,

2051 "I don't give a sloe-berry [that is, I care nothing at all] for them."
2070 "Might lay in wait to slay you."
2078 "Except a partition made of fir wood."

Hise wif and his sergaunz thrinne,   *three*
Aboute the middel of the night
Wok Ubbe and saw a mikel light
In the bour ther Havelok lay
095 Also bright so it were day.   *just as*

"Deus," quoth Ubbe, "what may this be?
Betere is I go myself and see
Whether he sitten nou and wessailen   *carouse*
Or any sotshipe to-deile,   *folly/partake in*
00 This tid nightes also foles;   *ought/pools*
Than birth men casten hem in poles   *ought/pools*
Or in a grip or in the fen;   *ditch/mud*
Nou ne sitten none but wicke men,   *wicked*
Glotuns, reveres, or wicke theves,   *robbers*
05 By Christ, that alle folk on leves!"   *believes*

He stood and totede in at a bord   *peeped/board*
Er he spack anlepy word   *single*
And saw hem slepen faste ilkon   *each one*
And lie stille so the ston;
10 And saw that all that mikel light
Fro Havelok cam, that was so bright.
Of his mouth it com ilk del–   *from/every/bit*
That was he war full swithe well.   *aware of/indeed*
"Deus," quoth me, "what may this mene!"
15 He calde bothe arwe men and kene,   *timid/bold*
Knightes and sergaunz swithe sleye,   *very/perceptive*
Mo than an hundred, withuten leye,   *more/denial*
And bad hem alle comen and see
What that selcuth mighte be.   *wonder*

20 Als the knightes were comen alle,
Ther Havelok lay, ut of the halle,   *there where*
So stood ut of his mouth a glem,   *gleam*
Right all swilk so the sunnebem,   *just/exactly/like*
That all so light was thare, by hevene,
25 So ther brenden serges sevene   *as if/burned
                                                            /candles*

And an hundred serges ok–   *also*
That durste hi sweren on a book!
He slepen faste alle five   *they/soundly*
So he weren brought of live;
30 And Havelok lay on his lift side,   *left*
In his armes his brighte bride.

——

2100 "[At] this time of night like fools."
2129 "As if they had been reft of life."

By the pappes he layen naked;
So faire two weren nevere maked
In a bed to lyen samen.   *together*
2135 The knightes thought of hem good gamen,   *sport*
Hem forto shewe and loken to.   *see/look/at*
Right also he stoden alle so   *just/as*
And his back was toward hem wend,   *turned*
So weren he war of a croiz full gent
2140 On his right shuldre swithe bright,
Brighter than gold again the light
So that he wiste, heye and lowe,
That it was kunrik that he sawe.
It sparkede and full brighte shon   *sparkled*
2145 So doth the gode charbuncle ston   *as/carbuncle*
That men see moughte by the light
A penny chesen so was it bright.
Thanne bihelden he him faste
So that he knewen at the laste
2150 That he was Birkabeines sone,
That was here king, that was hem wone   *accustomed*
Well to yemen and well were   *rule/defend*
Againes uten-laddes here.   *foreigners/army*
"For it was nevere yet a brother
2155 In all Denemark so lich another   *like*
So this man, that is so fair,
Als Birkabein; he is hise eir."

He fellen sone at hise feet;
Was non of hem that he ne greet.
2160 Of joye he weren alle so fawen   *glad*
So he him haveden of erthe drawen.
Hise feet he kisten an hundred sithes—   *times*
The tos, the nailes, and the lithes—   *tips*
So that he bigan to wakne   *awaken*
2165 And with hem full sore to blakne,
For he wende he wolden him slo   *slay*
Or elles binde him and do wo.

Quoth Ubbe, "Loverd, ne dred thee nought,

2132 "Down to the breasts they lay naked" [that is, uncovered].
2139 "They were thus aware of a very fair cross."
2143 "That it was a mark of kingship that they saw"; the word *kunrik* is probably
    an error for *kynemerk* of line 604.
2146–47 "[So] that men might see by the light to pick out a penny it was so bright."
2154–57 "For there was never yet a brother so like another [brother] in all Denmark
    as this man, who is so handsome, [is] like Birkabein; he is his heir."
2161 "As if they had recovered him from earth" [that is, from the grave].
2165 "And to grow very much pale in their presence."

Me thinkes that I see thy thought.
70 Dere sone, well is me
That I thee with eyen see.
Manred, loverd, bede I thee.   *fealty/offer*
Thy man aught I full well to be;   *retainer*
For thu art comen of Birkabein,
75 That havede many knight and swain,
And so shalt thou, loverd, have,
Though thou be yet a full yung knave.
Thou shalt be king of all Denemark–
Was therinne never non so stark.
80 Tomorwen shaltu manrede take   *shall you/fealty*
Of the brune and of the blake–
Of alle that aren in this tun,
Bothe of erl and of barun
And of dreng and of thain   *tenant/thane*
85 And of knight and of swain.
And so shaltu been maken knight
With blisse, for thou art so wight."   *joy/courageous*

Tho was Havelok swithe blithe
And thankede God full fele sithe.   *many/times*
90 On the morwen, whan it was light,
And gon was thisternesse of night,   *darkness*
Ubbe dide upon a stede   *caused*
A ladde lepe and thider bede   *to leap/to*
                                         summon

Erles, barouns, drenges, thaines,
95 Clerkes, knightes, burgeis, swaines,
That he sholden comen anon
Biforen him sone everilkon,   *quickly/everyone*
Also he loveden here lives   *if*
And here children and here wives.

100 His bode ne durste he non atsitte   *command/resist*
That he ne neme for to wite
Sone what wolde the justise;   *straightway*
And he bigan anon to rise
And saide sone, "Lithes me,   *listen to*
105 Alle samen, theu and free,   *together/serf*
A thing ich wile you here shauwe   *show*
That ye alle full well knawe.
Ye witen well that all this lond   *know*
Was in Birkabeines hond

2179   "[There] was never [before] anyone so strong [as you are]."
2181   Compare line 1909.
2201   "In that they went in order to learn."

2210 The day that he was quick and ded,
And how that he by youre red   *advice*
Bitaughte hise children three   *committed*
Godard to yeme, and all his fee.   *govern/property*
Havelok his sone he him bitaughte
2215 And hise two doughters and all his aughte.   *possessions*
Alle herden ye him swere
On boke and on messe-gere   *vestments*
That he shulde yeme hem well   *care for*
Withuten lack, withuten tel.   *fault/blame*

2220 He let his oth all overgo–   *go*
Evere wurthe him ivel and wo!–
For the maidnes here lif
Refte he bothen with a knif;   *reft/both*
And him shulde ok have slawen.   *also*
2225 The knif was at his herte drawen.
But God him wolde well have save;
He havede reunesse of the knave   *pity*
So that tho he with his hend   *then/hand*
Ne drop him nought, that sorry fend!   *killed/fiend*
2230 But sone dide he a fishere   *made/fisherman*
Swithe grete othes swere
That he sholde drenchen him   *drown*
In the se, that was full brim.   *furious*

Whan Grim saw that he was so fair
2235 And wiste he was the righte eir,   *heir*
Fro Denemark full sone he fledde
Intill Englond and ther him fedde   *raised*
Many winter that till this day
Haves he been fed and fostred ay.
2240 Lokes, whare he stondes her–
In all this werd ne haves he peer,   *world*
Non so fair, ne non so long,   *tall*
Ne non so mikel, ne non so strong.   *big*
In this middelerd nis no knight   *earth*
2245 Half so strong, ne half so wight.   *courageous*
Bes of him full glad and blithe   *be*
And cometh alle hider swithe,   *quickly*
Menrede youre loverd forto make,   *homage/give*
Bothe brune and the blake!
2250 I shall myself do first the gamen

2210   "[Until] the day he died" [literally, the day that he was alive and dead].
2221   "[May] ever evil and woe be his [lot]."
2249   See line 1909.
2250   "I shall myself first perform the sport"—where *gamen* may carry the connotation "happy ceremony" in the manner of slang substitution.

And ye sithen alle samen." *afterwards*
/altogether

O knees full faire he him sette, *on*
Moughte nothing him therfro lette, *from it/hinder*
And bicam his man right thare– *retainer*
255 That alle sawen that there ware.

After him stirt up laddes ten
And bicomen hise men;
And sithen everilk a baroun
That evere weren in all that toun,
260 And sithen drenges and sithen thaines
And sithen knightes and sithen swaines;
So that or that day was gon, *before*
In all the tun ne was nought on *one*
That ne was his man bicomen–
265 Manrede of alle havede he nomen. *fealty/taken*

Whan he havede of hem alle
Manrede taken in the halle,
Grundlike dide he hem swere *solemnly*
That he sholden him god feith bere *bear*
270 Againes alle that woren on live;
Ther-yen ne wolde never on strive, *a one*
That he ne maden sone that oth,
Riche and poure, lef and loth. *dear/hostile*
Whan that was maked, sone he sende,
275 Ubbe, writes fer and hende,
After alle that castels yemede, *governed*
Burwes, tunes, sibbe and fremde
That thider sholden comen swithe
Till him and heren tithandes blithe, *hear/tidings*
/glad
280 That he hem alle shulde telle.
Of hem ne wolde nevere on dwelle, *tarry*
That he ne come sone plattinde;
Who hors ne havede, com gangande. *walking*
So that withinne a fourtenight
285 In all Denemark ne was no knight,
Ne conestable, ne shireve, *sheriff*
That com of Adam and of Eve,

2260–61 See lines 2194–95, where similar social groups appear.
2271–72 "Never [a] one would strive against that [Havelok's demand for loyalty]
 in that they quickly swore that oath."
2274–75 "When that was done, he—Ubbe—quickly sent writs far and near."
2277 "Towns, villages, kinsmen and strangers"
2282 "In that they quickly came hastening."

That he ne com biforn sire Ubbe–
He dredden him so thef doth clubbe.

2290 Whan he the king haveden y-gret,   *saluted*
And he weren alle dune set,
Tho saide Ubbe, "Lokes here   *see*
Ure loverd swithe dere,
That shall been king of all the lond
2295 And have us alle under hond!   *in*
For he is Birkabeines sone,
The king that was umbe stonde wone   *once/accustomed*
Us for to yemen and well were   *govern/defend*
With sharpe swerd and longe spere.
2300 Lokes nou, hu he is fair!
Sikerlike he is hise eir.
Falles alle to his feet;
Bicomes hise men full sket."   *retainers*
    /immediately

He weren for Ubbe swithe adrad
2305 And dide sone all that he bad;
And yet he deden sumdel more: *something*
O book full grundlike he swore   *on/solemnly*
That he sholde with him halde   *hold*
Bothe againes stille and bolde   *timid*
2310 That evere wolde his body dere–   *harm*
That dide he hem o boke swere.   *made*

Whan he havede manrede and oth
Taken of lef and ek of loth,   *dear/also/hostile*
Ubbe dubbede him to knight
2315 With a swerd full swithe bright;
And the folk of all the lond
Bitaughte him all in his hond,   *committed*
The kuneriche everilk del   *kingdom*
And made him king heylike and well.   *solemnly*
2320 When he was king, ther moughte men see
The moste joye that moughte be:
Buttinge with the sharpe speres,   *thrusting*
Skirming with talevas that men beres,   *fencing/shields*
Wrastling with laddes, putting of ston,   *wrestling*
2325 Harping and piping, full good won,   *indeed/aplenty*
Leik of mine, of hasard ok,
Romanz-reding on the book;   *romance-reading*
Ther moughte men here the gestes singe,   *tales*
The gleumen on the tabour dinge.

2289   "They held him in awe as [does] a thief a club."
2326   "Game of backgammon, also of dice."
2329   "Which minstrels beat out on the drum."

330 Ther moughte men see the boles beite,   *bulls/baited*
    And the bores, with hundes teite.
    Tho moughte men see everilk glew;   *sport*
    Ther moughte men see hu grim grew.   *excitement*
    Was nevere yete joye more
335 In all this werd than tho was thore.   *world/then*
    /there

    Ther was so mikel yeft of clothes   *giving away*
    That, though I swore you grete othes,
    I ne wore never therof troud;   *believed*
    That may I full well swere, by God!
340 There was swithe gode metes   *foods*
    And of win, that men fer fetes,   *from afar/fetches*
    Right all so mikel and gret plenté
    So it were water of the se.   *as if*
    The feste fourty dawes sat,   *feast/days*
345 So riche was nevere non so that.
    The king made Roberd there a knight,
    That was full strong and ek full wight;   *courageous*
    And William Wendut ek, his brother,   *also*
    And Huwe Raven, that was that other;
350 And made hem barouns alle three
    And yaf hem lond and other fee,   *property*
    So mikel that ilker twenty knightes   *each*
    Havede of genge, dayes and nightes.   *in/retinue*

    Whan that feste was all don,
355 A thusand knightes well o bon   *equipped*
    Withheld the king, with him to lede,
    That ilkan havede full good stede,
    Helm and sheld and brinie bright   *mail jacket*
    And all the wepne that fell to knight.   *weapons/belong*
360 With hem ek five thusand gode
    Sergaunz that weren to fighten wode,   *retainers/eager*
    Withheld he ther, all of his genge–   *retained/retinue*
    Wile I namore the storie lenge!   *lengthen*
    Yet whan he havede of all the lond
365 The casteles alle in his hond
    And conestables don therinne,   *placed*
    He swor he ne sholde never blinne   *cease*
    Till that he were of Godard wreken,   *avenged*
    That ich have of ofte speken.
370 Half hundred knightes dede he calle
    And hise fif thusand sergaunz alle   *retainers*
    And dide hem sweren on the book

2331   "And boars [baited] by active hounds."
2356–57   "The king retained to escort him in that each one had a very fine mount."

Sone–and on the auther ok–   *altar*
That he ne sholde nevere blinne,   *cease*
2375 Ne for love ne for sinne,
Till that he haveden Godard funde
And brought biforn him faste bunde.   *bound*

Thanne he haveden sworn this oth,   *when*
Ne leten he nought, for lef ne loth,
2380 That he ne foren swithe rathe
Ther he was, unto the pathe   *where*
Ther he yet on hunting for   *went*
With mikel genge and swithe stor.   *retinue/strong*
Robert, that was of all the ferd   *army*
2385 Maister, girt was with a swerd
And sat upon a full god stede,
That under him right wolde wede.
He was the firste that with Godard
Spak and saide, "Hede, caynard!   *heed/rogue*
2390 What dost thu here at this pathe?
Cum to the kinge swithe and rathe,   *quickly/soon*
That sendes he thee word, and bedes
That thu thenke what thou him dedes
Whan thu reftes with a knif   *bereft*
2395 Hise sistres here lif
And sithen bede thou in the se   *afterwards*
     /ordered

Drenchen him–that herde he!   *drown*
He is to thee swithe grim;   *angry*
Cum nu swithe unto him
2400 That king is of this kunerike,   *kingdom*
Thou fule man, thou wicke swike!   *foul/wicked*
     /scoundrel

And he shall yelde thee thy mede,   *give/reward*
By Christ that wolde on rode blede!"   *cross/bleed*

Whan Godard herde that he ther thrette,   *that which*
     /threatened

2405 With the neve he Robert sette   *fist/struck*
Biforn the teeth a dint full strong.
And Robert kipt ut a knif long   *whipped*
And smot him thoru the righte arum–   *arm*
Therof was full litel harum.

2379–80   "They did not stop for anything [literally, for dear or hostile] in that they
went very quickly."
2387   "That under him would gallop furiously."
2392   "He who sends you word, and commands."
2409   "Of that [there] was little harm" (that is, that no one would feel sorry about).

410 Whan his folk that saw and herde
    Hou Robert with here loverd ferde,   *carried on*
    He haveden him well ner brought of live,
    Ne weren his brethren and othre five
    That slowen of here laddes ten,
2415 Of Godardes alther-beste men.   *very best*
    Whan the othre sawen that, he fledden,
    And Godard swithe loude gredde,   *shouted*
    "Mine knightes, what do ye?
    Shule ye thus-gate fro me flec?   *in this manner*
2420 Ich have you fed and yet shall fede,
    Helpeth me nu in this nede
    And late ye nought my body spille,   *destroy*
    Ne Havelok don of me hise wille.
    Yif ye it do, ye do you shame
2425 And bringeth youself in mikel blame!"
    Whan he that herden, he wenten again,   *turned/back*
    And slowen a knight and ek a swain   *also*
    Of the kinges oune men
    And woundeden abuten ten.

2430 The kinges men, whan he that sawe,
    Shuten on hem, heye and lowe,   *rushed*
    And everilk foot of hem he slowe
    But Godard one, that he flowe,
    So the thef that men dos henge,
2435 Or hund men shole in dike slenge.
    He bunden him full swithe faste,
    While the bondes wolden laste,
    That he rorede als a bole   *roared/bull*
    That wore parred in an hole   *confined*
2440 With dogges forto bite and beite–   *bait*
    Were the bondes nought to leite!
    He bounden him so fele sore   *very/hard*
    That he gan crien Godes ore   *plead for/grace*
    That he ne sholde his hend of-plette;
2445 Wolden he nought therfore lette   *stop*
    That he ne bounden hond and fet–   *until*
    Datheit that on that therfore let!

2412–14 "They very nearly took his life were [it] not for his brothers and the other
        five [men] who killed ten of the fellows."
2432–33 "And every foot [that is, person] of them they killed except Godard alone,
        whom they [afterwards] flayed, like the thief whom men do hang or dog men
        sling in [a] ditch."
2437   For the idiom, see note to line 538.
2441   "The bonds were not to seek"—that is, they were present when needed.
2444   "That they should not cut off his hands"; see line 2755.
2447   "Cursed [be] that one who hinders that."

But dunten him so man doth bere   *beat/bear*
And keste him on a scabbed mere;   *mangy/mare*
2450 Hise nese went unto the crice.   *cleft*
So ledden he that fule swike   *foul/traitor*
Till he biforn Havelok was brought,
That he havede full wo wrought,
Bothe with hungre and with cold
2455 Or he were twelve winter old,   *before*
And with many hevy swink,   *labor*
With poure mete and feeble drink,   *scanty*
And with swithe wicke clothes,   *wretched*
For all hise manye grete othes.   *despite*
2460 Nu beyes he his olde blame: *atones for/guilt*
Old sinne makes newe shame.
Whan he was brought so shamelike
Biforn the king, the fule swike,   *foul/traitor*
The king dede Ubbe swithe calle   *had/quickly*
     /called

2465 His erles and hise barouns alle,
Dreng and thain, burgeis and knight,
And bad he sholden demen him right,   *judge*
For he knew the swike dam—
Everilk del, God was him gram!
2470 He setten hem dune by the wawe,   *wall*
Riche and pouere, heye and lowe,
The olde men and ek the grom,   *also/young*
And made ther the righte doom   *judgment*
And saiden unto the king anon,
2475 That stille sat also the ston,   *quietly*
"We deme that he be all quick flawen   *alive/flayed*
And sithen to the galwes drawen   *afterwards*
At this foule mere tail,   *mare's*
Thoru his feet a full strong nail,
2480 And thore been henged with two fetteres
And thare be writen thise letteres:
'This is the swike that wende well   *rob*
The king have reft the lond ilk del,   *traitor/intended*
And hise sistres with a knif
2485 Bothe refte here lif.'
This writ shall henge by him thore;
The dom is demd, saye we na more."

Whan the dom was demd and give,   *given*
And he was with the prestes shrive,   *shriven*
2490 And it ne moughte been non other,

2468 "For they knew the treacherous fellow."
2469 "In every way, God was angry with him."
2490 "And it might be no otherwise."

Ne for fader ne for brother,
But that he sholde tharne lif, *lose*
Sket cam a ladde with a knif *quickly*
And bigan right at the toe
495 For to ritte and for to flo *cut/flay*
So it were goune or gore.
And he bigan tho for to rore *roar*
That men mighte thethen a mile *thence*
Here him rore, that fule file! *wretch*
500 The ladde ne let no wight forthy, *stopped/whit/for*
that

They he criede "Merci! Merci!" *although*
That he ne flow him everilk del
With knive mad of grunden steel.
They garte bringe the mere sone, *made/to be*
brought

505 Skabbed and full ivele o bone,
And bunden him right at hire tail
With a rop of an old sail *rope*
And drowen him unto the galwes, *dragged*
Nought by the gate, but over the falwes, *road/fields*
510 And henge him thore by the hals– *hanged/neck*
Datheit who recke! he was fals. *cursed be/cares*

Thanne he was ded, that Sathanas, *when*
Sket was saised all that his was *quickly/invested*
In the kinges hand ilk del,
515 Lond and lith and other catel; *folk/chattels*
And the king full sone it yaf
Ubbe in the hond, with a fair staff,
And saide, "Her ich saise thee *invest*
In all the lond, in all the fee." *with*
520 Tho swor Havelok he sholde make,
All for Grim, of monekes blake *monks/black*
A priorie to serven in ay *forever*
Jesu Christ, till domesday,
For the good he havede him don
525 Whil he was povere and ivel o bon. *wretchedly*
/situated

And therof held he well his hot,
For he it made, God it wot!

2496 "As if it [the skin] were a gown or garment"; the emendation of the MS's *grim or gore*, which makes no sense, to *goun or gore* is suggested by Skeat–Sisam.
2502 "In that he flayed him every bit."
2505 "Scabby and very wretched in condition."
2526 "And thereof he held his promise well"; the reading *hot* 'promise' (from OE *hāt*) rather than *oth* 'oath' (from OE *āth*) of the MS is suggested by Skeat–Sisam.

In the tun ther Grim was graven,   *where/buried*
That of Grim yet haves the name.
2530 Of Grim bidde ich na more spelle.   *offer/story*
But whan Godrich herde telle,
Of Cornwaile that was erl,
(That fule traitour, that mixed cherl!)   *filthy*
That Havelok king was of Denemark,
2535 And with a ferde strong and stark   *army*
Was comen Engelond withinne,
Engelond all for to winne;   *conquer*
And that she, that was so fair,
That was of Engelond right eir,
2540 Was comen up at Grimesby,
He was full sorrwfull and sorry
And saide, "What shall me to rathe?   *counsel*
Goddot! I shall do slon hem bathe!
I shall don hengen hem full heye
2545 (So mote ich brouke my righte eye!)
But-yif he of my londe flee.   *unless*
What! Wenden he desherite me?"
He dide sone ferd ut bede,   *had/army/called*
                                                                      out

That all that evere moughte o stede   *on/steed*
2550 Ride or helm on heved bere,   *head*
Brini on back, and sheld and spere,   *mail jacket*
Or any other wepne bere,
Hand-ax, sythe, gisarm, or spere,   *halberd*
Or aunlaz and good long knif,   *dagger*
2555 That, als he lovede leme or lif,
That they sholden comen him to,
With full good wepne y-boren so,
To Lincolne, ther he lay,
Of Marz the seventeenthe day,
2560 So that he couthe hem good thank;
And yif that any were so rank   *presumptuous*
That he thanne ne come anon,
He swor by Christ and by Saint Johan,
That he sholde maken him thrall   *serf*
2565 And all his offspring forth withall.

The Englishe men that herde that,

2532 "Who was Earl of Cornwall."
2543 "By God, I shall have them both slain."
2545 "If I may use my right eye!"—an asseveration.
2547 "What! Do they intend to disinherit me?"
2555-56 "Who, if they loved limb and life, should come to him"; the *that they*
       of line 2556 is pleonastic.
2560 "So that he would be grateful to them."

Was non that evere his bode at-sat;   *command /withstood*

For he him dredde swithe sore,
So runcy spore, and mikle more.
570 At the day he come sone
That he hem sette, full well o bone,   *equipped*
To Lincolne with gode stedes,
And all the wepne that knight ledes.   *carries*
Whan he wore come, sket was the erl yare   *straightway/eager*
575 Againes Denshe men to fare,   *set out*
And saide, "Lithes nu alle samen,   *listen/altogether*
Have ich you gadred for no gamen,   *game*
But ich wile sayen you forwhy:
Lokes whare here at Grimesby
580 Is uten-laddes here comen   *foreigners/army*
And haves the priorie numen.   *taken*
All that evere mighten he finde,
He brenne kirkes and prestes binde.   *burns/churches*
He strangleth monkes and nunnes bothe—
585 What wile ye, frendes, herof rede?   *counsel*
Yif he regne thusgate longe,   *continues/in such manner*

He moun us alle overgange,   *may/subject*
He moun us alle quick henge or slo   *alive/slay*
Or thrall maken and do full wo   *serf*
590 Or elles reve us ure lives   *else/rob*
And ure children and ure wives.
But dos nu als ich wile you lere,   *instruct*
Als ye wile be with me dere.
Nimes nu swithe forth and rathe   *set out/quickly*
595 And helpes me and youself bathe   *both*
And slos upon the dogges swithe.   *strike/out at /wretches*

For shall I nevere more be blithe,
Ne hoseled been ne of prest shriven
Till that he been of londe driven.
600 Nime we swithe and do hem flee
And follwes alle faste me.   *follow/closely*
For ich am he of all the ferd   *army*
That first shall slo with drawen swerd.
Datheit who ne stonde faste   *cursed be*
605 By me while hise armes laste!"
"Ye! lef, ye!" quoth the erl Gunter;   *dear one*

2569 "As does a nag [fear] the spur, and much more."
2578 "But I desire to tell you the reason."
2593 "If you will be faithful to me."
2598 "Nor receive the sacrament nor be shriven by priest."
2600 "Let us go quickly and make them flee."

"Ya!" quoth the erl of Chestre, Reyner.
And so dide alle that ther stode
And stirte forth so he were wode.   *dashed forth /insane*

2610 Tho moughte men see the brinies brighte   *mail jackets*
On backes ceste and late righte,   *cast/straightened*
The helmes heye on heved sette.   *high/head*
To armes all so swithe plette,
That they wore on a litel stunde
2615 Greithed, als men mighte telle a pund,
And lopen on stedes sone anon   *raced/steeds*
And towards Grimesby, full good won,   *vigorously*
He foren softe by the sty   *rode/quietly /road*

Till he come ney at Grimesby.   *near/to*

2620 Havelok, that havede spired well   *learned*
Of here fare, everilk del,   *journey*
With all his ferd cam hem again;   *army/toward*
Forbar he nother knight ne swain.   *spared*
The firste knight that he ther mette
2625 With the swerd so he him grette   *in such manner /greeted*

That his heved off he plette–   *head/struck*
Wolde he nought for sinne lette.
Roberd saw that dint so hende,   *handy*
Wolde he nevere thethen wende,   *from there/go*
2630 Till that he havede another slawen
With the swerd he held ut-drawen.
William Wendut his swerd ut-drow
And the thredde so sore he slow   *third/struck*
That he made upon the feld
2635 His lift arm fleye with the swerd.   *left/fly*

Huwe Raven ne forgat nought
The swerd he havede thider brought.
He kipte it up and smot full sore   *whipped*
An erl, that he saw priken thore   *riding*
2640 Full noblelike upon a stede,
That with him wolde all quick wede.
He smot him on the heved so   *head*
That he the heved clef atwo.
And that he by the shuldre-blade   *near*
2645 The sharpe swerd let dune wade   *down/plow*

2613–15 "All [having] hastened thus quickly to arms, they were in as little while prepared as men might count out a pound."
2627   "He wouldn't stop for anything."
2641   "Who was going to gallop furiously at him."

Thoru the brest unto the herte;
The dint bigan full sore to smerte
That the erl fell dun anon
Also ded so any ston.

2650 Quoth Ubbe, "Nu dwell ich too longe!"   *tarry*
And let his stede sone gonge   *straightway*
                                                              /gallop

To Godrich with a full good spere,
That he saw another bere;
And smot Godrich and Godrich him,
2655 Hetelike with herte grim,   *bitterly*
So that he bothe felle dune
To the erthe, first the croune.   *headfirst*
Thanne he woren fallen dune bothen,   *both*
Grundlike here swerdes he utdrowen,   *vehemently*
2660 That weren swithe sharp and gode,
And foughten so they woren wode,   *crazy*
That the swot ran fro the crune   *sweat*
To the feet right there adune.
Ther moughte men see two knightes bete   *strike*
2665 Either on other dintes grete   *blows*
So that with the altherleste dint   *very least*
Were all to-shivered a flint.
So was bitwenen hem a fight
Fro the morwen ner to the night,   *almost*
2670 So that they stinted nought ne blunne   *stopped*
Till that to sette bigan the sunne.
Tho yaf Godrich thoru the side   *gave*
Ubbe a wunde full unride   *quite/ugly*
So that thoru that ilke wounde
2675 Havede he been brought to grunde
And his heved all ofslawen,   *head/struck off*
Yif God ne were–and Huwe Rauen,
That drow him fro Godrich away
And barw him so that ilke day.   *saved/very*
2680 But er he were fro Godrich drawen,   *withdrew*
Ther were a thousind knightes slawen
By bothe halve and mo y-nowe,   *on/sides/more*
                                                              /enough

Ther the ferdes togidere slowe.   *where/armies*
                                                              /fought

Ther was swilk dreping of the folk   *killing*
2685 That on the feld was nevere a polk   *pool*
That it ne stood of blood so full

2653   "Who he saw was bearing another [good spear]."
2667   "A stone would be cracked to pieces."
2687   "That the stream [of blood] ran downhill."

'That the strem ran intill the hull.
Tho tarst bigan Godrich to go
Upon the Danshe and faste to slo
2690 And forthright also leun fares   straightway/like
                                                          /lion

That nevere kines best ne spares,
Thanne is he gon, for he garte alle   made
The Denshe men biforn him falle.
He felde browne, he felde blake,
2695 That he moughte overtake.
Was nevere non that moughte thave   survive
Hise dintes, noither knight ne knave,
That he ne felden so dos the gres
Biforn the sythe that full sharp is.
2700 Whan Havelok saw his folk so brittene   broken
And his ferd so swithe littene,   army/diminished
He cam drivende upon a stede   galloping
And bigan till him to grede   cry
And saide, "Godrich, what is thee,
2705 That thou fare thus with me   against
And mine gode knightes slos?   slay
Sikerlike thou misgos.   certainly/do
                                                          wrong
                                            know/perceive
Thou wost full well, yif thou wilt wite,
That Athelwold thee dide sitte
2710 On knees and sweren on messe-book,
On caliz and on patein ok,   chalice/paten
                                                          /also

That thou hise doughter sholdest yelde,   grant
Than she were wimman of elde,   when/age
Engelond all everilk del.
2715 Godrich the erl, thou wost it well!   know
Do nu well withuten fight;
Yeld hire the lond, for that is right.
Wile ich forgive thee the lathe,   enmity
All my dede and all my wrathe,   dead/anger
2720 For I see thu art so wight   courageous
And of thy body so good knight."   person/such a
"That ne wile ich nevere mo,"
Quoth erl Godrich, "for ich shall slo

2688   "Then first Godrich began to go"; *tarst* "at first" (from *at arst*) may suggest
       something like German *nun erst recht* "now [furiously] for the first time."
2691   "Which never spares any kind of beast."
2694   Compare line 1909.
2698   "In that they fell as does the grass."
2704   "And said, 'Godrich, how is it with you.' "
2709-10   "That Athelwold had you kneel down and swear on a massbook."

Thee—and lure for-henge heye.
2725 I shall thrist ut thy righte eye   *thrust*
      That thou lokes with on me,
      But thou swithe hethen flee."   *unless/hence*
      He grop the swerd ut sone anon   *drew*
      And hew on Havelok full good won,   *vigorously*
2730 So that he clef his sheld ontwo.   *cleft/atwo*
      Whan Havelok saw that shame do   *done*
      His body, ther biforn his ferd,   *person/army*
      He drow ut sone his gode swerd
      And smote him so upon the crune
2735 That Godrich fell to the erthe adune.
      But Godrich stirt up swithe sket—   *jumped/quickly*
      Lay ne nought longe at hise feet—
      And smot him on the sholdre so
      That he dide thare undo
2740 Of his brinie ringes mo   *mail jacket/more*
      Than that ich can tellen fro;   *enumerate*
      And woundede him right in the flesh,
      That tendre was and swithe nesh,   *soft*
      So that the blood ran till his to.
2745 Tho was Havelok swithe wo   *very/distressed*
      That he havede of him drawen
      Blood and ek so sore him slawen.   *wounded*
      Hertelike till him he wente   *vehemently*
      And Godrich ther fullike shente.   *foully/injured*
2750 For his swerd he hof up heye   *lifted/high*
      And the hand he dide of-fleye,
      That he smot him with so sore.
      Hu mighte he don him shame more?

      Hwan he havede him so shamed,
2755 His hand ofplat and ivele lamed,   *cut off/vilely*
                                                        /maimed
      He took him sone by the necke
      Als a traitour—datheit who recke!—   *accursed/cares*
      And dide him binde and fettere well   *had*
      With gode feteres all of steel;
2760 And to the queen he sende him,
      That birde well to him been grim,   *ought/angry*
      And bad she sholde don him gete   *ordered/guard*
      And that non ne sholde him bete,   *beat*
      Ne shame do, for he was knight,
2765 Till knightes haveden demd him right.   *judged/properly*
      Than the Englishe men that sawe,   *when*

2724   "You—and execute her by hanging [her] high."
2751   "And he made his hand fly off."

That they wisten, heye and lawe,   *high/low*
That Goldeboru, that was so fair,
Was of Engelond right eir,   *heir*
2770 And that the king hire havede wedded
And haveden been samen bedded,   *together*
He comen alle to crye "Merci!"
Unto the king, at one cry,
And beden him sone manrede and oth   *offered/fealty*
2775 That he ne sholden, for lef no loth,
Nevere more again him go,
Ne ride, for wele ne for wo.

The king ne wolde nought forsake
That he ne shulde of hem take
2780 Manrede that he beden and ok
Hold-othes sweren on the book.
But or bad he that thider were brought   *prior to that*
                                                            /ordered
The queen, for hem—swilk was his thought—   *before/them*
For to see and forto shawe,   *observe*
2785 Yif that he hire wolde knawe.   *recognize*
Thoru hem witen wolde he   *them/know*
Yif that she aughte queen to be.   *ought*

Sixe erles weren sone yare   *ready*
After hire for to fare.
2790 He nomen anon and comen sone   *set out*
                                                        /immediately
And broughten hire, that under mone   *moon*
In all the werd he havede per   *world/peer*
Of hendeleike fer ne ner.   *in/courtesy*
Whan she was come thider, alle
2795 The Englishe men bigunne falle
O knees and greten swithe sore   *wept/bitterly*
And saiden, "Levedy, Christes ore
And youres! We haven misdo mikel
That we again you have be fikel,   *in that/disloyal*
2800 For Englond aughte forto been   *ought*
Youres and we youre men.
Is non of us, ne yung ne old,
That he ne wot that Athelwold   *know*

2775–77   "That they would never for anything march or ride against him for weal
          or woe."
2778–81   "The king would not neglect that he should take the fealty which they
          offered from them, and also [that they should] swear oaths of loyalty on the
          book."
2797–98   "And said, 'Lady, [may we have] the grace of Christ and yours! We have
          transgressed greatly.'"

Was king of all this kunerike   *kingdom*
2805 And ye his eir, and that the swike   *traitor*
Haves it halden with mikel wronge–
God leve him sone hey to honge!"   *grant/high*

Quoth Havelok, "Whan that ye it wite,   *since/know*
Nu wile ich that ye doune sitte,
2810 And after Godrich haves wrought,   *according as*
       /done

That haves himself in sorrwe brought,   *who*
Lokes that ye demen him right,   *see to it*
For doom ne spareth clerk ne knight.   *judgment*
And sithen shall ich understonde   *afterwards*
       /receive

2815 Of you, all after lawe of londe,
Manrede and holde-othes bothe,   *fealty/oaths of*
       loyalty

Yif ye it wilen and ek rothe."   *wish/advise*
Anon ther dune he hem sette,
For non the doom ne durste lette   *no one/dared*
       /neglect

2820 And demden him to binden faste
Upon an asse swithe unwraste,   *filthy*
Andelong, nought overthwert,   *endwise/athwart*
His nose went unto the stert,   *turned/tail*
And so unto Lincolne lede,
2825 Shamelike in wicke wede,   *wretched/clothes*
And, whan he come unto the boru,
Shamelike been led therthoru,
Bisouthe the boru, unto a grene,   *south of*
That thare is yete, als I wene,
2830 And there be bunden till a stake,
Abouten him full gret fir make,
And all to dust be brend right thore.   *burned*
And yete demden he ther more,
Other swikes for to warne,   *traitors*
2835 That hise children shulde tharne   *lose*
Everemore that eritage   *heritage*
That his was, for his utrage.   *because of*

Whan the doom was deemd and said,
Sket was the swike on the asse laid,   *quickly*
2840 And led untill that ilke grene   *very*
And brend till asken all bidene.   *ashes/forthwith*
Tho was Goldeboru full blithe;
She thanked God fele sithe   *many/times*
That the fule swike was brend,   *foul/traitor*
       /burned

2845 That wende well hire body have shend;   *intended/shamed*
And saide, "Nu is time to take
Manrede of brune and of blake,   *fealty*
That ich ride see and go—   *whom/walk*
Nu ich am wreken of my foe."   *avenged*

2850 Havelok anon manrede took   *fealty*
Of alle Englishe on the book
And dide hem grete othes swere
That he sholden him good faith bere
Again hem all that woren lives   *alive*
2855 And that sholde been born of wives.   *women*

Thanne he havede sikernesse   *surety*
Taken of more and of lesse,
All at hise wille, so dide he calle
The erl of Chestre and hise men alle,
2860 That was yung knight withuten wif,
And saide, "Sire erl, by my lif,
And thou wile my conseil tro,   *if/trust*
Full well shall ich with thee do;
For ich shall yeve thee to wive   *as*
2865 The fairest thing that is olive.   *alive*
That is Gunild of Grimesby,
Grimes doughter, by saint Davy,
That me forth broughte and well fedde   *reared*
And ut of Denemark with me fledde,
2870 Me for to berwen fro my ded;   *rescue/death*
Sikerlike, thoru his red   *surely/help*
Have ich lived into this day,
Blissed worthe his soule ay!   *blessed/be/ever*
I rede that thou hire take   *advise*
2875 And spuse and curteisie make;
For she is fair and she is free   *noble*
And all so hende so she may be.   *gracious*
Thertekene, she is well with me,   *moreover*
That shall ich full well shewe thee.
2880 For ich wile give thee a give
That everemore, whil ich live,
For hire shaltu be with me dere,
That wile ich that this folk all here."

2847   See note to line 1008.
2857   "Taken from people of all station."
2863   "I shall do very well by you."
2875   "And marry [her] and treat her in a courteous way."
2880   "For I shall give you assurance."
2882   "You will be held dear to me because of her."
2883   "That I desire all this folk to hear."

The erl ne wolde nought again   *against*
2885 The kinge be, for knight ne swain,
Ne of the spusing sayen nay,   *marriage*
But spusede hire that ilke day.   *very*
That spusinge was in good time maked,
For it ne were nevere clad ne naked
2890 In a thede samened two
That cam togidere, livede so,
So they diden all here live.
He geten samen sones five,   *begot/together*
That were the beste men at nede
2895 That moughte riden on any stede.
Whan Gunild was to Chestre brought,
Havelok the gode ne forgat nought
Bertram, that was the erles cook,
That he ne dide him callen ok,
2900 And saide, "Frend, so God me rede,   *as/advise*
Nu shaltu have riche mede   *reward*
For wissing and thy gode dede   *guidance/deeds*
That tu me dides in full gret nede.   *you/dire/need*
For thanne I yede in my covel   *when/went/cloak*
2905 And ich ne havede bred ne sowel.   *bread/relish*
Ne I ne havede no catel,   *possessions*
Thou feddes and claddes me full well.
Have nu forthy of Cornwaile   *for that*
The erldom ilk del, withuten faile,   *each/part*
2910 And all the lond that Godrich held,
Bothe in towne and ek in feld;   *also*
And therto wile ich that thou spuse,   *wed*
And faire bring hire untill huse,
Grimes doughter, Levive the hende,   *gracious*
2915 For thider shall she with thee wende.   *go*
Hire semes curteis forto be,   *she/seems*
For she is fair so flour on tree;   *as*
The hew is swilk in hire ler   *complexion/face*
So is the rose in roser,   *as/on/rose-bush*
2920 Whan it is faire sprad ut newe   *fresh*
Again the sunne bright and lewe."   *warm*
And girde him sone with the swerd
Of the erldom, biforn his ferd,   *army*
And with his hond he made him knight
2925 And yaf him armes, for that was right,
And dide him there sone wedde   *had*
Hire that was full swete in bedde.

2889–2892   "For there were never of all in the world [literally, of the clad and naked] two united in a land that came together[and] lived as they did all their life."
2899   "In that he also summoned him."

After that he spused wore,   *they/married*
Wolde the erl nought dwelle thore,   *tarry*
2930 But sone nam untill his lond   *went*
And saised it all in his hond   *received*
And livede therinne, he and his wif,
An hundred winter in good lif,
And gaten many children samen   *begot/together*
2935 And liveden ay in blisse and gamen.   *joy*
Whan the maidens were spused bothe,
Havelok anon bigan full rathe   *straightway*
His Denshe men to feste well   *endow*
With riche landes and catel   *property*
2940 So that he weren alle riche,
For he was large and nought chiche.   *generous/stingy*

Thereafter sone, with his here,   *army*
For he to Lundone forto bere   *journeyed*
Corune, so that it sawe
2945 Englishe and Denshe, heye and lowe,
Hou he it bar with mikel pride
For his barnage, that was unride.

The feste of his coruning   *feast/at*
Lastede with gret joying
2950 Fourty dawes and sumdel mo.   *days/somewhat*
Tho bigunnen the Denshe to go   *then*
Unto the king to aske leve;   *permission to*
                                                        depart
And he ne wolde hem nought greve;   *offend*
For he saw that he woren yare   *eager*
2955 Into Denemark for to fare;   *go*
But gaf hem leve sone anon
And bitaughte hem saint Johan;   *commended*
And bad Ubbe, his justise,
That he sholde on ilke wise   *in/each*
2960 Denemark yeme and gete so   *govern/guard*
That no plainte come him to.   *complaint*

Whan he wore parted alle samen,   *altogether*
Havelok bilefte with joye and gamen   *remained*
In Engelond and was therinne
2965 Sixty winter king with winne,   *joy*
And Goldeboru queen, that I wene   *so that/think*
So mikel love was hem bitwene   *much*
That all the werd spak of hem two;   *world*
He lovede hir and she him so

2947 "In the presence of his nobles, who were many."

2970 That neither other mighte be   *away from/nor*
      Fro other ne no joye see
      But-yif he were togidere bothe;   *unless*
      Nevere yete no weren he wrothe   *at odds*
      For here love was ay newe;   *ever/fresh*
2975 Nevere yete wordes ne grewe
      Bitwene hem wharof no lathe   *from which/any*
      *   /enmity*

      Mighte rise ne no wrathe.   *nor/any/anger*

      He geten children hem bitwene
      Sones and doughtres right fivetene,
2980 Wharof the sones were kinges alle,
      So wolde God it sholde bifalle,   *occur*
      And the doughtres alle quenes:
      Him stondes well that good child strenes.
      Nu have ye herd the gest all thoru   *story*
2985 Of Havelok and of Goldeboru–
      Hou he weren boren and hu fedde   *reared*
      And hou he woren with wronge ledde   *unjustly*
      *   /managed*

      In here youthe with trecherie,
      With tresoun, and with felounie;   *wickedness*
2990 And hou the swikes haveden tight   *traitors*
      *   /intended to*
      Reven hem that was here right   *rob/of that which*
      And hou he weren wreken well,   *avenged*
      Have ich said you everilk del.   *bit*
      Forthy ich wolde biseken you   *therefore/beseech*
2995 That haven herd the rime nu,
      That ilke of you, with gode wille,   *each*
      Saye a pater noster stille   *quietly*
      For him that haveth the rime maked
      And therfore fele nightes waked   *many*
      *   /stayed awake*
3000 That Jesu Christ his soule bringe   *so that*
      Biforn his fader at his endinge.

2983   "It is well for him who begets a good child."

Athelston

HE romance that follows is often given unqualified praise—in a sense, deserved; but reaction varies with repeated reading. It appears much better the first time around than it does on the second or third. A fourth reading, say, when its thin verse, it righteous bishop, and its silly king appear for what they are, can push the initial good impression quite out of mind. The observation should be remembered. "Athelston" is, taken as a whole, not so good really as its plot; nor is it quite so bad, again taken as a whole, as some of its essential features.

The story convinces immediately because it has the appearance of a modern historical novel. Its world is elemental, brutish, and bloody. There is nothing to do with enchantment or courtly love. It convinces again because, once set in motion, it hurtles along unchecked until its horrendous end. In the beginning we find four royal messengers—Athelston, Egelond, Alryke, and Wymond—swearing blood-brotherhood at a crossroads. One—Athelston—becomes king and endows his "brothers" fittingly —Egelond with the Earldom of Stane, Alryke with the Archbishopric of Canterbury, and Wymound with the Earldom of Dover. The last named is envious; he tells the king that Egelond plots to depose and murder him. The king is gullible; he imprisons Egelond and his wife Edif and their two boys. The queen intercedes, but is kicked by the king (their unborn child dies from the blow) and in desperation sends for aid from Canterbury. Finding the king intransigent, Alryke, at first banished by the king, in turn threatens to excommunicate him and put the land under interdict. The barons reject the authority of the king and support the bishop—and Athelston submits. A trial by fire is arranged and the accused—man and wife and their two children—walk through a fire nine ploughshares in length unscathed. Athelston, again under the threat of excommunication, reveals in confession that it was Wymound who caused all the trouble. The culprit is summoned, fails to pass the ordeal by fire, and undergoes a spectacular—and thoroughly medieval—execution.

Where "Athelston" suffers notably is in its verse. The twelve-line stanza belongs to the east Midland tail-rhyme tradition. (See the comment on the verse of "Sir Launfal.") Its tail-rhyme lines (those lacing the stanza together after every couplet and doing so on a single rhyme per stanza) draw the poet into flat, sterile phrases—like the conventional "It is nought to hide" and "In romance as we rede"—and such do no good in enhancing the drama of the story. Further, "Athelston" in its motivation and characterization can bear little scrutiny. The king is petulant and altogether weak; the bishop is powerful and oppressively righteous. Yet it would not be fair to let consideration rest on obvious features, good and bad. Somehow, other details, less obvious and less essential, make the poem worth its salt.

"Athelston" is, first and last, a poem of the mid-fourteenth century whose audience cannot have been made up of people other than small tradesmen, very conscious of the history of their country, very well aware of its traditions, and very sensitive to the authoritarian habit of kings. The minstrel, consequently, echoes (but does not reproduce historically) features of national life which would appeal to such an audience. The name of the king, for example, does not make him identical with the Old English King AEthelstan, the victor of Brunanburg; but it has a national flavor about it which the more usual William or Henry would not have. Peculiarly national also is the care taken in detailing the towns along the old pilgrim route from London to Canterbury. The Athelston-Alryke confrontation, in particular, would recall perhaps Becket and Henry II or even more Stephen Langdon's stand against King John. Even Dame Edif's walk over the fiery pit echoes an English legend, current at the time, concerning Emma, mother of Edward the Confessor, who was falsely accused of crimes by a favorite of the king and who exculpated herself by a similar ordeal. To be sure, the poem appears to be the product of church-state friction with all sense and justice on the side of the church. But the time in which the poem was written would make any protest take such a form and to the audience of the time "Athelston" would appear chiefly as something directed against tyranny and not as what it might appear to us today—namely, as an apology for the secular power of the church.

Unfortunately, there is only one manuscript of "Athelston"; it is No. 175 in Gonville and Caius College, Cambridge. The spelling is somewhat erratic, although it may not appear so here because oddities (like the strange doubling of consonants) have been removed. The dialect is Midland with a few Northern features and its date of composition usually placed between 1350 and 1400. Inflections and forms are standard Middle English; difficulties of language arise primarily from racy syntax and elliptical expression, and these are taken care of in notes.

REFERENCES: Brown and Robbins, No. 1973; Billings, pp. 32–36; CBEL, I: 150–151; Hibbard, pp. 143–146; Kane, p. 54; Wells, pp. 23–25.

—The one authoritative, modern, and available edition is A.
MCI. Trounce's *Athelston: A Middle English Romance* (Oxford
1951; Early English Text Society, No. 224 Orig. Series).

Lord that is of mightis most,	*powers*
	/most great
Fadir and Sone and Holy Gost,	
Bring us out of sinne	
And lene us grace so for to wirke	*grant*
5 To love bothe God and Holy Kirke	
That we may hevene winne.	*attain*
Lystnes, lordingis that been hende,	*gracious*
Of falsnesse, hou it will ende	
A man that ledes him therin.	
10 Of foure weddid bretherin I wole you tell	*sworn*
That wolden in Ingelond go dwell,	*were supposed to*
That sibbe were nought of kinde.	
And alle foure messangeres they were,	
That wolden in Ingelond lettris bere,	*should*
15 As it wes here kinde.	*was/occupation*
By a forest gan they mete	*meet*
With a cross, stood in a strete	
Be lef undir a linde,	
And, as the story telles me,	
20 Ilke man was of divers cuntré,	*each*
In book y-wreten we finde.	*written*
For love of here meting thare	
They swoor hem weddid bretherin for evermare,	
In trewthe trewely dede hem binde.	
25 The eldeste of hem ilkon,	*each*
He was hight Athelston,	*called*
The Kingis cosin dere;	
He was of the Kingis blood,	
His eemes sone, I undirstood;	*uncle's*
30 Therfore he neighid him nere.	
And at the laste, weel and fair,	*well*
The King him diid withouten air.	*died/heir*

---

12 "Who were not by family related."
17-18 "By a cross [which] stood on a highway under the leaf of a linden."
30 "Therefore he was closely related" [literally, approached him nearer].
31 Despite the double *e*, *weel* since it rhymes with *dwelle* (line 231) probably had
    a short *e* sound.
32 "The King died without an heir"; the *him* is probably a dative of interest.

Thenne was ther non his pere   *equal*
But Athelston, his eemes sone;
35 To make him king wolde they nought shon   *refuse*
    To coroune him with gold so clere.

Now was he king semely to see;   *handsome*
                                /behold
He sendes aftir his bretherin three
    And gaf hem here warisoun.   *gave/reward*
40 The eldest brothir he made Erl of Dovere,
And thus the pore man gan covere,
    Lord of tour and toun.
That other brother he made Erl of Stane,
Egelond was his name,
45   A man of gret renoun;
And gaf him till his weddid wif
His owne sustri, Dame Edif,
    With gret devocioun.

The ferthe brothir was a clerk;   *fourth/cleric*
50 Mekil he coude of Goddis werk.   *knew*
    His name, it was Alryke.
Cauntirbury was vacant
And fell into that Kingis hand.
    He gaf it him, that wike,   *office*
55 And made him bishop of that stede.   *place*
That noble clerk on book coude rede;
    In the world was non him liche.   *like*
Thus avaunsid he his brother thorugh Godis gras,   *advanced*
And Athelston himselven was
60   A good king and a riche.

And he that was Erl of Stane—
Sere Egeland was his name—
    Was trewe, as ye shall here.   *true*
Thorugh the might of Godis gras,   *grace*
65 He gat upon the Countas   *begot*
    Two knave-children dere.   *boys*
That on was fiftene wintir old,   *one*
That other thritene, as men me told.
    In the world was non here pere—
70 Also whit so lilie-flour,   *just as*
Red as rose of here colour,
    As bright as blosme on brere.   *blossom/briar*

---

41 "And thus the poor man did rise in station" [literally, recover].
43 Stane, or Stone, is seventeen miles from London on the way to Canterbury.
44 In the MS, *Egelond* appears frequently without the -d.
56 "That worthy ecclesiastic knew about ritual."

Bothe the Erl and his wif,
The King hem lovede as his lif,
75   And here sones two;
And often-sithe he gan hem calle   *oftentimes*
Bothe to boure and to halle,
    To counsail whenne they sholde go.
Therat Sere Wymound hadde gret envie,
80 That Erl of Dovere, wittirlie.   *certainly*
    In herte he was full wo.   *heart*
He thoughte all for here sake
False lesingis on hem to make,   *lies*
    To don hem brenne and slo.

85 And thanne Sere Wymound him bethoughte,   *reflected*
    "Here love thus endure may noughte;
    Thorugh wurd oure werk may springe."
He bad his men maken hem yare;   *ready*
Unto Londone wolde he fare   *go*
90   To speke with the Kinge.
Whenne that he to Londone come,
He mette with the King full sone.   *straightway*
    He saide, "Welcome, my dereling."   *dear one*
The King him frainid soone anon,   *asked*
95 Be what way he hadde y-gon,   *road/gone*
    Withouten ony dwelling.   *without delay*

    "Come thou ought be Cauntirbery,   *at all/by*
    There the clerkis singen mery   *merry*
        Bothe erly and late?
100 Hou farith that noble clerk,   *ecclesiastic*
    That mekil can on Goddis werk?   *much/knows*
        Knowest thou ought his state?   *anything*
    And come thou ought be the Erl of Stane,   *at all*
    That wurthy lord in his wane?   *dwelling*
105   Wente thou ought that gate?   *road*
    Hou fares that noble knight
    And his sones fair and bright?
        My sustir, yif that thou wate?"   *know*

    "Sere," thanne he saide, "withouten les,   *falsehood*
110 Be Cauntirbery my way I ches.   *chose*
    There spak I with that dere.   *spoke/dear one*
    Right weel gretes thee that noble clerk,

---

77   "Both to private and to public counsel."
84   "To cause them to be burned and slain."
86–87 "Their love may not endure thus; by means of word [that is, through false
      rumor] our plan may advance."

That mikil can of Godis werk–
  In the world is non his pere.   *peer*
115 And also be Stane my way I drough;   *went*
  With Egeland I spak y-nough   *enough*
    And with the Countesse so clere.
They fare weel, is nought to laine,
And bothe here sones." The King was faine   *glad*
120   And in his herte made gald chere.

"Sere King," he saide, "yif it be thy wille
To chaumbir that thou woldest wenden tille,
    Counsail for to here,
I shall thee telle a swete tidande–
125 Ther comen nevere non swiche in this lande   *such*
    Of all this hundrid yere."
The Kingis herte than was full wo
With that traitour for to go.
    They wente bothe forth in fere;   *together*
130 And whenne that they were the chaumbir withinne,
  False lesingis he gan beginne
    On his weddid brother dere.

"Sere King," he saide, "wo were me,
Ded that I sholde see thee,
135   So moot I have my lif!
For by Him that all this worl wan,   *saved*
Thou hast makid me a man,
    And y-holpe me for to thrif.   *helped/thrive*
For in thy land, sere, is a fals traitour.
140 He wole do thee mikil dishonour
    And bringe thee of live.
He wole deposen thee slyly;
Sodainly than shalt thou dy   *die*
    Be Christis woundis five!"

145 Thenne saide the King, "So moot thou thee,
Knowe I that man and I him see?
    His name thou me telle."
"Nay," says that traitour, "that wole I nought
For all the gold that evere was wrought,
150   Be masse-book and belle,

---

118   "They fare well—[there] is nothing to hide."
124   "I shall tell you a sweet bit of news."
131   "He [Wymond] did begin [to relate] treacherous lies."
134   "[If] I should see you dead, as may I have my life."
137   An idiom probably to be understood as "You have made my fortune for me."
141   "And kill you."
145   "As you may thrive"—a frequent asseveration.

But-yif thou me thy trouthe will plight
That thou shalt nevere bewreye the knight   *betray*
    That thee the tale shall telle."
Thanne the King his hand up raughte.
155 That false man his trouthe betaughte–
    He was a devil of helle!

"Sere King," he saide, "thou madist me knight,
And now thou hast thy trouthe me plight
    Oure counsail for to laine: *conceal*
160 Certainly, it is non othir
But Egelond, thy weddid brothir.
    He wolde that thou were slaine.
He dos thy sustyr to undirstand   *causes*
He wole be king of thy lande,   *will*
165   And thus he beginnes here traine.
He wole thee poisoun right slyly;
Sodainly thanne shalt thou dy,   *die*
    Be Him that suffrid paine."

Thanne swoor the King, "Be cross and roode,
170 Meete ne drink shall do me goode   *food*
    Till that he be dede.   *dead*
Bothe he and his wif, his sones two,
Shole they nevere be no moo
    In Ingelond on that stede."   *place*
175 "Nay," says the traitour, "so moot I thee,
Ded wole I nought my brother see–
    But do thy beste rede!
No longere there then wolde he lende;   *remain*
He takes his leve–to Dovere gan wende.   *go*
180   God geve him shame and dede!   *death*

Now is that traitour hom y-went.   *gone*
A messanger was aftir sent   *summoned*
    To speke with the King.
I wene he bar his owne name–
185 He was hoten Athelstane;

---

151 "Unless you will give me your promise."
154 "Then the King raised up his hand"—a gesture common in taking an oath.
155 "[To] that false man [he] entrusted his faith."
158 "And now you have given me your word."
165 "And thus he begins to lead her [astray]."
169 Both words of the asseveration mean 'cross,' one being from Latin (via OF *crois*), the other from OE.
175 See line 145.
177 "But follow your best advice"—meaning "Do as you see fit [and I wash my hands of the whole business]."

He was foundeling.
The lettris were y-maad fulliche thare
Unto Stane for to fare,   *go*
    Withouten ony dwelling,   *delay*
190 To fette the Erl and his sones two   *fetch*
And the Countasse also,
    Dame Edive, that swete thing.

And in the lettre yit was it tolde
That the King the Erlis sones wolde
195   Made hem bothe knight
And therto his seel he sette.
The messanger wolde nought lette;   *delay*
    The way he rides full right.   *immediately*

The messanger, the noble man,
200 Takes his hors and forth he wan   *sets off*
    And hies a full good spede.   *hastens*
The Erl in his halle he fande.
He took him the lettre in his hande;   *gave*
    Anon he bad him rede.
205 "Sere," he saide also swithe,   *straightway*
    "This lettre oughte to make thee blithe;
        Thertoo thou take good hede.   *heed*
The King wole for the Countas sake
Bothe thy sones knightes make.
210   To London I rede thee spede.   *advise/hurry*

The King wole for the Countas sake
Bothe thy sones knightes make–
    The blithere thou may be.
Thy faire wif with thee thou bring,
215 And ther be right no letting,
    That sighte that she may see."
Thenne saide that Erl with herte milde,   *gentle*
"My wif goth right gret with childe,
    And forthinkes me
220 She may nought out of chaumbir win   *get out*
To speke with non ende of here kin   *part*
    Till she deliverid be."

185–186 This curiously extraneous information has called forth various comments—
    such as that in Celtic tales foundlings are named after their foster parents and
    that here is a possible indication the "Athelstan" poet was working from an
    original now lost.
213   "[By such] may you be the happier."
215   "And there should be no delay."
219   "And I suspect" [or: 'regret'] that."

But into chaumbir they gunne wende   *go*
To rede the lettris before that hende   *gracious one*
225   And tidingis tolde here sone.
Thenne saide the Countasse, "So moot I the,
I will nought lette till I there be   *stop*
    To morwen or it be noone.   *ere*

To see hem knightes, my sones free,   *noble*
230 I wole nought lette till I there be;
    I shall no lengere dwelle.   *tarry*
Christ foryelde my lord the King,   *requite*
That has grauntid hem here dubbing.   *knighting*
    Min herte is gladid welle."
235 The Erl his men bad make hem yare;   *ready*
He and his wif forth gunne they fare;   *did/go*
    To London faste thy wente.
At Westeminstir was the Kingis wone;   *dwelling*
There they mette with Athelstone,
240   That aftir hem hadde sente.

The goode Erl soone was hent   *seized*
And fetterid faste, verraiment,   *in truth*
    And his sones two.
Full loude the Countasse gan to cry   *began*
245 And saide, "Goode brothir, mercy!
    Why wole ye us slo?
What have we ayens you done   *against*
That ye wole have us ded so soone?
    Me thinkith ye arn oure foe."
250 The King as wood ferde in that stede;
He garte his sustir to presoun lede;   *had/lead*
    In herte he was full wo.

Thenne a squier, was the Countasses frende,
To the Quene he gan wende,   *did/go*
255   And tidingis tolde here soone.
Gerlondes of chiries of she caste;   *cherries*
Into the halle she come at the last,
    Longe or it were noone.   *ere*
"Sere King, I am before thee come
260 With a child, doughter or a sone.
    Graunte me my bone,   *request*
My brothir and sustir that I may borwe

---

250   "The King there behaved as though he were out of his wits."
253   A relative should be understood [by the modern reader] after *squier*.
262–264   "[That] I may act as surety for my brother and sister till the morning of the
       next day [to relieve them] of their severe anxieties."

Till the nexte day at morwe,
Out of here painis stronge,

265 That we mowe wete be comoun sent
In the plaine parlement. . . ."   *full*
"Dame," he saide, "go fro me!
Thy bone shall nought y-grauntid be,   *request*
I do thee to undirstande.   *cause*
270 For be Him that weres the coroune of thorn,
They shole be drawen and hangid to-morn,
Yif I be king of lande!"   *if*

And whenne the Quene these wurdes herde   *words*
As she hadde be beten with yerde,   *as if/beaten/rod*
275   The teeres she let doun falle.
Certainly as I you telle,
On here bare knees doun she felle,
And praide yit for hem alle.   *prayed/still*
"A, dame," he saide, "verraiment,   *in truth*
80 Hast thou broke my comaundement;
Abiid full dere thou shalle."   *pay for*
With his foot he wolde nought wonde;
He slough the child right in here wombe;   *killed*
She swounid amonges hem all.   *swooned*

85 Ladiis and maidenis that there were
The Quene to here chaumbir bere,   *bore*
And there was dool y-nough.   *lamentation*
Soone withinne a litil spase
A knave-child y-born ther wase,   *boy*
90   As bright as blosme on bough;
He was bothe white and red.
Of that dint was he ded;
His owne fadir him slough!
Thus may a traitour baret raise   *turmoil*
95 And make manye men full evele at aise—   *ease*
Himself nought aftir it lough.

But yit the Quene, as ye shole here,
She callid upon a messangere,
Bad him a lettre fonge,   *carry*
00 And bad him wende to Cauntirbery,   *go*
There the clerkis singen mery   *where*

---

265   "[So] that we may know by common assent."
266   Here four lines are missing in the MS.
282   "He would not refrain from kicking [her]."
296   "[But he] himself [the traitor] did not laugh afterwards"—implying he got his
      just deserts.

Bothe masse and evensonge.
"This lettre thou the Bishop take,
And praye him, for Goddis sake,
305   Come borewe hem out of here bande.   *rescue/bonds*
He wole do more for him, I wene,
Thanne for me, though I be Quene,
   I do thee to undirstande.

   An erldom in Spaine I have of land;
310 All I sese into thin hand,
     Trewely, as I thee hight–   *promise*
And hundrid besauntis of gold red.   *coins*
Thou may save hem from the ded,
     Yif that thin hors be wight."   *worthy*
315 "Madame, brouke weel thy moregeve
Also longe as thou may leve.   *live*
     Therto have I no right.
But of thy gold and of thy fee,
Christ in hevene foryelde it thee!   *reward*
320   I wole be there to night.   *shall*

   Madame, thritty miles of hard way
I have reden sith it was day.   *since*
     Full sore I gan me swinke.   *did/toil*
And for to ride now five and twenty thertoo,
325 An hard thing it were to do,
     For soothe, right as me thinke.
Madame, it is nerhande passid prime,
And me behoves all for to dine,
     Bothe win and ale to drinke.
330 Whenne I have dinid, thenne wole I fare.
God may covere hem of here care   *relieve*
     Or that I slepe a winke."   *ere*

   Whenne he hadde dinid, he wente his way
Also faste as that he may.
335   He rod be Charinge Cross
And entrid in to Flete Strete
And sithen thorough Londone, I you hete,   *then/assure*

---

310 "All I shall give legally to you."
315 "Madam, use well your dowery"; the *moregeve* was, strictly, a gift given a bride
      by the groom on the morning after the wedding.
318 "But [for the offer] of gold and property."
326 "In truth, it seems to me indeed."
327 "Madame, it is nearly past prime"—*prime* denoting the time between 9 A.M.
      and 10 A.M. The detail of the messenger putting breakfast before duty is sur-
      prising and prompts Trounce (see *References*) to comment on lines 327–330:
      "John Bull wants his dinner."

Upon a noble hors.
The messanger, that noble man,
340 On Loundone Brigge sone he wan   *reached*
   (For his travaile he hadde no los).
From Stone into Steppingebourne,   *Sittingbourne*
For sothe, his way nolde he nought tourne–   *change*
   Sparid he nought for mire ne moss.   *nor/bog*

345 And thus his way wendes he
   Fro Ospringe to the Blee.
     Thenne mighte he see the toun
   Of Cauntirbery, that noble wike,   *town*
   Therin lay that bishop rike,   *powerful*
350   That lord of gret renoun.
   And whenne they rungen undernbelle,   *morning bell*
   He rod in Londone, as I you telle
     He was non er redy;   *before*
   And yit to Cauntirbery he wan   *arrived*
355 Longe or evensong began;   *ere*
     He rod milis fifty.

The messanger nothing abod.   *not at all/delayed*
   Into the palais forth he rod
     There that the Bishop was inne.
360 Right welcome was the messanger,
   That was come from the Quene so cleer,   *radiant*
     Was of so noble kinne.
   He took him a lettre full good speed   *gave*
   And saide, "Sere Bishop, have this and reed,"
365   And bad him come with him.
   Or he the lettre hadde half y-redde,   *read*
   For dool him thoughte his herte bledde;   *grief*
     The teeres fill ovir his chin.

The Bishop bad sadele his palfray:
370 "Also faste as they may,
     Bidde my men make hem yare,   *ready*
   And wendes before," the Bishop dede say,   *go/ahead*
     "To my maneres in the way–   *manors*

---

341   "For his effort he had no praise" would seem likely; but some editors suggest
     "had no loss" (*los* can come from either OF *los* 'praise' or OE *los* 'destruction')
     on the grounds that "loss" restates in negative form what has just been said
     in the affirmative, a habit common in the more popular romances.
346   *Ospringe* was once a town on the road to Canterbury and *Blee* formerly a
     wooded hill very near Canterbury.
362   The relative *who* should be understood, but its referent can be either *Quene*
     or *messanger*.
365   The subject of *bad* 'asked' is probably "the messanger."

For no thing that ye spare–
375 And loke at ilke five miles ende   *see to it/each*
    A fresh hors that I finde
      Shod and nothing bare.   *not/unsaddled*
    Blithe shall I nevere be
    Till I my weddid brother see,
380   To cevere him out of care."   *recover/from*

    On nine palfrays the Bishop sprong,
    Ar it was day from evensong,   *ere*
      In romaunce as we rede.
    Certainly, as I you telle,
385 On Londone Bridge ded doun felle   *dead*
      The messangeres stede.   *steed*
    "Allas," he saide, "that I was born!
    Now is my goode hors forlorn,
      Was good at ilke a nede.
390 Yistirday upon the grounde
    He was wurth an hundrid pounde
      Ony king to lede."

    Thenne bespak the Erchebishop,   *remonstrated*
    Oure gostly fadir undir God,   *spiritual*
395   Unto the messangere.
    "Lat be thy mening of thy stede,   *lament*
    And think upon oure mikil nede
      The whilis that we been here;   *time*
    For-yif that I may my brother borwe   *provide that/save*
400 And bringen him out of mekil sorwe,
      Thou may make glad chere,
    And thy warisoun I shall thee geve,   *reward*
    And God have grauntid thee to leve
      Unto an hundrid yere."

405 The Bishop thenne nought ne bod.   *tarried*
    He took his hors and forth he rod
      Into Westeminstir so light–   *in haste*
    The messanger on his foot also.
    With the Bishop come no mo,

---

374 "Don't spare anything [in your haste]."
383 A line filler, common in tail-rhyme stanzas, whose sense does not imply any-
      thing in particular—as, for example, a source from which the "Athelston"
      poet was working.
389 "[It] was good in every need."
392 "To bear any king."
403–404 "[Enough, even if] God would have granted you up to a hundred years to
      live."
408 "The messenger [went] along afoot."

410   Nether squier ne knight.
    Upon the morwen the King aros   *morning*
    And takes the way to the kirke; he gos   *church*
        As man of mekil might.
    With him wente bothe preest and clerk,
415 That mikil coude of Goddis werk,   *who/knew*
        To praye God for the right.

    Whenne that he to the kirke com,
    Tofore the rode he knelid anon,   *cross*
        And on his knees he felle:
420 "God, that sit in Trinité,
    A bone that thou graunte me,   *request*
                                           /may gran:

    Lord, as thou harewid helle:
    Giltless men yif they be
    That are in my presoun free   *redoubtable*
425 Forcursid there to yelle,   *condemned*
                                           /shriek

    Of the gilt and they be clene,
    Leve it moot on hem be sene
        That garte hem there to dwelle."

    And whenne he hadde maad his prayer,
430 He loked up into the queer;   *choir*
        The Erchebishop saugh he stande.   *saw*
    He was forwondrid of that caas,   *surprised*
    And to him he wente apas   *hurriedly*
        And took him be the hande.
435 "Welcome," he saide, "thou Erchebishop,
    Oure gostly fadir undir God."   *spiritual*
        He swoor be God levande,
    "Weddid brother, weel moot thou spede,   *fore*
    For I hadde nevere so mekil nede,
440 Sith I took cross on hande.   *since*

    "Goode weddid brother, now turne thy rede:
    Do nought thin owne blood to dede   *cause/death*
        But-yif it wurthy were.   *unless/just*
    For Him that weres the corounc of thorn,
445 Lat me borwe hem till to morn,   *stand surety for*
        That we mowe enquere   *may*
    And weten alle be comoun assent   *know*

---

422   "Lord, as [surely as] you harrowed Hell."
426–428   "If of guilt they are free, allow that it may be seen [by him] who made
       them dwell there."
437   "He swore by the living God"; the *he* refers to the archbishop, as seen in line
       440.

In the plaine parlement   *full*
  Who is wurthy be shent.   *punished*
450 And but-yif ye wole graunte my bone,   *unless/request*
It shall us rewe bothe or none,
  Be God that alle thing lent."   *things/gave*

Thanne the King wax wroth as winde;   *grew/angry*
A wodere man mightee no man finde   *more angry*
455 Than he began to be.
He swoor othis be sunne and mone,   *moon*
"They sholen be drawen and hongid or none–   *ere*
  With eyen thou shalt see!
Lay doun thy cross and thy staff,
460 Thy mitir and thy ring that I thee gaf!
  Out of my land thou flee!
Highe thee faste out of my sight!   *hie*
Wher I thee mete, thy deth is dight.   *ready*
  Non othir then shall it be!"

465 Thenne bespak that Erchebishop,   *remonstrated*
Oure gostly fadir undir God,
  Smertly to the King:
"Well I wot that thou me gaf   *know/gave*
Bothe the cross and the staff,
470 The mitir and eke the ring.
My bishopriche thou reves me,
And christindom forbede I thee!
  Preest shall ther non singe;
Neither maidinchild ne knave   *girl/boy*
475 Christindom shall ther non have.
  To care I shall thee bringe!

I shall gare crye thorugh ilke a toun   *have/proclaimed /each*

That kirkis shole be broken doun
And stoken again with thorn.
480 And thou shalt ligge in an old dike,   *lie/ditch*
As it were an heretike,
  Allas that thou were born!

Yif thou be ded that I may see,   *dead*
Assoilid shalt thou nevere be;   *absolved*
485 Thanne is thy soule in sorwe.

---

451 "Both of us shall be sorry ere noon."
464 "None other [than that] shall it be!"
471–472 "[If] you deprive me of my bishopric, I shall deny you Christianity" (that is, place you under interdict).
479 "And overgrown with thorns"; just what *again* may mean is conjectural.

And I shall wende in uncouthe lond   *go/foreign*
And gete me stronge men of hond–
  My brothir yit shall I borwe!   *save*
I shall bringe upon thy lond
90 Hungir and thirst full strong,
  Cold, droughthe, and sorwe.
I shall nought leve on thy lond   *leave*
Wurth the gloves on thy hond   *worth*
  To begge ne to borwe."

95 The Bishop has his leve tan;   *leave/taken*
  By that, his men were comen ilkan;
    They saiden, "Sere, have good day."
He entrid into Flete Strete.
With lordis of Ingelond gan he mete
00   Upon a nobil array.
On here knees they kneleden adoun
And prayden him of his benisoun,   *blessing*
  He nikkid hem with nay.   *nodded*
Neither of cross neither of ring
05 Hadde they non kins weting;
  And thanne a knight gan say–

A knight thanne spak with milde vois,
"Sere, where is thy ring? Where is thy crois?   *cross*
  Is it fro thee tan?"   *from/taken*
10 Thanne he saide, "Youre cursid King
Hath me reft off all my thing   *bereft*
  And off all my worldly wan,   *store*
And I have entirditid Ingelong.   *interdicted*
Ther shall no preest singe masse with hond,
15   Child shall be christenid non,
But-yif he graunte me that knight,   *unless*
His wif and childrin fair and bright,
  He wolde with wrong hem slon."

The knight saide, "Bishop, turne again;
520 Of thy body we are full fain;   *person*
  Thy brothir yit shole we borwe.   *save*
And but he graunte us oure bone,   *unless/request*
His presoun shall be broken soone,
  Himself to mekil sorwe.
525 We sholen drawe doun bothe halle and boures,   *chambers*

---

496   "Just then each of his men arrived"; those referred to are probably the arch-
    bishop's followers.
505   "Had they any sort of recognition."
518   "[Whom] he would unjustly slay."
524   "To his [the King's] great sorrow."

Bothe his castelles and his toures.
   They shole ligge lowe and holewe.   *lie/empty*
Though he be King and were the coroun,
We sholen him sette in a deep dunioun.
530   Oure Christindom we wole folewe."   *follow*

Thanne, as they spoken of this thing,
Ther comen two knightes from the King
   And saiden, "Bishop, abide
And have thy cross and thy ring,
535 And welcome whil that thou wilt ling: *stay*
   It is nought for to hide.
Here he grauntis thee the knight,   *commits to*
His wif and childrin fair and bright.
   Again I rede thou ride.   *back/advise*
540 He prayes thee par charité
That he mighte assoilid be,   *absolved*
   And Ingelond long and wide."

Hereof the Bishop was full fain
And turnis his bridil and wendes again;   *returns*
545   Barouns gunne with him ride   *did*
Unto the Brokene-Cross of ston.
Thedir com the King full soone anon,
   And there he gan abide.
Upon his knees he knelid adoun
550 And praide the Bishop of benisoun,   *blessing*
   And he gaf him that tide.
With holy watir and orisoun,   *prayer*
He assoilid the King that werid the coroun, *absolved*
   And Ingelond long and wide.

555 Thenne saide the King anon right,
"Here I graunte thee that knight
   And his sones free,
And my sustir hende in halle.   *gracious*
Thou hast savid here livis alle.
560   Y-blessyd moot thou be."
Thenne saide the Bishop also soone,   *immediately*
"And I shall geven swilke a dome—
   With eyen that thou shalt see!–
Yif they be gilty of that dede,

---

536   The implication is "We cannot conceal the matter."
546   Trounce (see *References*) locates the landmark near St. Paul's and indicates it
      was removed in 1390.
562–566 "And I shall pass such judgment—that you will see with [your own] eyes!
      —[that] if they be guilty of the deed, they will fear the penalty more grievously
      than [they would fear] revealing their guilt to me."

565 Sorrere the doome they may drede,
    Than shewe here shame to me."

Whanne the Bishop hadde said so,
A gret fir was maad right tho,
    In romance as we rede.
570 It was set that men mighte knawe,
Nine plough-lengthe on rawe,   *row*
    As red as ony glede.   *coal*
Thanne saide the King, "What may this mene?"
"Sere, of gilt and they be clene,
575   This doom hem thar nought drede."   *trial/need/fear*
Thanne saide the good King Athelston,
"An hard doome now is this on;   *one*
    God graunte us alle weel to spede."   *well/prosper*

They fetten forth Sere Egelan–   *fetched*
580 A trewere erl was ther nan–   *truer*
    Before the fir so bright.
From him they token the rede scarlet,
Bothe hosin and shoon, that were him met,   *hose/shoes*
                                           suitable
    That fell for a knight.
585 Nine sithe the Bishop halewid the way   *times*
                                       /consecrated
That his weddid brother sholde go that day,
    To praye God for the right.
He was unblemeshid, foot and hand.
That saugh the lordes of the land   *saw*
590   And thankid God of His might.

They offerid him with milde chere
Unto Saint Poulis heighe autere,
    That mekil was of might.
Doun upon his knees he felle
595 And thankid God that harewede helle   *harrowed*
    And His Modir so bright.

And yit the Bishop tho gan say,   *then*
"Now shall the childrin gon the way
    That the fadir yede."   *went*
600 Fro hem they tooke the rede scarlete,

---

569   See gloss for line 383.
574   "Sir, if they are free of guilt."
584   "[And] that were appropriate for a knight."
591   "They offered him reverently at the high altar of Saint Paul's"; the "offering"
        may be part of the ordeal ceremony, and it may not. Just what significance
        lines 591 to 596 have, if any significance at all, is not evident.

The hosen and shoon that weren hem mete,
   And all here worldly wede.   *clothes*
The fir was bothe hidous and red;
The childrin swounid as they were ded.   *swooned/as if*
605   The Bishop till hem yede,   *went*
With careful herte on hem gan look.   *anxious*
Be his hand he hem up took:
   "Childrin, have ye no drede."   *fear*

Thanne the childrin stood and lough: *laughed*
610 "Sere, the fir is cold y-nough."
   Thoroughout they wente apase.   *quickly*
They weren unblemeshid, foot and hand.
That saugh the lordis of the land
   And thankid God of his grace.

615 They offerid hem with milde chere
To Saint Poulis that highe autere–
   This miracle shewid was there.
And yit the Bishop eft gan say,   *again*
"Now shall the Countasse go the way
620   There that the childrin were."

They fetten forth the lady milde;   *fetched*
She was full gret y-gon with childe,
   In romaunce as we rede.
Before the fir when that she come,
625 To Jesu Christ he prayde a bone,   *boon*
   That leet His woundis blede:
"Now, God lat nevere the Kingis fo
Quick out of the fir go."   *alive*
   Therof hadde she no drede.

630 Whenne she hadde maad here prayer,
She was brought before the feer,   *fire*
   That brennid bothe fair and light.
She wente fro the lengthe into the thridde;
Stille she stood the fir amidde   *stockstill/amidst*
635   And callid it merye and bright.
Harde shouris thenne took here stronge   *bitter/labor-pains*
Bothe in back and eke in wombe,
   And sithen it fell at sight.

---

615   See note to line 591.
633   "She went along the length as far as the third [ploughshare]."
638   The line is a mystery. It may be that *sight* is a form of ME *siken* 'to sigh,' but
      such a sense offers no convincing reading. Since the line is a tail-rhyme verse,
      it may say something conventional and general like "And then everythng be-
      came clear."

Whenne that here painis slakid was   *abated*
640 And she hadde passid that hidous pas,   *course*
    Here nose barst on bloode.
She was unblemeshid foot and hand–
That saugh the lordis of the land,   *saw*
And thankid God on rode.   *cross*
645 They comaundid men here away to drawe,
As it was the landis lawe;
    And ladiis thanne till here yode.   *went*
She knelid doun upon the ground
And there was born Saint Edemound–
650   Y-blessid be that foode.   *child*

And whanne this child y-born was,
It was brought into the plas;
    It was bothe hool and sound.
Bothe the King and Bishop free
655 They christnid the child, that men might see,
    And callid it Edemound.
"Half my land," he saide, "I thee geve,
Also longe as I may leve,
    With markis and with pounde;   *marks*
660 And all aftir my dede,
Ingelond to wisse and rede."   *guide/direct*
    Now y-blessid be that stounde!   *time*

Thenne saide the Bishop to the King,
"Sere, who made this grete lesing,   *lie*
665   And who wroughte all this bale?"   *grief*
Thanne saide the King, "So moot I thee,
That shalt thou nevere wete for me,   *know*
    In burgh neither in sale;
For I have sworn be Saint Anne
670 That I shall nevere bewreye that manne   *reveal*
    That me gan telle that tale.
They arn savid thorugh thy red.   *are/counsel*
Now lat all this be ded,
    And kepe this counseil hale."

675 Thenne swoor the Bishop, "So moot I thee,
Now I have power and dignyté
    For to assoile thee as clene   *absolve*
As thou were hoven off the fount-ston.   *lifted*
                                               /baptismal font

---

641   "Her nose began to bleed."
668   "Neither in town [hence, in public] nor in hall [hence, in private]."
673–674   "Now let all this lie [literally, be dead] and [let] this information be kept
       undisclosed [literally, whole]."

Trustly trowe thou therupon
680 And holde it for no wene.
I swere bothe be book and belle,
But-yif thou me his name telle,   *unless*
   The right doom shall I deme:
Thy-self shalt go the righte way
685 That thy brother wente to day,
   Though it thee evele beseme!"   *ill/suit*

Thenne saide the King, "So moot I thee,
Be shrifte of mouthe telle I it thee;   *confession*
   Therto I am unblive.   *reluctant*
690 Certainly, it is non othir
But Wymound, oure weddid brother;
   He wole nevere thrive."   *prosper*
"Allas," saide the Bishop than,
"I wende he were the treweste man
695 That evere yit levid on live.
And he with this ateint may be,
He shall be hongid on trees three,
   And drawen with hors five."

And whenne that the Bishop the soothe hade,   *truth*
700 That that traitour that lesing made,   *lie*
   He callid a messaungere,
Bad him to Dovre that he sholde founde   *hasten*
For to fette that Erl Wymounde: *fetch*
   "That traitour has no pere.
705 Say Egelond and his sones be slawe,
Bothe y-hangid and to-drawe;
   Do as I thee lere.   *instruct*
The Countasse is in presoun done;
Shall she nevere out of presoun come
710 But-yif it be on bere."   *unless/bier*

Now with the messanger was no badde;   *delay*
He took his hors, as the Bishop radde,   *instructed*
   To Dovere till that he come.
The Erl in his halle he fand;
715 He took him the lettre in his hand   *gave*
   On high—wolde he nought wonde.   *in/haste/hesitate*
"Sere Egelond and his sones be slawe,
Bothe y-hangid and to-drawe;
   Thou getist that erldome.

---

680 With *wene* meaning something like "opinion," the line can be understood as
     "And do not doubt it at all."
696 "If he is proved guilty of this."

720 The Countasse is in presoun done;
Shall she nevere more out come,
   Ne see neither sunne ne mone."   *moon*

Thanne that Erl made him glade
And thankid God that lesing was made:
725   "It hath gete me this erldome."
He saide, "Felawe, right weel thou be.
Have here besauntis good plenté.   *coins*
   For thin hedir-come."   *coming hither*
Thanne the messanger made his mon: *complaint*
730 "Sere, of youre goode hors lende me on.   *horses/one*
   Now graunte me my bone;   *request*
For yistirday deide my nobil stede   *died*
On youre arende as I yede,   *went*
   Be the way as I come."

735 "Min hors be fatte and corn-fed,
And of thy lif I am adred,"   *anxious*
   That Erl saide to him than,
"Thanne yif min hors sholde thee slo,   *for/if*
My lord the King wolde be full wo
740   To lese swilk a man."   *such*

The messanger yit he broughte a stede,
On of the beste at ilke a nede   *each/need*
   That evere on grounde dede gange,   *go*
Sadelid and bridelid at the best;
745 The messanger was full preste;   *quite/ready*
   Wightly on him he sprange.   *vigorously*
"Sere," he saide, "have good day;
Thou shalt come whan thou may.
   I shall make the King at hande."
750 With sporis faste he strook the stede;   *struck*
To Gravisende he come good spede,   *Gravesend*
   Is fourty mile to fande.

There the messanger the traitour abood,   *awaited*
And sethin bothe in same they rod   *then/together*
755   To Westeminstir-wone.
In the palais there they light,   *alighted*
Into the halle they come full right,   *immediately*
   And mette with Athelstone.

---

726   The "Right well [may] you be" is a form of salutation.
749   "I shall make the King aware [of your coming]."
752   "[Which] is forty miles to travel."
755   "To the [King's] residence at Westminster."

He wolde have kissid his lord swete;
760 He saide: "Traitour, nought yit lete,
   Be God and be Saint John!
For thy falsnesse and thy lesing
I slough min heir, sholde have been king
   When my lif hadde been gon."

765 There he deniid faste the King   *denied to/firmly*
That he made nevere that lesing,
   Among his peres alle.
The Bishop has him be the hand tan;   *taken*
Forth in same they are gan   *together*
770   Into the wide halle.
Mighte he nevere with craft ne ginne
Gare him shriven of his sinne
   For nought that mighte befalle.
Thenne saide the goode King Athelston,
775 "Lat him to the fir gon
   To preve the trewethe indede."   *prove*

Whenne the King hadde said so,
A gret fir was maad tho,
   In romaunce as we rede.
780 It was set, that men mighten knawe,
Nine plough-lenge on rawe   *length/row*
   As red as ony glede.   *coal*
Nine sithis the bishop halewes the way   *times/consecrates*
That that traitour shole go that day–
785   The wers him gan to spede.
He wente fro the lengthe into the thridde
And doun he fell the fir amidde;
   His eyen wolde him nought lede.

Than the Erlis childrin were war full smerte   *aware/sharply*
790 And wightly to the traitour sterte   *quickly/ran*
   And out of the fir him hade,
And sworen bothe be book and belle:
"Or that thou deye, thou shalt telle   *before*
   Why thou that lesing made."
795 "Certain, I can non other red,   *know/recourse*
Now I wot I am but ded: *realize/all but*
                              /dead

---

760 The King's sharp greeting is idiomatic; essentially it says something like "Do not
    indeed allow," to which we should perhaps add "yourself familiarities with me."
771–773 "He might never [either] with deceit or trickery have himself absolved of sin
    for anything at all."
785 "The worst outcome fell his lot."
786 "He walked the course up to the third [ploughshare]."

I telle you nothing gladde.
Certain, ther was non other wite:
He lovid him to mekil and me to lite;   *much/little*
800 Therfore envie I hadde."

Whenne that traitour so hadde saide,
Five goode hors to him were taide–   *tied*
Alle men mighten see with ighe.   *eye*
They drowen him thorugh ilke a strete,   *each*
805 And sithen to the elmes, I you hete,   *then/assure*
And hongid him full highe.
Was ther nevere man so hardy   *bold*
That durste felle his false body.
This hadde he for his lye.
810 Now Jesu, that is Hevene-king,
Leve nevere traitour have betere ending,
But swich dome for to dye.   *sentence*

797 "Reluctantly I [must] confess."
798 *Wite* means essentially 'injury' or 'punishment,' but here context would make it
"reason [for injury]."

Gamelyn

OTH Shakespeare and Chaucer have a prominent place in the literary history of *Gamelyn* and for this reason it is perhaps the most widely known of all romances of the Matter of England. It is present in several of the *Canterbury Tale* manuscripts, usually placed just after the Cook's "Prologue" and abortive "Tale" of Perkyn Revelour—and hence sometimes called, incorrectly, "The Cook's Tale of Gamelyn." Undoubtedly Chaucer knew about it, was probably going to rework it (for the Yeoman and not the Cook), but never touched its bumpy seven-stress-per-line verses. Whatever Chaucer might have done with it, his product most certainly would lack the forthrightness it now possesses. One would have to read into "Gamelyn," and hence the delight of accepting just exactly what the poem is and says would be lost. Another great poet, however, did rework the story, although not the poem, and from a revamped version. In 1590 Thomas Lodge produced his *Rosalynde or Euphues Golden Legacie*, a prose romance wherein Gamelyn appears as Rosader, the evil eldest brother as Saladyne, and the good middle brother as Fernandyne. The setting is no longer an English manor north of London, but the home of a French Knight of Malta resident in Bordeaux. It is from Lodge's *Rosalynde* that Shakespeare drew the essential motifs for his *As You Like It* and it is in Shakespeare's version primarily that the mid-fourteenth-century romance is known and read today.

Gamelyn itself has no sources that can be readily identified. It does fall into clearly defined segments and most of them have their literary or historical associations. In the beginning, we find the knight Sir John of Boundys dying and summoning friends to help him parcel out his property to his three sons—John, Ote, and Gamelyn the young. Just as in *Havelok*, the rightful—or more appropriately here, the favored—heir is slighted. Gamelyn is duly put aside by the knight's executors. Further, as in *Havelok*, the "male Cinderella" proves his worth in an athletic contest: Gamelyn excells in a wrestling bout with a local champion. After a roistering time in celebration of his victory in his eldest brother's house and at his eldest brother's expense, Gamelyn lets himself be bound hand and foot on the grounds that the aggrieved brother had vowed to do so and had to do so in order to maintain his moral integrity. During a banquet, old Adam (the) Spencer releases poor Gamelyn and the two soundly beat up the abbots, priors, and canons who failed to help the youth out of his bonds, presumably because they believed what the eldest brother had told them—that Gamelyn was mad. Both Gamelyn and Adam are obliged to withdraw in the face of numerical superiority (one posse from the sheriff is taken care of, a second is just too much to handle) and flee to the greenwood to live as outlaws. (The greenwood is, of course, Shakespeare's Forest of Arden.) It is here that Robin Hood associations arise. Is the Gamelyn of romance the prototypic Robin? The romance is certainly older than the extant Robin Hood ballads and Skeat, for one, assumes that the latter somehow derive from it. The assumption is questionable because in several ballads Gamelyn is drawn into the Robin Hood complex not as Robin, but as an equal and rival. In the ballad "Robin and Gandelyn," he avenges Robin's murder; in the later ballad "Robin Hood Newly Revived," he gets the better of Robin and is received into the outlaw band under the name of Will Scarlet. Yet *Gamelyn* culminates not in a forest, but, like several Icelandic sagas, in a courtroom brawl. Sir John, the eldest brother, becomes sheriff in a neighboring shire and declares Gamelyn "wolf's head," whereby anyone has leave to kill him on sight. Gamelyn visits his brother's courtroom and is seized, only to be let off on bail when the good middle brother Sir Ote stands in for him. On the day appointed for the trial, Gamelyn and a strong force of outlaws appear before the bar. They turn tables on established order; they hang the corrupt judge, the bribed jury, and the malodorous John. The King sanctions their action and rewards them: Sir Ote becomes justice, the outlaws are pardoned, and Gamelyn is given supervision of all the King's free forest. Few literary associations can be found for the courtroom scene, but historical analogues are many. In government records of the thirteenth century in particular, there are instances of corrupt judges and bribed juries being called to account and ultimately suffering for their misdeeds. And the final scene in *Gamelyn* probably arises, not from any one particular legal scandal, but from the general impression many such legal crises would have had on any right-thinking onlooker.

The *Gamelyn* poet is anonymous. His language is generally that of Chaucer's time. Skeat would like to assume that a French source existed (none of the extant manuscripts is the original) on the unconvincing grounds that there are some words of French origin in the poem and that names like John and Ote are of French derivation. Others would like to see a poem of Northern origin; but Scandinavian words (unlike the situation pertaining in *Havelok*) are few and the language is certainly not that of Yorkshire or Northumberland. In the end, dating and origin must be adduced by the not-here and not-there method, meaning that *Gamelyn* is essentially a Midland poem composed prior to Chaucer's period of literary activity—or somewhere around the year 1350—and in a locale perhaps to the north of, but not awfully far removed from the London area.

The line is a seven-stress affair, like some of Middle English alliterative poetry, although *Gamelyn* is written in rhymed couplets and alliteration is only incidental and confined chiefly to stock, conventional phrases. The stresses in the individual line are significant; unstressed syllables vary both in number and location so that a half line made up of iambs can be followed by another made up of trochees. This fact plus the presence of instances where a stressed syllable is followed immediately by another stressed syllable make the verses seem rough and unpolished in the extreme. The surprise comes, however, when *Gamelyn* is read aloud; its lines then appear, if not elegant, certainly competent and quite appropriate to the matter of the poem.

The version of *Gamelyn* which follows combines features of several editions, although the raised full stop used by both Skeat and French and Hale to indicate the line caesura has been omitted in favor of the triple space between half lines—a usage present in all modern editions of "Sir Gawain and the Green Knight," Langland's "Piers," and the bulk of Old English poetry. The annotations and glosses utilize the line division. An annotation for the first half line (the *a* line) is indicated by a lower-case *a* beside the arabic line number and a note for the second half line (the *b* line) is similarly indicated. With *Gamelyn*, in contrast to the practice in the other romances, a marginal gloss and a foot-of-the-page annotation can be present for one particular line, but in such cases a gloss always refers to a half-line different from that of the foot-of-the-page annotation.

REFERENCES: Brown and Robbins, No. 1913; Billings, pp. 425–427; *CBEL*, I:151; Hibbard, pp. 156–163; Kane, p. 48; Wells, p. 25. A quasi-diplomatic printing of *Gamelyn* is in French and Hale, pp. 207–235; a critical edition with many textual comments was published by W. W. Skeat as *The Tale of Gamelyn* (Oxford, 1884 and later, revised printings.)

Litheth and lestneth   and herkneth aright
And ye shull heere a talking   of a doughty knight.   *tale*

---

1 All three plural imperatives mean "listen," the first being rare and of Norse origin.

Sire John of Boundis   was his right name;
He coude of norture y-nough   and mochil of game.
5 Three sones the knight had   that with his body he wan;   begot
The eldest was a moche shrewe   and sone he began.
His bretheren loved well here fader   and of him were agast;
The eldest deserved his faders curs   and got it at the last.
The goode knight his fader   livede so yore   long
10 That deth was comen him to   and handled him full sore.   tormented
                                                                     /bitterly

The goode knight cared sore,   sik ther he lay,   was anxious
How his children sholde liven   after his day.
He hadde been wide-wher,   but non housbond he was;   far and wide
All the lond that he had   it was verrey purchas.
15 Fain he wold it were   dressed amonges hem alle,   divided
That ech of hem had his part   as it might falle.   happen
Tho sent he into cuntré   after wise knightes   then
To helpe delen his londes   and dressen hem to rightes.   divide/justly
He sent hem word by lettres   they shulden hie blive,   quickly
20 If they wolde speke with him   whil he was on live.   alive

Tho the knightes herden   sick that he lay,
Hadde they no reste   nother night ne day,   neither
Till they comen to him   ther he lay stille
On his deth-bedde   to abide Goddes wille.
25 Than saide the goode knight,   sick ther he lay,
"Lordes, I you warne   for-soth withoute nay,   denial
I may no lengere liven   heer in this stounde.   longer/time
For thurgh Goddes wille   deth draweth me to grounde."
Ther nas non of hem alle   that herd him aright
30 That they hadden rewthe   of that ilke knight.   pity/same
And saide, "Sir, for Goddes love,   ne dismay you nought.
God may do bote of bale   that is now y-wrought."
Then spak the goode knight,   sick ther he lay
"Boote of bale God may sende,   I wot it is no nay;
35 But I biseke you, knightes,   for the love of me,
Goth and dresseth my lond   among my sones three.
And, sires, for the love of God,   deleth hem nat amiss,
And forgetith nat Gamelin,   my yonge sone that is.
Taketh heed to that on   as well as to that other;   one
40 Selde ye see ony eir   helpen his brother."   seldom/heir

---

3   *Boundis* (in one MS *Burdeuxs*) may mean "border lands."
4   "He knew enough of good breeding and much concerning sport."
6   "The eldest was a great rogue and early began [to show it]."
13–14   *Housbond* seems to imply a farm-bound individual (perhaps *but* should read
        and); *verrey purchas* "true purchase" implies the land was not inherited.
21   "When the knights heard that he lay sick."
32   "God may work remedy for evil that now has been wrought."
34b   "I know there is no denying it."

Tho leete they the knight lyen,   that was nought in hele,   *health*
And wenten into counseil,   his londes for to dele.   *divide*
For to delen hem alle   to oon, that was her thought.   *intent*
And for Gamelyn was yongest,   he should have nought.   *because*
45 All the lond that ther was,   they dalten it in two,
And leeten Gamelyn the yonge   withoute lond go,
And ech of hem saide   to other full loude
His bretheren might yeve him lond   whan he good coude.
Whan they hadde deled   the lond at here wille,
50 They come ayein to the knight   ther he lay full stille   *back*
And tolden him anon right   how they hadden wrought.   *acted*
And the knight there he lay   liked it right nought.   *not at all*
Than saide the knight,   "By Saint Martin,
For all that ye have y-doon,   yit is the lond min.
55 For Goddes love, neihebours,   stondeth alle stille,
And I will dele my lond   after my wille.
Johan, min eldest sone,   shall have plowes five,
That was my fadres heritage   while he was on live.
And my middeleste sone   fif plowes of lond.
60 That I halp for to gete   with my right hond;
And all min other purchas   of londes and leedes,   *tenants*
That I biquethe Gamelyn   and alle my goode steedes.
And I biseke you, goode men,   that lawe conne of londe,
For Gamelynes love   that my queste stonde."   *bequest*
65 Thus dalte the knight   his lond by his day,   *divided/life-time*
Right on his deth-bed   sick ther he lay.
And sone aftirward   he lay stoon stille,
And deide whan time com,   as it was Christes wille.   *died*
And anon as he was deed   and under grass y-grave,   *as soon as*
70 Sone the elder brother   giled the yonge knave.   *beguiled/boy*
He took into his hond   his lond and his leede   *tenants*
And Gamelyn himselfe   to clothen and to feede.
He clothed him and fed him   ivel and eek wrothe   *poorly/also/ill*
And leet his londes forfare   and his houses bothe,   *go to ruin*
75 His parkes and his woodes,   and dede nothing well;
And sethen he it abought   on his faire fell.
So longe was Gamelyn   in his brotheres halle,   *as long as*
For the strengest, of good will,   they doutiden him alle.

48b   "When he knew good" [that is, knew right from wrong].
57   A *plow* was a measure of land presumably covering the area a man could plow in
one day.
60   A line which can be taken to mean the knight received the land for military
service.
63b   "Who know the law of the land."
72   "And [took to] himself the duty to clothe and feed Gamelyn."
76   "And afterwards he paid for it with his own hide" [that is, suffered the conse-
quences].
78   "For the strongest [one] they all feared him of their own accord."

Ther was non therinne,   nouther yong ne olde,

80 That wolde wrathe Gamelyn,   were he never so bolde.   *anger*

Gamelyn stood on a day   in his brotheres yerde   *one day*

And bigan with his hond   to handlen his berde.

He thought on his londes   that layen unsawe   *unsown*

And his faire okes   that doun were y-drawe.   *drawn*

85 His parkes were y-broken   and his deer bireeved.   *broken into /robbed*

Of alle his goode steedes   noon was him bileved.   *left*

His houses were unhiled   and full ivel dight.   *unroofed /repaired*

Tho thoughte Gamelyn   it went nought aright.   *then*

Afterward cam his brother   walkinge thare

90 And saide to Gamelyn,   "Is our mete yare?"   *meal/ready*

Tho wrathed him Gamelyn   and swor by Goddes book,   *grew angry*

"Thou shalt go bake thiself;   I will nought be thy cook!"

"How? Brother Gamelyn,   how answerest thou now?

Thou spake never a word   as thou dost now."

95 "By my faith," saide Gamelyn,   "now me thinketh neede;

Of alle the harmes that I have,   I took never ar heede.   *before/notice*

My parkes been tobroken   and my deer bireved,

Of min armure and my steedes   nought is me bileved.

All that my fader me biquath,   all goth to shame,   *ruin*

100 And therfor have thou Goddes curs,   brother, by thy name!"

Than bispack his brother,   that rape was of rees,

"Stond stille, gadeling,   and hold right thy pees.

Thou shalt be fain for to have   thy mete and thy wede.   *eager/clothes*

What spekest thou, Gamelyn,   of lond other of leede?"   *tenants*

105 Thanne saide Gamelyn,   the child that was ying,   *young*

"Christes curs mot he have   that clepeth me gadeling!   *may/calls*

I am no worse gadeling   ne no worse wight,   *fellow*

But born of a lady   and geten of a knight."   *begot*

Ne durst he not to Gamelyn   ner a foote go,

110 But clepid to him his men   and saide to hem tho,   *called*

"Goth and beteth this boy   and reveth him his wit   *beat*

And lat him leren another time   to answere me bet."   *learn/better*

Thanne saide the child,   yonge Gamelyn,   *boy*

"Christes curs mot thou have!   Brother art thou min,   *may*

115 And if I shall algate   be beten anon,   *anyway*

82b   "To stroke his beard," an action suggestive of both thought and [newly arrived] maturity.

95b   "Now it seems to me necessary."

100b   "Brother in name only" is the implication.

101   "Then said his brother, who was quick to anger."

102   *Gadeling*, according to Skeat's notes, is not only a term of reproach, but also a slurring pun on the hero's name.

109   "He dare not go on foot nearer to Gamelyn."

111b   "And rob him of his wits," the implication being "beat him senseless."

Christes curs mot thou have, but thou be that oon!"
And anon his brother in that grete hete   *heat*
Made his men fette staves Gamelyn to bete.   *fetch*
Whan that everich of hem a staf had y-nome, *every/taken*
120 Gamelyn was war anon tho he seigh hem come. *aware/when*
Tho Gamelyn seigh hem come, he loked overall *saw*
And was war of a pestel stood under a wall.
Gamelyn was light of foot and thider gan he lepe *leap*
And drof alle his brotheres men right on an hepe. *heap*
125 He loked as a wilde lioun and laide on good woon. *vehemently*
Tho his brother say that, he bigan to goon. *saw/run*
He fley up intill a loft and shette the dore fast. *fled/shut*
Thus Gamelyn with the pestel made hem alle agast. *terrified*
Some for Gamelynes love and some for his eighe,
130 Alle they drowe by halves tho he gan to pleighe.
"What! how now!" saide Gamelyn, "evil mot ye thee! *prosper*
Will ye biginne conteck and so sone flee?" *fight*
Gamelyn sough his brother whider he was flowe *saw/fled*
And saugh wher he loked out at a windowe.
135 "Brother," saide Gamelyn, "com a litel ner, *nearer*
And I will teche thee a play atte bokeler."
His brother him answerde and swor by Saint Richer,
"Whil the pestel is in thin hond, I will come no neer.
Brother, I will make thy pees, I swere by Christes ore.
140 Cast away the pestel and wrathe thee namore."
"I mot neede," saide Gamelyn, "wrathe me at oones, *grow angry*
                  /indeed*

For thou wolde make thy men to breke mine boones.
Ne had I hadde main and might in min armes,
To have y-put hem fro me, he wolde have do me harmes." *they*
145 "Gamelyn," saide his brother, "be thou nought wroth; *angry*
For to seen thee have harm, it were me right looth. *loath*
I ne dide it nought, brother, but for a fonding, *except/test*
For to loken or thou were strong and art so ying."
"Com adoun than to me and graunte me my bone *request*
150 Of thing I will thee aske and we shull saughte sone."
Doun than cam his brother that fikil was and felle *deceitful/cruel*

---

116 "Unless you be the one" [that is, dare to be the one to beat me].
122 "And was aware of a pestle [which] leaned by a wall." The *pestel* might be one
   for grinding grain or pounding meat.
129 "Some out of affection and some out of fear for Gamelyn."
130 "All sidled to one side or another when he began to play." Repeatedly in
   "Gamelyn" *play* is understatement for "fight."
136 *Atte bokeler* "at the buckler" [small arm shield] is a sarcastic allusion to the sport
   of fencing with wooden sword and shield.
140b "And don't be furious any longer."
143a "[If] I had not had power."
148 "[Just] to see whether you were strong [who] are so young."
150 "Of matters I wish to ask you about and we shall be quickly reconciled."

And was swithe sore   agast of the pestelle.   *very/much/afraid*
He saide, "Brother Gamelyn,   aske me thy boone   *request*
And loke thou me blame,   but I graunte sone."
155 Thanne saide Gamelyn,   "Brother, y-wis,   *indeed*
And we shulle been at oon,   thou most me graunte this: *if*
All that my fader me biquath,   while he was on live,   *alive*
Thou most do me it have,   yif we shull not strive."
"That shalt you have, Gamelyn–   I swere by Christes ore!–   *grace*
160 All that thy fader thee biquath,   though thou woldest have
     more.   *even if*
Thy lond that lith laye,   full well it shall be sowe,   *untilled/sown*
And thin houses raised up,   that been laid so lowe."
Thus saide the knight   to Gamelyn with mouthe
And thought eek of falsnes   as he well couthe.   *also/could*
165 The knight thought on tresoun   and Gamelyn on noon
And went and kisst his brother   and whan they were at
     oon,   *reconciled*
Allas, yonge Gamelyn,   nothing he wiste   *knew*
With which a false tresoun   his brother him kisste.

Litheth and lestneth   and holdeth your tonge
170 And ye shull heer talking   of Gamelyn the yonge.
Ther was ther bisiden   cried a wrastling   *announced*
And therfor ther was sette up   a ram and a ring
And Gamelyn was in good will   to wende therto   *desirous*
For to preven his might   what he couthe do.
175 "Brother," saide Gamelyn,   "by Saint Richer,   *Richard*
Thou most lene me tonight   a litel courser   *loan*
That is freish to the spore   on for to ride.
I most on an erande   a litel her biside."
"By God," said his brother,   "of steedes in my stalle
180 Go and chese thee the best   and spare non of alle   *choose*
Of steedes or of coursers   that stonden hem biside;
And tell me goode brother,   whider thou wolt ride."
"Her biside, brother,   is cried a wrastling,
And therfor shall be set up   a ram and a ring;
185 Moche worship it were,   brother, to us alle,   *honor*
Might I the ram and the ring   bring home to this halle."
A steede ther was sadeled   smertely and skeet;   *quickly*
Gamelyn did a paire spores   fast on his feet.   *put*
He set his foot in stirop,   the steede he bistrood,

---

154   "And see to it you blame me unless I grant it at once."
158   "You must have it granted to me if we are not to quarrel."
163b   "To Gamely with [his] mouth" [that is, deceptively].
168   "With such deceptive treachery."
169   See note to line 1.
172b   "A ram and ring" [as prizes].
174b   "[And] what he could do."

190 And toward the wrasteling   the yonge child rood.   *boy*
    Tho Gamelin the yonge   was ride out at the gate,   *when*
    The fals knight his brother   locked it after thate,
    And bisoughte Jesu Christ,   that is Hevene-king,
    He mighte breke his necke   in that wrastling.
195 As sone as Gamelyn com   ther the place was,   *king*
    He lighte doun of his steede   and stood on the gras.
    And ther he herd a frankelein   wayloway sing,
    And bigan bitterly   his hondes for to wring.
    "Goode man," saide Gamelyn,   "why makestou this fare?
200 Is ther no man that may you helpe   out of this care?"
    "Allas!" said this frankelein,   "that ever was I bore!   *born*
    For tweye stalworthe sones   I wene that I have lore.   *two/suspect/lost*
    A championn is in the place   that hath y-wrought me sorwe,
    For he hath slain my two sones,   but if God hem borwe.   *unless/save*
205 I wold yeve ten pound,   by Jesu Christ, and more,
    With the nones I fand a man   to handil him sore!"
    "Goode man," saide Gamelyn,   "wilt thou well doon,
    Hold min hors whil my man   draweth of my shoon;   *shoes*
    And help my man to kepe   my clothes and my steede,   *guard*
210 And I will into place go   to loke if I may speede."   *win*
    "By God!" saide the frankelein,   "anon it shall be doon;
    I will myself be thy man   and drawen of thy shoon;
    And wende thou into the place–   Jesu Christ thee speede!–
    And drede not of thy clothes   nor of thy goode steede."   *fear*

215 Barfoot and ungert   Gamelyn in cam;
    Alle that weren in the place   heede of him they nam;   *took*
    How he durst auntre him   of him to doon his might
    That was so doughty championn   in wrastling and in fight.
    Up sterte the championn   raply and anoon;   *quickly*
220 Toward yonge Gamelyn   he bigan to goon
    And saide, "Who is thy fader   and who is thy sire?
    For sothe thou art a gret fool   that thou come hire."   *in that*
    Gamelyn answerde   the championn tho,   *then*
    "Thou knewe well my fader   whil he couthe go;   *walk*
225 Whiles he was on live,   by Saint Martin!
    Sir John of Boundis was his name   and I, Gamelyn."
    "Felaw," saide the championn,   "also mot I thrive!
    I knew well thy fader   whil he was on live;
    And thiself, Gamelyn,   I will that thou it heere,

---

197   "And there he heard a franklin [a man ranking just below a knight] make lamen-
       tation."
199b   "Why do you carry on so?"
206   "[If] I found a man immediately to handle him [the champion] roughly."
207b   "[If] you wish to do well" [that is, do me a favor].
217   "How he dared take a chance to prove his strength on him."

230 Whil thou were a yong boy   a moche shrewe thou were."   *great/rogue*
    Than saide Gamelyn   and swor by Christes ore,   *grace*
    "Now I am older woxe,   thou shalt me find a more!"   H·
    "By God," saide the champioun,   "welcome mote thou be!   *may*
    Come thou ones in min hond,   shalt thou never thee."   *once/thrive*
235 It was well withinne the night   and the moone shon,
    Whan Gamelyn and the champioun   togider gon to goon.   *did/go*
    The champioun caste tornes   to Gamelyn, that was prest,
    And Gamelyn stood stille   and bad him doon his best.
    Thanne saide Gamelyn   to the champioun,
240 "Thou art fast aboute   to bringe me adoun;   *trying/hard*
    Now I have y-proved   many tornes of thine,   *withstood/holds*
    Thou most," he saide, "proven   on or two of mine."   H·
    Gamelyn to the champioun   yede smartly anon;   *went*
    Of alle the tornes that he couthe   he shewed him but oon   *knew*
245 And cast him on the left side   that three ribbes tobrack   *broke*
    And therto his oon arm,   that yaf a gret crack.   *gave*
    Thanne said Gamelyn   smertly anoon,
    "Shall it be holde for a cast   or elles for noon?"   H·   *considered/throw*
    "By God," said the champioun,   "whether that it be,
250 He that comes ones in thin hand   shall he never thee!"   *once/prosper*
    Than saide the frankelein,   that had his sones there,
    "Blessed be thou, Gamelyn,   that ever thou bore were."   *born*
    The franklein said to the champioun–   of him stood him
        noon eye–
    "This is yonge Gamelyn   that taughte thee to playe."
255 Ayein answerd the champioun,   that liked nothing well,
    "He is alther maister   and his play is right fell.   *of all/cruel*
    Sith I wrastled first,   it is y-go full yore,
    But I was nevere my lif   handled so sore."   *sorely*
    Gamelyn stood in the place   allone withoute serk   *shirt*
260 And said, "If ther be eny mo,   lat hem come to werk!   *more*
    The champioun that pained him   to werke so sore,
    It semeth by his continaunce   that he will nomore."   H·   *wants*
    Gamelyn in the place   stood as stille as stoon
    For to abide wrasteling,   but ther com noon.
265 Ther was noon with Gamelyn   wolde wrastle more,
    For he handled the champioun   so wonderly sore.   *exceedingly/hard*
    Two gentilmen ther were   that yemede the place   *had charge of*
    Comen to Gamelyn–   God yeve him goode grace!–   *give*

---

232   "Now I've grown older, you'll find me a greater [rogue]."
237   "The champion tried [various] holds on Gamelyn, who was prepared."
249b   "However it be [taken]."
253b   "He [the franklin] stood in no fear of him."
255b   "Who was much displeased."
257b   "It is very long ago."
261   "The champion who took pains to labor so hard."

And saide to him, "Do on   thin hosen and thy shoon;   *put/hose/shoes*
270 For soth, at this time   this feire is y-doon."
And than saide Gamelyn,   "So mot I well fare,
I have nought yet halvendel   sold up my ware."   *by half*
Tho saide the champioun,   "So brouk I my sweere,
He is a fool that therof beyeth,   thou sellest it so deere."   *buys/dearly*
275 Tho saide the frankelein,   that was in moche care,
"Felaw," he saide,   "why lackest thou his ware?   *find fault with*
By Saint Jame in Galis,   that many man hath sought,
Yet it is to good cheep   that thou hast y-bought."
Tho that wardeines were   of that wrastling   *those/who*
280 Come and broughte Gamelyn   the ram and the ring,
And saiden, "Have, Gamelyn,   the ring and the ram
For the best wrasteler   that ever here cam."
Thus wan Gamelyn   the ram and the ring
And wente with moche joye   home in the morning.
285 His brother seih wher he cam   with the grete route   *saw/company*
And bad shitte the gate   and holde him withoute.   *ordered/to be shut*
The porter of his lord   was full sore agast   *afraid*
And stert anon to the gate   and locked it fast.

Now litheth and lestneth,   both yong and olde,   *hearken*
290 And ye shull heere gamen   of Gamelyn the bolde.   *sport*
Gamelyn com therto   for to have comen in   *went*
And thanne was it y-shet   faste with a pin.   *shut*
Than saide Gamelyn,   "Porter, undo the yate,   *gate*
For many good mannes sone   stondeth therate."
295 Than answerd the porter   and swor by Goddes berd,
"Thou ne shalt, Gamelyn,   come into this yerde."   *yard*
"Thou lixt," saide Gamelyn,   "so brouke I my chin!"
He smot the wiket with his foot   and brack away the pin.
The porter seih tho   it might no better be;   *saw/then*
300 He sette foot on erthe–   he bigan to flee.
"By my faith," saide Gamelyn,   "that travail is y-lore,   *effort/lost*
For I am of foot as light as thou,   though thou haddest   *fleet*
    swore."
Gamelyn overtook the porter   and his teene wrack   *anger/avenged*
And gert him in the necke   that the bon tobrack   *struck/bone*
    /broke

270b   "This fair is over"; here to line 278, the wrestling match is spoken of (with the heavy-handed irony common in *Gamelyn*) as a country fair.
273b   "As I may use my neck"—an asseveration.
277   "By Saint James in Galicia" [a saint whose shrine "many a man has visited" was located in northern Spain].
278   "Indeed it is a bargain that which you have bought."
297   "You lie," said Gamelyn, "as I may use my chin!"
298   A wicket is the small door in a large gate.
302b   "[Ever] if you had sworn [to the contrary]."

305 And took him by that oon arm   and threw him in a welle–
    Seven fadmen it was deep,   as I have herd telle.   *fathoms*
    Whan Gamelyn the yonge   thus hadde plaid his play,
    Alle that in the yerde were   drewen hem away.
    They dredden him full sore   for werkes that he wroughte   *feared*
310 And for the faire company   that he thider broughte.
    Gamelyn yede to the gate   and leet it up wide;   *went/let*
    He leet in all maner men   that gon in wold or ride,
    And saide, "Ye be welcome   withouten eny greeve,
    For we wiln be màistres heer   and aske no man leve.   *permission*
315 Yestirday I lefte,"   saide yonge Gamelyn,
    "In my brother seller   five tonne of win;   *cellar/barrels*
    I will not that this compaignye   parten atwinne,
    (And ye will doon after me)   while eny sope is thrinne.
    And if my brother grucche   or make foul cheere,   *grumble*
320 Other for spense of mete or drink   that we spenden heere,   *either/cost*
    I am oure catour   and bere oure aller purs;   *caterer*
    He shall have for his grucching   Saint Maries curs!   *grumbling*
    My brother is a niggoun,   I swer by Christes ore,   *niggard/grace*
    And we will spende largely   that he hath spared yore.   *generously*
325 And who that maketh grucching   that we here dwelle,
    He shall to the porter   into the draw-welle."
    Seven dayes and seven night   Gamelyn held his feste,
    With moche mirth and solas   that was ther and no cheste;   *quarreling*
    In a litel toret   his brother lay y-steke,   *turret/hidden*
330 And say hem wasten his good,   but durst he not speke.   *saw*
    Erly on a morning   on the eighte day,
    The gestes come to Gamelyn   and wolde gon here way.   *would/depart*
    "Lordes," saide Gamelyn,   "will ye so hye?   *hurry off*
    All the win is not yet y-dronke,   so brouk I min ye."
335 Gamelyn in his herte   was he full wo,
    Whan his gestes took her leve   from him for to go.
    He wold they had lenger abide   and they saide nay,   *longer/tarried*
    But bitaughte Gamelyn   God and good day.
    Thus made Gamelyn his fest   and brought it well to ende,
340 And after his gestis   took leve to wende.   *afterward*

---

308   "All [the eldest brother's men] who were in the yard withdrew."
312b   "Who wished to walk in or ride."
313b   "Without reservation" [literally, without any vexation].
317b   "Go [its] various ways" [literally, depart asunder].
318   "(If you will act according to my desire) while any draught is therein."
321b   "And [shall] pay [literally, bear the purse] for all of us."
324b   "That which he long ago saved."
326a   "He will [join] the porter."
334b   An idiom probably near "If I thus [can] use my eye."
335   Dialect, old and new, often uses a name and then a pronoun, a usage which the standard language cannot duplicate.
338   "But commended Gamelyn [to] God and [said] good-bye."
340b   "Received permission to depart."

Litheth and lestneth   and holdeth youre tonge
And ye shull heere gamen   of Gamelyn the yonge.   *sport/about*
Herkneth, lordinges,   and lestneth aright,
Whan alle gestes were goon   how Gamelyn was dight.   *treated*
345 All the whil that Gamelyn   heeld his mangerye,   *feast*
His brother thought on him be wreke   with his treccherie.   *to be avenged/by*
Tho Gamelyns gestes   were riden and y-goon,   *when/guests*
Gamelyn stood allone;   frendes had he noon.
Tho after full soone   withinne a litel stounde,   *thereafter/space*
350 Gamelyn was y-take   and full hard y-bounde.
Forth com the fals knight   out of the selleer;   *cellar*
To Gamelyn his brother   he yede full neer,   *went*
And saide to Gamelyn,   "Who made thee so bold
For to stroye my stoor   of min housholde?"   *waste/supplies*
355 "Brother," saide Gamelyn,   "wrathe thee right nought,   *anger*
For it is many day y-gon   sithen it was bought;   *since/paid for*
For, brother, thou hast y-had,   by Saint Richer,   *Richard*
Of fiftene plowes of lond   this sixtene yer,
And of alle the beestes   thou hast forth bred,
360 That my fader me biquath   on his deth-bed,
Of all this sixtene yeer   I yeve thee the prow,   *profit*
For the mete and the drink   that we have spended now."
Thanne saide the fals knight—   evel mot he thee—
"Herkne, brother Gamelyn,   what I wol yeve thee;
365 For of my body, brother,   geten heir have I noon,
I will make thee min heir,   I swere by Saint John."
"Par ma foy," said Gamelyn,   "and if it so be,   *by my faith*
And thou thenke as thou saist,   God yelde it thee!"   *reward*
Nothing wiste Gamelyn   of his brotheres gile;   *knew/guile*
370 Therfore he him bigiled   in a litel while.
"Gamelyn," saide he,   "o thing I thee telle;   *one*
Tho thou threwe my porter   in the draw-welle,   *when*
I swor in that wrathe   and in that grete moot   *anger*
That thou shuldest be bounde   bothe hand and foot.
375 Therfore I thee biseche,   brother Gamelyn,
Lat me nought be forsworn,   brother art thou min.   *perjured*
Lat me binde thee now,   bothe hand and feet,
For to holde min avow   as I thee biheet."   *vow/promised*
"Brother," saide Gamelyn,   "also mot I thee,   *prosper*
380 Thou shalt not be forsworen   for the love of me."
Tho made they Gamelyn to sitte—   might he nat stonde—
Till they had him bounde   bothe foot and honde.
The fals knight, his brother,   of Gamelyn was agast

---

341   Compare lines 1, 169, and 289.
363b   "May you have ill luck."
373   Moot seems to imply "anger," but its form indicates the meaning "assembly."
376b   "[As] you are my brother."

And sent aftir feteres to feteren him fast.		*fetters*
385 His brother made lesinges on him ther he stood		*lies*
And told hem that comen in that Gamelyn was wood.		*mad*
Gamelyn stood to a post bounden in the halle;		
Tho that comen in ther loked on him alle.		*those/who*
Ever stood Gamelyn even upright,		*bolt*
390 But mete ne drink had he non neither day ne night.		
Than saide Gamelyn, "Brother, by min hals,		*neck*
Now I have aspied thou art a party fals;		*person*
Had I wist that tresoun that thou haddest y-found,		*known/concocted*
I wolde have yeve thee strokes or I had be bounde."		*given/ere*
395 Gamelyn stood bounden stille as eny stoon;		
Two dayes and two nightes mete had he noon.		*food*
Thanne saide Gamelyn, that stood y-bounde stronge,		
"Adam Spencer, me thinkth I faste too longe.		
Adam Spencer, now I biseche thee,		
400 For the mochel love my fader loved thee,		*great*
If thou may come to the keyes, lese me out of bond,		*come upon /release*
And I will parte with thee of my <u>free lond</u>."		*divide*
Thanne saide Adam, that was the Spencer,		*steward*
"I have served thy brother this sixtene year;		
405 If I leete thee goon out of his bour,		*chamber*
He wolde say afterward I were a traitour."		
"Adam," saide Gamelyn, "so brouk I min hals,		
Thou shalt finde my brother atte laste fals;		
Therfor, brother Adam, louse me out of bond		*free*
410 And I will parte with thee <u>of my free lond</u>."		
"Up swich a forward," saide Adams, "y-wiss,		*agreement /certainly*
I will do therto all that in me is."		
"Adam," saide Gamelyn, "also mot I thee,		
I woll hold thee covenaunt and thou will lose me."		*if/release*
415 Anon as Adames lord to bedde was y-gon,		*had/gone*
Adam took the keyes and leet Gamelyn out anoon.		*let*
He unlocked Gamelyn bothe hand and feet		
In hope of avauncement that he him biheet.		*advancement /promised*
Than saide Gamelyn, "Thanked be Goddes sonde!		*providence*
420 Now I am loosed bothe foot and honde;		
Had I now eten and dronken aright,		
Ther is noon in this hous shulde binde me this night."		
Adam took Gamelyn as stille as ony stoon		*stone*
And ladde him into spence rapely and anon		*pantry/quickly*

407b "As I may use my neck"—an asseveration.
413b "As I may prosper."

425 And sette him to soper right in a privé stede. *supper/private*
/place

He bad him do gladly and Gamelyn so dede.
Anon as Gamelyn hade eten well and fin *fine*
And therto y-dronke well of the rede win,
"Adam," saide Gamelyn, "what is now thy reed? *advice*
430 Wher I go to my brother and girde of his heed?"
"Gamelyn," saide Adam, "it shall not be so;
I can teche thee a reed that is worth the two. *plan*
I wot well, for sothe, that this is no nay; *know/denying*
We shull have a mangery right on Sonday. *banquet*
435 Abbotes and priours many heer shall be
And other men of holy chirche as I telle thee.
Thou shalt stonde up by the post as thou were hond-fast,
And I shall leve hem unloke— awey thou may hem cast.
Whan that they have eten and waishen here hondes, *washed*
440 Thou shalt biseke hem alle to bring thee out of bondes; *beseech*
And if they will borwe thee, that were good game;
Then were thou out of prisoun and I out of blame.
And if everich of hem say unto us nay,
I shall do another, I swere by this day.
445 Thou shalt have a good staf and I will have another
And Christes curs have that oon that faileth that other!"
"Ye, for Gode," saide Gamelyn, "I say it for me,
If I faile on my side, ivel mot I thee. *may/prosper*
If we shull algate assoile hem of here sinne, H ,
450 Warne me, brother Adam, whan I shall biginne."
"Gamelyn," saide Adam, "by Sainte Charité,
I will warne thee biforn whan that it shall be.
Whan I twink on thee, loke for to goon *wink/at*
And cast away the fetteres and com to me anoon."
455 "Adam," saide Gamelyn, "blessed be thy bones!
That is a good counseil yeven for the nones. *give/occasion*
If they werne me thanne to bringe me out of bendes, *deny/bonds*
I woll sette goode strokes right on here lendes." *loins*
Tho the Sonday was y-come and folk to the feste, *when*
460 Faire they were welcomed bothe lest and meste;

---

430 "Shall I go to my brother and strike off his head?" *Wher* is merely an interrogative sign.
432b "That is worth two [of your plans]."
437b "As if your hands were fettered."
438a "And I shall leave them [the fetters] unlocked."
441 "And if they will go bail for you, that would be a good turn"; here the context gives the legal term *borwe* a colloquial quality and the modern equivalent of Adam's *good game* is hard to find.
444a "I shall try something else."
449 "If we shall indeed absolve them of their sins" [that is, beat them up]; such heavy jocularity continues throughout the fight.
460b "Both low [ranking people] and high."

And ever as they atte halle   dore comen in,
They caste their eye   on yonge Gamelyn.
The fals knight his brother,   full of trechery,
Alle the gestes that ther wer¢   atte mangery   *at the/banquet*
465 Of Gamelyn his brother   he tolde hem with mouthe
All the harm and the shame   that he telle couthe.   *could*
Tho they were served   of messes two other three,   *when/courses/or*
Than saide Gamelyn   "How serve ye me?
It is nought well served,   by God that all made,
470 That I sitte fasting   and other men make glade."
The fals knight his brother   ther that he stood
Tolde alle his gestes   that Gamelyn was wood;   *insane*
And Gamelyn stood stille   and answerde nought,
But Adames wordes   he held in his thought.
475 Tho Gamelyn gan speke   dolfully with-alle   *pitifully/indeed*
To the grete lordes   that saten in the halle:
"Lordes," he saide,   "for Christes passioun,
Helpeth bringe Gamelyn   out of prisoun."
Than saide an abbot–   sorwe on his cheeke–
480 "He shall have Christes curs   and Sainte Maries eeke   *also*
That thee out of prisoun   beggeth other borwe;
But ever worthe hem well   that doth thee moche sorwe."
After that abbot,   than spack another,
"I wold thin heed were off   though thou were my brother;
485 Alle that thee borwe,   foule mot hem falle!"
Thus they saide alle   that were in the halle.
Than saide a priour–   ivel mot he thrive–   *may*
"It is moche skathe, boy,   that thou art on live."   *harm/alive*
"Ow!" saide Gamelyn,   "so brouk I my bon!
490 Now I have aspied   that freendes have I non.
Cursed mot he worthe,   bothe fleish and blood,   *may/be*
That ever do priour   or abbot ony good!"   *may do*
Adam the Spencer   took up the cloth
And loked on Gamelyn   and say that he was wroth.   *saw/angry*
495 Adam on the pantrie   litel he thought,
But two goode staves   to hall-dore he brought.
Adam loked on Gamelyn   and he was war anoon   *aware/at once*
And cast away the fetteres   and he bigan to goon.   *walk*
Tho he com to Adam,   he took that oo staf   *when/one*
500 And bigan to worche   and goode strokes yaf.   *act/gave*

465b "He spoke to them with his mouth" [that is, hypocritically].
479b "[May there be] sorrow on his cheek."
481–482 "Who begs [to get you free] or stands bail [for you]; but ever may he thrive
        who causes you much sorrow."
485b "May ill luck befall them."
489b "As I may use my bones!"—an asseveration.
495 The phrase "little did he think" implies that Adam did not think twice about
        fetching the staves.

Gamelyn cam into the halle   and the spencer bothe
And loked hem aboute   as they had be wrothe.   *as if/crazed*
Gamelyn sprengeth holywater   with an oken spire   ⊢|.
That some that stoode upright   fell in the fire.
505 Ther was no lewede man   that in the halle stood
That wolde do Gamelyn   enything but good,
But stood beside   and leet hem bothe werche,   *aside/act*
For they hadde no rewthe   of men of holy cherche.   *pity*
Abbot or priour,   monk or chanoun,
510 That Gamelyn overtook   anon they yeeden doun.   *went*
Ther was non of hem alle   that with his staf mette
That he made him overthrowe   and quit him his dette.
"Gamelyn," saide Adam,   "for Sainte Charité.
Pay large liverey   for the love of me;   ⊢|.
515 And I will kepe the dore   so ever here I masse!   *guard*
Er they been assoiled,   there shall noon passe."   *before/absolved*
"Dout thee nought," saide Gamelyn,   "whil we been in   *fear/*
    feere,   *together*
Keep thou well the dore   and I woll werche heere;   *operate*
Stere thee, good Adam,   and lat ther noon flee,
520 And we shull telle largely   how many ther be."
"Gamelyn," saide Adam,   "do hem but good;
They been men of holy chirche,   draw of hem no blood.   ⊢|.
Save well the croune   and do hem non harmes,
But brek bothe her legges   and sithen here armes."   *then*
525 Thus Gamelyn and Adam   wroughte right fast
And playden with the monkes   and made hem agast.   *sported/terrified*
Thider they come riding   jolily with swaines
And hom ayen they wer y-lad   in cartes and in waynes.
Tho they hadden all y-don,   than saide a gray frere,
530 "Allas! sire abbot,   what dide we now heere?
Tho that we comen hider,   it was a cold reed;   *when*
Us hadde been better at home   with water and breed."
Whil Gamelyn made ordres   of monkes and frere,

503   "Gamelyn sprinkles holy water with an oak twig"—he beats up the abbots and priors.
505   *Lewede man* "ignorant man" is here probably equivalent to "layman."
512b   "And paid him his due."
514a   "Pay [them] a generous allowance"—beat them royally.
515b   "As sure as I [shall] hear mass!"
520   "And we shall count liberally how many there are"; the adverb carries the implication of savage beating.
521b   "Do them no harm" [literally, do them (nothing) but good].
523a   "Save [or: respect] their tonsure."
527–528   "They [the abbots, priors, canons, monks] came there riding jauntily with their servants and were brought back [unconscious] in carts and wagons."
531b   "It was a baleful choice"; *cold* often has overtones implying "fatal" or "pernicious" in ME idiom.
533a   "Make orders of" refers to the ceremony of ordaining priests, here implying that Gamelyn and Adam fulfilled the rite with their staves.

Ever stood his brother   and made foul chere.   *acted/distraught*
35 Gamelyn up with his staf   that he well knew
And gert him in the necke   that he overthrew.   *struck/fell down*
A litel above the girdel   the riggebon tobarst;   *waist/backbone*
                                                            /broke

And sette him in the fetteres   ther he sat arst.
"Sitte ther, brother,"   saide Gamelyn,   H.
40 "For to colin thy blood,   as I dide min."   *cool*
As swithe as they hadde   y-wroken hem on here foon,   *avenged/foes*
They askeden watir   and wisshen anoon.   *asked for/washed*
What some for here love   and some for awe,
Alle the servants served hem   of the beste lawe.   *manner*
45 The sherreve was thennes,   but a five-mile,   *distant/only*
And all was y-told him   in a litel while,
How Gamelyn and Adam   had doon a sorry rees,   *made/grievous*
                                                            /attack

Bounden and y-wounded men   ayein the kinges pees.   *contrary to*
Tho bigan sone   strif for to wake   *then/arise*
50 And the sherref aboute   Gamelyn for to take.   *went about*

Now litheth and lestneth,   so God yif you goode fin!
And ye shull heere good game   of yonge Gamelyn.
Four and twenty yonge men   that heelden hem full bolde   *considered*
                                                            /themselves

Come to the shirref   and saide that they wolde
55 Gamelyn and Adam   fetten away.   *fetch*
The sherref yaf hem leve,   soth as I you say.   *gave*
They hieden faste–   wolde they nought bilinne   *hastened/tarry*
Till they come to the yate   ther Gamelyn was inne.   *gate/where*
They knocked on the gate,   the porter was ny,   *near*
60 And loked out at an hol,   as man that was sly.   *cautious*
The porter hadde biholde   hem a litel while;
He loved well Gamelyn   and was adrad of gile   *fearful/guile*
And leet the wiket stonden   y-steke full stille.   *fastened*
And asked hem withoute   what was here wille.
65 For all the grete company   thanne spack but oon,
"Undo the gate, porter,   and lat us in goon."
Than saide the porter,   "So brouke I my chin,
Ye shull say your errand   er ye comen in."
"Say to Gamelyn and Adam,   if here wille be,
70 We will speke with hem   wordes two or three."
"Felaw," saide the porter,   "stond there stille,
And I will sende to Gamelyn   to witen his wille."   *know*

---

543   "Some partly out of love for them and some because of fear."
551b   "As God may give you a good ending!"
567b   "As I may use my chin."
569b   "If it be their will."

In went the porter   to Gamelyn anoon
And saide, "Sir, I warne you,   her been come your foon;   *foes*
575 The sherreves meiné   been atte gate   *posse*
For to take you bothe–   shull ye na skape."   *escape*
"Porter," saide Gamelyn,   "so moot I well thee!   *may/prosper*
I will allowe thee thy wordes   when I my time see.
Go again to the yate   and dwell with hem a while   *back/tarry*
580 And thou shalt see right sone,   porter, a gile."   *stratagem*
"Adam," saide Gamelin,   "looke thee to goon;   *get ready*
We have foomen atte gate   and frendes never oon.   *enemies/not a*
    /one

It been the shirrefes men   that hider been y-come;   *hither*
They been swore togidere   that we shull be nome."   *taken*
585 "Gamelyn," saide Adam,   "hie thee right blive   *hasten/quickly*
And if I faile thee this day,   evel mot I thrive!   *H.*
And we shull so welcome   the sherreves men
That som of hem shull make   here beddes in the fen."   *shall/mud*
Atte posterne gate   Gamelyn out went   *rear*
590 And a good cart staf   in his hand he hent;   *seized*
Adam hente sone   another gret staf
For to helpe Gamelyn   and goode strokes yaf.   *gave*
Adam felde tweine   and Gamelin felde three;   *felled/two*
The other setten feet on erthe   and bigonne flee.
595 "What," saide Adam,   "so ever here I mass!
I have a draught of good win–   drink er ye passe!"
"Nay, by God!" saide they,   "thy drink is not good;   *H.*
It wolde make mannes brain   to lien in his hood."
Gamelin stood stille   and loked him aboute
600 And seih the sherreve come   with a gret route.   *saw/troop*
"Adam," saide Gamelyn,   "what be now thy reedes?   *suggestions*
Here comth the sherreve   and will have oure heedes."
Adam saide, "Gamelin,   my reed is now this,   *advice*
Abide we no lenger   lest we fare amiss.
605 I rede that we to wode goon   are that we be founde;   *ere*
Better is us ther loos   than in town y-bounde."
Adam took by the hond   yonge Gamelyn
And everich of hem two   drank a draught of win   *each*
And took her coursers   and wenten her way.   *H.*
610 Tho fond the sherreve   nest but non ay.   *then/eggs*

---

578   "I shall reward you for your words when I see opportunity [to do so]."
589   One has to assume that Gamelyn and Adam go out the back door and around to the front, where they take the posse by surprise.
596   "I have [for you] a draught of good wine—drink before you go"—again the irony of the initial fight.
598b   Perhaps a pun is involved: the wine [meaning the staff] would make a man's brains lie [meaning either tell lies or lie within the hood because knocked out of the brain pan].
606   "It is better for us to be free there than [be] in town bound."

The sherreve lighte adoun   and went into the halle
And fond the lord y-fettered   faste with-alle.
The sherreve unfettered him   sone and that anoon
And sent after a leche   to hele his rigge-boon.   *doctor/backbone*

615 Lete we now this fals knight   lien in his care   *misery*
And talke we of Gamelin   and loke how he fare.   *see/fares*
Gamelin into the woode   stalkede stille   *went cautiously*
And Adam the Spenser   liked full ille.
Adam swor to Gamelyn   by Saint Richer,   *Richard*
620 "Now I see it is merry   to be a spencer.
That lever me were   keyes for to bere
Than walken in this wilde woode   my clothes to tere."
"Adam," saide Gamelyn,   "dismay thee right nought;
Many good mannes child   in care is y-brought."   *G.*
625 And as they stoode talking   bothen in feere,   *together*
Adam herd talking of men   and neih him thought they   *near*
    were.
Tho Gamelyn under the woode   loked aright;
Seven score of yonge men   he saugh well adight;   *equipped*
Alle satte atte mete   compas aboute.
630 "Adam," saide Gamelyn,   "now have we no doute;   *fear*
After bale cometh boote   thurgh grace of God Almight. *G.* *evil/remedy*
Me thinketh of mete and drink   that I have a sight."
Adam lokede tho   under woode-bough
And whan he seih mete,   he was glad y-nough;   *saw/enough*
635 For he hopede to God,   for to have his deel;   *portion*
And he was sore alonged   after a good meel.
As he saide that word,   the maister outlawe
Saugh Gamelyn and Adam   under woode-shawe.   *wood-thicket*
"Yonge men," saide the maister,   "by the goode roode,   *cross*
640 I am war of gestes—   God send us non but goode!   *aware/guests*
Yonder been two yonge men   wonder well adight   *very/equipped*
And paraventure ther been mo,   who-so loked aright.   *perhaps*
Ariseth up, ye yonge men,   and fetteth hem to me;   *fetch*
It is good that we witen   what men they bee."   *find out*
645 Up ther sterten sevene   fro the diner
And metten with Gamelyn   and Adam Spenser.
Whan they were neih hem,   than saide that oon,   *near*
"Yeldeth up, yonge men,   your bowes and your floon."   *arrows*

615a   "Let us now leave this false knight."
618   "And Adam the Spenser was not well pleased."
621a   "That would be more pleasant for me."
624   Either a proverbial remark or a reference to the condition of the sheriff's men—
       or both.
629b   "In a circle."
636a   "And he was suffering from desire"; *alongen* denotes painful longing.
642b   "Whosoever looked carefully [might see more]."

Thanne saide Gamelyn,   that yong was of elde,   *age*
650 "Moche sorwe mot he have   that to you hem yelde!   *may*
I curse non other,   but right myselve;
They ye fette to you five,   thanne ye be twelve."
Tho they herde by his word   that might was in his arm,
Ther was non of hem alle   that wolde do him harm;
655 But said unto Gamelyn   mildely and stille,
"Com afore our maister   and say to him thy wille."   *tell*
"Yonge men," saide Gamelyn,   "by your lewté,   *loyalty*
What man is your maister   that ye with be?"   *what kind of a*
Alle they answerde   withoute lesing,   *deception*
660 "Our maister is y-crouned   of outlawes king."
"Adam," saide Gamelyn,   "go we in Christes name;
He may neither mete ne drink   werne us for shame.   *deny*
If that he be heende   and come of gentil blood,   *courteous*
He woll yeve us mete and drink   and doon us some good."
665 "By Saint Jame," said Adam,   "what harm that I gete,
I will auntre to the dore   that I hadde mete."
Gamelyn and Adam   wente forth in feere   *together*
And they grette the maister   that they founde there.   *saluted*
Than saide the maister,   king of outlawes,
670 "What seeke ye yonge men   under woode-shawes?"   *wood-thickets*
Gamelyn answerde   the king with his croune,
"He moste needes walke in woode   that may not walke in
    toune.
Sire, we walke not heer   noon harm for to do,
But if we meete with a deer   to sheete therto   *shoot/at*
675 As men that been hungry   and mow no mete finde   *may/food*
And been harde bistad   under woode-linde."   *beset /linden-woo(*

Of Gamelynes wordes   the maister hadde routhe   *sympathy*
And saide, "Ye shall have y-nough–   have God my trouthe!" *enough*
He bad hem sitte ther adoun   for to take reste,
680 And bad hem ete and drink   and that of the beste.
As they sete and eeten   and dronke well and fin,   *fine*
Than said that oon to that other,   "This is Gamelyn."
Tho was the maister outlawe   into counseil nome   *taken*
And told how it was Gamelyn   that thider was y-come.
685 Anon as he herde   how it was bifalle,   *happened*

650b "Who gives them up to you."
651–652 "I curse no other [person] but just myself [implying he is not hostile toward anyone, including outlaws]; although you might add five [to your seven men], then you would number twelve [and we still would not be afraid of you]."
661b "Let us go in Christ's name."
665b "Whatever the harm I may get."
666 "I shall take my chances at the door where I obtained food."
674a "Unless [it be that] we encounter a deer."
678b "God may have my pledged word [on that]!"

He made him maister under him   over hem alle.
Within the thridde wike   him com tiding,   *third/week*
                                               /to him

To the maister outlawe,   that tho was her king,   *who/then/their*
That he shulde come hom,   his pees was y-made;
90 And of that goode tiding   he was tho full glad.
Tho saide he to his yonge men,   soth for to telle,
"Me been comen tidinges,   I may no lenger dwelle."   *tarry*
Tho was Gamelyn anon   withoute tarying   *delay*
Made maister outlawe   and crouned her king.

95 Tho was Gamelyn crouned   king of outlawes
And walked a while   under woode-shawes.
The fals knight his brother   was sherreve and sire
And leet his brother endite   for hate and for ire   *had/indicted*
                                                 /out of
Tho were his bonde-men   sorry and nothing glade   *farm hands*
700 Whan Gamelyn, her lord,   wolves-heed was cried and made;
And sent out of his men   wher they might him finde   *wherever*
For to seke Gamelyn   under woode-linde   *linden-wood*
To telle him tidinges   how the wind was went
And all his good reved   and his men shent.   *badly treated*
705 When they had him founde   on knees they hem sette
And adoun with here hood   and here lord grette: *saluted*
"Sire, wrathe you nought   for the goode roode,   *cross*
For we have brought you tidinges,   but they be nat goode.
Now is thy brother sherreve   and hath the baillie   *bailiff's office*
710 And he hath endited thee   and wolves-heed doth thee crie."   *indicted*
"Allas!" saide Gamelyn,   "that ever I was so slak   *careless*
That I ne hadde broke his necke   tho his rigge brak!   *in that/when*
                                                 /back
Goth, greteth hem well,   min housbondes and wif;
I woll been atte nexte shire,   have God my lif!"
715 Gamelyn came well redy   to the nexte shire
And ther was his brother,   both lord and sire.
Gamelyn com boldelich   into the moot-halle   *boldly*
                                                 /assembly hall

---

689b   "His peace was made" [meaning, pardon had been granted him].
691b   "To tell the truth [about the matter]."
696   The sense is that Gamelyn then lived as an outlaw for a time.
700b   "Was declared and made wolf's head" [that is, declared outlaw and his life set
        at the value of the life of a wolf].
701a   "And his [farm hands] sent out [some of their number]."
703b   "How the wind had turned" [that is, which way the wind was blowing].
704a   "And [how] all his property had been despoiled."
706a   "And [drew] off their hoods"—as a sign of respect.
713b   "My farm hands and [their] wives."
714a   "I shall go into the next shire" [that is, into the next county where the eldest
        brother has bailiff's authority].

And put adoun his hood   among the lordes alle:
"God save you alle, lordinges, that now here be,
720 But brokebak sherreve–   evel mot thou thee!   *broken-back*
                                                    /prosper

Why hast thou do me   that shame and vilonie   *done*
For to late endite me   and wolves-heed me crie?"   *have/indicted*
Tho thought the fals knight   for to been awreke   *then/avenged*
And leet take Gamelyn–   most he no more speke.   *had/seized*
725 Might ther be no more grace,   but Gamelyn atte last   *finally*
Was cast into prisoun   and fettered full fast.
Gamelyn hath a brother   that highte Sir Ote,   *was called*
As good a knight and heende   as mighte gon on foote.   *gracious/walk*
Anon ther yede a messager   to that goode knight   *went*
730 And told him altogidere   how Gamelyn was dight.   *treated*
Anon as Sire Ote herde   how Gamelyn was adight,
He was wonder sorry–   was he nothing light–   *extremely*
                                                    /not at all

And leet sadle a steede   and the way he nam   *had/saddled*
                                                    /took

And to his tweyne bretheren   anon right he cam.   *two*
735 "Sire," saide Sire Ote   to the sherreve tho,   *then*
"We been but three bretheren–   shull we never be mo–   *more*
And thou hast y-prisoned   the best of us alle;
Swiche another brother   ivel mot him bifalle!"
"Sir Ote," saide the fals knight,   "lat be thy curs;
740 By God, for thy wordes,   he shall fare the wurs!   *because of/worse*
To the kinges prisoun   anon he is y-nome   *summarily/taken*
And ther he shall abide   till the justice come."
"Par dé!" saide Sir Ote,   "better it shall be;   *by God*
I bidde him to mainpris   that thou graunt him me   *so that*
745 Till the nexte sitting   of deliveraunce
And thanne lat Gamelyn   stande to his chaunce."
"Brother, in swich a forthward,   I take him to thee;   *on/agreement*
                                                    /commit

And by thy fader soule   that thee bigat and me,
But-if he be redy   whan the justice sitte,   *unless*
750 Thou shalt bere the juggement   for all thy grete witte."   *judgment*
"I graunte well," saide Sir Ote,   "that it so be.   *concede/indeed*
Let deliver him anon   and tak him to me."   *commit*

---

718   "And pulled down his hood [to reveal his identity]."
724b   "He [Gamelyn] was permitted to say nothing further."
725a   "No further consideration was allowed."
738   "May evil befall [any] other brother such [as you are]!"
743b   The implication is "It shall not remain as bad as that."
744a   "I demand [or: ask] bail for him."
745b   *Deliverance* apparently refers to the legal hearing given prisoners at a particular
        date.
750b   *For* may mean either 'in spite of' or 'because of,' probably the latter since the
        remark would then be appropriately sarcastic.

Tho was Gamelyn delivered   to Sire Ote, his brother,
And that night dwellede   that on with that other.   *stayed*
55 On the morn saide Gamelyn   to Sir Ote the heende,   *courteous*
"Brother," he saide, "I moot   forsothe fro thee wende   *go*
To loke how my yonge men   leden here lif,   *see/lead*
Whether they liven in joye   or elles in strif."
"By God," saide Sire Ote,   "that is a cold reed!
60 Now I see that all the cark   shall fallen on min heed;   *responsibility*
                                                      /head

For whan the justice sitte   and thou be nought y-founde,
I shall anon be take   and in thy stede y-bounde."   *taken/place*
"Brother," saide Gamelyn,   "dismaye thee nought,
For by Saint Jame in Gales,   that many man hath sought,
65 If that God almighty   hold my lif and witt,   *maintain*
I will be ther redy   whan the justice sitt."   *sits*
Than saide Sir Ote to Gamelyn,   "God shilde thee fro   *shield*
     shame;
Com whan thou seest time   and bring us out of blame."

Litheth and lestneth   and holdeth you stille
70 And ye shull here how Gamelyn   had all his wille.
Gamelyn wente ayein   under woode-ris   *back*
                                                     /wood branches

And fond there playing   yonge men of pris.   *sporting/value*
Tho was yonge Gamelyn   glad and blithe y-nough   *enough*
Whan he fond his merry men   under woode-bough.
75 Gamelyn and his men   talked in feere   *together*
And they hadde good game   here maister to heere;   *great/pleasure*
They tolden him of aventures   that they hadde founde
And Gamelyn hem tolde agein   how he was fast y-bounde.   *in turn*
Whil Gamelyn was outlawed   had he no cors;
80 There was no man that for him   ferde the wors
But abbots and priours,   monk and chanoun;   *except*
Of hem left he nothing   whan he might hem nom.   *overtake*
Whil Gamelyn and his men   make merthes rive,
The fals knight his brother–   ivel mot he thrive!–
85 For he was fast about   bothe day and other,   *much/busied*
For to hire the quest   to hangen his brother.   *bribe/inquest*
Gamelyn stood on a day   and as he biheeld
The woodes and the shawes   in the wilde feeld,   *groves*

759b   "That is dismal news"; for a similar use of *cold* 'baleful,' see line 531.
764a   See note on line 277.
779   "While Gamelyn was [legally] outlawed, he suffered no [one's] curse"; the sense is that he never abused anyone except those individuals noted in the line following.
783b   "Make mirths rife" [that is, amuse themselves royally].
785a   *For*, though ungrammatical, is suggested fittingly by the "Evil may he thrive" in the line above.

He thought on his brother   how he him beheet — *promised*
790 That he wolde be redy   whan the justice seet. — *should sit*
He thoughte well that he wolde   withoute delay
Come afore the justice   to kepen his day. — *go/appointment*
And saide to his yonge men,   "Dighteth you yare, — *make/ready*
For whan the justice sitt,   we moote be thare; — *sits/must*
795 For I am under borwe   till that I come — *pledge*
And my brother for me   to prisoun shall be nome." —
"By Saint Jame," saide his yonge men,   "and thou rede — *if/advise*
     therto, — */so*
Ordaine how it shall be   and it shall be do." — *done*
Whil Gamelyn was coming   ther the justice sat, — *going*
800 The fals knight his brother   foryat he nat that — *overlooked*
To huire the men on his quest   to hangen his brother; — *bribe/inquest*
Though he hadde nought that oon,   he wolde have that
     other.
Tho cam Gamelyn   fro under woode-ris — *wood branches*
And broughte with him   his yonge men of pris. — *value*
805 "I see well," saide Gamelyn,   "the justice is sette;
Go aforn, Adam,   and loke how it spette." — *in advance*
Adam went into the halle   and loked all aboute;
He seih there stonde   lordes gret and stoute — *saw/proud*
And Sir Ote his brother   fettered well fast.
810 Tho went Adam out of halle   as he were agast. — *as if/terrified*
Adam said to Gamelyn   and to his felaws alle,
"Sir Ote stant y-fettered   in the moot-halle." — *assembly hall*
"Yonge men" saide Gamelyn,   "this ye heeren alle;
Sir Ote stant y-fettered   in the moot-halle. — *stands*
815 If God yif us grace   well for to doo, — *gives/succeed*
He shall it abegge   that broughte thertoo." — *pay for*
Thanne saide Adam,   that lockes hadde hore, — *whose/grey*
"Christes curs most he have   that him bond so sore!
And thou wilt, Gamelyn,   do after my red, — *if/act/plan*
820 Ther is noon in the halle   shall bere away his heed."
"Adam," saide Gamelyn,   "we wilne nought don so;
We will slee the giltif   and lat the other go. — *guilty*
I will into the halle   and with the justice speke;
On hem that been giltif   I will been awreke. — *avenged*
825 Lat non skape at the dore;   take, yonge men, yeme; — *escape/heed*
For I will be justice this day   domes to deme.

796   "And my brother must be taken to prison in my place."
802   "If he [could] not have the one [Gamelyn], [he was determined] to have the
        other [Sir Ote]."
806b   "And see how things are proceeding."
816b   The sense must be "Who brought matters to such a pass."
820b   "[Who] shall bear away his head [unbroken]."
826b   "To hand down verdicts."

God spede me this day   at my newe werk!
Adam, com on with me,   for thou shalt be my clerk."
His men answereden him   and bad him doon his best,   *told/to do*
830 "And if thou to us have neede,   thou shalt find us prest;   *of/ready*
We wiln stande with thee   whil that we may dure;   *endure*
And but we werke manly,   pay us non hure."   *unless/wages*
"Yonge men," saide Gamelyn,   "so mot I well thee!   *may/prosper*
As trusty a maister   ye shall finde of me."
835 Right there the justice   sat in the halle,   *where*
In wente Gamelyn   amonges hem alle.

Gamelyn leet unfettere   his brother out of beende.   *had/unfettered /bonds*

Thanne saide Sir Ote,   his brother that was heende,   *courteous*
"Thou haddest almost, Gamelyn,   dwelled too longe,   *tarried*
840 For the quest is out on me   that I shulde honge."   *verdict*
"Brother," saide Gamelyn,   "so God yif me good rest,   *give*
This day they shuln been hanged   that been on thy quest;   *inquest*
And the justice bothe,   that is jugge-man,   *also*
And the sherreve bothe–   thurgh him it bigan."
845 Than saide Gamelyn   to the justise,
"Now is thy power y-don;   thou most nedes arise;   *finished*
Thou hast yeven domes   that been ivel dight;   *unjustly /arrived at*

I will sitten in thy sete   and dressen hem aright."   *seat*
The justice sat stille   and roos nought anoon;   *immediately*
850 And Gamelyn   clevede his cheeke boon.   *split open*
Gamelyn took him in his arm   and no more spak,   *nothing/further /said*

But threw him over the barre   and his arm tobrak.   *broke*
Durste non to Gamelyn   saye but good,
Forfered of the company   that withoute stood.   *terrified*
855 Gamelyn sette him doun   in the justices sete   *seat*
And Sire Ote his brother by him   and Adam at his feet.
Whan Gamelyn was y-set   in the justices stede,   *place*
Herkneth of a bourde   that Gamelyn dede.   *listen/jest*
He leet fettre the justice   and his fals brother   *had/fettered*
860 And dede hem come to the barre,   that oon with that other.   *had*
Tho Gamelyn hadde thus y-doon,   had he no rest   *when*
Till he had enquered   who was on the quest   *found out/jury*
For to deme his brother   Sir Ote to honge;
Er to wiste which they were,   he thoughte full longe.

827a   "[May] God [help] me [to] succeed this day."
834   "You will find in me [just] as dependable a master [as I find in you loyal followers]."
848b   "And rearrange them [the unjust verdicts] correctly."
864   "He thought [it] over long before he found out which [ones] they were."

865 But as sone as Gamelyn wiste   wher they were,   *knew*
He dede hem everichone   fettere in feere   *had/fettered*
                                                                             /together
And bringen hem to the barre   and sette hem in rewe.
"By my faith," saide the justice,   "the sherreve is a shrewe!"   *rogue*
Than saide Gamelyn   to the justise,
870 "Thou hast y-yeve domes   of the wors assise;
And the twelve sisours   that weren of the queste,   *jurymen/inquest*
They shull been hanged this day,   so have I reste!"
Thanne saide the sherreve   to yonge Gamelyn,
"Lord, I crie thee mercy,   brother art thou min!"
875 "Therfore," saide Gamelyn,   "have thou Christes curs,
For and thou were maister,   yit I shulde have wors."   *for if*
For to make short tale   and nought to tarie longe,
He ordained him a queste   of his men so strong.   *established*
                                                                            /inquest

The justice and the sherreve   bothe honged hie   *high*
880 To waiven with ropes   and with the wind drie.   *swing/on/in/dry*
And the twelve sisours—   sorwe have that recke!—   *jurymen*
Alle they were hanged   faste by the necke.
Thus ended the fals knight   with his treccherie
That ever had y-lad his lif   in falsnes and folie.   *led/folly*
885 He was hanged by the neck   and nought by the purs;
That was the meede that he had   for his faders curs.   *reward*
Sir Ote was eldest   and Gamelyn was ying;   *young*
They wenten with here freendes   even to the king.   *straight*
They made pees with the king   of the best assise;
890 The king loved well Sir Ote   and made him justise.
And after, the king made Gamelyn   bothe in est and west   *afterwards/east*
Chef justice   of all his free forest.
Alle his wighte yonge men   the king foryaf here gilt   *bold*
And sithen in good office   the king hem hath y-pilt.   *after/put*
895 Thus wan Gamelyn   his lond and his leede   *tenants*
And wrack him of his enemies   and quit hem here meede;   *avenged/gave/*
                                                                            reward
And Sire Ote his brother   made him his heir

867a "And [had them] brought to the bar."
870   "You have handed down verdicts appropriate to the worst possible court of law."
872b "[If] I [ever shall] have peace!"
876b "I would indeed have worse" [that is, no mercy at all].
881b "[May they have] sorrow who show concern [over it]!"
885   The expression is difficult; Skeat (see *References*) says the false eldest brother was "rewarded by being hanged . . . instead of having a purse hang at his girdle"; French and Hale (see *References*) say, more convincingly, that "nought by the purs" means he "did not buy off" the jury.
889b *Assise* here probably means not 'court of law,' but within the phrase 'of the best assise' something equivalent to 'legality.' Hence, the half-line would read "in the best legal manner."

And sithen wedded Gamelyn   a wif bothe good and fair.
They liveden togidere   whil that Christ wolde;
900 And sithen was Gamelyn   graven under molde.   *buried/earth*
And so shall we alle–   may ther no man flee;
God bring us to the joye   that ever shall be.

PART 2

The Breton Lai

Sir Orfeo

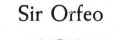

WO fifteenth-century manuscripts exist for *Sir Orfeo* (Harley 3810 and Ashmole 61) and a third (the Auchinleck manuscript) which antedates the two by over a hundred years and which may have been seen by—may, indeed,* have belonged to—Geoffrey Chaucer. The poem is anonymous; its dialect, by no means purely one thing or the other, would localize its poet in the south or, more narrowly as far as the Auchinleck manuscript is concerned, somewhere in the general area around London. Whether the *Orfeo* poet and the *Lai le Freine* poet are one and the same is debatable; the two poems are inextricably associated chiefly because the twenty-four line comment on the Breton *lai* which begins *Le Freine* also appears in the two later manuscripts of *Orfeo*. But *Orfeo* possesses a skillfully contrived accretion of motifs; its artlessness conceals high narrative skill; and it is not a reworking of anything in Marie. Chaucer's "Wife of Bath's Tale" and "Franklin's Tale" aside, it stands as the all-around success among English poems classed as Breton *lais*.

The immediate, or distant, source of *Orfeo* does not exist today and the English poem points to no definite source at all, be it Old French or Celtic or medieval Latin. Yet cumulative indications there are which make editors see behind *Orfeo* an Old French *conte* and behind that a Celtic *lai*. Ultimately, of course, the Orpheus and Eurydice story, known in the Middle Ages through Ovid's *Metamorphoses X* and Virgil's *Georgics IV* (or through reworkings of the pair), provides the seminal motifs: a harper —actually the son of the muse Calliope—whose wife dies of a snake bite ventures into the Lower World to regain her; his music charms the infernal deity into allowing the pair to return to earth provided Orpheus does not look back—but he does (the Lot's wife motif) and thereby loses Eurydice forever. But the Celtic *lai* and the Old French *conte*— certainly the Middle English poem—change matters: Orpheus becomes a king as well as harper; Eurydice dies, not of a snake, but from innocently taking a nap under an unnatural thing, an *ympe-tre*—a tree with grafted branches—thereby giving the king of the (Celtic) other world (*pace* his tendency to abduct the mortally wounded) opportunity to abduct her. Orfeo, unlike his classic counterpart, who goes to seek his spouse straightway, enters a sort of rustic *moniage:* he lives with beasts and off rough herbs and gives over his kingdom (it is at the same time in Middle English in both Thrace and Winchester) to his stewart. In the wilderness, he sees by chance a fairy retinue (reminiscent of the Germanic *wilde Jagd*) and it is curiosity, not specifically the desire to retrieve Eurydice, which prompts him to follow the host into the other world. By chance again, he sees among the beings abducted into the other world his beloved spouse (the Middle English poem calls her Herodis) and by his harping charms the king into promising one specific boon— the return of his wife. And when the pair return to the world of light, there is no mention of looking back. Orfeo must redeem and resume his kingship. A happy ending—the cachet of the Celtic *lai*—occurs when Orfeo in disguise as palmer and harper tests the fidelity of his vice-regent, the stewart, who, along with all his subjects, welcomes him back. With all the good-natured Celtic modifications to the sad classical story, one is prompted to wonder whether any purely English additions are present. There may be and if so, they might derive from the peculiarly English version of the Orfeus story in the Old English translation (usually attributed to or associated with King Alfred) of the *Consolatione Philosophiae* by Boethias, even though in the Old English rendering the Orpheus story is used to illustrate the sin of backsliding into old sins.

Meter and language in *Orfeo* should offer no difficulty. The former is basically iambic and the line four-stress. Feminine rhymes are frequent and lines lacking an unstressed syllable to make up an initial iamb—as in "Traciens withouten no"—are also frequent. For reading aloud one can often used a caesural pause (as noted earlier) where an unstressed syllable is apparently lacking—as in the second line of the couplet "Orfeo most of ony thing / Lovede the gle || of harpyng." For the modern reader, it must be admitted, a number of lines defy analysis and the best one can do is to get through them as gracefully as possible. As for language, inflections are simple, noun plurals being mostly in -(e)s, only occasionally in -en. Infinitives end in e or nothing at all; inflectional suffixes for the present (singular -e/-est/-eth and plural -eth) and for the preterite are more or less standard Middle English. The present participle is either in -ing or -and and the past participle prefixes y. Pronouns are less regular: *I* alternates with *ich, she* with *he* and *hie,* and *they* once with *he* and once with *hie; thou, he, it,* and *ye* are stable.

The high praise usually allotted *Orfeo* is implicit in the foregoing comment; certainly few narrative poems conceal artfullness under such disarming artlessness so well. Unlike *Aethelstan*, it can stand close scrutiny. And one way of indicating the fine craftsmanship is to note its high number of common folklore motifs. There is a musician capable of charming beasts; an abduction and descent into the under- or other world; a period of rustic *moniage*; a rash promise; a return home in disguise; a retainer tested and rewarded for faithfulness. Somehow all fit in and make up the story and leave no rough edges whatsoever.

REFERENCES: Brown and Robbins, No. 3868; *CBEL*, I:151–152; Hibbard, pp. 195–199; Kane, pp. 80–84; Wells, pp. 128–129.—The most recent and best edition of *Sir Orfeo* is that by A. J. Bliss (Oxford 1954), which prints all three manuscripts; a recent detailed study of the sources of *Sir Orfeo*, one which stresses the possible contributions of the Middle English poet to the structure of the piece, is that by J. Burke Severs, "The Antecedents of Sir Orfeo" in *Studies in Medieval Literature in Honor of Professor Albert Croll Baugh*, edited by MacEdward Leach (Univ. of Penn. Press 1961), pp. 187–207.

Orfeo was a king,
In Inglond an heighe lording, *high*
A stalworth man and hardy bo; *both*
Large and curteis he was also. *generous*
5 His fader was comen of King Pluto
And his moder of King Juno,
That sum time were as godes y-hold
For aventours that they dede and told.
Orfeo most of ony thing
10 Lovede the gle of harping.
Siker was every gode harpoure
Of him to have moche honoure.
Himself loved for to harpe
And laide theron his wittes sharpe; *applied*
15 He lernid so ther nothing was *not at all*
A better harper in no plas.
In the world was never man born
That ever Orfeo sat biforn,
And he might of his harping here,
20 He shulde thinke that he were
In one of the joys of Paradis:–
Such joy and melody in his harping is.

5–6 The genealogy has no basis in other literature nor does the association in lines 25 and 26 of Winchester with Thrace.

This king sojournd in Traciens, — *dwelled*
That was a cite of noble defens; — *fortifications*
25 For Winchester was cleped tho — *called/then*
Thraciens withouten no. — *denial*
The king hadde a Quen of priis — *excellence*
That was y-cleped Dame Herodis,
The fairest levedy for the nones — *lady/indeed*
30 That might gon on body and bones,
Full of love and godenisse, — *goodness*
Ac no man may telle hir fairnise. — *but*
Bifell so in the comessing of May, — *beginning*
When miry and hot is the day — *merry*
35 And oway beth wintershours,
And every feld is full of flours,
And blosme breme on every bough — *blossoms/bright*
Overall wexeth miry anough, — *grows/enough*
This ich Quen, Dame Herodis, — *same*
40 Tok two maidens of priis
And went in an undrentide — *morning time*
To play by an orchardside–
To see the floures sprede and spring
And to here the foules sing.
45 They set hem doun all three
Under a fair ympe-tree; — *grafted tree*
And well sone this fair Quene — *very/quickly*
Fell on slepe opon the grene.
The maidens durst hir nought awake,
50 Bot lete hir ligge and rest take.
So she slepe till afternone, — *slept*
That undertide was all y-done. — *until/past*
Ac as sone as she gan awake,
She crid and lothly bere gan make; — *horrible/outcry*
55 She froted hir honden and hir feet — *rubbed*
And crached hir visage–it bled wete. — *scratched/wet*
Hir riche robe hie all to-rett — *tore to pieces*
And was reveysed out of hir wit. — *driven*
The two maidens hir biside
60 No durst with hir no leng abide; — *longer*
Bot urn to the palais full right — *ran/immediately*
And told bothe squier and knight
That her Quen awede wold — *go mad*
And bad hem go and hir at-hold. — *seize*
65 Knightes urn and levedis also, — *ran*
Damisels sexty and mo. — *more*
In the orchard to the Quen hie come — *go*
And her up in her armes nome — *took*
And brought hir to bed atte last
70 And held hir there fine fast. — *very*

Ac ever she held in o cry
And wold up and owy.   *away*
When Orfeo herd that tiding,
Never him nas wers for no thing.
75 He come with knightes tene   *ten*
To chaumber right bifor the Quene
And biheld and said with grete pité,
"O lef lif, what is te,
That ever yete hast ben so stille   *who/quiet*
80 And now gredest wonder shille?
Thy body, that was so white y-core,   *such/excellent*
With thine nailes is all to-tore!   *rent*
Alas, thy rode, that was so red,   *complexion*
Is all wan as thou were ded!
85 And also thine fingers smale   *slender*
Beth all blody and all pale!
Allas! thy lovesum eyghen two   *eyes*
Loketh so man doth on his fo!
A dame, ich biseche, merci!
90 Lete ben all this rewefull cry   *pitiful*
And tell me what thee is and hou
And what thing may thee help now!"
Tho lay she stille atte last
And gan to wepe swithe fast   *very/hard*
95 And said thus the King to,
"Allas, my lord, Sir Orfeo!
Sethen we first togider were,   *since*
Ones wroth never we nere;   *once/at odds*
Bot ever ich have y-loved thee
100 As my lif, and so thou me.
Ac now we mot delen atwo.   *must/part*
Do thy best, for I mot go!"
"Allas," quath he, "forlorn icham!   *I am*
Whider wiltow go and to wham?   *will you*
105 Whider thou gost, ichill with thee,
And whider I go, thou shalt with me."
"Nay, nay, sir, that nought nis,
Ichill thee telle all hou it is: *I shall*
As ich lay this undertide
110 And slepe under our orchardside,
Ther come to me two fair knightes
Wele y-armed all to rightes   *quite/properly*

---

74 "He was never [so] distressed at anything."
78 "O dear life, what is wrong with you!"
80 "And now cries out [so] strangely shrill."
91 "And tell me what is wrong and how."
105 "Whither you go, I shall [go] with you."
107 "No, no, sir, that would not help."

And bad me comen an heighing   *in/haste*
And speke with her lord the King.
115 And ich answerd at wordes bold,   *with*
     I durst nought no I nold.
     They priked oyain as they might drive;
     Tho com her King all so blive   *just as/quickly*
     With an hundred knightes and mo,
120 And damisels an hundred also,
     All on snowewhite stedes.
     As white as milke were her wedes.   *garments*
     I no seighe never yete bifore   *saw*
     So fair creatours y-core.   *excellent*
125 The King hadde a croun on hed.
     It nas of silver no of gold red,
     Ac it was of a precious ston–
     As bright as the sonne it shon.
     And as soon as he to me cam,
130 Wold ich, nold ich, he me nam   *took*
     And made me with him ride
     Opon a palfray by his side
     And brought me to his palais,
     Wele atird in ich ways,
135 And shewed me castels and tours,
     Rivers, forestes, frith with flours,   *woodland*
     And his riche stedes ichon.   *each one*
     And sethen me brought oyain hom   *afterwards/back*
     Into our owhen orchard
140 And said to me thus afterward,
     'Loke, dame, to morwe thatou be   *that you*
     Right here under this ympe-tree
     And than thou shalt with us go
     And live with us ever-mo.
145 And yif thou makest us y-let,   *hindrance*
     Whar thou be, thou worst y-fet,
     And to-tore thine limes all   *torn asunder*
     That nothing help thee no shall;
     And they thou best so to-torn,   *although*
150 Yete thou worst with us y-born.' "   *shall be/carried*
     When King Orfeo herd this cas,   *event*
     "O we," quath he, "allas, allas!   *woe*
     Lever me were to lete my lif
     Than thus to lese the Quen, my wif!"
155 He asked conseil at ich man,

116 "I dared not nor would I."
117 "They rode back as [fast as] they might go."
134 "Well-appointed in every respect."
146 "Wherever you are, you will be fetched."
153 "I would rather lose my life."

Ac no man him help no can.
Amorwe the undertide is come
And Orfeo hath his armes y-nome   *taken*
And wele ten hundred knightes with him,
160 Ich y-armed stout and grim;
And with the Quen wenten he
Right unto that ympe-tree.
They made sheltrom in ich a side
And said they wold there abide
165 And die ther everichon   *every one*
Er the Quen shuld fram hem gon.
Ac yete amiddes hem full right   *straightway*
The Quen was oway y-twight,   *snatched*
With fairy forth y-nome.   *magic/taken*
170 Men wist never wher she was bicome.   *knew/gone*
Tho was ther crying, wepe, and wo!
The King into his chaumber is go
And oft swooned opon the ston   *floor*
And made swiche diol and swiche mon   *lamentation*
                                                        /sorrow

175 That neighe his lif was y-spent;
Ther was non amendement.
He cleped togider his barouns,   *called*
Erls, lordes of renouns.
And when they all y-comen were,
180 "Lordinges," he said, "bifor you here
Ich ordainy min heighe steward   *appoint/high*
To wite my kingdon afterward.   *rule*
In my stede been he shall
To kepe my londes overall.
185 For now ichave my queen y-lore,
The fairest levedy that ever was bore.   *born*
Never eft I nill no woman see.
Into wilderness ichill te   *go*
And live ther ever-more
190 With wilde bestes in holtes hore.   *woods/grey*
And when ye understond that I be spent,   *dead*
Make you than a parlement
And chese you a newe king.
Now doth your best with all my thing!"   *affairs*
195 Tho was ther wepeing in the halle
And grete cry among hem alle.
Unnethe might old or yong   *with difficulty*
For wepeing speke a word with tong.
They kneled adoun all y-fere   *together*
200 And preid him, yif his wille were,

163   "They made on each side a rank of armed men."

That he no shuld nought fram hem go.
"Do way," quath he, "it shall be so."   *enough*
All his kingdom he forsoke;
Bot a sclavin on him he toke.   *pilgrim mantle*
205 He no hadde kirtel no hode,   *hood*
     Shert ne no nother gode.   *goods*
     Bot his harp he tok algate   *at any rate*
     And dede him barfot out atte yate.   *gate*
     No man most with him go.
210 O way, what ther was wepe and wo,   *woe/lamentation*
     When he that hadde been king with croun
     Went so poverlich out of toun!   *wretchedly*
     Thurch wode and over heth   *heath*
     Into the wilderness he geth.
215 Nothing he fint that him is ais,   *finds/comfort*
     Bot ever he liveth in gret malais.   *distress*
     He that hadde y-werd the fowe and gris
     And on bed the purper bis,   *linen*
     Now on hard hethe he lith;   *lies*
220 With leves and gresse he him writh.   *covers*
     He that hadde had castels and tours,
     River, forest, frith with flours,   *woodland*
     Now, they it comency to snewe and frese   *although*
     This King mote make his bed in mese.   *must/moss*
225 He that had y-had knightes of pris
     Bifor him kneland and levedis,
     Now seth he nothing that him liketh,   *sees/pleases*
     Bot wilde wormes by him striketh.   *glide*
     He that had y-had plenté
230 Of mete and drink, of ich deynté,
     Now may he all day digge and wrote,   *dig/grub*
     Er he finde his fille of rote.   *root*
     In somer he liveth by wild frut
     And berien bot gode lite;
235 In winter may he nothing finde
     Bot rote, grases, and the rinde.   *except/bark*
     All his body was oway dwine   *dwindled*
     For missais, and all to-chine.   *hardship*
                                    /chapped

     Lord! who may telle the sore   *pain*
240 This King sufferd ten yere and more!
     His here of his berd, black and rowe,   *hair/rough*
     To his girdel-stede was growe.   *waist*
     His harp, whereon was all his glee,   *pleasure*
     He hidde in an holwe tree.

---

217   "He who had worn the variegated and grey fur."
234   "And berries of little worth."

245 And when the weder was clere and bright,   *weather*
    He took his harp to him well right
    And harped at his owhen wille;
    Into alle the wode the soun gan shille   *resound*
    That alle the wilde bestes that ther beth
250 For joye abouten him they teth.   *gather*
    And alle the foules that ther were   *birds*
    Come and sete on ich a brere
    To here his harping afine,
    So miche melody was therin.   *much*
255 And when he his harping lete wold,   *cease*
    No best by him abide nold.
    He might see him bisides   *near*
    Oft in hot undertides
    The King o fairy with his rout   *fairyland/troop*
260 Com to hunt him all about
    With dim cry and bloweing,   *faint*
    And houndes also with him berking.
    Ac no best they no nome,   *took*
    No never he nist wheder they bicome.
265 And otherwhile he might him see   *at other times*
    As a gret ost by him te   *army/pass*
    Wele atourned ten hundred knightes,   *equipped*
    Ich y-armed to his rightes,   *properly*
    Of cuntenaunce stout and fers,
270 With many desplaid baners,
    And ich his swerd y-drawe hold;
    Ac never he nist whider they wold.   *wither*
    And otherwhile he seighe other thing;   *saw*
    Knightes and levedis com daunceing
275 In quaint atire, gisely,   *elegant/skillfully*
    Quaint pas and softly.   *step*
    Tabours and trumpes yede hem by   *tabors/trumpets
                                                                 /went*

    And all maner menstracy.   *sorts of*
    And on a day he seighe him biside   *saw*
280 Sexty levedis on hors ride,
    Gentil and jolif as brid on ris;   *bird/bough*
    Nought o man amonges hem ther nis.
    And ich a faucoun on hond bere
    And riden on haukin by o rivere;   *a-hawking/a*
285 Of game they founde well gode haunt–   *great/plenty*
    Maulardes, hayroun, and cormeraunt.   *mallards/heron*
    The foules of the water ariseth,

---

253 "To listen to his harping to the end."
256 "No beast would stay by him."
264 "Nor did he ever know where they went."

The faucouns hem wele deviseth; *descry*
Ich faucoun his pray slough. *killed*
290 That seigh Orfeo and lough. *saw/laughed*
"Parfay," quath he, "ther is fair game; *indeed*
Thider ichill, by Godes name.
Ich was y-won swiche werk to see." *accustomed*
  /sport

He aros and thider gan te. *approach*
295 To a levedy he was y-come,
Biheld and hath wele undernome *perceived*
And seth by all thing that it is *sees*
His owhen queen, Dam Herodis.
Yern he biheld hir, and she him eke, *eagerly/also*
300 As noither to other a word no speke. *but*
For messais that she on him seighe, *sorrow/saw*
That had been so riche and so heighe, *exalted*
The teres fell out of her eighe. *eye*
The other levedis this y-seighe
305 And maked hir oway to ride;
She most with him no lenger abide.
"Allas," quath he, "now me is wo!
Why nill deth now me slo! *slay*
Allas, wreche, that I no might
310 Die now after this sight!
Allas! too long last my lif,
When I no dar nought with my wif,
No hie to me, o word speke. *she/one*
Allas, why nill min hert breke!
315 Parfay," quath he, "tide what bitide,
Whider-so this levedis ride,
The selve way ichill streche— *go*
Of lif no deth I me no reche!"
His sclavin he dede on all so spack *quickly*
320 And henge his harp opon his back
And had well gode will to gon— *very/desire*
He no spard noither stub no ston.
In at a roche the levedis rideth *rock*
And he after and nought abideth.
325 When he was in the roche y-go,
Wele three mile other mo,
He com into a fair cuntray,
As bright so sonne on somers day,
Smothe and plain and all grene,

---

292 "Thither I shall [go], in God's name."
314 "Allas, why wont my heart break!"
315 "Indeed," he said, "happen what may."
318 "I do not care about life or death."
322 "He spared neither tree trunk nor stone"—meaning, he hastened.

330 Hille no dale was ther non y-sene.
   Amidde the lond a castel he sighe,   *saw*
   Riche and real and wonder heighe.   *regal/wondrous*
   All the utmast wall   *outer*
   Was clere and shine as cristal.   *bright*
335 An hundred tours ther were about
   Degiselich and bataild stout.
   The butras com out of the diche,   *moat*
   Of rede gold y-arched riche.
   The vousour was avowed all   *vaulting/adorned*
340 Of ich maner divers aumal
   Within ther wer wide wones   *spacious*
                                          /dwellings

   All of precious stones.
   The werst piler on to biholde
   Was all of burnist gold.
345 All that lond was ever light,
   For when it shuld be therk and night,   *dark*
   The riche stones light gonne
   As bright as doth at none the sonne.   *noon*
   No man may telle no thenche in thought   *think*
350 The riche werk that ther was wrought.
   By all thing, him think that it is
   The proude court of paradis.
   In this castel the levedis alight.
   He wold in after, yif he might.   *if*
355 Orfeo knocketh atte gate;
   The porter was redy therate
   And asked what he wold have y-do.   *done*
   "Parfay," quath he, "icham a minstrel, lo!
   To solas thy lord with my glee,   *minstrelsy*
360 Yif his swete wille be."
   The porter undede the yate anon
   And lete him into the castel gon.
   Than he gan bihold about all
   And seighe liggeand within the wall   *lying*
365 Of folk that were thider y-brought
   And thought dede and nare nought.
   Sum stode withouten hade   *head*
   And sum non armes nade,
   And sum thurch the body hadde wounde, *through*
370 And sum lay wode, y-bounde,   *mad*
   And sum armed on hors sete,
   And sum astrangled as they ete,

---

336   "Wonderful and strongly crenelated."
340   "With each sort of various enamel."
347   "The precious stones did shine."
366   "And seemed dead and were not."

And sum were in water adreint,   *drowned*
And sum with fire all forshreint.   *shriveled*
375 Wives ther lay on child-bedde,
 Sum ded and sum awedde;   *insane*
 And wonder fele ther lay bisides,   *very/many*
 Right as they slepe her undertides.
 Eche was thus in this warld y-nome,
380 With fairy thider y-come.
 Ther he seighe his owhen wif,
 Dame Herodis, his lef lif,   *dear/life*
 Slepe under an ympe-tree.
 By her clothes he knewe that it was he.   *she*
385 And when he hadde bihold this mervails alle,
 He went into the Kinges halle.
 Than seighe he ther a seemly sight,   *fair*
 A tabernacle blisseful and bright,   *canopy*
 Therin her maister King sete
390 And her Quen fair and swete.
 Her crounes, her clothes shine so bright,
 That unnethe bihold he hem might.   *scarcely*
 When he hadde biholden all that thing,
 He kneled adoun bifor the King.
395 "O lord," he said, "yif it thy wille were,
 My menstracy thou shust y-here."   *hear*
 The King answerd, "What man artow,   *are you*
 That art hider y-comen now?
 Ich no non that is with me,   *nor/anyone*
400 No sent never after thee.
 Sethen that ich here regny gan,   *since/reign*
 I no fond never so folehardy man
 That hider to us durst wende
 Bot that ichim wald ofsende."   *unless/summon*
405 "Lord," quath he, "trowe full well,   *believe*
 I nam bot a pover menstrel;
 And, sir, it is the maner of us
 To seche many a lordes hous.   *visit*
 They we nought welcom no be,   *although*
410 Yete we mot profery forth our glee."   *must/offer*
 Bifor the King he sat adoun
 And tok his harp so miry of soun   *merry/sound*
 And trempreth his harp, as he wele can,   *tunes*
 And blisseful notes he ther gan   *began*
415 That all that in the palais were
 Com to him forto here,

379–380 "Each had been seized in this world [and] gone thither through enchantment."
399–400 "I nor no one who is with me ever sent for you."

And liggeth adoun to his fete,   *lie*
Hem thenketh his melody so swete.
The King herkneth and sit full stille;
420 To here his glee he hath gode wille.
Gode bourde he hadde of his glee;   *pleasure*
                                                      /minstralsy

The riche Queen al-so hadde he.   *she*
When he hadde stint his harping,   *ceased*
Than said to him the King,
425 "Menstel, me liketh wele thy glee;
Now aske of me what it be,
Largelich ichill thee pay.   *generously*
Now speke, and tow might assay."
"Sir," he said, "ich biseche thee
430 Thatou woldest yive me   *that you/give*
That ich levedy, bright on ble,   *same/complexion*
That slepeth under the ympe-tre."
"Nay," quath the King, "that nought nere!
A sorry couple of you it were,   *ill-matched*
435 For thou art lene, rowe, and black   *rough*
And she is lovesum withouten lack.   *blemish*
A lothlich thing it were forthy   *therefore*
To seen hir in thy compayny."
"O sir," he said, "gentil King,
440 Yete were it a wele fouler thing   *much*
To here a lesing of thy mouthe!   *lie*
So, sir, as ye said nouthe,   *just now*
What I wold asky, have I shold,
And nedes thou most thy word hold."   *by necessity*
445 The King said, "Sethen it is so,   *since*
Take hir by the hond and go.
Of hir ichill thatou be blithe."   *happy*
He kneled adoun and thonked him swithe.   *greatly*
His wif he took by the hond
450 And dede him swithe out of that lond   *quickly*
And went him out of that thede.   *land*
Right as he come, the way he yede.   *went*
So long he hath the way y-nome,   *taken*
To Winchester he is y-come,
455 That was his owhen cité.
Ac no man knew that it was he.
No forther than the tounes ende
For knoweleche he durst wende;   *because of*
                                                       /recognition

---

418 "His melody seems to them so sweet."
428 "Now speak, and you may find out."
433 "No," said the King, "that would not be!"

Bot with a begger, y-bilt full narwe,
460 Ther he took his herbarwe
    To him and to his owhen wif   *for*
    As a minstrel of pover lif;
    And asked tidings of that lond,
    And who the kingdom held in hond.
465 The pouer begger in his cote   *cottage*
    Told him everich a grot–   *bit*
    Hou her Queen was stole owy,
    Ten yer gon, with fairy,   *by/enchantment*
    And hou her King en exile yede,   *went*
470 Bot no man nist in wiche thede;
    And hou the steward the lond gan hold,   *did*
    And other many thinges him told.
    Amorwe, oyain none tide,   *toward/noon*
    He maked his wif ther abide;
475 The beggers clothes he borwed anon
    And heng his harp his rigge opon,   *back*
    And went him into that cité
    That men might him bihold and see–
    Erls and barouns bold,
480 Buriays and levedis him gun bihold.   *burgesses*
    "Lo," they said, "swiche a man!
    How long the here hongeth him opan!   *hair*
    Lo, hou his berd hongeth to his knee!
    He is y-clongen also a tree!"   *shriveled/like*
485 And as he yede in the strete,   *went*
    With his steward he gan mete
    And loude he set on him a crie,
    "Sir steward," he said, "merci!
    Icham an harpour of hethenisse;   *I am
                                                         /heathendom*

490 Help me now in this destresse!"
    The steward said, "Com with me come;
    Of that ichave, thou shalt have some.   *I have*
    Everich gode harpour is welcom me to
    For my lordes love, Sir Orfeo."   *because of*
495 In the castel the steward sat atte mete,   *table*
    And many lording was by him sete.
    Ther were trompours and tabourers,   *drummers*
    Harpours fele and crouders.
    Miche melody they maked alle,
500 And Orfeo sat stille in the halle

459–460 "But with a beggar, housed very poorly, there he took his lodging."
470   "Except no man knew into what country."
487   "And loudly cried out to him."
498   "Many harpers and crowd-players."

And herkneth. When they been all stille,
He toke his harp and tempred shille.   *tuned/sharply*
The blissefulest notes he harped there
That ever any man y-herd with ere.
505 Ich man liked wele his glee.   *minstrelsy*
The steward biheld and gan y-see   *did/perceive*
And knewe the harp als blive.
"Menstrel," he said, "so mot thou thrive,
Where hadestow this harp and hou?
510 I pray that thou me telle now."
"Lord," quath he, "in uncouthe thede   *foreign/land*
Thurch a wildernes as I yede,   *went*
Ther I founde in a dale
With liouns a man to-torn smale,   *by/rent*
515 And wolves him frete with teeth so sharp.   *ate*
By him I fond this ich harp;   *very*
Wele ten yere it is y-go."
"O," quath the steward, "now me is wo!
That was my lord, Sir Orfeo.
520 Allas wreche, what shall I do,
That have swiche a lord y-lore!   *lost*
A way, that ich was y-bore!   *woe*
That him was so hard grace y-yarked
And so vile deth y-marked!"   *allotted*
525 Adoun he fell aswoon to grounde;
His barouns him toke up in that stounde   *moment*
And telleth him hou it geth—
It is no bot of manes deth!
King Orfeo knewe wele by than
530 His steward was a trewe man
And loved him as he aught to do
And stont up and sait thus, "Lo,
Steward, herkne now this thing!
Yif ich were Orfeo the King,
535 And hadde y-suffred full yore   *very/long ago*
In wildernisse miche sore,   *much/sorrow*
And hadde y-won my queen owy   *gotten*
Out of the lond of fairy,
And hadde y-brought the levedy hende   *gracious*
540 Right here to the tounes ende,
And with a begger her in y-nome,
And were myself hider y-come
Poverlich to thee, thus stille,

507   "And straightway recognized the harp."
509   "From where did you get this harp and how?"
523   "That for him such bitter fate was appointed."
528   "There is no remedy for man's death."
541   "And [had] taken her into [the house of] a beggar."

For to assay thy gode wille;   *test*
545 And ich founde thee thus trewe,
    Thou no shust it never rewe–   *should/regret*
    Sikerlich for love or ay   *fear*
    Thou shust be king after my day.
    And yif thou of my deth hadest been blithe,
550 Thou shust have voided also swithe."
    Tho all tho that therin sete   *Then/those*
    That it was King Orfeo underyete,   *perceived*
    And the steward him wele knewe,
    Over and over the bord he threwe
555 And fell adoun to his feet;
    So dede everich lord that ther sete
    And all they said at o crying,   *in/one/cry*
    "Ye beth our lord, sir, and our king!"
    Glad they were of his live.   *life*
560 To chaumber they ladde him als belive   *immediately*
    And bathed him and shaved his berd
    And tired him as a king apert.   *clothed/openly*
    And sethen with gret processioun   *afterwards*
    They brought the Queen into the toun
565 With all maner menstracy.
    Lord, ther was grete melody!
    For joye they wepe with her eighe   *eye*
    That hem so sounde y-comen seighe.
    Now King Orfeo newe coround is
570 And his queen, Dame Herodis,
    And lived long afterward,
    And sethen was king the steward.
    Harpours in Bretaine after than
    Herd hou this mervaile bigan
575 And made herof a lay of gode likeing   *great/delight*
    And nempned it after the King.   *named*
    That lay "Orfeo" is y-hote.   *called*
    God is the lay, swete is the note.
    Thus com Sir Orfeo out of his care.
580 God graunt us alle wele to fare!

---

550 "You should have left immediately."
554 The steward, in his excitement, overturns the trestle tables.
568 "That [they] saw him come so sound."

Sir Launfal

PART from romances by Chaucer and his followers, *Sir Launfal* bears the distinction of being one of the few Middle English romances whose author's name is known. Just before the terminal prayer we are told that Thomas Chestre wrote the tale, but verifiable particulars about the man have failed to appear. Inferences* are that he was native to the southeast of England and a contemporary of Chaucer. The unique copy of *Launfal* (it is in MS Cotton Caligula A ii in the British Museum) is early fifteenth century, but its language is that of the last quarter of the fourteenth and shows some dialect feaures which would localize it in Kent. Chestre may have been the author of two other romances *Octavian* and *Libeaus Desconus*, because the one precedes and the other follows *Launfal* in the MS and both are linguistically and stylistically similar enough to the piece they enclose to be attributable to the author of *Launfal* and hence to Chestre himself. Finally, *Launfal* shows an outsider's admiration for and ignorance of wealth and rank and there is no reason to believe that Chestre was other than a humble and talented minstrel.

The source of Chestre's poem is an earlier anonymous *Sir Landevale*, written in tetrameter couplets and numbering 538 lines: identical rhymes and phrases are too numerous for the dependence of the one on the other to be doubted. *Landevale* takes as its source a *Lai de Lanval* by Marie de France. But Chestre's version is 398 lines longer than *Landevale* and contains material from an anonymous Old French romance *Graelant*. From it Chestre appears to have taken Guinevere's enmity toward Launfal, the incidents of the mayor's daughter, the bringing of gifts to Launfal's lodging, and the disappearance of Gyfre and Blaunchard. Two additional items—the episodes of the tournament at Carlisle and the challenge and defeat of Valentine—can be explained as having their origin in a third source now lost, possibly of Old French origin and existing in analogue form in a tale by Andreas Capellanus. Only the account of Arthur's wooing and the appearance of Arthur's nephews Hugh and John seem to be Chestre's own.

Launfal is one of the twenty-three "tail-rhyme" romances which were written primarily in the fourteenth century and especially in the East Midlands. Unlike the earlier alliterative tales of the West Midlands, these are popular in authorship and appeal. "Tail-rhyme" stanzas show a series of couplets laced together by individual lines based on one rhyme. The *Launfal* stanza (here printed with a break after each sixth line) consists of twelve lines rhyming usually *aabccbddbeeb*, although the patterns *aabaabccbddb* and *aabaaccbccb* appear occasionally. The line with the *b*-rhyme is the "tail-rhyme" line. It frequently tucks away descriptive and otherwise secondary detail and can serve an extranarrative function, for with it the poet can protest the truth of his words "Certain withouten othe", demand attention "Now harkeneth how it was," even indicate sources, although always with disarming vagueness "Thus seid the French tale." For practical purposes it is best to consider the lines in *Launfal* four-stress in the couplets and three-stress in the "tail-rhyme" lines since the number of unaccented syllables per line vary while the number of stresses per line are fairly constant. Although Old French shows examples of "tail-rhyme" structure earlier than Middle English, the tendency to write whole romances in "tail-rhyme" is peculiarly English.

Chestre's language, if one overlooks its few southeastern peculiarities, is not very much different from Chaucer's. Certain orthographic peculiarities exist in the manuscript which here are normalized: the sporadic *d* for *th* and *th* for *d*, for example, and the occasional *w* for *v* and *aw* for *au*. The diphthongs *ey* and *ay* have been left quite as they appear in the manuscript except *y* becomes *i* where correspondence with late fourteenth-century usage permits. Present participles are in *-ing* and second and third person presents in *-st* and *-th*. The past participle (usually in *y-*), the infinitive, and the present and preterit plurals of strong and weak verbs usually lack *-n*. Pronouns are standard late Middle English, *she* being present although *hi* "she" appears in lines 352 and 701. *They, the, thay, ham,* and *hem* have been normalized to *they* and *hem*.

Launfal has been edited ten times since 1800 and the number of editions may in part be a tribute to its charm. The most recent and by all odds the finest critical edition, A. J. Bliss's *Sir Launfal* (London, Nelson, 1960), has much to say about sources, language, and meter, and little in the way of praise for Chestre's talent and taste. Bliss emphasizes the idea that *Launfal's* appeal would be to the shameless wish-fulfillment of the petty tradesman and notes that wealth, power, and physical satisfaction are unalloyed by any selfless and chivalric ideal. He notes further a peculiar bloodthirsty quality: Guenevere is blinded for her pettishness and Launfal not only unhorses all adversaries but slaughters them as well. The strictures are true. We do not feel sympathy with Launfal's predicament as we do with Orfeo's; we miss the genuineness which pervades the love of hero and heroine in *The Squire of Low Degree;* we tend nowadays to impute to generosity such as Launfal's motives of a not altogether disinterested cut. But *Launfal* does not bore as do a number of other romances with higher aims and more adroit technique, the chief reason being that each step in the tale contributes quite naturally to narrative progress and offers as well a distinctive and often surprising motif. The promiscuous Guinevere's niggardliness toward Launfal at her bridal and her ultimate malice toward him when rebuffed somehow make her human as well as nasty. Tryamour's seduction of Launfal via semi-nudity is an uncommon thing in Middle English romance. Arthur's nephews Hugh and John suggest that Launfal has some genial social qualities. The legal proceedings over Launfal's fate have, perhaps only to us, their comic side since they are interrupted by a succession of beautiful damsels whose presence shatters decorum and turns discussion into hot-headed argument.

REFERENCES: Brown and Robbins, No. 567; Billings, pp. 144–153; *CBEL*, I:152; Kane, pp. 34–35; Wells, pp. 131–133.—Bliss's edition (noted above), prints not only *Launfal*, but also *Lanval* and *Landevale* and on pp. 47–52 gives the fullest bibliographic coverage to date, including editions, articles, and background materials.

B̲e doughty Artours dawes   *days*
That helde Engelond in good lawes
   There fell a wondire cas
Of a ley that was ysette,
5 That hight Launval and hatte yette.   *was called*
                                        /is called

   Now herkeneth how hit was!

Doughty Artoure som while   *at one time*
Sojournede in Kardevyle,
   With joye and greet solas,
10 And knightes that were profitable   *worthy*
With Artour of the Rounde Table–
   Nevere noon bettere ther nas!

Sere Perseval and Sere Gawain,
Sir Gyheries and Sir Agrafrain
15   And Launcelet du Lake;

3–4   "There befell a strange event of which a lay was composed."
8   *Kardevyle*, the town of Carlisle in Cumberland.
14   Gaheres and Agravaine, two of Gawain's brothers.

Sir Kay and Sir Ewain,
That well couthe fight in plain — *in the field*
   Bateles for to take. — *engage in*

King Banbooght and King Bos
20 (Of ham ther was a greet los— — *renown*
   Men sawe tho nowhere here make), — *equal*
Sire Galafre and Sir Launfale,
Whereof a noble tale
   Among us shall awake.

25 With Artoure ther was a bachelere,
And hadde y-be well many a yere.
   Launfal for soth he hight.
He gaf giftis largeliche, — *prodigally*
Golde and silvere and clothes riche,
30   To squier and to knight.

For his largesse and his bounté — *gift giving/*
                     generosity
The kinges stuward made was he
   Ten yere, I you plight; — *assure*
Of alle the knightes of the Table Rounde,
35 So large ther nas noone y-founde
   Be dayes ne be night.

So hit befill in the tenthe yere
Marlin was Artours counsalere; — *Merlin*
   He radde him for to wende — *advised*
40 To King Rion of Irlond right
And fette him ther a lady bright, — *fetch*
   Gwenere, his doughtir hende.

So he dede and hom her brought,
But Sir Launfal likede her nought,
45   Ne other knightes that were hende; — *gracious*
For the lady bar los of swich word — *reputation/repor*
That she hadde lemannis under her lord, — *lovers/besides*
   So fele there nas noon ende. — *many*

---

19   *Bos* is King Bors of Gaul and *Banbooght* must be his brother King Ban of Benwich, although the second syllable of the *Launfal* name is a mystery.

22   *Galafre* appears in ME only here, although in OF occasionally as a Saracen name.

40–42   *Rion* is King Ryence of Ireland. In other Arthurian tales, it is Ryence who attacks Leodegen, King of Carmelide and father of Guinevere, and it is to Leodegen's aid that Arthur goes and thus meets his future wife.

42   *Gwenere*, a syncopated form of Guenevere, appears once in the MS as *Gonnore* (164), elsewhere as here.

They were y-wedded, as I you say,
50 Upon a Witsonday,
   Before princes of moch pride.
No man ne may telle in tale
What folk ther was at that bredale   *marriage festival*
   Of countreys fere and wide!

55 No nother man was in halle y-sette
But he were prelat other baronette   *unless/or*
   (In herte is noght to hide).
If they satte noght alle y-like,   *even if*
Hare servise was good and riche,
60   Certein in ech a side.

And whan the lordes hadde ete in the halle
And the clothes were drawen alle,   *table linen*
                                       /removed
   As ye mowe her and lithe,   *harken*
The botelers sentin win   *served*
65 To alle the lordes that were therin,
   With chere bothe glad and blithe.

The Quene yaf giftes for the nones,
Gold and selvere and precious stonis
   Here curtasie to kithe.   *make known*
70 Everich knight she yaf broche other ring,
But Sir Launfal she yaf no thing–
   That grevede him many a sithe.   *time*

And whan the bredale was at ende,
Launfal tok his leve to wende
75   At Artoure the king,
And seide a lettere was to him come
That deth hadde his fadir y-nome–
   He most to his beryinge.

Tho seide King Artour, that was hende,
80 "Launfal, if thou wilt fro me wende,
   Tak with the greet spending,   *costly gifts*
And my sustere sones two–
Bothe they shull with the go
   At hom the for to bring."

---

57   One of many metrical expetives in *Launfal*, this one best rendered perhaps as "No
      reason to hide anything."
78   After auxiliaries, verbs of motion are often omitted, but understood, as is here the
      verb "go."
83   The two nephews are the Hugh and John of line 136; they are peculiar to the
      Launfal poem.

85 Launfal tok leve, withoute fable,   *deceit*
    With knightes of the Rounde Table,
      And wente forth in his journé
    Til he com to Karlyoun,
    To the meyris hous of the toune,   *mayor's*
90   His servaunt that hadde y-be.

    The meyr stod, as ye may here,
    And sawe him come ride up anblere   *ambling*
      With two knightes and other mainé.   *retinue*
    Agains him he hath wey y-nome
95 And seide, "Sire, thou art welcome.
      How farith oure King, tel me?"

    Launfal answerede and seide than,
    "He farith as well as any man
      And elles greet ruthe hit wore.
100 But, Sir Meyr, without lesing,   *deceit*
    I am departid from the King,   *estranged*
      And that rewithe me sore.

    Nether thare no man, benethe ne above,   *nor/need*
    For the King Artours love
105   Onoure me never more.   *esteem/any more*
    But, Sir Meyr, I pray the, par amoure,
    May I take with the sojoure?   *lodging*
      Som time we knewe us yore."   *at one time*
                                        /long ago

    The meyr stod and bethoghte him there
110 What might be his answere
      And to him than gan he sain,
    "Sir, seven knightes han here hare in y-nome
    And ever I waite whan they wil come,
      That arn of Litill Bretaine."   *are*

115 Launfal turnede him self and lough;
    Therof he hadde scorn inough
      And seide to his knightes tweine,

---

88   *Karlyoun*, the town Caeleon-on-Usk in Monmouthshire, sometimes considered the
      site of Camelot.
90   "That had been his [Launfal's] servant."
94   "Toward him he [the mayor] took his way."
99   "Or else it were a great pity."
112–114   "Sir, seven knights have here lodged, and ever I await when they will come
      who are from Brittany." The expected guests are mere excuse; they do not
      materialize.

"Now may ye se, swich is service
Under a lord of litill prise–
120   How he may therof be fain!"

Launfal awayward gan to ride.   *away*
The meyr bad he shuld abide
   And seide in this manere:
"Sir, in a chamber by my orchard side
125 Ther may ye dwelle with joye and pride
   Yif hit your will were."

Launfal anoon rightes,   *at once*
                                            /thereupon

He and his two knightes,
   Sojournede ther in fere.   *together*
130 So savagelich his good he besette   *spent*
   That he ward in greet dette   *fell*
     Right in the ferst yere.

So hit befell at Pentecost
Swich time as the Holy Gost
135 Among mankend gan light,   *descend*
   That Sir Huwe and Sir Jon
   Tok here leve for to gon
     At Sir Launfal the knight.

They seid, "Sir, our robes beth torent,   *torn to pieces*
140 And your tresoure is all y-spent
   And we goth evil y-dight."   *clothed*
Thanne seide Sir Launfal to the knightes fre,
"Tellith no man of my poverté,
   For the love of God Almight!"

145 The knightes answerede and seide tho
   That they nolde him wreye nevir-mo,   *would/betray*
                                              /never

   All this world to winne.
With that word they wente him from
To Glastinbery, bothe two,

118–121 "Now you may see [that] such is the [reward of] service from a lord of little
      value—how grateful he may be thereof." Launfal sarcastically refers to his ex-
      servant as "lord" and the "thereof" probably indicates past favors from Launfal
      which the mayor forgets.
133   Since Hugh and John leave on Pentecost [Whitsunday], the implication is that
      Launfal has been away a year.
147   "[Even] to gain all this world."
149   *Glastinbery*, the town Glastonbury in SW England, although sometimes associ-
      ated with Avelon, is here indicated simply as one of Arthur's residences.

150   Ther King Artoure was inne.   *resident*

The king sawe the knightes hende
And agens ham he gan wende,
   For they were of his kenne.   *kin*
Noon other robes they ne hadde
155 Than they out with ham ladde
   And tho were totore and thinne.   *those*
                                                           /torn to pieces

Than seide Quene Gwenere, that was fel,   *cruel*
"How farith the proude knight Launfel?
   May he his armes welde?"
160 "Ye, madame," saide the knightes than,
"He farith as well as any man,
   And ellis God hit shelde!"

Moche worchip and greet honour
To Gwenere the Quene and King Artoure
165   Of Sir Launfal they telde,   *related*
And seide, "He lovede us so
That he wolde us evir-mo
   At will have y-helde.

But upon a rainy day hit befel
170 An-huntinge wente Sir Launfel
   To chasy in holtes hore;   *hunt/woods*
                                                           /ancient

In oure old robes we yede that day
And thus we beth y-went away,
   As we before him wore."

175 Glad was Artoure the king
That Launfal was in good liking.   *comfort*
   The quene hit rew well sore,
For she wold with all here might
That he hadde be bothe day and night
180   In painis more and more.

Upon a day of the Trinité
A feste of greet solempnité   *festival*

---

159   "Can he still bear arms?"
162   "If otherwise—God prevent it!"
168   "Have retained willingly."
174   A disputed line whose crux is *wore*, either 'wore' or 'were,' either interpretation
        being possible. The sense is probably "[dressed just] as we were in his presence."
180   "In ever greater pains."
181   The "day" could be any one of those in the octave of Trinity Sunday, the first
        Sunday after Pentecost.

In Carlyoun was holde;
Erles and barones of that countré,
85 Ladies and borieies of that cité,   *burgesses*
    Thider come, bothe yongh and olde.

But Launfal, for his poverté,
Was not bede to that semblé.   *invited/gathering*
    Lite men of him tolde.   *little/thought*
90 The meyr to the feste was ofsent;   *invited*
The meyr's doughter to Launfal went
    And axede if he wolde   *asked*

In halle dine with here that day.
"Damesele," he saide, "nay,
95   To dine have I no herte.
Thre dayes ther been agon,   *passed*
Mete ne drinke eet I noon,
    And all was fore povert.   *poverty*

Today to cherche I wolde have gon,
200 But me fautede hosin and shon,   *lacked/stockings*
                                    /shoes*
    Clenly brech and sherte.   *breeches*
And fore defaute of clothinge,
Ne mighte I in the peple thringe.   *press*
    No wonder though me smerte!

205 But o thing, damesele, I pray the:
Sadel and bridel lene thou me   *loan*
    A while for to ride,
That I mighte confortede be
By a launde under this cyté
210   Al in this underntide."   *morning time*

Launfal dighte his courser
Withoute knave other squier.
    He rood with litill pride;
His hors slod and fel in the fen,   *slipped/mud*
215 Wherefore him scornede many men
    Aboute him fere and wide.

Poverly the knight to hors gan spring.   *wretchedly*
For to drive away lokinge,   *dispel/curiosity*

---

185   The MS reads *boriaes*, but the emendation *borieies* is used because closer to the
      ME and OF *burgeis*.
204   "No wonder that I smart," the *though* being absent in modern idiom.
209   "In a park near this city," *Launde* being cognate to MnE "lawn" and meaning
      in ME "forest clearing."

He rood toward the west.
220 The wether was hot the underntide;   *that/morning*
He lighte adoun and gan abide   *dismounted*
Under a fair forest.   *beside*

And for hete of the wedere
His mantel he felde togidere   *folded*
225   And sette him doun to reste.
Thus sat the knight in symplité   *innocence*
In the shadwe under a tre,
Ther that him likede beste.

As he sat in sorow and sore
230 He sawe come out of holtes hore
Gentil maidenes two.
Har kerteles were of Inde-sandel   *gowns*
                                                         /Indian silk
Ylased smalle, jolif, and well.   *laced/narrowly*
                                                         /neatly
Ther might noon gayere go.

235 Hare manteles were of grene felvett,   *velvet*
Y-bordured with gold, right well ysett,   *arranged*
Y-pelured with gris and gro.   *furred/gray*
                                                         /white
Hare heddis were dight well withalle: *coifed*
Everich hadde on a jolif coronall   *coronet*
240   With sixty gemmis and mo.   *more*

Hare faces were whit as snow on downe;
Har rode was red, here eyn were browne.   *complexion*
I sawe nevir non swiche!
That on bare of gold a basin
245 That other a towaile white and fin,   *towel*
Of selk that was good and riche.

Hare kercheves were well shire,   *very/bright*
Arayd with riche golde wire.
Launfal began to siche.   *sigh*
250 They com to him ovir the hoth;   *heath*
He was curteis and agens hem goth
And grette hem mildeliche.   *gently*

250–252 The audience would assume that the maidens, being supernatural, have
   foreknowledge of Launfal's poverty and excellence. His sigh is wistful, perhaps
   also tinged with self-pity.

"Damesels," he seide, "God you se!"
"Sir Knight," they seide, "well the be!
255   Oure lady, Dame Tryamour,
Bad thou shuldest com speke with here
Yif hit were thy wille, sere,
    Withoute more sojour."   *delay*

Launfal hem grauntede curteisliche   *assented*
260 And went with hem mildeliche.
    They werin whit as floure.
And when they come in the forest an high,   *above*
A paviloun y-teld he sigh,   *pitched/saw*
    With merthe and mochel honoure.   *great*

265 The paviloun was wrouth, fore sothe y-wis,   *wrought*
All of werk of Sarsinis.   *Saracens*
    The pomelles of crystal;   *pole knobs*
Upon the toppe an ern ther stode   *eagle*
Of bournede golde riche and goode,   *burnished*
270   Yflorished with riche amall–   *decorated*
                                            /enamel

His eyn were carbonkeles bright,
As the mone they shon anight,
    That spreteth out ovir all.   *spreads*
Alisaundre the conqueroure
275 Ne King Artoure in his most honour
    Ne hadde non swich juell!   *jewel*

He fond in the paviloun
The kinges doughter of Olyroun,
    Dame Triamoure that highte.   *who/was called*
280 Here fadir was King of Fairie
Of Occient, fere and nyie,   *near*
    A man of mochel mighte.

In the paviloun he fond a bed of pris
Y-heled with purpur bis,   *canopied/linen*

253–254   The two conventional greetings amount to "[May] God watch over you"
and "[May] it be well with you."
255   The heroine's name, made up of OF elements meaning 'choice' and 'love' (the
Try- being related to Fr. *trier* 'to choose' rather than to Lat. *tri-* 'three'), appears
in ME again as the name of the hero of the fifteenth century romance *Sir
Triamour*.
278   *Olyroun* was probably—and appropriately—Avalon originally, but reformed here
on the basis of the Ile d'Oléron, an island off the coast of Brittany.
281   *Occient* can be either OF *Occiant*, the name of a Saracen land in OF poetry,
or ME *occient*, a rare word meaning 'the west.'

285   That semilé was of sighte.   *seemly*
      Therinne lay that lady gent
      That aftere Sir Launfal hedde y-sent,
         That lefsom lemede bright.   *delightful one*
                                                   /shone

      For hete her clothes down she dede
290 Almest to here gerdilstede;   *waist*
         Than lay she uncovert.
      She was as whit as lilie in May
      Or snow that sneweth in winteris day–
         He seigh nevere non so pert.   *charming*

295 The rede rose, whan she is newe,
      Agens here rode nes naught of hewe,
         I dar well say in cert.   *with/certainty*
      Here here shon as gold wire;
      May no man rede here atire   *reckon*
300   Ne naught wel thenke in hert.

      She seide, "Launfal, my lemman swete,   *darling*
      Al my joye for the I lete,   *abandon*
         Sweting paramour.   *sweet/lover*
      Ther nis no man in Cristenté   *Christian lands*
305 That I love so moche as the,
         King neither emperoure!"

      Launfal beheld that swete wighth–   *being*
      All his love in her was lighth   *had settled*
         And keste that swete flour   *kissed*
310 And sat adoun her biside
      And seide, "Sweting, what so betide,
         I am to thin honoure."   *service*

      She seide, "Sir Knight, gentil and hende,
      I wot thy stat, ord and ende.   *condition*
                                           /beginning

315   Be naught ashamed of me.   *before*
      If thou wilt truly to me take   *cleave*
      And alle wemen for me forsake,
         Riche I will make the.

      I will the yeve an alner   *purse*
320 Y-mad of silk and of gold cler
         With faire images thre.

---

296   "In comparison with her complexion is [as] nothing in color."
300   "Nor well imagine in [his] heart."

As oft thou puttest the hond therinne,
A mark of gold thou shalt winne
   In wat place that thou be."   *whatever*

325 Also she seide, "Sir Launfal,
   I yeve the Blaunchard, my stede lel,   *loyal*
      And Gyfre, my owen knave;
   And of my armes o pensel,   *banner*
   With thre ermins y-peinted well   *pictured*
330   Also thou shalt have.

   In werre ne in turnement
   Ne shall the greve no knightes dent,   *harm/blow*
      So well I shall the save."
   Than answerede the gantil knight   *gentle*
335 And seide, "Gramarcy, my swete wight,   *thank you/thing*
      No better kepte I have."

   The damesel gan here up sette,   *did/sit herself*
   And bad here maidenes here fette   *fetch*
      To hir hondis watir clere.
340 Hit was y-do without lette.   *delay*
   The cloth was spred, the bord was sette,
      They wente to hare sopere.

   Mete and drink they hadde afin,   *of the best*
   Piement, claré, and Reinish win
345   And elles greet wondyr hit were.
   Whan they had soupeth and the day was gon,
   They wente to bedde and that anon,
      Launfal and she in fere.   *together*

   For play litill they slepte that night,
350 Till on morn hit was day light.
      She badde him arise anon;
   Hi seide to him, "Sir gantil Knight,
   And thou wilt speke with me any wight,   *at any time*
      To a derne stede thou gon.   *secret/place*

---

323 A late fourteenth-century mark would be worth exactly what eight ounces of
     gold would be worth—at any event, a considerable sum.
326–327 Bliss notes that the name *Blaunchard* is probably of Chester's choosing (it
     is an occasional animal name elsewhere in ME) and that *Gyfre* is also his, be-
     ing suggested probably by the name of a dwarf *Guivret* in Chrestien de Troyes'
     Erec.
336 "No better have I received." An obsolete sense "to receive" for keep is attested.
344 *Piement* and *claré* are spiced wines, but in what they differ is unknown.
345 "Or otherwise it were very strange."
352 *Hi,* the older by-form of ME *she.*

355 Well privily I woll come to the
    (No man alive ne shall me se)
      As stille as any stone."
    Tho was Launfal glad and blithe
    (He coude no man his joye kithe)   *make known*
360   And keste here well good won.   *many/times*

    "But of o thing, Sir Knight, I warne the
    That thou make no bost of me
      For no kennes mede.   *kind of*
                             /recompense

    And if thou dost, I warny the before,
365 All my love thou hast forlore!"   *lost*
      And thus to him she seide.

    Launfal tok his leve to wende.
    Gyfre kedde that he was hende   *made known*
      And brought Launfal his stede.
370 Launfal lepte in to the arsoun   *saddle*
    And rood hom to Karlyoun
      In his povere wede.   *clothes*

    Tho was the knight in herte at wille.   *ease*
    In his chaunber he hild him stille   *held*
375   All that underntide.
    Than come ther thorugh the cité ten
    Well y-harneisid men   *equipped*
      Upon ten somers ride.   *pack horses*

    Some with silver, some with golde,
380 All to Sir Launfal hit sholde.
      To presente him with pride
    With riche clothes and armure bright,
    They axede aftir Launfal the knight,
      Whare he gan abide.

385 The yong men wer clothed in inde;   *indigo*
    Gyfre he rod all behinde
      Up Blaunchard whit as flour.
    Tho seide a boy that in the market stod,
    "How fere shall all this good?
390   Tell us, par amour."   *by all means*

    Tho seide Gyfre, "Hit is y-sent
    To Sir Launfal in present   *as a*
      That hath leved in greet doloure."   *misery*

---

380 "Go" must be understood, as also in line 389.

Than seide the boy, "Nis he but a wrecche!   *miscreant*
95 What thar any man of him recche?
    At the meyris hous he taketh sojoure."

At the meyris hous they gon alighte,
And presented the noble knighte
    With swich good as him was sent;
00 And whan the meyr seigh that richesse
And Sir Launfales noblenesse,
    He held himself foule yshent.   *abused*

Tho seide the meyr, "Sir, par charyté,
In halle today that thou wilt ete with me!
05   Yesterday I hadde y-ment   *intended*
And at the feste we wold han be in same   *together*
And y-hadde solas and game,
    And erst thou were y-went.

"Sir Meyr, God foryelde the!   *reward*
10 Whiles I was in my poverté,
    Thou bede me never dine.
Now I have more gold and fe,
That mine frendes han sent me,
    Than thou and alle thine!"

15 The meyr fro shame away yede.   *went*
Launfal in purpure gan him shrede,   *clothe*
    Y-pelured with whit ermine.   *trimmed*
All that Launfal hadde borwith before,   *borrowed*
Gyfre, be taile and be score,
20   Yald hit well and fine.   *repaid*

Launfal helde riche festes.
Fifty feede povere gestes,   *guests*
    That in mischef were.   *distress*
Fifty boughte stronge stedes;
25 Fifty yaf riche wedes   *clothes*
    To knightes and squiere.

---

395   "Why need any man take heed of him?"
404–405   "Sir, for the love of God, would that you might eat in the hall with me
      today!"
408   "But before [I had an opportunity to invite you] you had gone."
419   "According to tally and account." The two nouns, roughly synonymous, re-
      ferred originally to a tally stick on which notches were cut to indicate debts
      and which was split in two, debtor and creditor each taking a half.
422–430   The repetition of the same word at the beginning of a line is the rhetorical
      device anaphora; here each *fifty* must limit the noun at the end of the line.

Fifty rewardede religions;   *members of*
                                               religious orders

Fifty deliverede povere prisouns   *prisoners*
   And made ham quit and shere;
430 Fifty clodede gestours.   *minstrels*
   To many men he dede honours
     In countreys fere and nere.

Alle the lordes of Karlyoun
Lette crie a turnement in the toun
435   For love of Sir Launfel
(And for Blaunchard his good stede)
   To wite how him wold spede   *find out/succeed*
     That was y-made so well.

And whan the day was y-come
440 That the justes were in y-nome,
   They ride out also snell.   *as quickly as*
                                               possible

Trompours gan har hare bemes blowe.   *horns*
The lordes riden out arowe   *in a row*
   That were in that castell.

445 There began the turnement
And ech knight leyd on other good dent   *blows*
   With mases and with swerdes bothe.   *maces*
Me mighte y-se some therfore   *a person/at that*
Stedes y-wonne and some y-lore
450   And knightes wonder wroth.   *enraged*

Sithe the Rounde Table was,   *since*
A bettere turnement ther nas,
   I dare well say for sothe.
Many a lord of Karlioun
455 That day were y-bore adoun,   *thrust down*
   Certain withouten othe.   *oath*

Of Karlyoun the riche constable   *governor*
Rood to Launfal, without fable–   *to make it plain*
   He nolde no lengere abide.
460 He smot to Launfal and he to him;
Well sterne strokes and well grim
   Ther were, in eche a side.   *on every hand*

---

429 "And make them free and clear." *Shere* is the native form contrasting with the
    Scan. cognate *skere* of lines 881 and 915.
440 "On which the jousts were [to be] held."
448 *Some* modifies *stedes* in the following line.

Launfal was ot him yware.   *aware*
Out of his sadell he him bare
165   To grounde that ilke tide.   *very/moment*
And whan the constable was bore adoun,
Gyfre lepte into the arsoun   *saddle*
And awey he gan to ride.

The Erl of Chestere therof seigh;   *looked/on this*
170 For wrethe in herte he was wod neigh   *wrath/near mad*
And rod to Sir Launfale
And smot him in the helm on heigh
That the crest adoun fleigh
    (Thus seid the Frenshe tale).

175 Launfal was mochel of might.
Of his stede he dede him light   *from/caused*
                                                             /to fall

And bare him doun in the dale.
Than come ther Sir Launfal aboute
Of Walshe knightes a greet route,   *Welsh*
180   The numbre I not how fale.   *many*

Than mighte me se sheldes rive,   *one/broken*
Speres tobreste and todrive,   *smashed*
                                                             /splintered

Behinde and ek before.
Thorugh Launfal and his stedes dent   *because of*
185 Many a knight verement   *in truth*
    To ground was y-bore.

So the pris of that turnay
Was delivered to Launfal that day,
    Without oth I swore.
190 Launfal rood to Karlioun
To the meyris hous of the toun,
    And many a lord him before.

And than the noble knight Launfal
Held a feste riche and ryal
195   That leste fourtenight.   *lasted*
Erles and barouns fale   *many*
Semely were sette in sale   *hall*
    And ryally were adight.   *decked out*

---

472 "And struck him on the top of his helmet."
477 "And threw him down on the ground."
484 "Through the blows of Launfal and his steed," the implication being that
     Blaunchard fought along also.

And every day Dame Triamour,
500 She com to Sir Launfal boure   *private room*
    Aday when hit was night.
    Of all that ever were ther tho
    Seigh her non but they two,
        Gyfre and Launfal the knight.

505 A knight ther was in Lumbardie;
    To Sir Launfal hadde he greet envie–
        Sir Valentine he highte.
    He herde speke of Sir Launfal,
    How that he couth justy well
510   And was a man of mochel mighte.

    Sir Valentine was wondere strong;
    Fiftene feet he was longe.   **tall**
        Him thoughte he brente brighte
    But he mighte with Launfal pleye
515 In the feld, betwene ham tweye
        To justy other to fighte.

    Sir Valentine sat in his halle;
    Hiss messengere he let y-calle   *had/called*
        And seide he moste wende
520 To Sir Launfal, the noble knight,
    That was y-holde so michel of might.
        To Bretaine he wolde him sende.

    "And sey him, fore love of his lemman,
    If she be any gantile woman,
525   Courteis, fre, other hende,
    That he come with me to juste
    To kepe his harneis from the ruste,   *armor*
        And elles his manhod shende."

    The messengere is forth y-went
530 To do his lordis commaundement.
        He hadde winde at wille.
    Whan he was over the water y-come,
    The way to Sir Launfal he hath y-nome
        And grette him with wordes stille.

---

501   "Every day" of line 499 makes *aday* in the sense of each day questionable;
     "during the time when it was night" seems the best solution.
513–514   "It seemed to him he would consume himself utterly unless he were able to
     contend with Launfal."
528   "Or else disgrace his manhood."

535 And seid, "Sir, my lord, Sir Valentine,
   A noble werrour and queinte of ginne,   *clever/stratagem*
      Hath me sent the tille
   And praythe the, for thy lemanes sake,
   Thou shuldest with him justes take."   *undertake*
540   Tho lough Launfal full stille.

And seide, as he was a gentil knight,
   Thilke day a fourtenight,
      He wold with him play.   *joust*
   He yaf the messengere, for that tiding,
545 A noble courser and a ring   *charger*
      And a robe of ray.   *striped cloth*

Launfal tok leve at Tryamoure,
   That was the bright berde in boure,   *lady*
      And keste that swete may.   *maid*
550 Thanne seide that swete wight,   *thing*
   "Dreed the no thing, Sir gentil Knight!
      Thou shalt him sle that day."

Launfal nolde nothing with him have
   But Blaunchard his stede and Gyfre his knave,
555   Of all his faire mainé.   *from/retinue*
   He shipede and hadde wind well good
   And wente over the salte flod
      Into Lumbardie.

Whan he was ovir the watir y-come
560 Ther the justes shulde be nome
      In the cité of Atalie,
   Sir Valentin hadde a greet ost,   *host*
   And Sir Launfal abatede here bost   *lessened/boasting*
      With litil companie.

565 And whan Sire Launfal was y-dight   *ready*
   Upon Blaunchard, his stede light,
      With helm and spere and shelde,
   All that sawe him in armes bright
   Seide they sawe nevir swich a knight,
570   That him withe eyen behelde.

Tho ride togidere thes knightes two

---

542   "Two weeks from that very day."
561   *Atalie*, a city in the OF romance *Otinel*, where it is also in Lombardy and
     reputedly built by Saracens.

That hare shaftes tobroste bo   *shattered/both*
    And to*sh*iverede in the felde.   *splintered*
Another cours todgedere they rod
575 That Sir Launfal helm of glod,   *slipped off*
    In tale as hit is telde.

Sir Valentin lo*u*gh and hadde good game.
Hadde Launfal never so moche shame
    Beforhond in no fight.
580 Gyfre kedde he was good at nede   *made known*
And lept upon his maistris stede–
    No man ne se*i*gh with sight.

And er than thay togedere mette,
His lordes helm he on sette,
585   Faire and well adight.   *arranged*
Tho was Launfal glad and blithe
And thonkede Gyfre many si*the*   *times*
    For his dede so mochel of might.

Sir Valentine smot Launfal so
590 That his sheld fel him fro,
    Anoon right in that stounde.   *moment*
And Gyfre the sheld up hente
And brou*gh*te hit his lord to presente
    Ere hit cam *d*oune to grounde.

595 Tho was Launfal glad and blithe
And rode agen the thridde si*the*,
    As a knight of mochel mounde.   *strength*
Sir Valentine he smot so *d*ere   *fiercely*
That hors and man bothe deed **were,**
600   Groning with grisly wounde.

Alle the lordes of Atalie
To Sir Launfal hadde greet envie   *hostility*
    That Valentine was y-slawe.
And swore that he shold die
605 Er he wente out of Lumbardie
    And be hongede and todrawe.   *dismembered*

Sir Launfal braide out his fachon,   *whipped/sword*
And as light as dew he leide hem doune
    In a litil drawe.   *time*
610 And whan he hadde the lordes slain,
He wente agen in to Bretain
    With solas and with plawe.   *joy*

The tiding com to Artoure the King
Anon without lesing   *falsification*
615   Of Sir Launfales noblesse.
Anon he let to him sende
That Launfal shuld to him wende
    At Seint Jonis Masse.

For King Artoure wold a feste holde
620 Of erles and of barouns bolde,
    Of lordinges more and lesse.
Sir Launfal shud be stuard of halle
For to agie his gestes alle,   *handle*
    For couthe of largesse.
625 Launfal toke leve at Tryamoure
For to wende to King Artoure,
    His feste for to agie.
Ther he fond merthe and moch honour,
Ladies that wer well bright in boure,
630   Of knightes greet companie.

Fourty dayes leste the feste,   *lasted*
Riche, ryal, and honeste.   *decent*
    What help hit for to lie!
And at the fourty dayes ende,
635 The lordes toke har leve to wende,
    Everich in his partie.

And aftir mete Sir Gawein,
Sir Gyeries and Agrafain,
    And Sir Launfal also
640 Went to daunce upon the grene   *lawn*
Under to toure ther lay the Quene
    With sixty ladies and mo.

To lede the daunce Launfal was set.   *appointed*
For his largesse he was lovede the bet   *better*
645   Certain of alle tho.
The Quene lay out and beheld hem alle.   *leaned*
"I se," she seide, "daunce large Launfalle.
    To him than will I go.

---

616   The MS reads "a let," where *a* is probably an unstressed form of *he*; the mean-
        ing is "Immediately he had sent to him that Launfal should come to him."
618   If the birthday of John the Baptist is meant, the "feste" would fall toward the
        end of June.
624   "Because well-versed in magnanimity."
636   "Each to his [own] home area."

Of alle the knightes that I se there,
650 He is the faireste bachelere.
    He ne hadde never no wif.
Tide me good other ille,   *betide*
I will go and wite his wille.   *know*
    I love him as my lif!"

655 She tok with here a companie,
The fairest that she mighte aspie–
    Sixty ladies and fif–
And wente hem doun anon rightes,   *straightway*
Ham to pley among the knightes   *sport*
660   Well stille withouten strif.   *very/quietly/fuss*

The Quene yede to the formeste ende   *at/very front*
Betwene Launfal and Gawein the hende,   *gracious*
    And after here ladies bright.
To daunce they wente alle in same.   *together*
665 To se hem play, hit was fair game,   *pure joy*
    A lady and a knight.

They hadde menstrales of moch honours,
Fidelers, citolirs, and trompours,   *citole players*
        /trumpeters

    And elles hit were unright.
670 There they playde, for sothe to say,
After mete the someris day
    All-what hit was neigh night.   *until*

And whanne the daunce began to slake,   *abate*
The Quene gan Launfal to counsel take   *began*
        /in confidence

675   And seide in this mainere:
"Certainliche, Sire Knight,
I have the lovid with all my might
    More than this seven yere.

But that thou lovie me,
680 Certes I die fore love of the,   *unless*
    Launfal, my lemman dere."   *darling*
Than answerede the gentil knight,
"I nell be traitoure day ne night,   *will not*
    Be God, that all may stere!   *control*

685 She seide, "Fi on the, thou coward!
Anhongeth worth thou hie and hard!   *hanged/shall you*
        be/high

    That thou evir were ybore!

That thou livest, hit is pité!
Thou lovist no woman ne no woman the–
690 Thou were worthy forelore!"   *fittingly*
                                                    /destroyed

The knight was sore ashamed tho;
To speke ne mighte he forgo   *decline*
   And seide the Quene before,
"I have loved a fairir woman
695 Than thou evir leidest thin ey upon
   This seven yere and more.

Hire lothlokste maide withoute wene   *ugliest/doubt*
Mighte bet be a quene   *better*
   Than thou, in all thy live!"
700 Therefore the Quene was swithe wroth;   *very/angry*
She taketh hire maidenes and forth hi goth
   Into here tour also blive.   *as fast as possible*

And anon she ley doun in her bedde.
For wrethe, sik she hire bredde
705 And swore, so moste she thrive,
She wold of Launfal be so awreke   *avenged*
That all the lond shuld of him speke
   Withinne the dayes fife.

King Artour com fro huntinge
710 Blithe and glad in all thinge.   *every/way*
   To his chambere than wente he.
Anoon the Quene on him gan crie,
"But I be awreke, I shall die!   *avenged*
   Min herte will breke athre!   *into three*

715 I spak to Launfal in my game,   *sport*
And he besofte me of shame–   *besought*
   My leman fore to be.
And of a leman his yelp he made,   *boast*
That the lothlokest maide that she hadde
720 Might be a quene above me!"

King Artour was well wroth
And be God he swor his oth   *oath*
   That Launfal shuld be slawe.   *slain*
He went aftir doughty knightes
725 To bringe Launfal anoon rightes   *immediately*
   To be hongeth and to drawe.   *dismembered*

---

704 "Out of anger she made herself sick."
705 "And swore, if she were to live at all."

The knightes softe him anoon,   *sought*
But Launfal was to his chaumber gon
   To han hadde solas and plawe.
730 He softe his leef, but she was lore   *dear one/lost*
As she hadde warnede him before.
   Tho was Launfal unfawe!   *unhappy*

He lokede in his alnere,   *purse*
That fond him spending all plenere   *supplied/in full*
735 Whan that he hadde nede.
And ther nas noon, for soth to say;
And Gyfre was y-ride away
   Up Blaunchard, his stede.

All that he hadde before y-wonne,
740 Hit malt as snow agens the sunne,   *melted*
   In romance as we rede;
His armur, that was whit as floure,
Hit becom of blak coloure.
   And thus than Launfal seide:

745 "Alas," he seide, "my creature,   *darling*
How shall I from the endure,   *away from*
   Sweting Tryamoure?   *beloved*
All my joye I have forelore   *lost*
And the—that me is worst fore—
750 Thou blissful berde in boure!"   *delightful/lady*

He bet his body and his hedde ek   *beat/head*
And cursede the mouth that he with spek
   With care and greet doloure;
And for sorrow in that stounde   *moment*
755 Anon he fell aswowe to grounde.   *aswoon*
   With that come knightes foure

And bond him and ladde him tho
(Tho was the knighte in doble wo!)
   Before Artoure the King.
760 Than seide King Artoure,
  "File atainte traitoure,   *vile/guilty*
   Why madest thou swiche yelping?   *boasting*

That thy lemanes lothlokest maide
Was fairer than my wif thou seide.

---

729   "In order that he might have joy and sport."
749   "And you—that for me is the worst."

765   That was a foul lesinge!
And thou besoftest here before than
  That she shold be thy leman–
    That was misproud likinge!"   *arrogant/desire*

  The knight answerede with egre mode,   *angry*
770 Before the King ther he stode,
    The Quene on him gan lie.
  "Sithe that I evere was yborn,   *since*
  I besofte her here beforn   *besought of*
    Nevir of no folie.

775 But she seide I nas no man,
  Ne that me lovede no woman
    Ne no womannes companie.
  And I answerede her and saide
  That my lemannes lothlekest maide
780   To be a quene was bettere worthie.

  Certes, lordinges, his it so.   *indeed*
  I am aredy for to do
    All that the court will loke."   *ordain*
  To say the soth, without les,   *deception*
785 All togedere how hit was,
    Twelf knightis were drive to boke.

  All they seide ham betwene,   *among*
                                            themselves

  That knewe the maners of the Quene
    And the queste toke,   *inquiry*
                                           /undertook

790 The Quene bar los of swich a word
  That she lovede lemanes without her lord.
    Har nevir on hit foresoke.

  Therfor they seiden alle
  Hit was long on the Quene and not on Launfal.   *fault of*
795   Therof they gonne him skere;   *acquit*

784–786   The exact meaning is debatable. Some editors tend to overlook the obvious fact that lines 784 and 785 may simply be the poet asserting the veracity of his tale and interpret them as an introductory phrase of purpose, rendering them in such words as "In order to arrive indisputably at the truth as to how things stood"; they further interpret line 786 either as "Twelve knights had to swear an oath" or as "Twelve knights had to consult books," the latter being more likely since the knights seem to be adjudicators rather than witnesses.
787–792   "They all said among themselves who knew the habits of the Queen and [who] understood the inquest [that] the Queen bore reputation of such a kind that she had lovers in addition to her lord. Not one of them denied it."

And if he mighte his leman bringe,   *provided that*
That he made of swich yelpinge,   *boasting*
   Other the maidenes were

   Brightere than the Quene of hewe,
800 Launfal shuld be holde trewe
      Of that in all manere.   *by that*
   And if he mighte not bringe his leef,   *lover*
   He shuld be hongede as a theef,
      They seiden all in fere.   *in unison*
805 All in fere they made proferinge   *proposal*
   That Launfal shuld his leman bringe.
      His heed he gan to laye;
   Than seide the Quene, without lesinge,
   "Yif he bringeth a fairere thinge,
810   Put out my eyn gray!"

   Whan that waiour was take on hond,   *wager/taken up*
   Launfal therto two borwes fonde,   *pledges*
      Noble knightes twain,
   Sire Perceval and Sir Gawain.
815 They were his borwes, soth to sain,
      Till a certain day.   *appointed*

   The certain day, I you plight,   *promise*
   Was twelfe moneth and fourtenight
      That he shuld his leman bringe.
820 Sir Launfal, that noble knight,
   Greet sorow and care in him was light.   *arisen*
      His hondis he gan wringe.

   So greet sorowe him was upan,
   Gladliche he lif he wold a forgon
825   In care and in marninge.   *mourning*
   Gladliche he wold his heed forego.
   Everich man therfore was wo
      That wiste of that tidinge.

   The certain day was neighing;   *approaching*
830 His borowes him brought befor the King.
      The King recordede tho
   And bad him bring his leef in sight.   *dear one*

---

798   "Or the maidens [who] were."
807   "He pledged his head."
818   "Was [to be at the end of] a year and two weeks."
824   A is here an unstressed form of *have*.
831   *Recordede*, an awkward word in this context, probably means that the King's
      own words began the inquest.

Sir Launfal seide that he ne might–
Therfore him was well wo.

835 The King commaundede the barouns alle
To yeve jugement on Launfal
 And dampny him to slo.   *condemn/be slain*
Than saide the Erl of Cornewaile,
That was with ham at that counceile,
840 "We willith naught do so.

Greet shame hit wer us alle upon
For to dampny that gantilman
 That hath be hende and fre.
Therfore, lordinges, doth by my rede;   *advice*
845 Oure King we willith another wey lede:
 Out of lond Launfal shall fle."

And as they stod thus spekinge,
The barouns sawe come ridinge
 Ten maidenes bright of ble.   *fair of face*
850 Ham thoughte they were so bright and shene
That the lothlokest, without wene,   *doubt*
 Hare quene than mighte be.

Tho seide Gawain, that corteis knight,
"Launfal, brothir, drede the no wight.   *not at all*
855 Here cometh thy leman hende."
Launfal answerede and seide y-wis,   *indeed*
"Non of ham my leman nis,
 Gawain, my lefly frende!"   *devoted*

To that castel they wente right;
860 At the gate they gonne alight.
 Before King Artoure goone they wende
And bede him make aredy hastily   *ready*
A faire chambere for here lady,
 That was come of kinges kende.   *kin*

865 "Ho is your lady?" Artoure seide.   *who*
"Ye shull y-wite," seide the maide,   *know*
 "For she cometh ride."   *riding*
The King commaundede for here sake
The fairist chaumber for to take   *be prepared*
870 In his palis that tide.

And anon to his barouns he sente
For to yeve jugemente
 Upon that traitour full of pride.

The barouns answerede anon right
875 "Have we sein the maidenes bright,
   We shull not longe abide."

A newe tale they gonne tho,
Some of wele and some of wo,
   Har lord the King to queme.   *please*
880 Some dampnede Launfal there
And some made him quit and skere.   *free/blameless*
   Hare tales were well breme.   *fierce*

Tho saw they other ten maidenes bright,   *another*
Fairire than the other ten of sight,   *in/appearance*
885   As they gone him deme.
They rid upon joly moiles of Spaine   *mules*
With sadel and bridel of Champaine,
   Hare lorains light gonne leme.   *harness/brightly*
                             /gleam

They were y-clotheth in samit tire;   *samite/attire*
890 Ech man hadde greet desire
   To se hare clothinge.
Tho seide Gawain, that curtaise knight,
"Launfal, here cometh thy swete wight,
   That may thy bote bringe."   *salvation*

895 Launfal answerede with drery thought
And seide, "Alas, I knowe hem nought
   Ne non of all they of springe."
Forth they wente to that paleis
And lighte at the hie deis   *dismounted/high*
                             /dais

900   Before Artoure the Kinge.

And grette the King and Quene ek   *too*
And o maide this wordes speke   *these*
   To the King Artoure:
"Thin halle agraide and hele the walles   *prepare/cover*
905 With clothes and with riche palles   *cloths/drapes*
   Agens my lady Tryamoure."   *for the arrival of*

The King answerede bedene,   *at once*
"Well come, ye maidenes shene,   *beautiful*

875–876 Context seems to suggest "[Once] we have seen the radiant maidens, we
      shall no longer tarry," although they do not immediately make up their minds
      one way or the other since in the following stanza they fall into vigorous dispute.
885 "As they were passing judgment on him."
897 "Nor any one of all [those] they come from;" the MS reads *the*, which does
      not make sense.

Be oure lord the Savioure! *by*
910 He commaundede Launcelet du Lake to bringe hem in fere *together*
In the chamber there hare felawes were,
With merthe and moche honoure.

Anon the Quene supposed gile– *suspected/guile*
That Launfal shuld in a while
915 Be y-made quit and skere *free/clear*
Thorough his lemman that was comminge.
Anon she seide to Artoure the King,
"Sire, curtais if thou were,

Or if thou lovedest thin honoure,
920 I shuld be awreke of that traitoure *avenged*
That doth me changy chere.
To Launfal thou shuldest not spare.
Thy barouns driveth the to bismare– *humiliation*
He is hem leef and dere!"

925 And as the Quene spak to the King,
The barouns seigh come ridinge *saw*
A damesele alone
Upon a white comely palfrey.
They saw nevere non so gay
930 Upon the grounde gone:

Gentil, jolif as brid on bowe, *bird/bough*
In all manere faire y-nowe
To wonie in wordly wone. *dwell/earthly
/dwelling*

The lady was bright as blosme on **brere**, *briar*
935 With eyen gray, with lovelich chere. *appearance*
Her leire light shone. *countenance*

As rose on ris here rode was red. *twig/complexion*
The here shon upon here hed
As gold wire that shinith bright.
940 She hadde a crounne upon here molde *head*
Or riche stones and of golde
That lofsom lemede light. *beautifully
/gleamed*

The lady was clad in purpere palle, *cloth*
With gentil body and middil small, *slender*

---

910   Bliss explains the metrical irregularity of the line as being due to the scribe's sub-
        stitution of Lancelot, popular in his time, for an original Gawain, popular in
        earlier tradition.
921   "Who makes me change countenance"; but whether blushing with shame,
        flushing with anger, or losing composure is meant is not clear.

945 That semely was of sight.
Her mantil was furrid with white ermin,   *trimmed*
Y-reversid jolif and fin;   *lined*
 No richere be ne might.

Her sadel was semily set;   *seemly/adorned*
950 The sambus were grene felvet   *saddle-cloths*
                /velvet
 Y-painted with imagerie.   *pictures*
The bordure was of belles
Of riche gold and nothing elles
 That any man mighte aspie.

955 In the arsouns before and behinde   *saddle-bows*
Were twey stones of Inde,   *India*
 Gay for the maistrie.   *brilliant*
                /exceedingly
The paitrelle of her palfraye   *breast-trappings*
Was worth an erldome stoute and gaye, *magnificent*
960 The best in Lumbardie.

A gerfaucon she bar on here hond.   *gyrfalcon*
A softe pas here palfray fond   *slow/pace/went*
 That men here shuld beholde.
Thorugh Karlyoun rod that lady;
965 Twey white grehoundis ronne hire by;
 Hare colers were of golde.   *collars*

And whan Launfal sawe that lady,
To alle the folk he gon crie an hy,   *on/high*
 Bothe to yonge and olde,
970 "Here," he seide, "comith my laman swete!
She mighte me of my balis bete,   *misfortunes/cure*
 Yef that lady wolde."

Forth she wente into the halle,
There was the Quene and the ladies alle *there where*
975 And also King Artoure.
Here maidenes come agens here right– *toward*
To take here stirop whan she light–
 Of the lady Dame Tryamoure.

She dede of here mantil on the flet   *took off/floor*
980 That men shuld here beholde the bet *better*
 Withoute a more sojoure.   *further/delay*
King Artoure gan here faire grete

---

964 *Karlyon* is here an error for *Kardevyle* "Carlisle."

And she him again with wordes swete *in turn*
   That were of greet valoure. *courtesy*

985 Up stod the Quene and ladies stoute *stately*
   Her for to beholde all aboute
     How evene she stod upright. *straight*
   Than were they with here also donne
   As is the mone agen the sonne,
990   Aday whan hit is light.

Than seide she to Artour the King,
   "Sir, hidir I com for swich a thing: *hither*
     To skere Launfal the knight– *clear*
   That he never in no folie
995 Besofte the Quene of no drurie *shameful love*
   By dayes ne be night.

Therfor, Sir King, good kepe thou mine:
   He bad naught here, but she bad him
     Here leman for to be;
000 And he answerede here and seide
   That his lemannes lothlokest maide
     Was fairire than was she."

King Artoure seide withouten othe, *beyond a doubt*
   "Ech man may y-se that is sothe: *perceive*
005   Brightere that ye be."
   With that, Dame Tryamour to the Quene geth
   And blew on here swich a breth
     That never eft might she se.

The lady lep an hire palfray
010 And bad hem alle have good day–
     She nolde no lengere abide.
   With that com Gyfre all so prest *at once*
   With Launfalis stede out of the forest
     And stod Launfal beside.

015 The knight to horse began to springe
   Anon without any letting *delay*
     With his lemman away to ride.
   The lady tok here maidenis achon *each one*
   And wente the way that she hadde er gon
020   With solas and with pride.

988–990 "Then were they in comparison with her just as dark as the moon is in
      comparison with the sun during the time when it is light."
997   "Therefore, Sir King, take good heed of my words."

The lady rod thorugh Kardevyle
Fere in to a jolif ile,   *far/isle*
   Oliroun that highte.
Every yere upon a certain day
1025 Me may here Launfales stede nay   *a person/neigh*
   And him se with sight.

He that will ther axsy justus   *demand/jousts*
To kepe his armes fro the rustus   *rust*
   In turnement other fight
1030 Thare he never forther gon: *need/further*
Ther he may finde justes anon
   With Sir Launfal the knight.

Thus Launfal withouten fable,   *for a truth*
That noble knight of the Rounde Table,
1035   Was take in to fairie.   *enchanted land*
Sethe saw him in this lond no man   *since then*
Ne no more of him telle I ne can
   For sothe withoute lie.

Thomas Chestre made this tale
1040 Of the noble knight Sir Launfale,
   Good of chivalrie.
Jhesus, that is Heveneking,
Yeve us alle His blessing
   And His Modir Marie. AMEN
                    EXPLICIT LAUNFAL

1042–44   "May Jesus, who is heaven's king, and His mother Mary give us all their
          [lit., his] blessing."

Lay Le Freine

HE Middle English *Lay le Freine* is notable for two
features. Its first twenty-two lines give an excellent
definition of the genre Breton *lai* (they also appear
almost verbatim at the beginning of the Harley and
Ashmole manuscripts of *Sir Orfeo*, although not in
the Auchinleck manuscript, which is the basis of the
Orfeo version here); and its various motifs are those
which one would associate more readily with *fabliaux* than with Breton
lais, because here nothing really miraculous occurs and the locale is
definitely feudal western Europe and not a Celtic never-never-land. It
is a rather faithful translation of the third *lai* by Marie de France
and, with the exception of *Sir Launfal*, is the only extant Middle
English poem quite clearly deriving from Marie. Unfortunately the
Middle English version is defective; it lacks lines 121–133 and 341–408; but
these were supplied in 1810 by Henry William Weber in his *Metrical
Romances* from Marie's original. His lines appear here since his virtuosity
in translating the Old French into a counterfeit Middle English give us
the illusion of possessing *Le Freine* intact.

The sole copy of *Le Freine* is in the Advocates Library, Edinburgh;
it is in the Auchenleck manuscript, now designated Advocates 19.2.1, and
dated about 1330, give or take some twenty years. Its language is not
Northern nor west Midland, but Southern with some east Midland features which make it seem not very distant from Chaucer's, although less
sophisticated and more archaic. No editor has found evidence to date
the composition of the poem precisely, but it cannot have been written
much before the possible date of the manuscript itself. The prologue,
which appears in the two *Orfeo* manuscripts, is not in Marie's poem and
may be the English poet's creation. It suggests two things—that *Le Freine*
was written before *Sir Orfeo* and that both were written by the same
Middle English poet. Neither view can be convincingly demonstrated
nor completely disproved.

Le Freine progresses with the wrong-headed logic often attributed to
children. If a mother bears two children at the same time, it would seem

logical that each has a different father. The idea is current in much medieval folk literature; it is in the original of the Middle English poem, Marie's *Le lai del Fraisne*, which was written before 1190. But just what Marie's source was is not known; presumably it was then a common folk idea. It occurs, for example, in the late fourteenth century poem *Chevalere Assigne*, written in Middle English, but ultimately of Old French origin: here Beatrice, wife of King Oryens, declares a multiple birth adulterous and afterwards bears six children at one birth. The next move of such an unfortunate mother is also logical: to avoid scandal she must expose one or more of her children. Exposed children, of course, are always found and brought up by nuns, hermits, or other kind-hearted people. The final problem for the storyteller is to solve the ultimate recognition problem between mother and grown offspring. In *Le Freine*, the solution is typical: the girl, once mature, becomes the mistress of a young lord who eventually must marry someone else—someone with wealth and rank. The young lady chosen for marriage turns out to be the sister of the exposed child, recognition being triggered by the mother's catching sight of the cloak in which her rejected child had once been wrapped.

The version of *Le Freine* which follows appears pretty much as it does in Wattie's edition of the poem. No normalization nor regularization has been made because the language is not so primitive as that in *Horn* or *Havelok* nor so lexically varied as that in *Gamelyn* or *The Squire of Low Degree*. And if the original language were altered, then Weber's lines would also have to be altered and would then appear less of a tour de force than they actually are.

REFERENCES:

Brown and Robbins, No. 3869; *CBEL*, I:151; Hibbard, pp. 294–300; Kane, pp. 46–47; Wells, pp. 126–127. The best critical edition is Margaret Wattie, *The Middle English Lai le Fraine* (*Smith College Studies in Modern Languages* X, 3 [April 1929], xxii + 27 pp.), which also contains a bibliography (pp. xx–xxii) and prints the Middle English verses composed by Weber. The romance *Chevelere Assigne* is in French and Hale, pp. 859–873. Marie's *Le lai del Fraisne*, used occasionally in the following annotations, is in Karl Warnke, *Die Lais der Marie de France*, 3rd ed. (Halle: Niemeyer, 1925), pp. 54–74.

W e redeth oft and findeth y-write–
And this clerkes wele it wite–   *scholars/know*
Layes that ben in harping

---

2 *This*, here and in the following lines, "these."

Ben y-founde of ferli thing.
5 Sum bethe of war and sum of wo,   *war*
  And sum of joie and mirthe also,
  And sum of trecherie and of gile,
  Of old aventours that fel while;   *occurred/once*
  And sum of bourdes and ribaudy,   *jests/ribaldry*
10 And mani ther beth of fairy.
  Of al thinges that men seth,   *relate*
  Mest o love for sothe thai beth.   *most*
  In Breteyne bi hold time   *Brittany/olden*
  This layes were wrought, so seith this rime.
15 When kinges might our y-here   *anywhere/hear*
  Of ani mervailes that ther were,
  Thai token an harp in gle and game,   *mirth/sport*
  And maked a lay and gaf it name.
  Now of this aventours that weren y-falle
20 I can tel sum, ac nought alle.   *but/not*
  Ac herkneth, lordinges, soth to sain,   *truth*
  Ichil you telle Lay le Frayn.

    Bifel a cas in Breteyne
  Whereof was made Lay le Frain.
25 In Ingliche for to tellen ywis
  Of an asche for sothe it is,   *ash tree*
  On ensaumple fair with alle   *an/example*
  That sum time was bifalle.
  In the West Cuntre woned tvay knightes,   *dwelled*
30 And loved hem wele in al rightes;   *each other*
  Riche men in her best liif,
  And aither of hem hadde wedded wiif.
  That o knight made his levedi milde   *one/lady*
  That she was wonder gret with childe.   *very*
35 And when hir time was comen tho,   *then*
  She was deliverd out of wo.
  The knight thonked God almight,
  And cleped his messanger an hight.

3–4 "Lays which are for the harp [and] treat of miraculous stories."
10   *Fairy* is either 'enchantment' or 'fairyland,' although here the former is likely, since it is in sense parallel to *bourdes* and *ribaudry* and also to *love* two lines below.
19   "That have come to pass."
22   *Ichil*, here and in the following lines, 'I shall.'
23   "[There] befell an event."
25   "To put it in English, certainly."
29   The West Country could, of course, be Wales, which, like Brittany, is a Celtic area; but here the intent is probably to locate the tale in a distant and, for narrative purposes, appropriate land.
30   "In every respect."
31   "Powerful men in the prime of their life."
38   "And summoned his messenger in haste."

"Go," he seyd, "to my neighebour swithe,   *quickly*
40 And say I grete him fele sithe,
And pray him that he com to me,
And say he schal mi gossibbe be."   *godparent*
The messanger goth, and hath nought forgete,
And fint the knight at his mete.   *finds/table*
45 And fair he gret in the halle
The lord, the levedi, the meyné alle.   *household*
And sethen on knes doun him sett,   *thereupon*
And the Lord ful fair he gret:
"He bad that thou schust to him te,   *go*
50 And for love his gossibbe be."
"Is his levedi delived with sounde?"   *safely*
"Ya, sir, y-thonked be God the stounde."
"And whether a maidenchild other a knave?"   *girl/boy*
"Tvay sones, sir, God hem save."
55 The knight thereof was glad and blithe,
And thonked Godes sond swithe,
And graunted his erand in al thing,   *request*
And gaf him a palfray for his tiding.

Than was the levedi of the hous
60 A proude dame and an envieous,
Hokerfulliche missegging,
Squeymous and eke scorning.
To ich woman sche hadde envie;   *each*
Sche spac this wordes of felonie: *malice*
65 "Ich have wonder, thou messanger,
Who was thi lordes conseiler,
To teche him about to send   *direct*
And telle schame in ich an ende,
That his wiif hath to childer y-bore.
70 Wele may ich man wite therfore   *know/from that*
That tvay men hir han hadde in bour;   *bedchamber*
That is hir bothe deshonour."
The messanger was sore aschamed;

---

40 "And say I salute him many times."
42 The locution is now odd: the neighbor shall be a godparent in relation to the children, not to the knight himself.
50 "Out of affection."
52 "May God be thanked for the occasion."
53 *Whether* is an interrogative particle and would not appear in Mod E rewording.
56 "And straightway gave thanks for God's dispensation."
59 *Than* 'then' is more expletive than adverb, here and elsewhere, present only to indicate transition in narrative, and equivalent to Mod E 'now.'
61–62 "Maliciously slandering, disdainful, and also contemptuous."
65 "I marvel."
68 "And broadcast the disgrace everywhere."
72 "To both of them."

The knight himself was sore agramed,   *aggrieved*
75 And rebouked his levedy
To speke any woman vilainy.
And ich woman thereof might here
Curssed hir alle y-fere,   *together*
And bisought God in heven
80 For his holy name seven   *by*
That yif hie ever ani child schuld abide
A wers aventour hir shuld bitide.

Sone therafter bifel a cas
That hirself with child was.
85 When God wild, sche was unbounde   *disburdened*
And deliverd al with sounde.   *safely*
To maidenchilder sche hadde y-bore.
When hie it wist, wo hir was therefore.
"Allas," sche seid, "that this hap come!   *event*
90 Ich have y-goven min owen dome.
Forboden bite ich woman
To speken ani other harm opon.
Falsliche another I gan deme;   *did/judge*
The selve happe is on me sene.
95 Allas," sche seid, "that I was born!
Withouten ende icham forlorn.
Or ich mot siggen sikerly   *either/say*
                                                        /indeed

That tvay men han y-ly me by;
Or ich mot sigge in al mi liif
100 That I bileighe mi neghbours wiif;   *slandered*
Or ich mot–that God it schilde!–   *prevent*
Help to sle min owhen child.
On of this thre thinges ich mot nede
Sigge other don in dede.   *or/indeed*

105 "Yif ich say ich hadde a bilemon,   *lover*
Than ich leighe meselve opon;
And eke thay wil that me se
Held me wer than comoun be.
And yif ich knaweleche to ich man   *admit/each*

---

77   An instance where the relative is omitted.
80   Seven names are recognized in ancient Hebraic lore; among the more familiar are
     Elohim, Yahweh, and Adonai.
83   "It occurred."
90   "I have handed out my own doom."
91–92   "Be it forbidden for a woman to speak harm of another."
94   "The same event is seen with me."
99   "Or I shall be obliged to say throughout my life."
106 "Tell a lie about myself."
107–108   "And also they who see me will hold me to be worse than common."

110 That ich leighe the levedi opon,   *lied about*
    Than ich worth of old and yong   *shall be/by*
    Behold leighster and fals of tong.
    Yete me is best take mi chaunce,
    And sle mi childe, and do penaunce."

115 Hir midwiif hie cleped hir to:
    "Anon," sche seid, "this child fordo.   *destroy*
    And ever say thou wher thou go   *wherever*
    That ich have o child and namo."   *one/no more*
    The midwiif answerd thurchout al
120 That hie nil, no hie ne schal.

    The levedi hadde a maiden fre,   *noble*
    Who ther y-nortured hade y-be,   *fostered/been*
    And fostered fair ful mony a yere;
    Sche saw her kepe this sori chere,   *sad/countenance*
125 And wepe, and syke, and crye "Alas!"   *sigh*
    And thoghte helpen her in this cas.
    And thus sche spake, this maiden ying,   *young*
    "So nolde I wepen for no kind thing: *would not*
    But this o child wol I of-bare   *carry away*
130 And in a covent leve it yare.   *convent*
    Ne schalt thou be aschamed at al;
    And whoso findeth this childe smal,
    By Mary, blissful quene above,
    May help it for Godes love."
135 The levedi graunted anon therto,   *assented*
    And wold wele that it were y-do.
    Sche toke a riche baudekine   *brocaded cloth*
    That hir lord brought from Costentine   *Constantinople*
    And lapped the litel maiden therin,   *wrapped*
140 And toke a ring of gold fin,   *precious*
    And on hir right arm it knitt,   *fastened*
    With a lace of silke therin plit;   *entwined*
    And whoso hir founde schuld have in mende   *mind*
    That it were comen of riche kende.   *noble/family*

---

112 "Be considered a liar." *Leighster* means specifically 'female liar,' since it shows
     the feminine agential suffix present in many ME words, as *tapster*, *spinster*, and
     brewster.
120 "That she will not nor shall not." ME *will* suggests our 'wish' and ME *shall*
     our 'ought.'
128 "I would not weep thus for such a thing." The "maiden fre," incidentally, is not
     the reluctant midwife of 1. 115.
130 Weber's *yare* 'readily' translates Marie's *tut sein e salf* 'Quite healthy and safe.'
121–133 Lines missing in the Auchinleck MS.
136 "And wished indeed that it were done."
142 The MS reads *pilt* 'applied,' from ME *pilten*; the present *plit* (suggested by Ellis
     in 1848), from ME *plighten*, makes good sense and better rhyme.

45 The maide toke the child hir mide   *with*
   And stale oway in an eventide,   *stole*
   And passed over a wild heth.   *heath*
   Thurch feld and thurch wode hie geth   *goes*
   Al the winterlong night–
50 The weder was clere, the mone was light–
   So that hie com bi a forest side;   *until/beside*
   Sche wax al weri and gan abide.
   Sone after sche gan herk   *hear*
   Cokkes crowe and houndes berk.
55 Sche aros and thider wold.
   Ner and nere sche gan bihold.
   Walles and hous fele hie seighe,   *dwellings/many*
                                                /saw

   A chirche with stepel fair and heighe.
   Than nas ther noither strete no toun,
60 Bot an hous of religioun,
   An order of nonnes wele y-dight   *equipped*
   To servy God bothe day and night.
   The maiden abod no lengore,   *tarried/longer*
   Bot yede hir to the chirche dore,   *went*
65 And on knes sche sat adoun,
   And said wepeand her orisoun: *weeping/prayer*
   "O Lord," he seid, "Iesu Crist,
   That sinful man bedes herst,   *prayers/hears*
   Underfong this present,   *receive*
70 And help this seli innocent   *helpless*
   That it mot y-cristned be,   *may*
   For Marie love, thi moder fre."   *Mary's/mother*
                                                /blessed

   Hie loked up and bi hir seighe   *saw*
   An asche bi hir fair and heighe,
75 Wele y-bowed, of michel priis;   *branched/great*
                                                  /excellence

   The bodi was holow as moni on is.
   Therin sche leid the child for cold,
   In the pel as it was bifold,   *robe/enfolded*
   And blisced it with al hir might.   *blessed*
80 With that it gan to dawe light.
   The foules up and song on bough,   *birds*
   And acremen yede to the plough.   *farmers/went*

155–156   "She arose and would [go] thither. Nearer and nearer she did look."
159–160   "Now, [there] was there neither street nor town, but a religious house."
164   *Hir* is reflexive and unnecessary in a Mod E rewording.
177   "Because of the cold."
180   "Thereupon it became light."
181   Supply "woke."

The maiden turned ogain anon,   *back*
And tok the waye he hadde er gon.   *formerly*

185   The porter of the abbay aros,
And dede his ofice in the clos,
Rong the belles and tapers light,   *lighted*
Leid forth bokes and al redi dight.   *made*
The chirche dore he undede,
190 And seighe anon in the stede   *saw/place*
The pel liggen in the tre,   *lying*
And thought wele that it might be
That theves hadde y-robbed sumwhare,
And gon ther forth and lete it thare.   *left*
195 Therto he yede and it unwond,   *went/unwound*
And the maidenchild therin he fond.
He tok it up betven his hond,
And thonked Iesu Cristes sond;   *dispensation*
And hom to his hous he it brought,   *home*
200 And tok it his doughter and hir bisought
That hie schuld kepe it as she can,   *care for/knew*
                                                        how
For sche was melche and couthe theran.   *with milk*
Sche bad it souke and it nold,
For it was neighe ded for cold.

205   Anon fer sche alight   *fire/kindled*
And warmed it wele aplight.   *indeed/well*
Sche gaf it souk opon hir barm,   *bosom*
And sethen laid it to slepe warm.   *thereafter*

And when the masse was y-don,
210 The porter to the abbesse com ful son: *went/quickly*
"Madame, what rede ye of this thing?   *advise*
Today right in the morning,
Sone after the first stounde,   *hour*
A litel maidenchild ich founde
215 In the holwe assche ther out,
And a pel him about.
A ring of gold also was there.

---

186   Probably the sense is "And carried out his duties in the enclosure," although
one is tempted to say "And said morning prayer in the cloister," both inter-
pretations being, as far as the ME is concerned, quite feasible; but Marie's lines
(177–178) read *En l'abeie ot un portier; ovrir suleit l'us del mustier* "The abbey
had a porter; it was his custom to open the door of the church."
192–193   "And supposed that it might well be that thieves had stolen [it] somewhere."
202   Probably "and familiar with such things" (like nursing an infant).
203   "She offered it milk and it would not [have it]."

Hou it com thider I not nere."
The abbesse was awondred of this thing.   *amazed*
20 "Go," hie seid, "on heighing,   *in haste*
Ano feche it hider I pray the.   *fetch*
It is welcom to God and to me.
Ichil it help as I can
And sigge it is mi kinswoman."   *say*
25 The porter anon it gan forth bring   *did*
With the pal and with the ring.
The abbesse lete clepe a prest anon,
And lete it cristin in funston.
And for it was in an asche y-founde,
30 Sche cleped it Frain in that stounde.   *time*
The Freyns of the asche is a "freyn"
After the language of Breteyn;
Forthe "Le Frein" men clepeth this lay   *therefore*
More than "Asche" in ich cuntray.

35   This Frein thrived from yer to yer.
The abbesse nece men wend it were.   *assumed*
The abbesse hir gan teche and beld.   *instruct*
Bi that hie was of twelve winter eld   *by the time that*
In al Inglond ther nas non
40 A fairer maiden than hie was on.
And when hie couthe ought of manhed,   *human nature*
Hie bad the abbesse hir wis and rede   *direct/council*
Which were hir kin, on or other,
Fader or moder, soster or brother.
45 The abbesse hir in conseyl toke,
To tellen hir hie nought forsoke,   *neglected*
Hou hie was founden in al thing,
And tok hir the cloth and the ring,   *gave*
And bad hir kepe it in that stede: *place*
50 And ther whiles sche lived so sche dede.

     Than was ther in that contre
A riche knight of lond and fe,
Proud and yong and jolive,   *spirited*
And had nought yete y-wedded wive.

---

218   "I know nothing nearer"—that is, "nothing further."
227–228   "The abbess immediately had a priest called and had it [the child] christened
      at the font."
230   Marie's form is *Fraisne*, which corresponds to Mod F *frêne*.
231   *Freyns* could be an error for *Frensch* "French," which would make good sense;
      it could also be a scribal error for *name*, an error prompted by anticipation of
      freyn at the end of the line. Marie simply says *Pur ceo qu'el fraisne fu troves,
      Le Fraisne li mistrent a nun, e Le Fraisne l'apele hum.*
247   "In every detail how she was found."
250   "And while she lived there, so she did."

255 He was stout, of gret renoun,   *bold*
    And was y-cleped Sir Guroun.   *called*
    He herd praise that maiden fre,
    And seid he wald hir se.   *would like to*
    He dight him in the way anon,   *set out*
260 And joliflich thider he come;   *gaily*
    And bad his man sigge verrament   *say/truly*
    He schuld toward a turnament.
    The abbesse and the nonnes alle
    Fair him gret in the gest halle,
265 And damisel Freyn, so hende of mouth,   *gracious*
    Gret him faire as hie wele couthe;
    And swithe wele he gan devise   *discern*
    Her semblaunt and her gentrise,   *appearance*
        /breeding

    Her lovesum eighen, her rode so bright,   *lovely/eyes*
        /complexion
270 And comced to love hir anon right,   *began*
        /immediately

    And thought hou he might take on   *contrive*
    To have hir to his leman.   *as/lover*
    He thought, "Yif ich com hir to
    More than ichave y-do,
275 The abbesse wil souchy gile   *suspect/deceit*
    And voide hir in a litel while."   *dismiss*
    He compast another enchesoun:
    To be brother of that religioun.
    "Madame," he seid to the abbesse,
280 "I lovi wele in al godenisse,
    Ichil give on and other,
    Londes and rentes, to bicom your brother,
    That ye schul ever fare the bet   *better*
    When I com to have recet.   *reception*
285 At few wordes thai ben at on.   *are/in accord*
    He graithes him and forth is gon.   *gets ready*
    Oft he come by day and night
    To speke with that maiden bright.
    So that with his fair bihest,   *promise*
290 And with his gloseing atte lest,   *flattery/finally*
    Hie graunted him to don his wille

256 Marie's form of the name is *Gurun*.
259 *Him* is a reflexive.
262 "That he was obliged to attend a tournament."
273–274 "If I go to her more than I have reason to do."
277 "He devised a different approach."
278 "To become a brother of that [particular] religious order."
280 "I love [you] well in all faith."

When he wil, loude and stille.
"Leman," he seid, "thou most lat be   *forsake*
The abbesse, thi nece, and go with me.
295 For icham riche, of swich pouwere,   *power*
The finde bet than thou hast here."
The maiden grant and to him trist,   *acceded/trusted*
And stale oway that no man wist.
With hir tok hie no thing
300 Bot hir pel and hir ring.   *except*

  When the abbesse gan espie
That hie was with the knight owy,
She made morning in hir thought,
And hir biment and gained nought.   *lamented*
305 So long sche was in his castel
That al his meyné loved hir wel.   *household*
To riche and pouer sche gan hir dresse,
That al hir loved, more and lesse.
And thus sche lad with him hir liif   *led*
310 Right as sche hadde ben wedded wiif.

  His knightes com and to him speke,   *spoke*
And Holy Chirche comandeth eke,   *also*
Sum lordes doughter for to take,
And his leman al forsake;
315 And seid him were wel more feir
In wedlok to geten him an air   *heir*
Than lede his liif with swiche on
Of was kin he knewe non.
And seid, "Hir bisides is a knight   *nearby*
320 That hath a doughter fair and bright
That schal bere his hiritage;   *give birth to/heirs*
Taketh hir in mariage!"
Loth him was that dede to do,   *reluctant*
Ac atte last he graunt therto.

325   The forward was y-maked aright,   *agreement /properly*

291–292 "She allowed him to do his will whenever he wished, whatever the circumstance."
294 *Nece* 'niece,' but here quite general, '[female] relative.'
296 "To provide for you better than you have [it] here."
298 "And stole away so that no one knew."
307–308 "She did so conduct herself to rich and poor that all loved her, people of rank and people of humble station."
310 "Just as if she had been his wedded wife."
315–318 "And told him it were indeed more fitting to beget an heir in wedlock than to lead his life with such a one whose kin he knew not of."

And were at on, and treuthe plight.
Allas, that he no hadde y-wite,   *known*
Er the forward were y-smite   *was reached*
That hie and his leman also
330 Sostren were and tvinnes to!   *sisters/also*
Of o fader bigeten thai were,
Of o moder born y-fere.   *together*
That hie so ware nist non,
For soth I say, bot God alon.

335   The newe bride was graid with alle   *made ready/in*
                                   all
And brought hom to the lordes halle.
Hir fader com with hir also,
The levedi, hir moder, and other mo.   *many others*
The bischop of the lond withouten fail
340 Com to do the spusseayl.   *perform*
                                     /marriage

   Le Codre sche was y-hight: *called*
And ther the guestes had gamen and gle,   *merriment/mirth*
And said to Sir Guroun joyfully,
345 "Fairer maiden nas never seen;
Better than Ash is Hazle I ween!"   *suspect*
(For in Romance *le frain* "ash" is,   *French*
And *le codre* "hazle," y-wis.)

   A gret fest than gan they hold   *feast*
350 With gle and pleasaunce manifold.   *diversion*
And mo than al servauntes, the maid,
Y-hight Le Frain, as servant sped.   *called*
Albe her herte wel nigh to-broke,   *although/broke*
                                     completely
No word of pride ne grame sche spoke.   *resentment*
355 The levedi marked her simple chere,   *noted/bearing*
And gan to love her wonder dere.   *very dearly*
Scant could sche feel more pine or reuth   *pain/pity*
War it hir owen childe in sooth.
Than to the bour the damsel sped,
360 Whar graithed was the spousaile bed;   *made ready*
Sche demed it was ful foully dight,   *judged/prepared*
And ill besemed a may so bright;   *befitted/maiden*
So to her coffer quick sche cam,
And her riche baudekyn out-nam,   *withdrew*
365 Which from the abbesse sche had got;

---

326   "And [they] were agreed and troth [was] plighted."
333–334   "That they were so, for a truth I say, no one knew but God alone."
341   From this line to the end is Weber's rendering.

Fairer mantel nas ther not;
And deftly on the bed it laid;
Her lord would thus be well apaid. *pleased*
Le Codre and her mother thare
370 Insame unto the bour gan fare, *together*
But whan the levedi that mantill seighe,
Sche wel neighe swoned oway.
The chamberlaynt sche cleped tho, *summoned*
But he wist of it no mo. *knew/nothing*
375 Then came that hendi maid Le Frain, *gracious*
And the levedi gan to her sain, *speak*
And asked whose mantill it ware.
Then answered that maiden fair,
"It is mine without lesing; *a lie*
380 I had it together with this ringe. *received*
Mine aunte tolde me a ferli cas *strange/tale*
Hou in this mantill y-fold I was,
And hadde upon mine arm the ring,
Whanne I was y-sent to norisching." *for upbringing*

385 Than was the levedi astonied sore. *astonished /indeed*

"Fair child! My doughter! I the bore!"
Sche swoned and was wel neighe ded,
And lay sikeand on that bed. *sighing*
Her husbond was fet tho, *fetched*
390 And sche told him al her wo,
Hou of her neighbour sche had missayn, *spoken ill*
For sche was delivered of childre twain;
And hou to children herself sche bore;
"And that o child I of sent thore,
395 In a covent y-fostered to be;
And this is sche, our doughter free;
And this is the mantill and this the ring
You gaf me of yore as a love-tokening."

The knight kissed his daughter hende *gracious*
400 Oftimes, and to the bisschop wende: *went*
And he undid the mariage strate, *forthwith*
And weddid Sir Guroun alsgate
To Le Frain, his leman, so fair and hende.
With them Le Codre away did wend,
405 And sone was spousid with game and gle,
To a gentle knight of that countre.
Thus ends the lay of tho maidens bright,
Le Frein and Le Codre y-hight.

PART 3

Chivalry and Sentiment

The Squire of Low Degree

NLY one complete text of *The Squire of Low Degree* exists, and it is not a manuscript, but a printed book produced by William Copeland between 1555 and 1560. Wynkyn de Worde earlier (perhaps near 1520) also printed it, but of his version only 180 lines survive. (They correspond to lines 1–60 and 301–420 of Copeland's edition.) There is, further, a later, condensed version (170 lines) in the seventeenth-century Bishop Percy Folio, now in the British Museum as Manuscript Addit. 27879; its narrative is somewhat better motivated than that in Copeland's version, but transitions are abrupt, clumsy, or nonexistent. It seems like a summary of something longer and possibly very much better. The version in the Percy Folio, however, does let us know that the hero is "a squier of England borne" who "wrought a forfett against the crowne" and therefore flees England for Hungary, a detail lacking in the printed text. (Just why Hungary is chosen we never know; certainly there is nothing Hungarian about king or court in either the Copeland or the Percy version.) The original does not survive, but it must have been a mid-fifteenth-century creation. William Edward Mead, the only editor to do a painstaking edition of *The Squire* (see *References*), found a good two dozen words present in the poem that are not recorded in English until, roughly, 1450; he also collected evidence indicating that the final *e* is generally silent, or as silent as it probably had become by mid-fifteenth century. Be that as it may, the poem seems to have enjoyed a peculiar popularity a century after its creation—perhaps not of an altogether noteworthy kind—a popularity attested by numerous references to it by printers, pamphleteers, playwrights, and collectors of the time.

The Wynkyn de Worde edition of *The Squire* bears the title *Undo Youre Dore*, an indication of one of the two central motifs. The Squire and the daughter of the King of Hungary are in love, and closely watched by a false steward. In order to gain prestige, the Squire determines to perform deeds of chivalry in distant lands (Lumbardy, Tuscany, Spain,

Portugal) and then return to marry his lady. On the night of his departure, he pays a visit to her chamber, but is thwarted at her door by the steward and his men. (The steward, incidentally, is the only character given a name—Sir Maladose—who, perhaps in name only, appears elsewhere in Middle English romance in *Syr Tryamoure*, where he is the champion of the Emperor of Almayne.) The Squire, aware of his danger, cries "Undo thy dore! My lady swete!" One has to assume that he wished to gain some sort of advantage in the ensuing fight by, perhaps, standing at the threshold of her door. Presumably, the lady at first thinks he is the steward and will not let him in. One even has to assume a spirited fight takes place. At any event, the steward is killed and the Squire captured and taken to the King. The other motif is handled in a manner no less maladroit. Just after the capture of the Squire, the steward's men disfigure the steward's face, put the Squire's clothes on him, and leave his body before the lady's door. She finds him, thinks he is the Squire, em-head of her bed. A reader has to puzzle over motivation, a narrative balms him, and for seven years keeps him in a "marble stone" at the feature which the romance is decidedly weak in, as it presently exists. Why do the steward's men behave as they do? Perhaps the King, to test the love of the Squire and his daughter, ordered them to act as they did. We are not told. We must, however, assume something of the sort to give the narrative any coherence at all. We find that the King allows the Squire to journey into distant lands to win a knightly reputation and for seven years keeps from his daughter the fact that her beloved is still alive. Ultimately, revelation is made and the pair married—abruptly and without ado. Here, at least, we are informed that the King has been pulling the strings all along. He is satisfied with the Squire's doughtiness and his daughter's devotion and hands over his kingdom to the pair.

The motifs have their interest, particularly the macabre seven-year adoration. It is not, however, an isolated literary device. In the *Decameron*, a lady keeps the head of her beloved in a pot of basil; in the romance *Eger and Grime*, another lady keeps the head of her enemy Greysteel in a coffer. More recently, Faulkner's story—widely known, because often anthologized—"A Rose for Emily" rests entirely on a similar motif, although it is Emily who kills the lover, not intruders from without. But it is really the atmosphere and language of *The Squire* which merit attention. The poem is, in a way, a swan song of the romance. Gone is the naïve infatuation with names, with simple linear narrative, with fighting, jousting, amorous intrigue. What remains is a rather wistful echoing of the romantic sentiment (which was rarely ever profound) of the older stories and of the poetic devices in which it originally found expression. There are interminable catalogues of wines, birds, trees, musical instruments, household articles. There are interminable speeches, which rarely escape bathos, where inner sentiment is described, adorned, repeated, and underscored. Perhaps the most genuine literary response a reader today derives is a feeling of what the audience of the time wanted. One can sense their wistfulness and sympathize with it.

REFERENCES: Brown and Robbins, No. 1644; *CBEL*, I:159–160; Hibbard, pp. 263–266; Kane, pp. 95–99; Wells, pp. 149–150.—The only carefully edited text of *The Squire* is by William Edward Mead (Boston, Ginn & Company, 1904), which prints the Copeland version plus the de Worde fragments and the short version of the Percy Folio; French and Hale, pp. 719–755, print Copeland's version and use a good number of Mead's emendations.

It was a squier of lowe degree
That loved the Kings doughter of Hungré.
The squir was curteous and hend;   *gracious*
Ech man him loved and was his frend.
5 He served the King, her father dere,
Fully the time of seven yere;
For he was marshall of his hall
And set the lords both great and small.
An hardy man he was and wight,   *active*
10 Both in bataile and in fight.   *battle*
But ever he was still morning   *secretly*
                                                                    /mourning

And no man wiste for what thing;   *knew*
And all was for the lady,
The Kinges doughter of Hungry.
15 There wiste no wighte in Christenté   *knew/man*
Howe well he loved that lady free.   *noble*
He loved her more then seven yere,
Yet was he of her love never the nere.
He was not riche of gold and fee;   *property*
20 A gentill man forsoth was he.
To no man durst he make his mone,   *complaint*
But sighed sore himselfe alone.

And evermore whan he was so,
Into his chambre would he go;
25 And through the chambre he toke the waye
Into the gardin that was full gaye;
And in the garden, as I wene,   *think*
Was an arber faire and grene   *orchard*

---

2   ME idiom often splits a titular phase to accommodate the genitive object.
18   "Yet he was never the nearer to her love."

And in the arber was a tree,
30 A fairer in the world might none be.
The tree it was of cypresse,
The first tree that Jesu chose;
The sother-wood and sykamoure,   *wormwood*
The reed rose and the lyly-floure,
35 The boxe, the beche, and the larel-tree,
The date, also the damyse,   *damson plum*
The filbirdes hanging to the ground,   *filbert trees*
The figge-tree and the maple round,
And other trees there was mané one,
40 The piany, the popler, and the plane,   *peony/plane-tree*
With brode braunches all aboute,
Within the arbar and eke withoute.   *also*
On every braunche sate birdes three
Singinge with great melody,
45 The lavorocke and the nightingale,   *lark*
The ruddocke, the woodwale,   *robin*
                                  /woodpecker

The pee and the popinjaye,   *magpie/parrot*
The trustele sange both night and daye,   *thrush*
The marlin and the wrenne also,
50 The swalowe whippinge to and fro,
The jaye jangled them amonge,
The larke began that merry songe,
The sparowe spredde her on her spraye,
The mavis songe with notes full gaye,   *song thrush*
55 The nuthake with her notes newe,   *nuthatch/fresh*
The sterlinge set her notes full trewe,
The goldefinche made full merry chere,
Whan she was bente upon a brere,   *briar*
And many other foules mo,
60 The osill and the thrushe also;   *blackbird*
And they sange with notes clere
In conforting that squiere.

And evermore whan he was wo,
Into that arber wolde he go
65 And under a bente he laide him lowe,   *hillside/down*
Right even under her chambre windowe;
And lened his backe to a thorne
And said, "Alas, that I was borne!
That I were riche of golde and fee!
70 That I might wedde that lady free!
Of golde good or some treasure

---

32   No specific legend can be adduced to support the line; the suggestion is that Jesus, in his knowledge of the plan of redemption, chose cypress wood for the cross.

That I might wedde that lady floure!   *flower*
Or elles come of so gentill kinne,
The ladies love that I might winne.
75 Wolde God that I were a kinges sonne,
That ladyes love that I might wonne!   *win*
Or els so bolde in eche fight
As was Sir Libius, that gentell knight,
Or els so bolde in chivalry
80 As Sir Gawaine or Sir Guy;
Or els so doughty of my hande
As was the giaunte Sir Colbrande.
And it were put in jeoperde
What man shoulde winne that lady free,
85 Than should no man have her but I,
The Kinges doughter of Hungry."
But ever he saide, "Waile a waye!
For poverté passeth all my paye!"
And as he made this rufull chere,   *sorrowful/lament*
90 He sowned downe in that arbere.   *swooned*

That lady herde his mourning all,
Right under the chambre wall;
In her oriall there whe was   *oriel window*
                                 /where
Closed well with royall glass;   *enclosed*
95 Fulfilled it was with imagery.   *covered/pictures*
Every windowe by and by;
On eche side had there a ginne,   *latch*
Sperde with many a divers pinne.   *fastened*
Anone that lady, faire and free,
100 Undide a pinne of iveré   *ivory*
And wid the windowes she open set.   *wide*
The sunne shone in at her closet.   *chamber*
In that arber faire and gaye
She sawe where that squire lay.
105 The lady said to him anone,
"Sir, why makest thou that mone?   *complaint*
And why thou mournest night and day?
Now tell me, squire, I thee pray;
And as I am a true lady,
110 Thy counsail shall I never discry;   *reveal*

---

78 Libius is Lybeaus Desconus, "The Fair Unknown," an illegitimate son of Gawain
80 Sir Guy is the hero of the romance *Guy of Warwick*.
81 "Or else so courageous in combat."
82 Colbrande, a Danish giant, is slain by Guy of Warwick.
83 "If it were put to a test."
88 "Because of poverty all my pleasure passes."
96 "Every window one after the other."

And if it be no reprefe to thee,   *shame*
Thy bote of bale yet shall I be."   *remedy/harm*
And often was he in wele and wo,
But never so well as he was tho.

115 The squier set him on his knee
    And saide, "Lady, it is for thee:
    I have thee loved this seven yere
    And bought thy love, lady, full dere.
    Ye are so riche in youre array
120 That one word to you I dare not say;
    And come ye be of so hye kinne,   *high*
    No worde of love durst I beginne.
    My will to you if I had saide,   *desire*
    And ye therwith not well apaide,   *pleased*
125 Ye might have bewraied me to the Kinge   *betrayed*
    And brought me sone to my endinge.
    Therfore, my lady faire and free,
    I durst not shewe my harte to thee;   *heart*
    But I am here at your will
130 Whether ye will me save or spill;   *destroy*
    For all the care I have in be,   *because of/been*
    A worde of you might comfort me;
    And if ye will not do so,
    Out of this land I must nedes go.   *by necessity*
135 I will forsake both lande and lede   *people*
    And become an hermite in uncouth stede,   *foreign/land*
    In many a lande to begge my bread,   *beg for*
    To seke where Christ was quicke and dead.   *visit*
    A staffe I will make me of my spere;
140 Linen cloth I shall none were;
    Ever in travaile I shall wende   *hardship*
    Till I come to the worldes ende.
    And, lady, but thou be my bote,   *aid*
    There shall no sho come on my fote;   *shoe*
145 Therfore, lady, I thee praye,
    For Him that died on Good Fridaye,
    Let me not in daunger dwell,   *uncertainty*
    For His love that harrowed hell."

    Than said that lady milde of mode,
150 Right in her closet there she stode,   *chamber*
    "By Him that died on a tree,   *cross*
    Thou shalt never be deceived for me;

---

113   "And often [had] he been in happiness and dispair."
118   "And paid for [that is, suffered for] your love, lady, very grievously."
140   A pilgrim was supposed to wear rough wool, not fine linen.

Though I for thee should be slaine,
Squier, I shall thee love againe.   *in return*
155 Go forth and serve my father the Kinge
And let be all thy still mourninge.   *cease*
Let no man wete that ye were here,   *know*
Thus all alone in my arbere.
If ever ye will come to your will,   *arrive at/desire*
160 Here and see and hold you still.
Beware of the stewarde, I you praye!   *Steward in love, with her too?*
He will deceive you and he maye.   *wants to*
For if he wote of your woing,   *knew*
He will bewraye you unto the Kinge.   *betray*
165 Anon for me ye shall be take
And put in prison for my sake;
Than must ye nedes abide the lawe,
Peraventure both hanged and drawe.   *perhaps*
That sight on you I would not see
170 For all the gold in Christenté.
For and ye my love should winne,   *for if*
With chivalry ye must beginne
And other dedes of armes to done,
Through whiche ye may winne your shone
175 And ride through many a perilous place
As a venterous man to seke your grace
Over hilles and dales and hye mountaines
In wethers wete, both hail and raines,
And if ye may no harbough see,   *lodging*
180 Than must ye lodge under a tree,
Among the beastes wild and tame
And ever you will gette your name;
And in your armure must ye lie,
Eevery night than by and by
185 And your meny everychone   *followers /each one*

Till seven yere by comen and gone,
And passe by many a perillous see,   *sea*
Squier, for the love of me,
Where any war beginneth to wake,   *arise*
190 And many a bataill undertake,
Throughout the land of Lumbardy,
In every citie by and by.
And be avised, when thou shalt fight,   *advised*
Loke that ye stand aye in the right;

---

174   "Through which you may win your spurs" [literally, shoes].
182   "And constantly you will enhance the [glory of] your name."
184   "Every night then one after another."
194   "See [to it] that you are ever on the [side of] right."

195 And if ye will, take good hede,
    Yet all the better shall ye spede;   *succeed*
    And whan the warre is brought to ende,
    To the Rodes then must ye wende.
    And, Sir, I holde you not to prayes   *praise*
200 But ye there fight three Good Fridayes;   *unless*
    And if ye passe the batailes three,
    Than are ye worthy a knight to be;
    And to bere armes than are ye able,
    Of gold and goules sete with sable.
205 Then shall ye were a shelde of blewe,   *blue*
    In token ye shall be trewe,
    With vines of golde set all aboute
    Within your shelde and eke without,
    Fulfilled with imagery,   *covered/pictures*
210 And poudred with true loves by and by.   *sprinkled*
        /love knots

    In the middes of your sheld ther shall be set   *middle*
    A ladies head, with many a frete.   *ornament*
    Above the head written shall be
    A reason for the love of me: *motto*
215 Both O and R shall be therin;
    With A and M it shall beginne.
    The baudrike that shall hange therby   *baldric*
    Shall be of white, sikerly.   *certainly*
    A crosse of reed therin shall be   *red*
220 In token of the Trinité.
    Your basenette shall be burnished bright,
    Your ventall shall be well dight;   *ventail/adorned*
    With starres of golde it shall be set
    And covered with good velvet.
225 A coronall clene corven newe   *circlet/carved*
    And oystriche fethers of divers hewe.
    Your plates unto your body shall be enbraste,   *fastened*
    Shall sit full semely in your waste.   *waist*
    Your cote-armoure of golde full fine
230 And poudred well with good armine.
    Thus in your warres shall you ride
    With six good yemen by your side;   *yeomen*
    And whan your warres are brought to ende,

---

198   Rhodes was a traditional port of call on the pilgrim route to the Holy Land.
204   "Of gold and gules [the heraldic term for 'red'] set with sable" the [heraldic term for 'black'].
215–216   The motto *amor* 'love' is also that of Chaucer's Lady Prioress.
221   A bascinet was a steel headpiece over which a larger helmit was placed.
229–230   "Your tabard [coat placed over armor] [shall be] of very fine gold and well decorated with good ermine."

More ferther behoveth to you to wende,
235 And over many perellous streme
Or ye come to Jerusalem, *before*
Through feytes and feldes and forestes thicke,
To seke where Christe were dead and quicke. *visit/alive*
There must you drawe your swerde of were; *war*
240 To the sepulchre ye must it bere
And laye it on the stone
Amonge the lordes everychone; *every one*
And offre there florences five, *florins*
Whiles that ye are man on live;
245 And offre there florences three
In tokening of the Trinité; .
And whan that ye, sir, thus have done,
Than are ye worthy to were your shone;
Then may ye say, sir, by good right
250 That you ar proved a venturous knight.
I shall you geve to your ridinge
A thousande pounde to your spendinge;
I shall you geve hors and armure,
A thousande pounde of my treasure
255 Where-through that ye may honoure winn
And be the greatest of your kinne.
I pray to God and Our Lady,
Send you the whele of victory,
That my father so faine may be *pleased*
260 That he will wede me unto thee
And make thee king of this countré
To have and holde in honesté, *honor*
With welth and winne to were the crowne *wealth/success*
And to be lorde of toure and towne
265 That we might our dayes endure
In parfite love that is so pure.
And if we may not so come to,
Other wise then must we do;
And therfore, squier, wende thy way,
270 And hye thee fast on thy journay
And take thy leve of Kinge and Quene,
And so to all the courte bidene. *one after another*
Ye shall not want at your going *lack*

---

234 "It shall be necessary for you to go still farther."
237 Copeland's *feytes* may mean 'fights' or it may be an error, possibly for *frithes* 'fields.'
244 If the line may be more than just a filler, the sense might be "In gratitude that you are still alive."
248 Compare line 174.
258 *Whele* may be a play on "wheel of fortune" or Copeland's form of *wele* 'weal, benefit.'

Golde nor silver nor other thing.
275 This seven yere I shall you abide,   *await*
Betide of you what so betide.
Till seven yere be comen and gone
I shall be maide all alone."
The squier kneled on his knee,
280 And thanked that lady faire and free;
And thries he kissed that lady tho   *thrice/then*
And toke his leve and forth he gan go.

The Kinges steward stode full nye   *near*
In a chambre fast them bye   *closeby*
285 And hearde their wordes wonder wele   *very/well*
And all the woing every dele.   *part*
He made a vowe to Heaven-kinge
For to bewraye that swete thinge   *betray*
And that squier taken shoulde be
290 And hanged hye on a tree;
And that false stewarde full of ire,   *envy*
Them to betraye was his desire.
He bethought him nedely,   *took thought*
                                                                        /eagerly
Every daye by and by,   *continuously*
295 How he might venged be   *avenged*
On that lady faire and free,
For he her loved prively   *secretly*
And therfore did her great envye.
Alas! it tourned to wrotherheyle   *misfortune*
300 That ever he wiste of their counsayle.   *knew*

But leve we of the stewarde here
And speke we more of that squier,
Howe he to his chambre went
Whan he past from that lady gente.   *departed/elegant*
305 There he arraied him in scarlet reed
And set his chaplet upon his head,   *circlet*
A belte about his sides two,
With brode barres to and fro;
A horn about his necke he caste
310 And forth he went at the last
To do his office in the hall
Among the lordes both great and small.
He toke a white yeard in his hande;   *marshal's staff*
Before the Kinge than gane he stande   *did*

298   "And therefore caused her great harm."
301   "But let us turn from the steward here."
308   "With broad stripes from one end to the other."

315 And sone he sat him on his knee
And served the Kinge right loyally
With dainty meates that were dere,   *precious*
With partriche, pecoke, and plovere,
With birdes in bread y-bake,   *baked*
320 The tele, the ducke, and the drake,   *teal*
The cocke, the curlewe, and the crane,
With fesauntes faire–their were no wane–   *lack*
Both storkes and snites ther were also   *snipes*
And venison freshe of bucke and do,
325 And other daintes many one,   *a one*
For to set afore the Kinge anone.
And when the squier had done so,
He served the hall to and fro.
Eche man him loved in honesté.   *genuinely*
330 Hye and lowe in their degree;
So did the King full sodenly,
And he wist not wherfore nor why.   *knew*
The Kinge behelde the squier wele   *well*
And all his rayment every dele;   *part*
335 He thought he was the semiliest man   *handsomest*
That ever in the worlde he sawe or than.   *ere/then*
Thus sate the King and eate right nought,
But on his squier was all his thought.

Anone the stewarde toke good hede
340 And to the King full soone he yede,   *went*
And soone he tolde unto the Kinge
All their wordes and their woinge;
And how she hight him lande and fee,   *promised
                                                      /property*

Golde and silver great plentye,
345 And how he should his leve take
And become a knight for her sake:
"And thus they talked bothe in fere,   *together*
And I drewe me nere and nere.   *nearer*
Had I not come in, verayly,
350 The squier had laine her by;   *lies.*
But whan he was ware of me,   *aware*
Full fast away can he flee.
That is sothe: here my hand
To fight with him while I may stand!"

355 The King said to the steward tho,   *then*
"I may not beleve it should be so;

---

328 Compare *to and fro* in line 308.
352 *Can*, here and in lines 486, 502, and 662, doubles for the meaningless auxiliary
     gan 'did.'

Hath he be so bonaire and beningne,   *courteous/benign*
And served me sith he was younge,   *since*
And redy with me in every nede,
360 Bothe true of word and eke of dede,   *also*
I may not beleve, be night nor daye,
My doughter dere he will betraye,
Nor to come her chambre nye,   *go/near*
That fode to longe with no foly;
365 Though she would to him consente,
That lovely lady faire and gente,   *elegant*
I truste him so well, withouten drede,   *doubt*
That he would never do that dede
But if he might that lady winne   *unless*
370 In wedlocke to welde, withouten sinne;   *possess*
And if she assent him till,
The squier is worthy to have none ill;
For I have sene that many a page
Have become men by mariage;
375 Than it is semely that squier   *then/fit for*
To have my doughter by this manere,
And eche man in his degree
Become a lorde of ryaltye,
By fortune and by other grace,
380 By heritage and by purchace:
Therefore, stewarde, beware hereby;
Defame him not for no envy.   *malice*
It were great reuth he should be spilte   *pity/ruined*
Or put to death withouten gilte   *guilt*
385 (And more ruthe of my doughter dere,   *pity*
For chaunging of that ladyes chere.
I woulde not for my crowne so newe   *fresh*
That lady chaunge hide or hewe);   *color*
Or for to put thyselfe in drede,
390 But thou might take him with the dede.
For if it may be founde in thee   *discovered*
That thou them fame for enmité,   *defame/out of*
Thou shalt be taken as a felon   *arrested*
And put full depe in my prison,   *Threat*
395 And fettered fast unto a stone
Till twelve yere were come and gone,
And drawen with hors throughe the cité,

---

364   "To desire that child out of wontonnesse."
374   "Have become men [of stature] by marriage."
380   *Purchace* is a term for acquisition by various means (other than by inheritance),
      as by buying or by military deserts.
386   "For altering [to the worse] that lady's disposition."
389–390   "Or [it were a pity for you] to endanger yourself unless you might take
      him in the act."

And soone hanged upon a tree.
And thou may not thyselfe excuse,
400 This dede thou shalt no wise refuse;
And therfore, steward, take good hed
How thou wilt answere to this ded."   *deed*
The stewarde answered with great envy,   *malice*
"That I have said, that I will stand therby;
405 To suffre death and endlesse wo,
Sir Kinge, I will never go therfro;
For if that ye will graunt me here
Strength of men and great power
I shall him take this same night   *very*
410 In the chambre with your doughter bright;
For I shall never be gladde of chere
Till I be venged of that squier."   *avenged*

Than said the Kinge full curteisly
Unto the stewarde, that stode him by,
415 "Thou shalte have strength ynough with thee,
Men of armes three hundred and three
To watche that lady muche of price
And her to kepe fro her enemies.   *guard/from*
For there is no knight in Christenté
420 That wolde betray that lady free,
But he should die under his shelde,
And I might see him in the felde;   *if*
And therfore, stewarde, I thee pray,
Take hede what I shall to thee say;
425 And if the squiere come to-night
For to speke with that lady bright,
Let him say whatsoever he will,
And here and see and holde you still;
And herken well what he will say
430 Or thou with him make any fray;   *eve/trouble*
So he come not her chambre win,
No bate on him loke thou begin;
Though that he kisse that lady free   *even though*
And take his leave right curteisly,
435 Let him go, both hole and sounde,   *whole*
Without wemme or any wounde;   *injury*
But-if he will her chamber breke,   *unless/break into*
No worde to him that thou do speke.

399–400 "If you are unable to acquit yourself, such a death you can in no manner
    escape."
421 "Who would not die under his shield" [that is, fighting]
431–432 "So [long as] he does not go within her chamber, see that you start no
    strife with him."
438 "[I tell you] that you should speak no word to him."

But, if he come with company,
440 For to betraye that faire lady,
Loke he be taken soone anone
And all his meiné everychone   *followers*
And brought with strength to my prison   *under/guard*
As traitour, thefe, and false felon.
445 And if he make any defence,
Loke that he never go thence;
But loke thou hew him also small
As fleshe whan it to the potte shall.
And if he yelde him to thee,   *yield/himself*
450 Bringe him bothe saufe and sounde to me.   *safe*
I shall borowe for seven yere   *pledge/years*
He shall not wedde my doughter dere.
And therfore, stewarde, I thee praye
Thou watche that lady night and daye."
455 The stewarde saide the King untill,
"All your bidding I shall fulfill."

The stewarde toke his leave to go.
The squier came fro chambre tho;   *then*
Downe he went into the hall.
460 The officers sone can he call,   *did*
Both usher, panter, and butler,
And other that in office were;
There he them warned sone anone
To take up the bordes everychone.   *set up*
                                                 /trestle tables
465 Than they did his commaundement,   *then*
And sithe unto the King he went;   *afterwards*
Full lowe he set him on his knee
And voided his borde full gently.   *cleared/place*
And whan the squire had done so,
470 Anone he saide the Kinge unto,
"As ye are lorde of chivalry,
Geve me leve to passe the sea,   *permission*
To prove my strenthe with my right hande
On Godes enemies in uncouth land   *foreign*
475 And to be knowe in chivalry,
In Gascoyne, Spaine, and Lumbardy,
In eche bataile for to fight,   *battle*
To be proved a venterous knight."   *worthy*
The King said to the squier tho,
480 "Thou shalt have good leve to go;

447–448   "But see that you cut him to pieces just as small as meat when it is to go
to the pot."
461   An *usher* seems to have had charge of the door and the seating within the hall,
a *panter* charge of a "bread room," and a *butler* charge of a "bottle room."

I shall thee give both golde and fee
And strength of men to wende with thee: *go*
If thou be true in worde and dede,
I shall thee helpe in all thy nede."
485 The squier thanked the King anone
And toke his leve and forth can gone,   *did/go*
With joye and blisse and much pride,
With all his meiny by his side.   *followers*
He had not riden but a while,
490 Not the mountenaunce of a mile,   *length*
Or he was ware of a village.   *ere/aware*
Anone he saide unto a page,
"Our souper soone loke it be dight;   *supper/see*
                                                           /prepared
Here will we lodge all to-night."
495 They toke their innes in good intente,
And to their supper soone they wente.
Whan he was set and served at meate,
Than he said he had forgete   *forgotten*
To take leve of that lady free,
500 The Kinges doughter of Hungré.

Anone the squier made him yare   *ready*
And by himselfe forth can he fare;   *did/go*
Without strength of his meiné,   *followers*
Unto the castell than went he.   *then*
505 Whan he came to the posterne gate,   *rear*
Anone he entred in thereat,
And his drawen swerd in his hande.
There was no more with him wolde stande;
But it stode with him full harde,
510 As ye shall here nowe of the stewarde.
He wende in the worlde none had bene   *thought*
That had knowen of his privité;   *secret*
Alas! it was not as he wende,
For all his counsaile the stewarde kende.   *knew*
515 He had bewrayed him to the King   *betrayed*
Of all his love and his woing;
And yet he laye her chambre by,
Armed with a great company,
And beset it one eche side,   *surrounded*
520 For treason walketh wonder wide.
The squier thought on no mistruste;   *suspicion*

---

495   "They took their lodging with a good will."
508   The *no more* here may mean simply 'no one.'
517   "And even then he was waiting nearby her chamber."
520   Apparently proverbial, perhaps implying "treachery is strangely ubiquitous" or "extremely resourceful."

He wende no man in the worlde had wiste;   *known*
But if he had knowen, ne by Saint John,
He had not come theder by his owne!   *gone/alone*
525 Or if that lady had knowen his will,
That he should have come her chamber till,
She would have taken him golde and fee,   *given*
Strength of men and royalté.
But there ne wist no man nor grome   *knew/servant*
530 Where that squier was become,   *had/gone*
But forth he went himselfe alone,
Amonge his servauntes everychone.
Whan that he came her chambre to,
Anon he saide, "Your dore undo!
535 Undo," he saide, "now, faire lady!
I am beset with many a spy.   *surrounded*
Lady as white as whales bone,
There are thirty against me one.   *alone*
Undo thy dore, my worthy wife!
540 I am besette with many a knife.
Undo your dore, my lady swete!
I am beset with enemies great;
And, lady, but ye will arise,   *unless*
I shall be dead with mine enemies.
545 Undo thy dore, my frely flour!   *lovely/flower*
For ye are mine and I am your."

That lady with those wordes awoke;
A mantell of golde to her she toke.
She saide, "Go away, thou wicked wight;
550 Thou shalt not come here this night;
For I will not my dore undo
For no man that cometh therto.
There is but one in Christenté
That ever made that forwarde with me.   *agreement*
555 There is but one that ever bare life
That ever I hight to be his wife;   *promised*
He shall me wedde, by Mary bright,
Whan he is proved a venterouᴕ knight,
For we have loved this seven yere;
560 There was never love to me so dere,
There lieth on me both king and knight,
Duke, erles, of muche might.

---

532 [From] among each one of his servants."
549 One must assume that the lady here believes someone other than the squire is
     at her door.
561 "[Although] there woo me both king and knight."

Wende forth, squier, on your waye,
For here ye gette none other praye;   *reward*
565 For I ne wote what ye should be   *know*
That thus besecheth love of me."
"I am your owne squir," he saide,
"For me, lady, be not dismaide.
Com I am full prively   *secretly*
570 To take my leave of you, lady."
"Welcome," she said, "my love so dere,
Mine owne dere heart and my squier;
I shall you geve kisses three,
A thousand pounde unto your fee,
575 And kepe I shall my maidenhede right
Till ye be proved a venturous knight.
For if ye should me wede anone,   *immediately*
My father wolde make slee you soone.
I am the Kinges doughter of Hungré,
580 And ye alone that have loved me,
And though you love me never so sore,   *ever*
For me ye shall never be lore.   *lost*
Go forth and aske me at my kinne   *ask for/my hand*
And loke what graunt you may winne.   *see/favor*
585 If that ye gette graunt in faye   *faith*
Myselfe therto shall not say nay;
And if ye may not do so,
Otherwise ye shall come to.
Ye are bothe hardy, stronge, and wight;   *active*
590 Go forth and be a venterous knight.
I pray to God and our Lady
To send you the whele of victory,
That my father so leve ye be
That he will profer me to thee.
595 I wote well it is lightly said,   *know/easily*
'Go forth and be nothing afraide.'   *not*
A man of worship may not do so: *honor*
He must have what neds him unto;
He must have gold, he must have fee,
600 Strength of men and royalté.
Gold and silver spare ye nought
Till to manhode ye be brought;

---

563   *Squier* may here refer not to the lady's squier; it may simply be a form of address
      used for an unknown intruder.
588   "You must [then] achieve your goal in another manner."
592   See line 258.
593   "That to my father you will be so dear."
597–598   "A man of honor cannot do such [as you appear to be doing]; it is necessary
      for him to have what is fitting."

To what bataill soever ye go,   *whatever/battle*
Ye shall have an hundreth pounde or two;
605 And yet to me, sir, ye may saye
That I woulde faine have you awaye,   *gladly*
That profered you golde and fee,
Out of mine eye sight for to be.
Neverthelesse it is not so: *honor*
610 It is for the worship of us two.
Though you be come of simple kinne,   *humble*
Thus my love, sir, may ye winne.
If ye have grace of victory,
As ever had Sir Libius or Sir Guy,
615 Whan the dwarfe and maide Ely
Came to Arthoure, king so free.
As a king of great renowne
That wan the lady of Synadowne,
Libius was graunted the bataile tho;   *then*
620 Therfore the dwarfe was full wo,
And said, 'Authur, thou arte to blame.
To bidde this childe go sucke his dame
Better him semeth, so mote I thrive,
Than for to do these batailes five
625 At the chapell of Salebraunce!'
These wordes began great distaunce;   *strife*
They sawe they had the victory;
They kneled downe and cried mercy;
And afterward, sir, verament,
630 They called him knight absolent: *perfect*
Emperours, dukes, knightes, and quene,
At his commaundement for to bene.
Such fortune with grace now to you fall,   *befall*
To winne the worthiest within the wall,
635 And thinke on your love alone,
And for to love that ye chaunge none."

Right as they talked thus in fere,   *together*
Their enemies approched nere and nere,   *nearer*
Foure and thirty armed bright
640 The steward had arrayed him to fight.
The steward was ordained to spy
And for to take them utterly.

---

607 "[I] who [have] offered you wealth and property."
615 See line 78. The lady's references to the romance do not match altogether inci-
      dents present in the surviving ME *Libeans Desconus*, where a maiden Elene and
      a dwarf accompany Libeans to free a lady of Sinadoune.
622–624 "It would better befit this youth to command him to go to his mother, as
      I may thrive, than [command him] to perform these five battles."

He wende to death he should have gone;
He felled seven men against him one;
45 Whan he had them to grounde brought,
The stewarde at him full sadly fought.   *bitterly*
So harde they smote together tho,   *then*
The stewardes throte he cut in two,
And sone he fell downe to the grounde
50 As a traitour untrewe, with many a wound.
The squier sone in armes they hente,   *seized*
And off they did his good garmente,
And on the stewarde they it did,   *put*
And sone his body therin they hidde,
55 And with their swordes his face they share,   *disfigured*
That she should not knowe what he ware;   *who*
They cast him at her chambre dore,
The stewarde that was stiffe and store.   *large*
Whan they had made that great affraye,   *struggle*
60 Full prively they stale awaye.   *secretly/stole*
In arme they take that squier tho   *then*
And to the Kinges chambre can they go,   *did*
Without wemme or any wounde,   *injury*
Before the Kinge bothe hole and sounde.   *whole*
65 As soone as the Kinge him spied with eye,
He said, "Welcome, sonne, sikerly!   *son*
Thou hast cast thee my sonne to be;   *resolved*
This seven yere I shall let thee."
Leve we here of this squier wight   *active*
70 And speake we of that lady bright,
How she rose, that lady dere,
To take her leve of that squier.
Also naked as she was borne,
She stood her chambre dore beforne.
75 "Alas," she said, "and weale away!
For all too long nowe have I lay;
She said, "Alas, and all for wo!
Withouten men why came ye so?
If that ye wolde have come to me,
80 Other werninges there might have be.   *been*
Now all too dere my love is bought,
But it shall never be lost for nought."
And in her armes she toke him there;

---

643   The first *he* may refer to the steward, the second to the squier; in the following
        line, *he* must refer to the latter.
659   Motivation is not clear. The King may secretly have ordered the steward's re-
        tainers to act as they did.
668   "For seven years I am obliged to hinder you."
675   See the similar lamentation in line 87.

Into the chamber she did him bere;
685 His bowels soone she did out drawe
And buried them in Goddes lawe.
She sered that body with specery,   *covered/spices*
With virgin waxe and commendry;
And closed him in a maser tree   *maple*
690 And set on him lockes three.
She put him in a marble stone
With quaint ginnes many one   *devices*
And set him at hir beddes head;
And every day she kist that dead.
695 Soone at morne, whan she uprose,
Unto that dead body she gose;
Therfore wold she knele downe on her knee
And make her prayer to the Trinité
And kisse that body twise or thrise   *thrice*
700 Or fall in a swowne or she might rise.   *swoon/ere*
Whan she had so done,
To chirche than wolde she gone;   *go*
Than would she here masses five,   *hear*
And offre to them while she might live:
705 "There shall none knowe but Heven-kinge
For whome that I make mine offringe."

The King, her father, anone he saide:
"My doughter, why are you dismaide,   *distressed*
So feare a lady as ye are one   *fair*
710 And so semely of fleshe and bone?
Ye were white as whales bone;
Nowe are ye pale as any stone.
Your ruddy read as any cherry,   *complexion/red*
With browes bent and eyes full merry;   *arched*
715 Ye were wont to harpe and sing
And be the merriest in chambre coming;
Ye ware both golde and good velvet,   *wore*
Clothe of damaske with saphires set;
Ye ware the pery on your head,   *wore/jewelry*
720 With stones full orient, white and read;   *lustrous*
Ye ware coronalles of golde   *circlets*
With diamoundes set many a foulde;   *fold*
And nowe ye were clothes of blacke;
Tell me, doughter, for whose sake?
725 If he be so poore of fame   *reputation*
That ye may not be wedded for shame,

---

686   "And buried them according to the rites of the church."
688   Mead (see *References*) concludes *commendry* is for *cummin*, an herb, and *dry*
       'dry.'

Bringe him to me anone right.
I shall him make squier and knight.
And if he be so great a lorde
30 That your love may not accorde,
Let me, doughter, that lording see;
He shall have golde ynoughe with thee."
"Gramercy, father, so mote I thrive,
For I mourne for no man alive.
35 Ther is no man, by Heven-king,
That shall knowe more of my mourninge."

Her father knew it every deale,   *bit*
But he kept it in counsele: *secret*
"To-morowe ye shall on hunting fare,   *go*
40 And ride, my doughter, in a chare;   *litter*
It shall be covered with velvet recde,   *red*
And clothes of fine golde all about your hed,
With damaske white and asure-blewe,
Well diapred with lillies newe;   *figured/fresh*
45 Your pomelles shall be ended with gold,
Your chaines enameled many a folde;
Your mantel of riche degree,
Purpil palle and armine free;   *cloth/ermine*
Jennettes of Spaine, that been so wight,   *genets/active*
50 Trapped to the ground with velvet bright;
Ye shall have harpe, sautry, and songe,   *psaltery*
And other mirthes you amonge;
Ye shall have rumney and malmesine,   *white Spanish wine/malmsey*

Both ypocrasse and vernage wine,   *spiced wine/Italian white wine*

55 Montrose and wine of Greke,
Both algrade and respice eke,   *Cretan wine/raspis*

Antioche and bastarde,   *wine from Antioche/Spanish wine*

Piment also and garnarde;   *honey wine/Granada wine*

Wine of Greke and muscadell,   *Greek wine/muscatel*

---

733 "My thanks [literally, great thanks, from OF *grand merci*], father, as I may thrive."

745 The *pomelles* may refer to the knobs on the litter.

754 The terms which follow (as far as line 762) can each be given the gloss "a kind of wine"; the marginal glosses represent traditional editorial treatment.

755 *Montrose* is an unknown term.

760 Both claré, piment, and rochell.

The reed your stomake to defie,

And pottes of osey set you by.
You shall have venison y-bake,
The best wilde foule that may be take.
765 A lese of grehound with you to streke
And hert and hinde and other like.
Ye shall be set at such a trist
That herte and hinde shall come to your fist,
Your disease to drive you fro,
770 To here the bugles there y-blow
With their bugles in that place,
And sevenscore raches at his rechase;
Homward thus shall ye ride,
On hauking by the rivers side,
775 With goshauke and with gentill faucon,
With egle-horne and merlion.
Whan you come home, your men amonge,
Ye shall have revell, daunces, and songe;
Litle children, great and smale.
780 Shall sing as doth the nightingale.
Than shall ye go to your evensong,
With tenours and trebles among;
Threescore of copes, of damaske bright,
Full of perles they shall be pight;
785 Your aulter clothes of taffata
And your sicles all of taffetra.
Your sensours shall be of golde,
Endent with asure many a folde.
Your quere nor organ songe shall wante
790 With countre-note and discant,

The other halfe on orgains playing
With yonge children full faire singing.
Than shall ye go to your suppere,
And sitte in tentes in grene arbere,
795 With clothes of Aras pight to the grounde,
With saphires set and diamonde.
A cloth of golde abought your heade,

*claret/spiced
wine/wine from
LaRochelle
red/help in
digestion
Alsacian wine
baked*

three leashed/go

station

displeasure/from

beagles

*cloakes
decorated
altar-cloths*

*censers
ornamented
choir/lack
counterpoint
/descant*

*orchard
Arras/hung*

---

772 A *rache* refers to a hound that hunts by scent; *rechase* refers to the blast on a horn that recalls the hounds.
776 *Egle-horne* is a kind of hawk and *merlion* is the merlin.
785–786 The rhyme word in the second verse of the couplet is probably a scribal error; a *sicle* was a woman's upper garment.

With popinjayes pight, with pery read, *decorated/jewelry /red*

And officers all at your will:
300 All manner delightes to bring you till.
The nightingale sitting on a thorne
Shall singe you notes both even and morne.
An hundreth knightes truly tolde *accurately /numbered*

Shall play with bowles in alayes colde,
305 Your disease to drive awaye: *malaise*
To see the fishes in poles playe; *pools*
And then walke in arbere up and downe,
To see the floures of great renowne:
To a draw-bridge than shall ye,
310 The one halfe of stone, the other of tree; *wood*
A barge shall mete you full right
With four and twenty ores full bright,
With trompettes and with clarioune
The freshe water to rowe up and doune.
315 Than shall ye go to the salte fome, *foam*
Your maner to see, or ye come home, *manor/ere*
With four score shippes of large toure
With dromedaries of great honour, *dromonds*
And carackes with sailes two, *carracks*
320 The sweftest that on water may go,
With galies good upon the haven, *galleys*
With four score ores at the fore staven. *stem*
Your mariners shall singe arowe
'Hey, how, and rumbylawe.'
325 Than shall ye, doughter, aske the wine,
With spices that be good and fine,
Gentill pottes with genger grene, *ginger*
With dates and dainties you betwene,
Forty torches, breninge bright,
330 At your bridges to bringe you light.
Into your chambre they shall you bringe,
With muche mirthe and more liking. *delight*
Your costerdes covered with white and blewe *bed hangings*
And diapred with liles newe. *figured/fresh*
335 Your curtaines of camaca all in folde, *silk*
Your felioles all of golde. *bed posts*
Your tester-pery at your heed, *jeweled canopy*
Curtaines with popinjayes white and reed.
Your hillinges with furres of armine, *coverings/ermine*
340 Powdred with gold of hew full fine. *besprinkled*

---

817 *Toure* probably refers to the fighting tower on the mast of the ship.

Your blankettes shall be of fustiane,   *fustian*
Your shetes shall be of clothe of Rayne.   *Rennes*
Your head-shete shall be of pery pight   *jewelry/adorned*
With diamondes set and rubies bright.
845 Whan you are laide in bedde so softe,
A cage of golde shall hange alofte,
With longe pepper faire burning,
And cloves that be swete smelling,
Frankensence and olibanum,
850 That whan ye slepe the taste may come.
And if ye no rest may take,
All night minstrelles for you shall wake."
"Gramercy, father, so mote I thee,   *thrive*
For all these thinges liketh not me."   *please*
855 Unto her chambre she is gone,
And fell in sowning sone anone   *swoon*
With much sorrow and sighing sore;
Yet seven yeare she kept him thore.   *there*

But leve we of that lady here
860 And speake we more of that squier,
That in prison so was take   *taken*
For the Kinges doughters sake.
The King himselfe, upon a daye,
Full prively he toke the waye;
865 Unto the prison sone he came;
The squier sone out he name,   *took*
And anone he made him swere
His counsail he should never discure.   *disclose*
The squier there helde up his hand
870 His bidding never he should withstande:
The King him graunted ther to go
Upon his jorney to and fro,
And brefely to passe the sea   *in short/cross*
That no man weste but he and he.
875 And whan he had his jurnay done,   *completed*
That he wolde come full soone;   *should*
"And in my chambre for to be,
The whiles that I do ordaine for thee;   *time/designate*
Than shalt thou wedde my doughter dere
880 And have my landes, both farre and nere."

The squier was full merry tho
And thanked the Kinge and forth gan go.

---

849   The two terms are—and were—identical in meaning.
859   "But let us leave that lady here."
874   "[In such manner] that no man knew except he [the King] and he [the squire]."

The King him gave both lande and fee.   *property*
Anone the squier passed the se.
85 In Tuskayne and in Lumbardy,
There he did great chivalry.   *deeds of chivalry*
Portingale nor yet in Spayne   *Portugal*
There might no man stand him againe;   *against*
And where that ever that knight gan fare,   *did*
90 The worship with him away he bare.
And thus he travailed seven yere   *traveled*
In many a land, both farre and nere;
Till on a day he thought him tho   *then*
Unto the Sepulture for to go;
95 And there he made his offeringe soone,
Right as the Kinges doughter bad him don.
Than he thought him on a day
That the Kinge to him did saye.   *that which*
He toke his leve in Lumbardy
900 And home he came to Hungry,
Unto the King soone he rade,   *went*
As he before his covenaunce made;   *covenant*
And to the King he tolde full soone
Of batailes bolde that he had done
05 And so he did the chivalry
That he had sene in Lumbardy.   *experienced*
To the Kinge it was good tidande;
Anon he toke him by the hande,
And he made him full royall chere,   *gave/welcome*
10 And said, "Welcome, my sonne so dere!
Let none wete of my meiné
That out of prison thou shuldest be,
But in my chamber holde thee still
And I shall wete my doughters will."   *learn*

15 The Kinge wente forth himselfe alone
For to here his doughters mone   *hear/complaint*
Right under the chambre window,
There he might her counseile knowe.   *there where*
Had she wist, that lady free,   *known/noble*
920 That her father there had be,   *been*
He shulde not, withouten faile,
Have knowen so muche of her counsaile;   *secrets*
Nor nothing she knew that he was there.

---

894   The Holy Sepulchre in Jerusalem.
905   "And similarly he told the deeds of chivalry."
911   "Let none of my household know."
923   *Nor* would do well to read *For*.

Whan she began to carke and care   *sorrow/lament*
925 Unto that body she said tho,
"Alas that we should parte in two!"
Twise or thrise she kissed that body,
And fell in sowninge by and by.   *swoon/alongside*
"Alas!" than said that lady dere,
930 "I have thee kept this seven yere;
And now ye be in powder small,   *fine*
I may no lenger holde you with all.   *longer*
My love, to the earth I shall thee bringe
And preestes for you to reade and singe.
935 If any man aske me what I have here,
I will say it is my treasure.
If any man aske why I do so,
'For no theves shall come therto';   *because*
And, squier, for the love of thee,
940 Fy on this worldes vanité!
Farewell golde, pure and fine;
Farewell velvet and satine;
Farewell castelles and maners also;   *manors*
Farewell huntinge and hawkinge too;
945 Farewell revell, mirthe, and play;
Farewell pleasure and garmentes gay;
Farewell perle and precious stone;
Farewell my juielles everychone;   *every one*
Farewell mantell and scarlet reed;
950 Farewell crowne unto my heed;
Farewell hawkes and farewell hounde;
Farewell markes and many a pounde;
Farewell huntinge at the hare;
Farewell harte and hinde for evermare.
955 Nowe will I take the mantell and the ringe
And become an ancresse in my livinge;   *anchoress*
And yet I am a maiden for thee   *still*
And for all the men in Christenté.
To Christ I shall my prayers make,
960 Squier, onely for thy sake;   *solely*
And I shall never no masse heare
But ye shall have parte in feare;
And every daye whiles I live,
Ye shall have your masses five,
965 And I shall offre pence three,
In tokeninge of the Trinité."
And whan this lady had this saide,
In sowning she fell at a braide.   *at once*

---

934   "And [have] priests read and sing for you."
962   "But you shall have part together [with me]."

The while she made this great morninge,
70 Under the wall stode har father the Kinge.
"Doughter," he saide, "you must not do so,
For all those vowes thou must forgo."
"Alas, father, and wele awaye!
Now have ye harde what I dide saye."   *heard*
75 "Doughter, let be all thy mourninge;
Thou shalt be wedede to a kinge."
"Iwis, father, that shall not be   *indeed*
For all the golde in Christenté;
Nor all the golde that ever God made
80 May not my harte glade."   *gladden*
"My doughter," he saide, "dere derlinge,   *darling*
I knowe the cause of your mourning;
Ye wene this body your love should be.
It is not so, so mote I thee!   *thrive*
85 It was my stewarde, Sir Maradose,
That ye so longe have kept in close."
"Alas! father, why did ye so?"
"For he wrought you all this wo.   *because/sorrow*
He made revelation unto me
90 That he knew all your privité,   *secrets*
And howe the squier, on a day,   *once*
Unto your chambre toke the way,
And ther he should have lien you by,   *laid/with*
Had he not come with company;
95 And howe ye hight him golde and fee,   *promised*
Strengthe of men and royalté;
And than he watched your chambre bright,
With men of armes hardy and wight,   *bold*
For to take that squier,
300 That ye have loved this seven yere;
But as the stewarde strong and stout
Beseged your chambre rounde about,
To you your love came full right,   *straightway*
All alone about midnight.
305 And whan he came your dore unto,
Anone 'Lady,' he saide, 'undo,'
And soone ye bade him wende awaye,   *at once/go*
For there he gate none other praye;   *would get/reward*
And as ye talked thus in fere,   *together*
310 Your enemies drewe them nere and nere;   *nearer*
They smote to him full soone anone.   *at*
There were thirty against him one;   *alone*
But with a bastarde large and longe

1013 *Bastarde* 'canon' is probably an error for *baslarde* 'dagger' (see Mead in *Refer-ences.*)

The squier presed into the thronge;   *pressed*
1015 And so he bare him in that stounde,   *time*
His enemies gave him many a wounde.
With egre mode and herte full throwe,   *fierce/bold*
The stewardes throte he cut in two;
And than his meiné all in that place   *retinue*
1020 With their swordes they hurte his face,   *disfigured*
And than they toke him everichone   *each one*
And laid him on a marble stone
Before your dore, that ye might see,
Right as your love that he had be.
1025 And sone the squier there they hent,   *caught*
And they did off his good garment,   *took*
And did it on the stewarde there,   *put*
That ye wist not what he were.
Thus ye have kept your enemy here
1030 Palling more than seven yere;
And as the squier there was take   *and thus/taken*
And done in prison for your sake.   *put*
And therfore let be your mourning;
Ye shall be wedded to a king,
1035 Or els unto an emperoure,
With golde and silver and great treasure."
"Do awaye, father, that may not be,   *cease*
For all the golde in Christenté.
Alas, father," anone she saide,
1040 "Why hath this traitour me betraid?
Alas!" she said, "I have great wrong
That I have kept him here so long.
Alas! father, why did ye so?
Ye might have warned me of my fo;
1045 And ye had tolde me who it had be,   *if*
My love had never be dead for me."
Anone she tourned her fro the King,
And downe she fell in dead sowning.   *swoon*

The King anone gan go   *did*
1050 And hente her in his armes two.   *caught*
"Lady," he said, "be of good chere!
Your love liveth and is here;
And he hath bene in Lombardy

1024   "Just as if he had been your beloved."
1028   "So that you knew not who he was."
1030   If *palling* refers to *ye*, its sense is 'languishing,' if to *enemy*, its sense is 'de-
       caying.
1040   The remark presumably is directed toward the dead steward.
1046   Rephrased, the line might read "I would not have thought my lover dead."
       Compare line 1052.

And done he hath great chivalry;
55 And come againe he is to me. *back*
In life and health ye shall him see.
He shall you wede, my doughter bright;
I have him made squier and knight;
He shall be a lorde of great renowne
60 And after me to were the crowne."
"Father," she said, "if it so be,
Let me soone that squier see."

The squier forth than did he bringe,
Full faire on live and in likinge. *alive/appearance*
65 As sone as she saw him with her eye,
She fell in sowning by and by. *swoon /immediately*

The squier her hente in armes two *caught*
And kissed her an hundreth times and mo. *more*
There was mirth and melody
70 With harpe, getron, and sautry, *guitar/psaltery*
With rote, ribible, and clokarde, *fiddle/rebec/bells*
With pipes, organs, and bumbarde, *oboe*
With other minstrelles them amonge,
With sytolphe and with sautry songe,
75 With fiddle, recorde, and dowcemere, *recorder/dulcimer*
With trompette and with clarion clere,
With dulcet pipes of many cordes;
In chambre reveling all the lordes
Unto morne that it was daye. *until*

80 The King to his doughter began to saye,
"Have here thy love and thy liking, *pleasure*
To live and ende in Gods blessinge;
And he that will departe you two, *separate*
God geve him sorrow and wo!
85 A trewer lover than ye are one
Was never yet of fleshe ne bone;
And but he be as true to thee,
God let him never thrive ne thee." *prosper*
The King in herte he was full blithe;
90 He kissed his doughter many a sithe, *time*
With melody and muche chere;
Anone he called his messengere
And commaunded him soone to go
Through his cities to and fro
95 For to warne his chevalry *knights*
That they should come to Hungry

1074 "With songs to citole and psaltery."

That worthy wedding for to see
And come unto that mangeré.   *festival*
That messenger full sone he wente
1100 And did the Kinges commaundemente.
Anone he commaunded bothe olde and yonge
For to be at that wedding,
Both dukes and erles of muche might
And ladies that were faire and bright.
1105 As soone as ever they herde the crye,
The lordes were full soone redy;
With mirth and game and muche playe
They wedded them on a solempne daye.
A royall feest there was holde,
1110 With dukes and erles and barons bolde,
And knightes and squiers of that countré,
And sith with all the comunalté.   *afterwards*
                                               /common people

And certainly, as the story sayes,
The revell lasted forty dayes;
1115 Till on a day the King himselfe
To him he toke his lordes twelfe
And so he did the squier
That wedded his doughter dere;
And even in the middes of the hall,   *right/middle*
1120 He made him king among them all;
And all the lordes everychone,
They made him homage sone anon;   *immediately*
And sithen they revelled all that day   *afterwards*
And toke their leve and went their way,
1125 Eche lorde unto his owne countré,
Where that him semed best to be.
That yong man and the Quene his wife,
With joy and blisse they led their life;
For also farre as I have gone,
Suche two lovers sawe I none.
1130 Therfore blessed may their soules be,
Amen, Amen, for charité!

Floris and Blancheflour

PPENDIX V in Brown and Robbins's *Index of Middle English Verse* lists works of Middle English literature, both religious and secular, which appear in eight or more individual manuscripts. Religious texts predominate. There are a hundred and fourteen manuscripts of *The Prick of Conscience*, almost twice as many as there are for *The Canterbury Tales*, which, though its number is only sixty-four, does stand second. A surprising feature of Appendix V is the absence of titles of secular romances. Chaucer's *Troilus* has seventeen manuscripts, but *Troilus* transcends the genre. It is more something apart than genuine romance. An inference often drawn is that any Middle English work represented by two, three, or four manuscripts is likely to have been very popular, and popularity can equate with literary value: Chaucer's major works as well as Langland's *Piers* (with fifty manuscripts) stand high on the Brown and Robbins list. The fact, then, that four manuscripts exist for the romance *Floris and Blancheflour* may be an indication both of worth and appeal. Certainly *Floris* is one of the most international of romances. A. B. Taylor (see *References*) adduces much evidence to show that the story itself is Oriental in origin. But once given its "aristocratic" and "popular" versions in Old French, it spread throughout medieval Europe to Germany, Iceland, Sweden, Italy, Spain, the Netherlands, and England.

The version of Floris here followed is that in MS Egerton 2862, once owned by the Duke of Sutherland of Trentham Hall and hence sometimes called the Trenthan or the Sutherland manuscript. It is now in the British Museum (under its Egerton title) and is, although not in every way the best, the most usable of the four Middle English versions because its narrative is very nearly complete. Like the three other English manuscripts, it lacks the initial lines of the story (and has to be located in Brown and Robbins in the section at the end listing "acephalous poems") and initial exposition must be supplied from what is known from other versions, chiefly Continental. The Cambridge manuscript (designated as Gg. 4.27.2) contains a version of the story transcribed perhaps in the latter half of the thirteenth century, possibly a hundred years prior to the transcription of the Egerton manuscript. Its verse occasionally shows, in the view of some editors, better taste than does the verse of the Egerton manuscript. A third version is in Cotton Vitellius Diii in the British Museum. Like many other Cottonian manuscripts it suffered very badly in the great fire of 1731; of its 451 lines 180 are imperfect. Since it also may be dated sometime within the latter half of the thirteenth century, its readings are often noticeably close to the French original. A fourth version is that in the Auchinleck manuscript in the Advocates Library in Edinburgh, written down in the second quarter of the fourteenth century. Its treatment of the latter portion of the story is fuller than that in the Egerton manuscript, although it lacks 366 lines in the beginning which are present in the Egerton. None of the four versions is the original English poem. This may have been composed around 1250 and probably between it and the surviving manuscripts there once existed intervening copies, now lost and now held responsible for the numerous discrepancies existing among the four versions.

The seminal poem, the Old French original, was probably current in France some seventy-five to a hundred years prior to its appearance in English. It belongs to the "aristocratic," or earlier, of the two French versions; here there is no hero or villain, the simple affection between two adolescents being deemed sufficient to maintain narrative interest. The situation in the "popular," or later, French version is otherwise: Floris is seen to perform the usual, and often tedious, feats of knight errantry in order to win Blancheflour. Editors agree that the earlier French version is more linguistically even than any English redaction, that it possesses greater artistry. Certainly there is a pedestrian stamp to the English versions, particularly that in the Egerton manuscript. Where the French poem, however, tends toward mawkish protestation and elaborate description, the English versions, since they are much shorter, seem—perhaps just by chance—more natural and ingenuous.

It is hard to judge just how much note must be given the course of the narrative in order to make the Middle English *Floris* intelligible. The poet behind the Egerton scribe or the scribe himself occasionally lets totally inappropriate lines stand, lines which can only be explained by reference either to another English version or to the French itself. This fact plus richness of narrative incident can make *Floris* seem more difficult than it actually is. And it is from the French original that we know how the poem begins—with the capture of a Christian lady by heathen forces (Saracens) who, because of her evident breeding, commit her to the care and into the service of their queen. Both ladies give birth at the same time—the Christian to a girl, the heathen to a boy. Since it is the time of a festival of flowers, each child is given an appropriate name—the boy's being Floris, the girl's Blancheflour. They grow up together, inseparable. Distressed by his son's infatuation, the king proposes to kill Blancheflour, but is dissuaded by the queen. They send him away to a distant land, Montargis, to live with an aunt. Here he pines away and has to return at the end of a fortnight. Before his arrival, however, the royal couple sell Blancheflour to merchants, receiving for her a magnificent cup, and have a tomb made on which is inscribed "Here lies sweet Blancheflour." The boy attempts to kill himself before the tomb, but is thwarted by his mother, who then persuades her consort to reveal the truth—that the tomb is empty and Blancheflour sold into distant lands. The couple equip Floris for a journey in search of her, giving him not only money and palfreys, but the magnificent cup as well. In addition, the queen gives him a protective ring, which, along with the cup itself, plays its part in the development of the story. Floris, lodging near a harbor in a hostel where Blancheflour has stayed, learns from the host the general direction of her departure. At the end of the next leg of his journey, presumably in or near Babylon, he learns from a second host that Blancheflour now belongs to the Emir himself and that a certain Daris, a bridge porter or tollkeeper, will give advice as to how to get to her. It is from Daris that Floris finds that his beloved is in the Emir's tower along with some forty other maidens. He also is made aware of the Emir's custom of taking a new wife each year, his choice being made by the random falling of a blossom from a tree upon a particular maiden. He learns finally the ruse by which he himself can enter the tower: the Emir's porter is an obsessive chess player and miser; if allowed to win and if given money (and ultimately the magnificent cup), he will be won over and devise a method of spiriting Floris up to the harem. The boy goes through with the ruse and finds himself smuggled into the presence of his beloved in a basket of flowers. Claris, a confidant of Blancheflour's, first discovers him and with ambiguous remarks about flowers as symbolic of the Emir's choice and the flowers covering the boy before her (whom she recognizes as Floris) unites and protects the pair. Blancheflour immediately neglects her duty as handmaiden to the Emir and the couple are discovered in bed by a curious chamberlain. The Emir is furious and wishes only the consent of his counsellors before slaying them. The tale ends with the assembled nobles being touched with pity by the beauty of the pair and by their desire to sacrifice themselves the one for the other. Here the protective ring comes into play: a noble sees Floris trying to give it to Blancheflour and Blancheflour refusing it and relates the incident and its pathos to the Emir. Ultimately, Floris has to reveal how he got into the tower and why he has made so perilous a journey. Somewhat incongruously, the tale ends with the Emir knighting Floris and marrying him to Blancheflour in a church.

The language of the Egerton manuscript is primarily the language of its late fourteenth-century scribe. It is chiefly East Midland and its forms close to those in Chaucer's verse, although erratic spelling, particularly a tendency to indicate long *o* with a double *o* (as in *soo* and *goon*), make it at first sight appear much different. Further, scribal indication of final *e* is ambiguous and confusing in the manuscript itself; it is difficult to determine whether a terminal flourish on a word signals an *e* or is simply a flourish and nothing more. Here the readings of McKnight and French and Hale (see *References*) are in general followed. It is up to the prosodic taste of a reader to devise for difficult lines a suitable cadence. There are definite irregularities: three stress lines are common and six and seven syllable lines also. Here, however, a well-structured story is told in undistinguished verse and the virtue of one makes up for the minor inadequacies and uncertainties of the other.

REFERENCES: Brown and Robbins, No. *45; *CBEL*, I:153–154; Hibbard, pp. 184–194; Kane, pp. 47–48; Wells, pp. 47–48.—Since no one particular ME version of *Floris* is entirely satisfactory, the most accessible editions of each MS are here listed. The version in the Egerton (or Sutherland or Trenthan) MS (1083 lines) appears in French and Hale, pp. 823–855; it also appears in G. H. McKnight, *King Horn, Floriz and Blauncheflur, The Assumption of Our Lady*, 2nd ed. (London 1901, Early English Text Society, No. 14 Orig. Series), which prints as well the defective version in the Cotton Vitellius MS (451 lines) and the version in the Cambridge MS (824 lines). A. B. Taylor, *Floris and Blancheflour* (Oxford 1927) prints the romance as it appears in the Advocates (or Auchinleck) MS (861 lines), but with additions from both the Cotton and Cambridge MSS so that the line total reaches 1311.

N e thurst men never in londe   *need*
After fairer children fonde.   *seek*
The Christen woman fedde hem tho;   *nourished/then*
Full well she lovid hem both two.
5 So longe she fedde hem in fere   *together*
That they were of elde of seven yere.   *until/age*
The King behelde his sone dere
And saide to him on this manere:
That harme it were muche more
10 But his son were sette to lore   *unless/study*
On the book lettres to know,
As men don, both hye and lowe.   *high*
"Faire sone," she saide, "thou shalt lerne;

Lo, that thou do full yerne!"
15 Floris answerd with weeping,
As he stood bifore the King;
All weeping saide he,
"Ne shall not Blancheflour lerne with me?
Ne can I noght to scole goon   *school/go*
20 Without Blaunchefloure," he saide than,
"Ne can I in no scole sing ne rede   *read*
Without Blaunchefloure," he saide.
The King saide to his soon,
"She shall lerne, for thy love."
25 To scole they were put;
Both they were good of witte.
Wonder it was of hur lore,
And of her love well the more.
The children lovid togeder so
30 They might never parte a two.
When they had five yere to scole gon,
So well they had lerned tho,
Inough they couth of Latine   *knew*
And well write on parchemine.
35 The King understood the grete amoure   *perceived/love*
Bitwene his son and Blanchefloure
And thought when they were of age
That her love wolde noght swage   *lessen*
Nor he might noght her love withdrawe
40 When Floris shuld wife after the lawe.   *marry*
The King to the Quene saide tho   *then*
And tolde hur of his wo—
Of his thought and of his care
How it wolde of Floris fare.
45 "Dame," he saide, "I tell thee my reed: *advice*
I will that Blanchefloure be do to deed.
When that maide is y-slawe   *slain*
And brought of her lif-dawe,
As sone as Floris may it underyete,   *just as/know*
50 Rathe he wille hur foryete.   *quickly/forget*
Than may he wife after reed."   *marry/advisedly*
The Quene answerde then and said,
And thought with hur reed   *advice*

---

14   "Lo, do that very earnestly!"
26   "They were both of good intelligence."
27–28   "It was a marvel about their learning, but more a marvel about their love."
34   "And [could] write well on parchment."
44   "[Concerning] how Floris would fare."
46   "I wish that Blancheflour be done to death."
48   "And ended the days of her life."

Save the maide fro the deed.   *to save/dead*
55 "Sir," she saide, "we aught to fonde   *ought/try*
   That Florens lif with menske in londe,   *live/honor*
   And that he lese not his honour   *lose*
   For the maiden Blaunchflour.
   Who so might reve that maide clene
60 That she were brought to deth bidene,
   Hit were muche more honour
   Than slee that maide Blanchflour."
   Unnethes the King graunt that it be so: *hesitantly*
                                                         /granted
   "Dame, rede us what is to do."   *advise/to be done*
65 "Sir, we shull oure soon Floris
   Sende into the londe of Mountargis;
   Blithe will my suster be,   *glad*
   That is lady of that contree;
   And when she woot for whoom   *knows*
70 That we have sent him us froom,
   She will do all hur might,
   Both by day and by night,
   To make hur love so undo
   As it had never been so.
75 And, sir," she saide, "I rede eke   *advise/also*
   That the maidens moder make hur seeke.   *feign sickness*
   That may be that other resoun
   For that ilke encheson,
   That she may not fro hur moder go."
80 Now been these children swith wo,   *very/sad*
   Now they may not go in fere;   *together*
   Drewrier thinges never noon were.   *sadder*
   Floris wept bifore the King
   And saide, "Sir, without lesing,   *a lie*
85 For my harme out ye me sende,   *to/sorrow*
   Now she ne might with me wende;   *go*
   Now we ne mot togeder go,   *may*
   All my wele is turned to wo."   *pleasure*
   The King saide to his son aplight,   *at once*
90 "Sone, withinne this fourtenight,
   Be her moder quicke or deede,
   Sekerly," he him saide,
   "That maide shall com thee to."   *go*
   "Ye, sir," he said, "I pray you it be so.
95 Yif that ye me hur sende,

59–60   "Whosoever might take away that chaste girl in that she were killed at once
     [but in appearances only]." The significance of the lines is revealed later in
     the ruse of the false tomb created for Blanchflour.
73   "To make their love so dissolve."
77–78   "That may be a further reason for that same cause."

I recke never wheder I wende."   *care/whither/go*
That the child graunted, the King was fain,
And him betaught his chamburlain.   *committed to*
With muche honoure they theder coom,   *thither/go*
100 As fell to a riche kinges soon.   *was befitting*
Well faire him receivid the Duke Orgas,
That king of that castel was,
And his aunt with muche honour;
But ever he thought on Blanchefloure.
105 Glad and blithe they been him withe;
But for no joy that he seith   *saw*
Ne might him glade game ne glee,   *gladden*
For he might not his lif see.   *because/beloved*
His aunt sent him to lore   *study*
110 There as other children wore,   *there where/were*
Both maidons and grom;   *youths*
To lerne mony theder coom.   *thither/went*
Inough he sikes, but noght he lernes;   *sighs*
For Blauncheflour ever he mornes.
115 If eny man to him speke,   *speaks*
Love is on his hert steke.   *fastened*
Love is at his hert roote,
That no thing is so soote.   *sweet*
Galingale ne licoris   *spice/licorice*
120 Is not so soote as hur love is,   *sweet*
Ne no thing ne non other.
So much he thenketh on Blancheflour,
Of oon day him thinketh three
For he ne may his love see;
125 Thus he abideth with muche wo
Till the fourtenight were go.   *had/passed*
When he saw she was nought y-coome,
So muche sorrow he hath noome   *suffered*
That he loveth mete ne drinke,
130 Ne may noon in his body sinke.
The chamberlein sent the King to wete
His sones state, all y-wrete.   *completely*
                                       /written out

The King full sone the waxe to-brake   *quickly/seal*
                                       /broke
For to wete what it spake.   *know/said*
135 He beginneth to chaunge his moode,
And well sone he understode,

---

97   "[To] that the youth agreed, the King was glad."
121 "Nor anything [else] nor any other [person]."
123 "[That] one day seems three to him."
130 "Nor may take any into his body."
131 "The chamberlain sent to the King to let him know."

And with wreth he cleped the Quene   *anger/called*
And tolde hur alle his teene   *distress*
And with wrath spake and saide,
140 "Let do bring forth that maide!
Fro the body the heved shall go."   *from/head*
Thanne was the Quene full wo;
Than spake the Quene, that good lady,
"For Goddes love, sir, mercy!
145 At the next haven that here is,   *nearest/harbor*
Ther been chapmen riche, y-wis,   *merchants*
    /indeed

Marchaundes of Babyloin full riche,
That woll hur bye bletheliche.   *gladly*
Than may ye for that lovely foode   *child*
150 Have muche catell and goode;   *property/goods*
And so she may fro us be brought
So that we slee hur nought."
Unnethes the King graunted this,   *reluctantly*
But forsoth, so it is.
155 The King let sende after the burgeise,   *burgess*
That was hende and curtaise,   *gracious*
And welle selle and bigge couth,   *buy/could*
And moony langages had in his mouth.
Well sone that maide was him betaught   *committed*
160 And to the haven was she brought.
Ther have they for that maide yolde   *given*
Twenty mark of reed golde,   *red*
And a coupe good and riche;   *cup*
In all the world was non it liche.   *like*
165 Ther was never noon so well grave;   *engraved*
He that it made was no knave.   *ordinary workman*
Ther was purtraid on, I weene,   *depicted/suspect*
How Parise ledde away the Queene;   *Paris*
And on the covercle above   *lid*
170 Purtraide was ther bother love;
And in the pomel theron   *knob*
Stood a charbuncle stoon;
In the world was not so depe soler   *cellar*
That it nolde light the botelere
175 To fille both ale and wine;
Of silver and golde both good and fine.
Enneas the King, that nobel man,   *Aeneas*
At Troye in bataile he it wan

---

140   "Have the girl brought forth."
154   "But indeed, such is [the truth]."
170   "Depicted was the love of both."
174   "That it would not provide [sufficient] light for the butler."
176   "It was" understood.

And brought it into Lumbardy,
180 And gaf it his lemman, his amy.   *beloved/lover*
    The coupe was stoole fro King Cesar;
    A theef out of his tresour-hous it bar;
    And sethe that ilke same theef   *afterwards/very*
    For Blaunchefloure he it yeef;   *in exchange for*
                                    /gave

185 For he wist to winne suche three,
    Might he hur bring to his contree.
    Now these marchaundes sailen over the see
    With this maide, to her contree.   *their*
    So longe they han undernome   *journeyed*
190 That to Babylon they been coom.
    To the Amiral of Babyloine   *emir*
    They solde that maide swithe soone;   *straightway*
    Rath and soone they were at oon;   *quickly/agreed*
    The Amiral hur bought anoon
195 And gafe for hur, as she stood upright,
    Sevin sithes of golde her wight,   *times/weight*
    For he thought without weene   *doubt*
    That faire maide have to queene;   *as*
    Among his maidons in his bour   *harem*
200 He hur dide, with muche honour.   *put*
    Now these merchaundes that may belete   *maiden/left*
    And been glad of hur biyete.   *profit*

    Now let we of Blancheflour be
    And speke of Floris in his contree.
205 Now is the burgais to the King coom   *burgess*
    With the golde and his garison   *payment*
    And hath take the King to wolde   *given/in keeping*
    The selver and the coupe of golde.
    They lete make in a chirche
210 A swithe faire grave wirche
    And lete lay theruppon   *had/placed*
    A new faire painted ston
    With letters all aboute write   *engraved*
    With full muche worshippe.   *solemnity*
215 Whoso couth the letters rede,
    Thus they spoken and thus they saide:
    "Here lith swete Blaunchefloure,   *lies*
    That Floris lovid par amoure."   *passionately*
    Now Floris hath undernome   *departed*
220 And to his fader he is coome;
    In his fader halle he is light.   *at/alighted*

---

185   "For he knew how to obtain three such [cups]."
209–210   "They had made in a church a very beautiful tomb."

His fader him grette anoon right   *straightway*
And his moder, the Queene also,
But unnethes might he that do
225 That he ne asked where his leman be;
Nonskins answere chargeth he,
So longe he is forth noome
In to chamber he is coome.
The maidenis moder he asked right,   *immediately*
230 "Where is Blauncheflour, my swete wight?"   *being*
"Sir," she saide, "forsothe y-wis,   *in truth/indeed*
I ne woot where she is."   *know*
She bethought hur on that lesing   *remembered*
                                              /deception

That was ordained bifoore the King.
235 "Thou gabbest me," he saide tho;   *mock*
"Thy gabbing doth me muche wo!
Tell me where my leman be!"   *beloved*
All weeping saide thenne she,
"Sir," she saide, "deede." "Deed!" saide he.
240 "Sir," she saide, "for sothe, ye."   *yes*
"Allas, when died that swete wight?"
"Sir, withinne this fourtenight
The erth was laide hur about
And deed she was for thy love."
245 Flores, that was so faire and gent,   *gentle*
Sounid there, verament.   *swooned/truly*
The Christen woman began to crye
To Jesu Christ and Saint Marye.
The King and the Quene herde that crye;
250 Into the chamber they ronne on hye,   *in/haste*
And the Queene seye her biforne   *saw*
On sowne the childe that she had borne.   *swoon*
The Kinges hert was all in care,
That sawe his sone for love so fare.
255 When he awooke and speke moght,   *might*
Sore he wept and sore he sight,   *sighed*
And saide to his moder y-wis,   *indeed*
"Lede me there that maide is."
Theder they him brought on highe;   *thither/haste*
260 For care and sorrow he wolde dyghe.   *die*
As sone as he to the grave com,

224–225 "But he could hardly restrain himself from asking where his beloved might be."
226–228 The ME is confused, perhaps from maladroit translation from the French, but the sense is "He [does not wait] to demand an answer, [but] went forth until he got to the chamber."
254 "Who saw his son so act for love."

Sone there behelde he then
And the letters began to rede   *read*
That thus spake and thus saide:
265 "Here lith swete Blauncheflour,   *lies*
That Floris lovid par amoure."   *passionately*
Three sithes Floris sownidde nouth,   *times/swooned*
                                      /now

Ne speke he might not with mouth.
As sone as he awoke and speke might,
270 Sore he wept and sore he sight.   *sighed*
"Blauncheflour!" he said, "Blauncheflour!
So swete a thing was never in boure!   *chamber*
Of Blauncheflour is that I meene,
For she was com of good kin.
275 Litel and muche loveden thee   *low/high*
For thy goodnesse and thy beauté.
Yif deth were dalt aright,
We shuld be deed both on oo night.   *one*
On oo day born we were;
280 We shull be ded both in feere.   *together*
Deeth," he saide, "full of envie   *malice*
And of alle trechorie,
Refte thou hast me my leman;   *taken away*
                                      /beloved

For soth," he saide, "thou art to blame.
285 She wold have levid, and thou noldest,
And faine wolde I die, and thou woldest.
After deeth clepe no more I nille,   *call/shall not*
But slee my self now I wille."
His knife he braide out of his sheth;   *whipped*
290 Himself he wolde have do to deth   *done*
And to hert he had it smeten,
Ne had his moder it underyetèn;   *perceived*
Then the Queene fell him upon
And the knife fro him noom.   *took*
295 She reft him of his litel knif
And savid there the childes lif.
Forth the Queene ranne, all weeping,
Till she come to the King.
Than saide the good lady,
300 "For Goddes love, sir, mercy!
Of twelve children have we noon
On live now but this oon;   *alive/except/one*

---

262   "Quickly he then looked there."
277   "If death were handed down justly."
285–286   "She would want to have lived and you [Death] did not wish it, and I
        would gladly die and you would not [let me]."

And better it were she were his make	*mate*
Than he were deed for hur sake."	
305 "Dame, thou saist sooth," saide he;	
"Sen it may noon other be,	*since/otherwise*
Lever me were she were his wif	
Than I lost my sonnes lif."	
Of this word the Quene was faine	*glad*
310 And to her soon she ran againe.	*back*
"Flories, soon, glad make thee;	
Thy lef thou shalt on live see.	*dear one/alive*
Floris, son, through enginne	*a device*
Of thy faders reed and mine,	*counsel*
315 This grave let we make,	*had/made*
Leve sone, for thy sake,	
Yif thou that maide forgete woldest,	
After oure reed wif thou sholdest."	
Now every worde she hath him tolde	
320 How that they that maiden solde.	
"Is this sooth, my moder dere?"	
"For sooth," she saide, "she is not here."	
The rough stoon adoun they laide	
And sawe that there was not the maide.	
325 "Now, moder, I think that I leve may.	*leave*
Ne shall I rest night ne day—	
Night ne day ne no stounde—	*hour*
Till I have my leman founde.	*beloved*
Hur to seken I woll wende,	*wish/go*
330 Thaugh it were to the worldes ende!"	
To the King he goth to take his leve,	
And his fader bade him bileve.	*remain*
"Sir, I will let for no winne;	
Me to bidden it it were grete sinne."	
335 Than said the King, "Seth it is so,	*since*
Seth thou wilt noon other do,	*otherwise*
All that thee nedeth we shull thee finde.	*require*
Jesu thee of care unbinde!"	*release*
"Leve fader," he saide, "I telle thee	*dear*
340 All that thou shalt finde me.	*provide*
Thou mast me finde, at my devise,	*disposal*
Seven horses all of pris;	*excellence*
And two y-charged upon the molde	
Both with selver and with golde;	

307 "I had rather she were his wife."
317–318. "[To see] if you would forget that girl [and so that] you should marry according to our wish."
333–334 "Sir, I shall stop for no pleasure; [just] to ask me it [that is, to remain], it would be great harm."
343–344 "And two loaded with both silver and gold"; *upon the mold* "upon earth" merely supplies a rhyme.

345 And two y-charged with monay
    For to spenden by the way;
    And three with clothes riche,
    The best of all the kingriche;   *kingdom*
    Seven horses and sevin men,
350 And three knaves without hem;   *servants*
                                         /in addition to

    And thine owne chamburlaine,
    That is a well nobel swaine.   *very/man*
    He can us both wish and reede;   *guide/advise*
    As marchaundes we shull us lede."   *ourselves*
                                         /conduct
355 His fader was an hinde king;   *gracious*
    The coupe of golde he dide him bring, *cup*
    That ilke selfe coupe of golde   *very/same*
    That was Blaunchefloor for yolde.
    "Have this, soon," saide the King,
360 "Herewith thou may that swete thing   *with it*
    Winne, so may betide–
    Blaunchefloor with the white side,   *skin*
    Blaunchefloor, that faire may."   *maiden*
    The King let sadel a palfray,   *had/saddled*
365 The one half so white so milke
    And that other reed so silke.   *red*
    I ne can telle nought
    How richely that sadel was wrought.
    The arson was of golde fin;   *saddle-bow*
370 Stones of vertu stode therine,   *value*
    Bigon aboute with orfreis.   *fringed*
                                         /embroidery

    The Queene was kinde and curtais;
    Cast hur toward the King
    And of hur finger she braide a ring: *drew*
375 "Have now this ilke ring;   *very*
    While is it thine, dought no thing   *fear*
    Of fire brenning ne water in the see;
    Ne iren ne steele shall dere thee." *harm*
    He took his leve for to go;
380 Ther was full muche wo;
    They make him noon other chere
    Than her soon were laide in bere.

---

358   "For which Blaunchefloor was given."
361   "Obtain, if it so may happen."
365   Here the red and white colors apply to the saddle of line 368; in the French
      version, they apply to the horse itself.
373   Probably "[She] cast herself toward the king"—but the Advocates MS reads
      "She cast her hond to hire fingre," which is better despite the poor rhyme.
381–382   "They acted in no way different than they [would] were their son laid on
      [his] bier."

Furth he went with all his maine;   *forth/retinue*
With him went the chamberlaine.
385 So have they her havin nome
    That they been to the havin come   *until/harbor*
    There Blaunchefloure was all night.   *where*
    Well richely they been dight;   *received*
    The lord of the inne was welle hende;   *gracious*
390 The childe he sette next the ende   *nearest*
    In all the fairest seete.   *seat*
    Alle they dronken and all they yete.
    Ete ne drinke might he nought;
    On Blaunchefloure was all his thought.
395 The lady of that underyat   *perceived*
    That the childe morning sat   *mourning*
    And saide to her lord with still dreme,   *quiet/voice*
    "Sir, nim now goode yeme   *take/heed*
    How the childe mourning sittes.
400 Mete and drinke he foryetes;   *forgets*
    Litel he eteth and lasse he drinketh.   *less*
    He is no marchaund, as me thinketh."   *merchant*
    To Flores then saide she,
    "All full of mourning I thee see.
405 Ther sate ther this sender day
    Blaunchefloure, that swete may.   *maiden*
    Heder was that maide brought   *hither*
    With marchaundes that hur had bought;   *by*
    Heder they brought that maide swete;
410 They wold have solde hur for biyete;   *profit*
    To Babyloin they wille hur bring,
    Both of semblant and of morning."
    When Floris herd speke of his leman,   *beloved*
    Was he never so glad a man
415 And in his hert bigan to light;   *grow light*
    The coupe he let fulle anon right.   *cup/be filled*
    "Dame," he saide, "the fessel is thine,   *vessel*
    Both the coupe and the wine–
    The wine and the gold eke–   *also*
420 For thou of my leman speke.   *because*
    On hur I thought; for hur I sight;   *sigh*
    I ne wist where I hur finde might.   *know*

---

385 *Havin* is probably an error for *way*: "Thus they have taken their way."
392 "All of them drank and ate."
405 "There sat there only the other day."
412 In the Cambridge MS there precedes *Thou art hire y-lich of alle thinge* "You
     are like her in every way" and hence this line "both in appearance and in mourn-
     ing" would make sense.

Winde ne weder shall me assoine
That I ne shall seche hur in Babyloine."
425 Now Floris resteth him all a night.
At morn, when it was day light,
He dide him into the wilde floode.   *set out/on*
Winde and weder with him stoode;
Sone so Floris come to londe,   *as soon as*
430 There he thanked Goddes sonde–   *providence*
To the londe ther his lif inne is,   *where/beloved*
Him thought he was in paradise.
Sone to Floris tiding men tolde
That the Amiral wold fest holde.   *emir/festival*
435 His erls, barons, comin sholde,
And all that wolde of him lond holde,
For to herkin his hest,   *hear/behest*
And for to honoure his fest.
Glad was Floris of that tiding.   *news*
440 He hoped to com to that gestning,   *entertainment*
Yif he might in that halle
His leman see among hem alle.

Now to that citee Floris is come;
Faire he hath his inne y-noome   *appropriately
                                                       /quarters/taken*
445 At a palaise; was non it liche;   *like*
The lord of that inne was fulle riche;   *hostel*
He hadde been ferre and wide.
The childe he set next his side   *next to/him*
In all the fairest seete.   *seat*
450 Alle they dronken and ete,
All that therinne were;
All they made good chere;
They ete and dronke echoon with other;   *each one*
But Floris thought all another.   *quite/differently*
455 Ete ne drinke he might noght;
On Blauncheflour was all his thought.
Than spake the burgeis,   *burgess*
That was hende and curtais,   *gracious*
"Ow, child, me thinketh welle   *oh*
460 That muche thou thinkest on my catelle."   *possessions*
"Nay, sir, on catel thenke I nought"
(On Blauncheflour was all his thought),
"But I thinke on all wise   *expressly*

423–424   "Wind nor storm shall not prevent me from seeking her in Babyloine."
432   "It seemed to him he was in Paradise."
436   "And all who were supposed to hold land from him."

For to finde my marchaundise;
465 And yit it is the most wo,   *yet*
When I it find, I shall it forgo."
Than spack the lord of that inne,
"This sender day, ther sate herein   *recent*
That faire maide Blauncheflour,
470 Both in halle and in boure.
Ever she made morning chere,   *sad/mien*
And bement Floris, her lif fere;   *lamented for*
                                                          /dear/companion

Joye ne bliss made she noon,
But for Floris she made her moon."   *lament*
475 Floris toke a coupe of silver clere,   *cup/bright*
A mantil of scarlet with meniuere: *fur trim*
"Have this, sir, to thin honour:
Thou may thonke it Blauncheflour.   *for it*
He might make min hert glade
480 That couth me tell wheder she is ladde." *whither/taken*
"Child, to Babyloin she is brought;
The Amiral hur hath bought.
He gafe for hur, as she stood upright,
Seven sithes of gold hur wight;   *times/weight*
485 For he thenketh, without weene,   *denial*
That faire may have to Queene.
Among his maidons in his toure
He hur dide, with muche honoure."   *put*
Now Flores resteth him there all night,
490 Till on the morrow the day was light;
He roos on the morrowning.   *arose*
He gaf his ost an hundrid shelling,   *gave/shillings*
To his ost and to his ostesse,
And toke his leve, and feire dide kisse;
495 And yerne his ost he besought   *eagerly*
That he him help, yif he might ought–   *in any way*
Yif he might, with any ginne   *plan*
That faire may to him winne.   *maid/regain*
"Childe," he saide, "to a brigge thou shalt com; *bridge*
500 The senpere finde at hoom.
He woneth at the brigges ende;   *dwells/bridge's*
Curtais man he is and hende;   *gracious*
We arn bretheren and trouthes plight;

---

464 *Marchaundise* refers to what he would normally be after.
465–466 The Advocates MS reading is *And yit that is my meste wo/yif ich hit finde
and schal forgo* "And yet that is my greatest anxiety, if I [should] find it and be
obliged to do without [it]."
470 "[Fair] both in hall and chamber."
486 "To have that fair maiden as Queen."
500 "The good man [that is, the bridge keeper] [you] will find at home."
503 "We are brothers and sworn to be faithful."

He can thee wish and rede aright.   *direct/advise*
505 Thou shalt bere him a ringe
    Fro myself, to tokeninge,   *as a/sign*
    That he help thee in boure and halle
    As it were my self befalle."
    Floris taketh the ringe and nemeth leve,   *takes/leave*
510 For longe wolde he nought beleve.   *remain*
    By that it was undern highe,
    The brigge come he swith nye.   *bridge/very/near*
    The senperes name was Daris.   *good man's*
    Floris greet him well faire, y-wis,
515 And he him the ringe arought   *handed*
    And full faire it him betaught.   *very/committed*
    Through the token of that ilk ring
    Floris had full faire gestning   *entertainment*
    Of fish and flesh and tender breede,   *bread*
520 Of win, both white and reede;
    And ever Floris sate full colde
    And Dares bigan the childe beholde:
    "Leve child, what may this be,
    Thus thoughtful, as I thee see?
525 Art thou nought all in feere   *good health*
    That thou makist thus sorry chere—
    Or thou likest noght this in?"   *hostel*
    Than Floreis answerd him,
    "Yis, sir, by Goddes ore,   *grace*
530 So good ne had I mony day yore;   *for long*
    God let me abide that daye   *await*
    That I thee quite well may.   *requite*
    But I thenke on all wise   *in/every/way*
    Most upon my marchaundise;
535 And yit it is most wo,
    When I hit finde, I shall it forgo."
    "Childe, woldest thou telle me thy grif;   *grief*
    To hele thee, me were full lif."
    Every word he hath him tolde—
540 How the maide was fro him solde
    And how he was of Spain a kinges son,
    For grete love theder y-come   *thither*
    To fonde, with quaintyse and with gin,   *try/cleverness*
    /scheme

    Blauncheflour for to winne.
545 "Now," saith Dares, "thou art a folt"—   *stupid person*

---

508   "As [if] it were concerning myself."
511   "By the [time] it was high noon."
536   Compare lines 465–466.
538   "It would please me to heal you."

And for a foole the childe he halt–
"Now I woot how it gooth;   *know/goes*
Thou desirest thin own deeth.
The Amiral hath to his justinges   *tournaments*
550 Other half hundred of riches kinges;
And the alder-richest king   *most powerful*
Durst not beginne such a thing.   *would dare*
                                             /undertak

Yif Amiral might it understonde,   *perceive*
He shulde be drawe in his owne londe,
555 About Babyloin, I wene,
Six longe mile and tene.
At every mile is a walle therate,
Seven sithes twenty yate;   *times/gates*
And twenty toures ther been inne,
560 That every day cheping is inne;   *trading*
Every day and night throughout the yere
The cheping is y-liche plenere;   *alike/full-tilt*
And though all the men that been bore
Had on hur lif swore
565 To winne that maide faire and free,
All shull they die, so moot I thee.   *as/may/prosper*
In that bour, in midward pight,   *placed*
Stondeth a toure, I thee plight.   *assure*
A hundrid fathum it is hye;   *high*
570 Whoso beholdeth hit, fer or nere,
An hundred fathum it is y-fere;   *altogether*
It is made without pere,   *equal*
Of lime and of marbul stone;
In all this world is suche noone.
575 Now is the morter made so wele,
Ne may it breke iren ne steele.
The pomel that above is laide,   *tower finial*
It is made with muche pride
That man ne thar in the tour berne
580 Nouther torche ne lanterne,   *neither*
Suche a pomel was ther bigone–   *set*
Hit shined a-night so doth the soone.   *sun*
Now arn in that ilke toure   *same*
Two and fourty nobel boure;   *chambers*
585 Well were that ilke man

---

550 "One hundred fifty powerful kings" (literally, [a hundred and] a second half-hundred).
554–555 Probably "He [the culprit who attempts to steal Blancheflour] would be drawn [as a punishment] in his [the Emir's] own land." The scribe here confuses mention of punishment with a description of the Emir's city.
579 "That one does not need to burn in the tower"; the reason is given in lines 581 and 582.

That might woon in that onn!
Ne durst him never more, y-wis,   *indeed*
Covete after more blisse.   *yearn/for*
Naw arn ther serjauntes in that stage   *men at arms*
                                                   /upper floor
590 That serven the maidons of highe parage.   *lineage*
But no serjeaunt may serve therinne
That bereth in his breche that ginne   *device*
To serve hem day and night,
But he be as a capoun dight.   *unless/eunuch*
                                                   /made

595 At the yate is a yatewarde;   *guard*
He is not a cowarde;
He is wonder proude withalle–
Every day he goth in riche palle.   *clothes*
And the Amiral hath a wonder woon,   *strange/custom*
600 That he that is com of Christendom,
Every yere to have a new wif–
Then he lovith his Queene as his lif.
Then shull men bring doun of the toure   *from*
All the maidens of grete honoure
605 And bring hem into an orcharde,
The fairest of all midlerde.   *on/earth*
Therin is many fowles song;   *of many/birds*
Men might leve therin full long.   *remain*
About the orchard is a walle;
610 The foulest stone is cristall;   *meanest*
And a well springeth therinne
That is made with muche ginne.   *ingenuity*
The well is of muche pris;   *value*
The stremes com fo Paradise;
615 The gravel of the ground is precious stoones
And all of vertu for the noones.
Now is the well of muche aught: *power*
Yif a woman com that is forlaught   *unchaste*
And she be do to the streeme   *put/into*
620 For to weshe her hondes clene,   *wash*
The water wille yelle as it were woode   *crazed*
And bicome red as bloode.
On what maide the water fareth so,
Sone she shall to deth be do;

---

586 "Who might dwell in one [of them]."
600 A line peculiar to the Egerton MS and without any apparent sense. The Cambridge MS shows the line *In al the world nis such a sune* "In all this world [there] is not such a luminary [or: son, in the sense of "individual"]."
616 "And all [of the stones] indeed [have] power"—a reference to the medieval belief in the supernatural power of gems.

625 Tho that been maidens clene,   *those/who*
                                                                    /chaste

They may wesh therein, I wene;
The water woll stonde faire and clere;   *will/remain*
To hem maketh it no daungere.
At the walles hed stondeth a tree,
630 The fairest that on erthe may be;
It is cleped the Tree of Love;   *called*
Floures and blossomes springen above.
Then they that maidons clene bene,   *chaste*
They shull be brought under the trene,   *trees*
635 And which so falleth the floure   *on which*
Shall be queene with muche honour.
Yif any maiden ther is
That the Amiral telleth of more pris,   *account/value*
The flour shall be to her sent
640 Through art of enchauntement.
The Amiral cheseth hem by the flour,
And ever he herkeneth after Blauncheflour."
Three sithes Flores sownid anoon   *times/swooned*
Right bifore hem everychoon.   *everyone*
645 When he awoke and speke might,
Sore he wept and sore he sight,   *sighed*
And saide, "Dares, I worth now deede,   *shall be*
But that I hope of thee som reede."   *unless/plan*
"Leve soon, will ye see
650 That thy trust is muche on me.
Then is the best reed that I can–   *for*
Other reed ne can I noon–   *know/none*
Wende to-morn to the toure   *go*
As thou wer a good ginoure;   *craftsman*
655 Take on thy honde squier and scantlon   *square/measure*
As thou were a freemason.   *mason*
Behold the tour up and doun;
The porter is cruel and feloun;   *villainous*
Well sone he will come to thee
660 And ask what manner man thou be
And bere on thee felonie   *accuse*
And say thou art com to be a spie.
And thou shalt answere swetliche,   *sweetly*

---

629 At the walles hed may mean "above the wall," since the Cambridge MS reads
    aboue the walle.
635 The Cambridge MS (following the French) reads And wich-so falleth on that
    ferste flour "And on whomsoever falls that first flower."
642 The Cambridge MS reads Alle weneth hit shulle beo Blauncheflur "All suspect it
    shall be Blaunceflour."
649–650 The lines are strange, but probably mean "Dear son, [it] is well for you
    that your trust is firmly in me."

And say to him mildeliche–   *mildly*
65 Say thou art a ginoure   *craftsman*
To beholde that faire toure,
For to loke and for to fonde   *try*
To make suche another in thy londe.
Well sone he will com thee nere   *nearer*
70 And will bid thee play the chekere.   *chess*
When thou art at cheker brought,
Without selver be thou nought;   *silver coins*
Thou shalt have redy with thee
Twenty marke beside thy knee.
75 Yif thou winne ought of his,   *any*
Thou tell therof litel pris;
And if he winne ought of thin,
Loke thou leve it with him.
So thou shalt, all with ginne,   *deception*
80 The porters love forsoth winne
That he thee help on this day.
But he thee helpe, no man may.   *unless*
Well yerne he will thee bidde and pray   *very/eagerly/ask*
Com another day to playe;
85 Thou shalt saye thou wilt so;
Thou shalt take with thee suche two.
The thridde day, take an hundred pound
And thy coupe hool and sound;   *cup/whole*
Yeve him markes and poundes of thy male;   *give/from/wallet*
90 Of thy tresoure tell thou no tale.
Well yerne he will thee bidde and pray   *eagerly*
To lay thy coupe and to play.   *wager/cup*
Thou shalt answere altherfirst,   *at first*
Lenger to play thee ne list.   *longer/desire*
95 Full muche he wille for the coupe bede,   *offer*
Yif he might the better spede;
Thou shalt it blethly yeve him,   *gladly/give*
Yif it be of gold fine;   *even if*
And he woll full muche love thee   *very*
100 And to thee bowe also, pardé,   *indeed*
That he will falle to thy foote   *in that*
And becom thin, yif he moote;   *may*
And homage thou shalt fonge   *receive*
And the trouth of his honde.   *pledge*
105 As he saide, he dide y-wis;
And as he ordained, so it is:

---

676 "You [should] account it little gain."
686 "You shall take with you twice as much."
690 "Do not keep count of [pay little heed to] your treasure."
696 "[To see] if he might have better luck."

The porter is Floris man bicom
For his gold and his warisone.   *reward*
Floris saide, "Now art thou my moon,   *companion*
710 All my trust is thee upon;
Now my consel I will thee shewe;   *plan/reveal*
Rede me right, yif thou be trew."   *advise/true*
Now every word he hath him tolde–
How the maide was fro him solde
715 And how he was of Spain a kinges soon,
For grete love theder y-coom   *thither/come*
To fonden, with some ginne,   *attempt/ruse*
That faire maide for to winne.
The porter that herde, and sore sight,   *sighed*
720 And saide, "I am betraide aright;   *betrayed/indeed*
Though thy catel I am dismaide;   *goods
                                                   /brought low*

Therfore I am well evil apaide.   *ill/pleased*
Now I woot how it gooth;
For thee shall I suffer deth!
725 I shall thee faile nevermo,   *never*
The while I may ride and go.   *walk*
Thy forwardes shall I holde alle,   *agreements*
Whatsoever may befalle.
Winde now hoom to thin inne,   *go/hostel*
730 While I bethenke me of sum ginne;   *plan*
Betwene this and the thridde day,
Fonde I shall what I do may."   *try*
Flores spake and wept among,   *as well*
And thought the terme all too long.   *time*
735 The porter thought the best reed   *hit upon/plan*
And let geder floures in a meede;
He wist it was the maidons wille;
To lepes he lete of floures fille: *two/baskets*
That was the best reed, as him thought thoo,   *then*
740 Floures in that on lep to do.
Two maidens the lepe bore;
So hevy charged never they wore   *loaded*
And bade Gode yeve hem evil fine–   *end*
To mony floures he dide therinne!   *too/placed*
745 To Blauchefloures chamber they shulde tee;   *go*
They yede to another, and let that be.   *went/left*
They shuld have gon to Blaunchefloure,
And yede to swete Claris boure,   *went/chamber*
And cursed him so fele brought to honde;

---

736 "And had flowers gathered in a meadow."
740 "To put flowers in one basket [only]."
749 "And cursed him [who] brought so much [weight] together."

50 They yede hoom and lete hem stonde.
   Claris to the lepe com wolde,
   The flores to hondel and to beholde;   *flowers*
   Floris wende it hadde be his swete wight;   *thing*
   Of the lepe he stert upright   *out of/basket*
55 And the maide, all for drede,
   Bigan to shrelle and to grede.   *shriek/cry*
   When he saugh it was not she,   *saw*
   Into the lepe ayen stert he   *back/jumped*
   And held him betraide clene;   *clearly*
60 Of his lif tolde he not a bene.
   Ther com maidons, and to Claris lepe   *leapt*
   By ten, by twelf, on an heepe,   *altogether*
   And they asked what hur were,
   And why she made suche a bere.   *outcry*
65 Claris bithought hur anoon right
   That hit was Blauncheflour the white
   And gave the maidons answere anoon
   That to her chamber were goon   *who/had/gone*
   That to the lepe com she wolde   *go*
70 The flowres to hondel and to beholde;
   "And or I it evere wist,   *before/knew*
   A botterfleye cam against my brest!
   I was so soore adrad than   *afraid*
   That I loude crye can."
75 The maidons therof hadden gle,
   And turned hem and lete hur be.
   As sone as the maidons were gone,
   To Blauncheflour she yede anon,
   And said boldly to Blauncheflour,
80 "Fellow, come and see a faire flour!   *comrade*
   Suche a flour thee shall well like,   *please*
   Have thou it sene a lyte."
   "Away, Claris!" quod Blauncheflour;
   "To scorne me, it is none honoure.
85 I here, Claris, without gabbe,   *hear/mockery*
   That the Amiral will me to wif habbe;   *have*
   But that day shall never be
   That he shall ever have me–
   That I shall be of love so untrewe,
90 Ne chaunge my love for no newe;
   For no love ne for noon aye,   *awe*

---

760 "He accounted his life not [worth] a bean."
763 "And they asked her what was the matter."
774 "That I did cry aloud."
782 "[If] you have seen it a little." One must assume that Claris, by mentioning a
      "fair flower," is at once suggesting that the flower, symbol of the Emir's choice,
      is to be granted Blancheflour and that the boy in the basket is Floris.

Forsake Floris in his contraye.
Now I shall swete Floris misse,
Ne shall noon other of me have blisse."
795 Claris stood and beheld that rewth   *sorrow*
And the trewnesse of hur trewth   *trueness/word*
And said, "Lady Blaunchefloure,
Go we see that ilke floure!"
To the lepe they went both;   *basket*
800 Joyfull man was Floris tho,   *then*
For he had herde all this.
Of that lepe he stert y-wis;   *out of/jumped*
    /indeed

Well sone Blaunchefloure chaunged hewe;   *color*
Either of hem other knewe.   *recognized*
805 Withoute speche togeder they lepe   *leapt*
And klippt and kist wonder swete.   *embraced*
Claris beheld all this,
Her countenaunce and her blisse,   *their*
And saide then to Blaunchefloure,
810 "Fellow, knowist thou aught this flour?   *comrade/at all*
She shull conne full muche of art
That thou woldest therof geve part."
Now Blauncheflour and Floris,
Bothe these swete thinges y-wis,   *indeed*
815 Crien her mercy, all weeping,
That she ne wrey hem to the King.   *betray*
"Ne dought no more of me in alle   *fear/at/all*
Than it were myself bifalle.   *than if*
Wete ye well weturly,   *know/in truth*
820 Heele I will youre drury.   *conceal/love*
To a bedde they been brought
That is of palle and of silke wrought   *rich cloth*
And there they sette hem doun
And drough hemself all aroom;   *drew/themselves*
    /aside

825 Ther was no man that might radde   *estimate*
The joye that they two madde.   *made*
Floris then to speke bigan
And saide, "Lorde, that madest man,
I it thonke Goddes Sone
830 That all my care I have overcome.   *anxiety*
Now my leve I have y-founde;   *dear one*

793–794 [Since] now I am obliged to do without Floris, no other [man] shall have
    the pleasure of me."
798 "Let us go to see that very flower."
812–813 "She [another woman] would have to know much art [many wiles] to make
    you share part thereof" [that is, part of Floris].
829 "I give thanks for it to God's Son."

Of all my care I am unbounde."   *relieved*
Claris hem servid all at wille,
Both dernliche and stille.   *secretly*

35 Claris with the white side   *skin*
Rose up on morne tide
And cleped after Blaunchefloure   *called*
To wende with her in to the toure.   *go*
She saide, "I am commaunde";
40 But her answere was slepaunde.
The Amiral had suche a wone   *custom*
That every day shulde com
Two maidons of hur bour   *from/their
                                                        /chamber*

Up to him in to the toure
45 With water and clooth and basin
For to weshe his hondes inne.
That day they servid him faire;
Another day com another paire.
But most were wonid into the toure
50 Claris and Blaunchefloure.
Claris come thenne aloon.   *went/alone*
The Amiral asked anoon,
"Where is Blaunchefloure so free?   *noble*
Why cometh she not heder with thee?"   *hither*
55 "Sir," she saide anoon right,   *straightway*
"She hath wakid all this night
And y-cryde and y-loke   *gazed*
And y-redde on hur booke   *read/in*
And y-bede to God her orisone   *prayed/prayer*
60 That He geve thee his benisone   *might give
                                                        /blessing*

And that He holde long thy lif;
And now the maide slepeth swith.   *soundly*
She slepeth so fast, that maide swete,
That she may not com yete."
65 "Certes," saide the King,   *certainly*
"Now is she a swete thing!
Well aught me yerne her to wif
That so prayeth for my lif."
Another day Claris erly arist   *arose*
70 (That Blauncheflour well wist)   *knew*

---

833 *All at wille* is a vague phrase which could mean "quite willingly" or "completely
     to [their] pleasure."
839–840   "She [Blancheflour] said, 'I am coming'; but her answer was [given] sleepily."
849   "But chiefly were accustomed [to go] into the tower."
867   "I ought well to desire her for a wife."

And saide, "I com anoone,"		
When Claris her clepe bigan,		*to call*
And fell in a slepe newe;		*anew*
Sone after it made hem to rewe!		*suffer*
875 Claris to the piller cam;		
A basin of gold in hond she nam		*took*
And cleped after Blauncheﬂoure		*called*
To wende with hur into the toure.		*go*
The Amiral asked after Blaunchefloure,		
880 "What! is she not com yet?		
Now she me douteth all to lite."		
Forth he cleped his chamburlaine		
And bade him wende with his maine		*go/retinue*
"To wete why she will not com		*find out*
885 As she was wonid to doon."		*accustomed*
The chamburlain is forth noom;		*has/gone*
In to chamber he is coom,		*has/come*
And stondeth bifore hur bedde		*their*
And findeth there, nebbe to nebbe,		
890 Nebbe to nebbe and mouth to mouth.		
To the Amiral it was sone couth:		*quickly/known*
Up in to the toure he steigh		*climbed*
And told his lord all that he seigh.		*saw*
The Amiral lete him his swerd bring,		*be brought*
895 For wete he wolde of that tiding.		*learn*
He went to hem there they lay;		*there where*
Yit was she aslepe there ay.		*still*
The Amiral lete the clothes doun cast		*be cast*
A litel binethe hur brest		*below*
900 And sone he knew anoon		
That oon was woman and that other groom.		*man*
He quaked for tene there he stood;		*shook/anger*
Hem to sloon was in his moode;		*slay/mind*
Yit he thought, or he hem quelde,		*ere/killed*
905 What they were, they shuld him telle		
And seth he will with dome hem done.		
The children wakid swith soone		*very/quickly*
And saw the swerde over hem drawe;		*drawn*
They been adrad and in awghe.		*afraid/terror*
910 Than saide Floris to Blaunchefloor,		
"Of oure lif is no socour."		*help*
But they cryde him mercy swith		*vehemently*

---

871 "And [Blancheflour] said, "I'll come at once."
875 The *pillar*, as can be learned from other MSS, is the term for the place where the two girls draw water for the Emir.
881 "Now she fears me all to little" [that is, holds me in too little respect].
889 "And finds [them] there, face to face."
906 "And afterwards he would dispense justice to them."

For to length her live.   *lengthen/life*
Up he bade hem sitte booth
15 And do on both her cloth;   *put on/clothes*
Seth he dide hem binde fast   *afterwards/had*
                                       /bound

And in prison lete hem be cast.
Now hath he after his barons sent
To wreke him after jugement.   *avenge*
                                   /according to

20 Now han the barons undernome   *have/set out*
And to the Amiral they been coom.
He stood up among hem all
With semblaunt wroth withalle   *bearing/angered*
And saide, "Lordinges, with much honour,
25 Ye herde speke of Blaunchefloor–
That I bought hur dere aplight   *indeed*
For seven sithes of golde hur wight.   *times/weight*
For I wende, without wene,   *thought/doubt*
That faire maide to have had to quene.   *as*
30 Among my maidons in my toure
I hur dide, with muche honoure;   *put/graciously*
Bifore her bedde my self I coom;   *went*
I fonde therin a naked man.
Than were they to me so looth   *hateful*
35 I thought to have slain hem booth,   *intended*
I was so wroth and so woode;   *angry/maddened*
Yit I withdrough min hoot bloode
Till I have sende after you, by assent,
To wreke me with jugement.   *avenge/legally*
40 Now yit ye woot how it is goone;   *indeed/know*
Wreke me soon of my foon."   *foes*
Than spake a king of that londe,
"We have herd all this shame and shonde;   *disgrace*
But or we hem to deth deme,   *eve/condemn*
45 Lat us hem see, yif it thee queeme,   *pleases*
What they wolde speke or sigge,   *say*
Yif they will aught again us legge;
Hit were nought right jugement
Without answere make acoupement.   *to make*
                                 /accusation

50 Till this is herde of more and lasse,
What mister is to bere witnesse?"   *basis/pass*
                                 /judgment

---

924   If anything more than just a rhyme phrase, *with much honour* may mean "by your leave" or "with all due respect."
938   *By assent* can be expanded to "so that you by your common agreement will help me."
947   "If they will lay anything [in their defense] against us."

After the children have they sent–
To brenne hem was his entent.   *burn*
Two serjeauntes hem gan bring   *men-at-arms/did*
955 Toward hur deth all weeping.
Drery booth these children go;
Either bemeneth otheris wo.   *laments/sorrow*
Than saide Floris to Blaunicheflour,
"Of oure lif is no socour!   *help*
960 If kinde of man it thole might,
Twies I shuld die with right,
Oones for myself, another for thee,   *once*
For thy deeth thou hast for me."   *because of*
Blaunicheflour saide tho,   *then*
965 "The gilt is min of oure wo."
Floris drough forth that ring   *drew*
That his moder him gaf at her parting:
"Have this ring, lemman min;   *beloved*
Thou shalt not die while it is thin."
970 Blaunichefloure saide tho,   *then*
"So ne shall it never go
That this ring shall help me,
And the deed on thee see."
Floris that ring hur raught   *handed*
975 And she it him again betaught;   *back/gave*
Nouther ne will other deed seene;   *neither/see*
They let it falle hem bitwene.
A king com after; a ring he fonde   *went/behind*
And brought it forth in his honde.
980 Thus the children weeping com   *went*
To the fire and hur doom;
Bifore the folk they were brought.
Drery was her bothes thought;
There was noon so stern man
985 That the children looked oon   *who*
That they ne wolde, all well fawe,   *gladly*
He jugement have withdrawe
And with grete catel hem bigge,   *expense/ransom*
Yif they durst speke or sigge;
990 For Flores was so faire a yongling   *youth*
And Blaunichefloure so swete a thing
Ther wist no man whor hem were wo   *knew*
For no semblaunt that they made tho.

960–961   "If mankind might suffer such, I should by rights twice die."
971–973   "It shall never happen that the ring help me and I see you condemned to death."
983   "Sad was the thought of both of them."
989   "If they dared speak or say [as much]."
992–993   The expression is awkward; the reading suggests that the sense is "No man knew just how sad they were for any appearance that they made then."

The Amiral was so woode   *angry*
995 Ne might he nought cele his hoot bloode.   *cool*
He bade the children fast be bound
And in to the fire slong.   *thrown*
That ilke king that the ring fonde   *same*
To Amiral he spake and rounde   *whispered*
1000 And wolde hem save to the lif
And told how for the ring they gon strif.   *did/contend*
The Amiral lete hem again clepe,
For he wolde here hem speke   *because/hear*
And asked Floris what he heete   *was called*
1005 And he tolde him full skeete: *quickly*
"Sir," he saide, "if it were thy wille
Thou ne getest not that maide to spille;
But, good sir, quell thou me   *kill*
And late that maide on live be."   *alive*
1010 Blaunchefour saide bine,   *in between*
"The gilt of oure dedes is min."   *deeds*
The Amiral saide tho   *then*
"Y-wis, ye shull die bo!"   *both*
His swerd he breide out of his sheeth   *drew*
1015 The children to have don to deeth.   *put*
Blaunchefloure put forth hur swire   *neck*
And Floris dide her again to tire   *back/draw*
And saide, "I am man; I shall bifore;
With wrong hast thou thy lif loore!"
1020 Floris forth his swere putte,   *neck*
And Blaunchefour again him titte.   *back/drew*
The king saide, "Drery mot ye be,
This routh by this children to see!"
The king that the ring hadde
1025 For routh of hem sone he radde   *because of/pity*
                                        /advised

And at the Amiral will he spede
The children fro the deth to lede.   *lead*
"Sir," he saide, "it is litel pris   *honor*
These children for to slee, y-wis;   *indeed*
1030 And it is well more worship   *honor*
Floris counsel that ye weete: *plans/know*

1000   "And would have saved their life."
1002   "The Emir had them recalled."
1007   "You would not be able to destroy that maid"; the MS reading and its sense are faulty.
1018–19   "And said [to Blancheflour], "I am the one; I shall [die] before [you]; without justice you [would] lose your life."
1022–1023   "The King said, 'May you be ill-favored [if] you [unmoved] look upon this pitiful scene the children [make].' "
1026   "And at the Emir's will he hastened."

Who him taught that ilke ginne   *suggested/very*
                                                              /plan
Thy toure for to com inne
And who him brought thare,
1035 And other that ye may be ware."
Than saide the Amiral, "As God me save,
Floris shall his lif have
Yif he me telle who him taught therto."   *advised/to this*
Of Floris, "That shall I never do."
1040 Now they bidden all y-wis
That the Admiral graunted this,
To foryeve that trespass   *forgive*
Yif Floris told how it was.
Now every word he hath him tolde:
1045 How that maide was for him solde
And how he was of Spain a kinges sone,
For grete love theder y-com   *thither/gone*
For to fonde, with sum ginne,   *attempt/device*
That faire maide for to winne,
1050 And how the porter was his man bicom
For his gold and for his warisoun,   *reward*
And how he was in to Floris borne;
Alle the lordinges lough therforne.   *smiled/at that*
Now the Amiral–woll him tide!–
1055 Floris setteth next his side   *places/beside*
                                                              /him

And efte he made him stonde upright   *then*
And dubbed him there knight
And bade he shulde with him be
The furthermast of his meiné.   *chief/retinue*
1060 Floris falleth doun to his feet
And prayeth geve him his sweet.
The Amiral gaf him his leman;   *beloved*
All that there were thankid him thanne.
To a chirche he let hem bring   *had/brought*
1065 And dede let wed hem with a ring.
Both these two swete thinges, y-wis,   *indeed*
Fell his feet for to kisse;
And through consel of Blauncheflour,   *advice*
Claris was fet doun of the toure,   *taken*
1070 And Amiral wedded hur to queene.
There was fest swithe breeme;   *a festival/very*
                                                              /fine

---

1035 "And other [things also] so that you may be on guard."
1054 "Now the Emir—may he well prosper."
1061 "And entreats [him to] give him his sweet [love]."
1065 "And had them wedded with a ring."

I can not telle all the sonde,   *arrangements*
But richer fest was never in londe.
Was it nought longe after than
75 That to Floris tiding cam
That the King his fader was deed.
The baronage gaf him reed   *nobles/notice*
That he shuld wende hoom   *return*
And fonge his faire kingdoom.   *receive*
80 At the Amiral they toke leve   *from*
And he biddeth them bileve.   *tarry*
Hom he went with royal array
And was crownid within a short day.

PART 4

Burlesque and Grotesquerie

The Tournament of Tottenham

---◆◄◉►►---

HE town of Tottenham lies some six and a half miles north of London Bridge; it is now an urban district of no particular distinction and even in its long history down from Old English times no really significant item can be associated with its name. Just why an early fifteenth-century satire using the paraphernalia of the courtly tournament (so familiar to us through Malory) should choose Tottenham as its locale is puzzling, particularly so since the poem is in a Northern dialect. Effort has been made to localize it where its dialect belongs, and with no real success. But also puzzling, though to a lesser degree, is the question as to just what is being satirized, what, in other words, is the butt of all its absurdity. In part, it may be the romance itself, although not exclusively, as in Chaucer's *Sir Thopas*. In part also it may be chivalric tradition. The closer one looks at the poem, however, the less certain he may become as to its original purpose.

What happens in *The Tournament of Tottenham* is not very complex. It begins with a sort of proem which tells us that it would be a shame to let the deeds of such bold men as Hawkyn, Herry, Tomkyn, and Terry, all residents of Tottenham, go unsung. Then we are told that at a festival a certain Perkyn, a potter by trade, accosts Randolf the town bailiff with the question "Who is most worthy of all these bachelors to wed your daughter Tyb?" The bailiff asserts that only he who survives a tournament two weeks hence can have her, and not only her, but a setting hen and a brown cow to boot. The "bachelors" from Tottenham and from the neighboring Islington, Highgate, and Hackney go home to arm themselves. On the appointed day, Tyb is placed on a mare before a gap in a hedge overlooking the field where the affray is to take place. As each contestant enters—Herry, Hud, Hawkyn, Terry, Dudman, and Perkyn—he makes a vow that he will overcome. They lay on, the din is terrific, the carnage so great that the fallen creep on the grass like "crooked cripples." So vicious does the fight become that the champions steal each other's horses, which they would present to Tyb except that even the

313

horses are so weary they cannot amble as far as the hedge. The climax occurs when Perkyn (the hands-down favorite from the start) catches sight of Terry making off with Tyb; he pulls the miscreant off his horse and beats him mercilessly. The struggle ceases, wives come with improvised litters to carry off husbands who lie senseless on the ground (the "bachelry" seems not to have been made up entirely of eligible material), and Perkyn and Tyb go home together to spend a night in prenuptial bliss. The poem concludes with the note that all the battered and maimed attend the marriage feast, which is marked appropriately with much song and mirth.

The mechanics of the humor in *Tottenham* are, of course, quite simple. The Franco-Celtic names of Arthurian tradition are reduced to rustic English things, with the homely diminutive *-kyn* much in evidence. Weapons are not lances and swords, but flails and bats. Armor consists of black bowls, matting, and sheep skin. All this is, in its way, very funny and does indeed appear as a spoof directed at what Malory was to glorify a little later in the fifteenth century in his *Le Morte d'Arthur*. That *Tottenham* is first a funny poem and then a brickbat aimed at ancient chivalric practice may not, however, go far enough. The participants in the tournament are obviously rustics and their conduct is always gross and pretentious. A reader, giving the poem a second thought, can admit its good humor, but he may also wonder whether rustics in general are not just as much a target as jousting nobles. Northern European peasantry seem to have indulged at Shrovetide in genuine brawls on village greens, brawls replete with armor and weapons not far different from those described in *Tottenham*. Evidence to this effect adduced by G. F. Jones (see *References*) makes the poem appear almost exclusively as an anti-rustic satire. The conclusion may be overly restrictive, but it does indicate that the disrespect in *Tottenham* goes both up and down the social scale and that about the only people who must have laughed at it were medieval urbanites.

Two complete, but rather poor manuscripts of *Tottenham* exist—the Cambridge and the Harleian. They are poor in that the copyist of each seems to have allowed numerous errors to stand, probably as much from negligence as ignorance. Reverend William Bedwell, a rector of Tottenham, first printed the poem in 1631, thinking that it had historical value. It was repeatedly printed throughout the eighteenth and nineteenth centuries with one editor favoring one manuscript and another editor the other. Often an edition purports to be based on one manuscript, but shows so many readings from the other (and from earlier editions) that the result is a rather queer sort of conflation and not a true version of either manuscript. Here the same practice has been followed: the text straddles both French and Hale's printing and that of W. Carew Hazlitt (see *References*). Perhaps it is just as well. The language of *Tottenham* with its long *a*'s (where less Northern texts would show rounded *o*'s) and the prosody with its apparent disregard of syllabic count (stress seems paramount most of the time) are so hardy and durable that even the most wrong-headed editor could do them little harm.

REFERENCES: Brown and Robbins, No. 2615; *CBEL*, I:265—Wells, p. 180, lists *Tottenham* along with seventeen "late humorous tales," but gives no particulars. French and Hale, pp. 987–998, prints the Harley version of *Tottenham* with numerous readings from the Cambridge MS and from various old editions. Perhaps the most accessible of semidiplomatic editions of the Cambridge MS is in W. Carew Hazlitt's *Remains of Early Popular Poetry in England* (London 1866), Vol. III, pp. 82–93. The basic study of the peasant tournament as possible satire against the pretentions of rustics and nobles is George F. Jones's "The tournaments of Tottenham and Lappenhausen," *PMLA*, LXVI (December 1951), 1123–1140; related, and just as delightful, comment, especially on the possible historicity of peasant tournaments, is in Jones's " 'Christis Kirk,' 'Peblis to the Play,' and the German Peasant-Brawl," *PMLA*, LXVIII (December 1953), 1101–1125, which discusses two Middle Scots poems and analagous pieces in Middle High German literature.

O f all thes kene conquerours to carpe it were kinde;
Of fele feghting-folk ferly we finde;
The Turnament of Tottenham have we in minde:
It were harme sich hardiness were holden bihinde—   *a shame*
                                                    /concealed

5   In story as we rede—
     Of Hawkin, of Herry,
     Of Tomkin, of Terry,
     Of them that were doughty
     And stalworth in dede.

10 It befell in Totenham, on a dere day,   *memorable*
   Ther was mad a shurting be the hyway.   *festival*
   Theder com all the men of the contray—   *thither*
   Of Hyssyltoun, of Hygate, and of Hakenay,
       And all the swete swinkers.   *dear/workers*
15   Ther hopped Hawkin,

1–2   "It is natural to talk of all these bold conquerors; we find amazing things of many fighting folk."
13   Islington, Highgate, and Hackney, then suburbs of London.

Ther daunsed Dawkin,
Ther trumped Tomkin–   *trumpeted*
And all were trewe drinkers . . .

Till the day was gon and evin-song past,
20 That they shuld rekin ther scot and ther contes cast.   *recken/bill/cast*
                                                              up/accounts

Perkin the potter in to the press past
And said, "Rondol the refe, a doghter thou hast,   *bailiff*
   Tyb the dere.
   Ther-for wit wold I   *know*
25   Which of all this bachelery   *company*
   Were best worthy
      To wed hur to his fere."   *as/wife*

Up stirt thes gadelings with ther long staves   *started/fellows*
And said, "Randal the refe, lo! this lad raves!
30 Baldely amang us thy doghter he craves   *boldly*
And we er richer men then he and more good haves   *property*
   Of catel and corn."
   Then said Perkyn, "To Tybbe I have hight   *promised*
   That I shall be alway redy in my right,
35   If that it shuld be this day sevenight,
      Or ellis yet to-morn."   *tomorrow*

Then said Randolfe the refe, "Ever be he waried   *accursed*
That about this carping lenger wold be taried!
I wold not that my doghter that sho were miscarried,
40 But at hur most worship I wold sho were married.   *to/greatest/honor*
      Ther-for a turnament shall begin
   This day sevenight
   With a flail for to fight
   And he that is of most might   *greatest/power*
45   Shall brouke hur with winne.   *enjoy/pleasure*

"Whoso beris him best in the turnament,   *bears*
Him shall be granted the gree, be the comon assent,   *prize/by*
For to winne my doghter with dughtiness of dent   *courage/blows*
And Coppeld, my brode-henne, was broght out of Kent,
50   And my donnid cowe.   *brown*
   For no spens will I spare,   *expense*

34–35   "That I shall be ever ready to defend my rights [even] if it should be two
      weeks from today."
38   "Who would be delayed [any] longer over such higgling."
39   "I would not [wish] that my daughter would fare amiss"; the second *that* is un-
      necessary.
42   "Two weeks from today."
49   "And Coppeld, my brood hen, [which] was brought out of Kent."

For no catel will I care.
He shall have my gray mare
And my spottid sowe."

55 Ther was many bold lad ther bodies to bede.
Than they toke their leve and homward they yede   *went*
And all the woke afterward they graithed ther wede,   *week/prepared*
                                             /gear

Till it come to the day that they shuld do ther dede.   *deeds*
    They armed ham in mattis;   *themselves*
60   They set on ther nollis   *heads*
    For to kepe ther pollis   *polls*
    Gode blake bollis   *bowls*
    For battring of battis

They sowed tham in shepe-skinnes for they shuld not brest;   *sewed/burst*
65 Ilkon toke a blak hat insted of a crest,   *each*
A harrow brod as a fanne aboune on ther brest
And a flaile in ther hande for to fight prest.   *ready*
    Furth gon they fare.   *forth/do/go*
    Ther was kid mekil fors
70   Who shuld best fend his cors.   *defend/person*
    He that had no gode hors,
    He gat him a mare.

Sich another gadring have I not sene oft!   *such/gathering*
When all the gret cumpany com ridand to the croft.   *field*
75 Tyb on a gray mare was set upon loft,   *aloft*
On a sek full of seedis, for sho shuld sit soft . . .   *sack*
    And led hur to the gap.   *hedge-opening*
    For crieng of all the men
    Forther wold not Tyb then   *further*
80   Till she had hur gode brode-hen
    Set in hur lap.

A gay girdil Tyb had on, borrwed for the nonis,   *time being*
And a garland on hur hed, full of rounde bonis,   *bones*
And a broche on hur brest full of safer stonis–   *brooch/sapphire*
85 With the holy rode tokening was wrethin for the nonis.
    No catel was ther spared!   *expense*
    When joly Gyb saw hure thare,

---

52   "I shall not care at all about expenses."
55   "There was many a bold lad to hazard himself."
63   "For [protection against the] battering of bats."
66   "An arrow broad as a fan above on their breast."
69   "There was displayed much prowess."
78   "Because of the crying of all the men."
85   "With the symbol of the Holy Cross worked in as well."

He gird so his gray mere   *struck*
That she lete a faucon-fare   *wind*
90   At the rereward.

"I vow to God," quod Herry, "I shall not leve behende!   *remain*
May I mete with Bernard, on Bayard the blinde,
Ich man kepe him out of my winde!   *each/himself*
For whatsoever that he be befor me I finde
95   I wot I shall him greve!"   *know/harm*
"Wele said," quod Hawkyn.
"And I avow," quod Dawkyn,   *vow*
"May I mete with Tomkyn,
His flail him reve."

100 "I vow to God," quod Hud, "Tyb, sone shall thou see
Which of all this bachelery grant is the gree!   *granted/prize*
I shall scomfet thaim all, for the love of thy.   *discomfit/thee*
In what place so I come, they shall have dout of me,   *fear*
Min armes are so clere.   *coat of arms*
                                                                 /bright

105   I bere a reddil and a rake,
Poudred with a brennand drake
And three cantell of a cake
In icha cornare."

"I vow to God," quod Hawkyn, "if I have the gout,   *even if/gout*
110 All that I finde in the felde presand here about,   *pressing*
Have I twies or thries redin thurgh the route,   *ridden*
In icha stede ther they me see, of me they shall have doute   *each/place/where*
                                                                 /fear

When I begin to play.
I make a vow that I ne shall,
115   But-if Tybbe will me call,
Or I be thries doun fall,
Right onis com away."

Then said Terry and swore by his crede,   *creed*
"Saw thou never yong boy forth his body bede,
120 For when they fight fastest and most are in dredc,   *anguish*
I shall take Tyb by the hand and hur away lede.

---

92   *Bayard* is a steed in the romance *The Four Sons of Aymon* whose fury and blind-
       ness must at this time have made it a ridiculous item.
99   "[I] shall take away his flail."
105–108   "I carry a seive and a rake, decorated with a burning dragon and three sec-
       tions of a cake in each corner."
114–117   "I make a vow that I shall not even once withdraw before I fall down three
       times—unless Tyb wants to call me [away]."
119   "You never saw a young boy [so] offer forth his body." The Harleian MS reads
       forthy for *forth*.

I am armed at the full.
In min armis I bere wele   *coat of arms*
A dough trough and a pele,   *baker's shovel*
125   A sadill withouten a panel   *saddle cloth*
      With a fles of woll."   *fleece/wool*

"I vow to God," quod Dudman, "and swor be the stra,   *by/straw*
Whils me is left my mere, thou getis hur not swa!   *so*
For sho is wele shapen and light as the ro.   *well/shaped/roe*
130 Ther is no capul in this mile befor hur shall ga!
      She will me noght begile;
      She will me bere, I dar wele say,
      On a lang someris day,
      Fro Hyssyltoun to Hakenay,
135   Noght other half mile!"

"I vow to God," quod Perkyn, "thou spekis of cold rost!
I shall wirch wiselier, withouten any bost!   *act/more wisely*
Fif of the best capullis that ar in this ost,   *horses/host*
I wot I shall thaim winne and bring thaim to my cost;   *know/side*
140   And here I graunt tham Tybbe.
      Wele, boyes, here is he
      That will fight and not flee;
      For I am in my jolyté.   *fine spirits*
      With yo forth, Gybbe!"

145 When they had ther vowes made, furth gan they hye,   *hasten*
With flailes and hornes and trumpes made of tree.   *trumpets/wood*
Ther were all the bacheleris of that contré;
They were dight in array as thamselfe wold be.   *dressed*
      Their banners were full bright,
150   Of an old roten fell;   *rotten/hide*
      The cheverone, of a plow-mell   *plow mallet*
      And the shadow of a bell,   *silhouette*
      Poudred with mone-light.   *decorated*

I wot it is no childer-game whan they togedir met!   *know*
                                               /child's sport
155 When icha freke in tha feld on his felay bet
And laid on stifly; for nothing wold they let!   *stop*
And faght ferly fast till ther horses swet,

---

130   The humor dies in the shift of the praise from Tyb to Dudman's horse—his
      capul; *before hur shall ga* "shall excell her."
135   Probably "Not a mile and a half [more]."
136   *Cold roast* is a common term for something trivial, here perhaps meaning "non-
      sense."
155   "When each man in the field beat upon his fellow."
157   "And fought wondrously hard until their horses sweat."

    And fewe wordis spoken.
    Ther were flailes all to-slatred,   *split*
160 Ther were sheldis all to-clatred,   *smashed*
    Bollis and dishes all to-shatred,   *bowls/shattered*
      And many hedis brokin.   *heads*

    Ther was clinking of cart-sadellis and clattiring of cannes;   *cans*
    Of fele frekis in the feld, brokin were ther fannes;
165 Of sum were the hedis brokin, of sum the brain-panes;
    And ill ware it be sum or they went thens,   *ere/thence*
      With swipping of swepillis.   *swiping/flail ends*
    The boyes were so wery for-fught   *fought out*
    That they might not fight mare oloft,   *longer/on horse*
170 But creped then about in the croft   *crept/field*
      As they were crooked crepils.   *cripples*

    Perkyn was so wery that he began to loute;   *sink*
    "Help, Hud! I am ded in this ilk route!   *very/throng*
    A hors for forty pens, a gode and a stoute,
175 That I may lightly come of my noye out!
      For no cost will I spare."
    He stirt up as a snaile   *jumped up*
    And hent a capul be the taile   *caught/horse*
    And raght Dawkyn his flaile   *took from*
180   And wan ther a mare.   *won*

    Perkyn wan fif and Hud wan twa   *two*
    Glad and blithe they ware that they had don sa;   *so*
    They wold have tham to Tyb and present hur with tha.   *them*
    The capull were so wery that they might not ga,   *walk*
185   But still gon they stand.   *did*
    "Allas!" quod Hudde, "my joye I lese!   *lose*
    Me had lever then a ston of chese
    That dere Tyb had all these
    And wist it were my sand."   *knew/offering*

190 Perkyn turnid him about in that ich thrange;   *very/throng*
    Among thes wery boyes he wrest and he wrang.   *wrestled*
                                      /struggled

    He threw tham doun to the erth and thrast thaim amang,   *thrust*
    When he saw Tyrry away with Tyb fang,   *start*
      And after him ran.
195 Of his hors he him drogh   *off/drew*

---

164 "Broken were the winnowing shovels of many men in the field." A *fan* can also
      be a wicker shield used in mock combat.
175 "[So] that I may easily get out of my distress."
187 "I would rather than [have] a stone [that is, fourteen pounds] of cheese."

And gaf him of his flail inogh.
"We, te-he!" quod Tyb and lugh,
   "Ye er a dughty man."   *bold*

Thus they tugged and rugged till it was nere night;   *yanked*
200 All the wives of Tottenham come to see that sight,
With wispes and kexis and rishis ther light,
To fech hom ther husbandes that were tham trouth-plight.   *married to*
   And sum brought gret harwes   *sledges*
   Ther husbandes hom for to fech;
205 Sum on dores and sum on hech,   *gratings*
   Sum on hirdillis and sum on crech,   *hurdles/lattices*
   And sum on welebarraws.

They gaderid Perkyn about, everich side.
And graunt him ther the gre; the more was his pride.   *prize*
210 Tyb and he, with gret merthe homward con they ride,   *did*
And were all night togedir till the morn-tide;
   And they in fere assent: *together/agreed*
   So wele his nedis he has sped   *desires/achieved*
   That dere Tyb he has wed;
215 The prise folk that hur led   *fine*
   Were of the turnament.

To that ilk fest com many, for the nones.   *same/festival*
Some come hyp-halt and sum trippand on the stonis;   *limping*
                                            /stumbling
Sum a staf in his hand and sum two at onis.   *once*
220 Of sum were the hedis to-broken and sum the shulderbonis.
   With sorrow com they thedir!   *thither*
   Wo was Hawkyn, wo was Herry,
   Wo was Tomkyn, wo was Terry,
   And so was all the bachelary,
225 When they met togedir.

At that fest they were servid with a riche array:
Every fif and fif had a cokenay.
And so they sat in jolyté all the lang day;
And at the last they went to bed, with full gret deray.   *disarray*
230 Mekil mirth was them amang.   *much*

---

196 "And gave him enough [blows] with his flail."
197 " 'Whee, teehee!' said Tyb and laughed."
201 "With lit straw and flax and rushes there."
227 *Cockenay* is variously glossed. French and Hale (see *References*) assume the meaning is "cook" and hence that each fifth guest was served by an individual cook. The *Middle English Dictionary* suggests (questioningly) "bad egg," a sense that would at least fit the tone of the poem.

In every corner of the hous
Was melody delicious,
For to here precious,
   O six menis sang.

---

234   "Of a song for six voices."

The Wedding of Sir Gawain
and Dame Ragnell

OHN EDWIN WELLS in his treatment of *The Wedding of Sir Gawain and Dame Ragnell* says that the poem is "vivid and progresses well." He commends it for "excellent dialogue and good description of behavior." But he also says "it is not humorous" and this statement should be weighed carefully. Wells, perhaps, may have meant to imply that *Dame Ragnell* is not funny in the way Chaucer's "Miller's Tale" and "Reeve's Tale" are funny; if so, he is quite right. He may also have meant to imply that it deserves serious consideration, which it does. But the *Dame Ragnell* poet seems to have taken delight in grotesque characterization and absurd social situation and both features are staples of literary humor. Certainly, his intent is quite different from that of the poets who are responsible for two close analogues, both roughly contemporary with *Dame Ragnell*, namely, Chaucer's "The Wife of Bath's Tale" in the *Canterbury Tales* and Gower's "Tale of Florent" in the *Confessio Amantis*.

There is a literary virtuosity about Chaucer's tale which both enhances its esthetic potential and, in a sense, detracts from its effectiveness as a narrative. It tells us as much about the Wife of Bath as it does about the hero and heroine, who indeed remain quite shadowy characters. Also, as in "The Nun's Priest's Tale," matter extraneous to the main narrative takes up considerable space. There are 31 lines devoted to the tale of King Midas's wife; there is a bolster lecture on *gentillesse, poverté,* and *eld* of some 112 lines. The result is that the tale itself is reduced to meager proportions. The hero is nameless—a "lusty bacheler"—and he must seek the answer to the question "what thing is it that women most desire" because Guinevere says he should if he wishes to avoid the consequences of his chance ravishment of a stray maiden. He meets a "loathly lady" whom he promises to wed if she can tell him how to answer the queen's question. He does answer successfully with her "Women desire to have

323

sovereignty." Subsequently, the question posed in the marriage bed by the "loathly lady" is not the usual "would you have me foul by day and fair by night or visa versa," but a variation—essentially "would you have me foul and true or fair and adulterous." The whole, Chaucer has the Wife suggest, comes from ancient times when the land was still suffused with enchantment. Gower, in contrast, gives the tale a moral weight: he makes it point up the fact that a lover should obey his beloved since by doing so he may get more than he might otherwise get. Gower's Florent has to answer the first question because he has killed someone in battle. His "loathly lady" gives him the answer "all women most dearly desire to be sovereign in man's love." In the marriage bed, the usual question "fair by day and foul by night or visa versa" is posed. Florent lets the "loathly lady" have her own way and she turns out to be beautiful and the daughter of the King of Sicily. Gower's version, about as long as Chaucer's, is painfully verbose and maundering; its only narrative interruption is a page-long description of the lady's ugliness.

The short romance *Dame Ragnell* was composed by an indifferent artist who could tell a story with sufficient skill to make it effective. It has no esthetic complexities nor is it moral. It begins with King Arthur hunting out of Carlisle and stalking a hart until he wounds it with an arrow. He has just given the animal its death wound when a monstrous fellow who calls himself Sir Gromer Somer Jour (see the annotation to line 62) appears in full armor and threatens him with death because he has given Gawain land which originally belonged to Sir Gromer himself. The King's conduct is not craven, but it is not courtly or heroic. He is given a twelve-month span to answer the first question—what women most desire—and departs utterly crestfallen. Of his knights, only Gawain can draw the truth from him, and the modern reader may sense two things—that the audience had more respect for Gawain than for Arthur and that the King is selfish enough to foist his personal onus off on his nephew and best friend. Both men depart in separate directions to enquire about women; they set down their data in books—and this to us is funny and may have been so to listeners in the mid-fifteenth century. Ultimately, they come together again and compare notes, Gawain being sure that at least one of their answers will suffice, Arthur doubting and worrying like an old woman. With only a month to go, Arthur bumbles into Inglewood Forest, where he had originally shot the hart, and finds the "loathly lady." She shows him little respect; she says his life is in her hands; she asserts she can save him if he will have Gawain wed her. The King says as much as "Why, I couldn't do that"; but goes immediately to Gawain, who, seeing his uncle almost grovel before him, takes pity and says he would wed the Devil himself to save him. Arthur races back to Ragnell (here the "loathly lady" is given a name), gets the answer from her, gives it to Sir Gromer, and then brings Gawain's bride-to-be back to Carlisle. There follows much about Ragnell's officiousness, her hideousness, her bad manners at the wedding banquet. At this point, a leaf is missing from the manuscript, perhaps an indication that material indelicate to later taste prompted its removal. But the marriage-bed question—fair by day and foul by night or visa versa—is preserved and runs off broadly and well. We find, once Ragnell is beautiful, that she is really Sir Gromer's sister whom a wicked stepmother had transformed. Oddly, the romance ends on a note of pathos: the poet says Gawain, though often wed, loved Ragnell more than he ever loved any woman, but lost her within five years; and then he adds that he "that this tale did divine" is suffering bitterly in prison. He concludes with a prayer that God may deliver him from his present anguish.

The rhyme-scheme of *Dame Ragnell* runs *aabccbddeffe*; the couplets are essentially four stress and the tail-rhyme lines enclosing them usually three. The romance could be printed in stanzaic form like *Sir Launfal*, but here considerations of space make it seem practical to print it without a stanzaic break after the second tail-rhyme verse. The one copy is in the Rawlinson manuscript in the Bodleian Library, written down about 1500, although the language of the poem indicates that composition may antedate the manuscript by some fifty years. In reading *Dame Ragnell* aloud, one senses that if he ignores most of the final *e*'s he can still preserve a passable prosodic rhythm. The dialect of the copyist and hence probably of the poet is East Midland and offers fewer lexical difficulties than almost any of the romances which precede, although syntactic and idiomatic peculiarities are frequent, often challenging, and, it must be admitted, sometimes quite baffling.

REFERENCES: Brown and Robbins, No. 1916; Billings, pp. 217–221; CBEL, I:139; Kane, pp. 27–28; Wells, pp. 67–69. The only scholarly edition of the poem is Laura Sumner's *The Weddynge of Sir Gawen and Dame Ragnell* (Northampton, Mass., 1924, Vol. V, No. 4 in the Smith College Studies in Modern Languages). *Ragnell* is printed without glossary by B. J. Whiting, pp. 242–264, in his chapter on "The Wife of Bath's Tale" in *Sources and Analogues of Chaucer's Canterbury Tales*, edited by W. F. Bryan and Germaine Dempster (University of Chicago Press 1941); also printed in the same chapter are John Gower's "Tale of Florent," pp. 224–235, and the ballad "The Marriage of Sir Gawaine," pp. 235–241, a fragmentary version of the story closer to *Dame Ragnell* than to the poems by Chaucer and Gower.

Lithe and listenithe the lif of a lord riche,   *harken*
The while that he livid was none him liche,   *like*
Nether in boure ne in halle;
In the time of Arthoure this adventure betid,   *occurred*
5   And of the great adventure that he himself did,
That king curteis and royalle.
Of alle kinges Arture berithe the flowir,   *bears*
And of alle knightod he bare away the honour,
Where-so-evere he went.
10 In his contrey was nothing but chivalry
And knightes were belovid by that doughty,   *courageous one*
For cowardes were everemore shent.   *disgraced*
Nowe wille ye list a while to my talking,
I shalle you telle of Arthoure the king,
15 Howe ones him befelle.
On hunting he was in Ingleswood,   *Inglewood*
With alle his bold knightes good;
Nowe herken to my spelle!   *tale*
The king was set at his trestille-tree   *hunting station*
20 Withe his bowe to sle the wilde veneré   *slay/game*
And his lordes were set him beside;
As the king stode, then was he ware   *aware*
Where a great hart was and a faire,
And forthe fast did he glide.
25 The hart was in a braken ferne,   *fern thicket*
And hard the groundes, and stode fulle derne.
Alle that sawe the king.
"Hold you stille, every man,
And I wolle go myself, if I can
30 With crafte of stalking."
The king in his hand toke a bowe
And wodmanly he stoupid lowe
To stalk unto that dere.
When that he cam the dere fulle nere,
35 The dere lept forthe into a brere,   *briar patch*
And evere the king went nere and nere.
So King Arthure went a while,
After the dere, I trowe, half a mile,
And no man withe him went.
40 And at the last to the dere he let flye
And smote him sore and sewerly;   *sorely/surely*

---

15 "How [it] once befell him."
26 "And listened to the [noises of] the ground and stood very still" [literally, secret];
    groundes may be an error for *houndes.*
32 W*odmanly* may mean "like a woodsman" or, if it goes back to Old English *wǣth*
    "hunting," it means "like a hunter," a sense appropriate here.
36 "And the king drew ever nearer and nearer."

Such grace God him sent.
Doun the dere tumblid so deron,
And felle into a great brake of feron;   *thicket/fern*
45 The king followid fulle faste.
Anon the king bothe ferce and felle   *savage*
Was withe the dere and did him serve welle.
And after the grasse he taste.
As the king was withe the dere alone,
50 Streighte ther cam to him a quaint grome,   *strange/fellow*
Armid welle and sure,
A knighte fulle strong and of great mighte
And grimly wordes to the king he said,
"Welle y-met, King Arthour!
55 Thou hast me done wrong many a yere
And wofully I shalle quitte thee here.   *requite*
I hold thy life days nighe done;
Thou hast gevin my landes in certain   *indeed*
With great wrong unto Sir Gawen.
60 Whate sayest thou, king alone?"
"Sir Knight, whate is thy name withe honour?"
"Sir King," he said, "Gromer Somer Joure,
I telle thee nowe withe righte."   *straightway*
"A, Sir Gromer Somer bethink thee welle,
65 To slee me here honour getist thou no delle,   *slay/obtain*
                                                          /portion

Bethink thee thou art a knight;
If thou slee me nowe in this case,   *situation*
Alle knightes wolle refuse thee in every place,
That shame shalle nevere thee fro;
70 Let be thy wille and followe wit
And that is amiss I shalle amend it,   *that which*
And thou wolt, or that I go."
"Nay," said Sir Gromer Somer, "by hevin king!
So shalt thou not skape withoute lesing,   *escape/indeed*
75 I have thee nowe at availle.
If I shold let thee thus go withe mockery,

---

43   *Deron* is the *derne* of line 26; here it implies the deer tumbled "out of sight."
47   "Was at the deer and served him well" [that is, killed it].
48   A puzzling line, the difficulty being the referent of *he* (either the deer or Arthur)
     and the exact meaning of *taste* 'touch.' Perhaps "And afterwards he [the deer]
     touched the grass" [that is, died] is better than "And afterwards he [Arthur]
     touched the grass" [perhaps to wipe the deer's blood from his hands].
61   *Withe honour* probably is equivalent to "if you please."
62   An odd name, suggesting otherworldliness, *gromer* perhaps being from ME *grom*
     'man' (the Old Norse form is *gromr*), *somer* perhaps being ME *sumer* 'summer,'
     and *jour* suggesting Old French *jour* "day" or "time."
69   "[So] that shame shall never [go] from you."
72   "If you wish, before I go."
75   "I now have the advantage over you."
76   "If I should let you go thus with [only] mockery [of you]."

Anoder time thou wolt me defye;
Of that I shalle not faille."
Now said the king, "So God me save,
80 Save my life, and whate thou wolt crave,
I shalle now graunt it thee;
Shame thou shalt have to slee me in veneré,   *out/hunting*
Thou armid and I clothid but in grene, perdé."   *green/indeed*
"Alle this shalle not help thee, sekirly,   *surely*
85 For I wolle nother lond ne gold truly;
But if thou graunt me at a certain day   *unless*
Such as I shalle set, and in this same arraye."
"Yes," said the King, "lo, here my hand."
"Ye, but abide, King, and here me a stound;   *hear/moment*
90 First thou shalt swere upon my sword broun   *bright*
To shewe me at thy coming whate wemen love best in feld   *indicate/women*
and town;
And thou shalt mete me here witheouten send
Evin at this day twelve monethes end;
And thou shalt swere upon my swerd good
95 That of thy knightes shalle none com with thee, by the rood,   *cross*
Nouther frende ne freind.
And if thou bring not answere witheoute faille,
Thine hed thou shalt lose for thy travaille–   *head/effort*
This shalle nowe be thine othe.   *oath*
100 What sayst thou, King? Let see, have done!"
"Sir, I graunt to this, now let me gone;   *go*
Thoughe it be to me fulle lothe,   *distasteful*
I ensure thee, as I am true king,   *assure*
To com again at this twelve monethes end   *back*
105 And bring thee thine answere."
"Now go thy way, King Arthure;
Thy life is in my hand, I am fulle sure;
Of thy sorrowe thou art not ware.
Abide, King Arthure, a litelle while;
110 Loke not today thou me begile,
And kepe alle thing in close;
For and I wist, by Mary milde,   *if/knew*
Thou woldist betray me in the feld,
Thy lif first sholdist thou lose."

---

78 "In that I shall not fail [to enjoy my advantage]."
87 "Such as I shall require, and [dressed] in this same garb."
92 *Send*, perhaps "messanger," may here mean "armed guard."
93 "Exactly on this day twelve months hence."
96 *Frende* may derive from ON *fraendi* 'relative' and hence the line would mean "Neither relative nor friend"; it could also be an error for *fremde* 'stranger.'
100 The remark may be the elliptical equivalent of "What do you say [to that], king? Let [us] see [and] have done.'
108 "Of your [ultimate] sorrow you are [now] not aware."
110–111 "See to [it] you do not deceive me today and keep everything secret."

115 "Nay," said King Arthure, "that may not be;
Untrewe knighte shalt thou nevere finde me;
To dye yet were me lever.
Farwelle, Sir Knighte, and eville met,
I wolle com, and I be on live at the day set,   *if/alive*
                                                   /appointed
120 Thoughe I shold scape nevere."   *even though*
                                                 /escape

The king his bugle gan blowe;   *did*
That hard every knighte and it gan knowe;   *heard/did*
                                                 /recognize
Unto him can they rake;   *did/hasten*
Ther they fond the king and the dere,
125 Withe sembland sad and hevy chere,   *semblance/down-*
                                               cast/features
That had no lust to laik.   *who/desire*
                                               /sport
"Go we home nowe to Carlylle;   *Carlisle*
This hunting likis me not welle,"   *pleases*
So said King Arthure.
130 Alle the lordes knewe by his countenaunce
That the king had met withe sume disturbaunce.
Unto Carlylle then the king cam,
But of his hevinesse knewe no man;   *melancholy*
His hart was wonder hevy.   *heart/exceed-*
                                               ingly

135 In this hevinesse he did abide
That many of his knightes mervelid that tide,   *so that/then*
Tille at the last Sir Gawen
To the king he said than,
"Sir, me marvailithe righte sore,
140 Whate thing that thou sorrowist fore."
Then answerid the king as tighte,   *immediately*
"I shalle thee telle, gentille Gawen knighte.
In the forest as I was this daye,   *when*
Ther I met withe a knighte in his arraye
145 And sertain wordes to me he gan sain   *certain/did/say*
And chargid me I shold him not bewraine;   *commanded*
                                               /betray
His councelle must I kepe therfore,
Or els I am forswore."   *otherwise*
                                               /forsworn
"Nay, drede you not, lord, by Mary flower,   *fear*
150 I am not that man that wold you dishonour
Nother by evin ne by moron."   *neither/evening*
                                               /morning

---

117   "[I] would rather die first."
139   " 'Sir, I wonder indeed much.' "

"Forsothe I was on hunting in Inglcswood;
Thowe knowest welle I slewe an hart, by the rode,   *cross*
Alle myself alon;
155 Ther met I withe a knighte armid sure;   *well*
His name he told me was Sir Gromer Somer Joure:
Therfor I make my mone.   *because of this
                                                          /lament*

Ther that knighte fast did me threte   *threaten*
And wold have slain me withe great heat,   *in/passion*
160 But I spak faire again.   *except that/in
                                                          turn*

Wepins withe me ther had I none;
Alas, my worship therfor is nowe gone."   *honor*
"What thereof?" said Gawen,
"What nedis more I shalle not lye;
165 He wold have slain me ther witheoute mercy–
And that me was fulle lothe.
He made me to swere that at the twelve monethes end
That I shold mete him ther in the same kinde;   *manner*
To that I plighte my trouithe.   *gave/promise*
170 And also I shold telle him at the same day
Whate wemen desiren moste in good faye;   *women/indeed*
My life els shold I lese.   *otherwise/lose*
This othe I made unto that knighte,   *oath*
And that I shold nevere telle it to no wighte;   *man*
175 Of this I mighte not chese.
And also I shold com in none oder arraye,   *no/different
                                                          /garb*

But evin as I was the same daye;   *just*
And if I failid of mine answere,
I wot I shall be slain righte there.   *know*
180 Blame me not thoughe I be a wofulle man;   *chide/if*
Alle this is my drede and fere."
"Ye, Sir, make good chere;
Let make your hors redy   *be made*
To ride into straunge contrey;
185 And evere wheras ye mete outher man or woman, in faye, *either/indeed*
Ask of theim whate they therto saye.
And I shalle also ride anoder waye   *another*
And enquere of every man and woman and get what I may
Of every man and womans answere;
190 And in a boke I shalle theim write."   *book*
"I graunt," said the King as tite,   *immediately*
"It is welle advised, Gawen the good,

---

154 "All by myself."
164 "I shall not lie about what else need [be said]."
166 "And that was indeed hateful to me."
175 Loosely, "I had no choice in the matter."

Evin by the holy rood."	*indeed/cross*
Sone were they bothe redy,	
5 Gawen and the king witterly.	*certainly*
The king rode on way and Gawen anoder	*one/another*
And evere enquired of man, woman, and other,	*others*
Whate wemen desired moste dere.	*dearly*
Somme said they lovid to be welle arrayd,	
0 Somme said they lovid to be faire prayed;	
Somme said they lovid a lusty man	
That in their armis can clipp them and kisse them than;	*embrace*
Somme said one; somme said other;	*one thing*
And so had Gawen getin many an answere.	
5 By that Gawen had geten whate he maye	*with that/could*
And come again by a certain daye.	*went/back*
Sir Gawen had goten answeris so many	
That had made a boke great witterly.	*indeed*
To the courte he cam again.	
0 By that was the king comin withe his boke	
And either on others pamplett did loke.	*pages*
"This may not faile," said Gawen.	
"By God," said the King, "I drede me sore,	*afraid/extremely*
I cast me to seke a litelle more	
5 In Ingleswood Forest;	
I have but a monethe to my day set,	*appointed*
I may happen on somme good tidinges to hit–	
This thinkithe me nowe best."	*seems to*
"Do as ye list," then Gawen said,	*please*
0 "Whatesoevere ye do I hold me paid;	
Hit is good to be spyrring;	*enquiring*
Doute you not, lord, ye shalle welle spede;	*fear/succeed*
Sume of your sawes shalle help at nede,	*truths*
Els it were ille liking."	
5 King Arthoure rode forthe on the other day,	*following*
Into Ingleswood as his gate laye	*where/path/led*
And ther he met withe a lady.	
She was as ungoodly a creature	*ill-favored*
As evere man sawe witheoute mesure.	*in the extreme*
0 King Arthure mervailid securly.	*marveled/surely*
Her face was red, her nose snotid withalle,	
Her mouithe wide, her teethe yallowe overe alle,	*mouth*
Withe blerid eyen gretter then a balle;	*bleary*
Her mouithe was not to lak;	
5 Her teethe hing overe her lippes;	

---

200 *Prayed* 'supplicated' here may mean simply 'wooed.'
214 "I [shall] apply myself to look a little more."
220 "I[shall] be pleased with whatever you do."
224 "Otherwise it would be [indeed] ill luck."
234 "Her mouth was not out of tune [with other details]" [literally, to lack].

Her cheekis side as wemens hippes;   *broad/hips*
A lute she bare upon her back.
Her neck long and therto great;
Her here cloterid on an hepe;   *hair/clotted*
                                                       /heap

240 In the sholders she was a yard brode;
Hanging pappis to be an hors lode;
And like a barelle she was made;
And to reherse the foulnesse of that lady,   *describe*
Ther is no tung may telle, securly;   *surely*
245 Of lothinesse y-noughe she had.   *ugliness*
She sat on a palfray was gay begon,
With gold beset and many a precious stone.
Ther was an unsemely sighte;
So foulle a creature witheoute mesure
250 To ride so gayly, I you ensure,   *assure*
It was no reason ne righte.
She rode to Arthoure and thus she said,
"God spede, Sir King, I am welle paid   *pleased*
That I have withe thee met;
255 Speke withe me, I rede, or thou go,   *advise/before*
For thy life is in my hand, I warn thee so;
That shalt thou finde, and I it not let."
"Why, what wold ye, lady, nowe withe me?"   *want*
"Sir, I wold fain nowe speke withe thee
260 And telle thee tidinges good.
For alle the answeris that thou canst yelpe,   *speak*
None of theim alle shalle thee helpe
That shalt thou knowe by the rood.   *should/realize*
                                                       /cross

Thou wenist I knowe not thy councelle;   *think/secret*
265 But I warn thee I knowe it every dealle.   *bit*
If I help thee not, thou art but dead.   *as good as*
Graunt me, Sir King, but one thing,
And for thy life, I make warraunting,
Or elles thou shalt lose thy hed."   *otherwise*
270 "Whate mean you, lady, telle me tighte,   *quickly*
For of thy wordes I have great dispite;   *contempt*
To you I have no nede.   *of*
What is your desire, faire lady?

---

241 "Hanging paps [large enough] to be a load for a horse."
246 "She sat upon a palfrey [which] was gaily decked out."
249 "[For] so immeasurably foul a creature."
251 "There was neither right nor reason [to it]."
257 "That [your life being in my hands] you shall discover, if I do not prevent it"
      [namely, your demise].
268 "And I [shall] give guarantee for your life."

Let me wete shortly   *know*

5 Whate is your meaning

And why my life is in your hand;

Telle me and I shalle you warraunt

Alle your own asking."

"Forsothe," said the lady, "I am no qued.   *evil person*

o Thou must graunt me a knighte to wed—

His name is Sir Gawen.

And suche covenaunt I wolle make thee,

But thorowe mine answere thy lif savid be,   *so that/shall be*

Elles let my desire be in vaine.   *else*

5 And if mine answere save thy lif,

Graunt me to be Gawens wif.

Advise thee nowe, Sir King.

For it must be so, or thou art but ded;

Chose nowe, for thou maiste sone lose thine hed.   *may*

o Telle me nowe in hying."   *haste*

"Mary," said the king, "I maye not graunt thee

To make warraunt Sir Gawen to wed thee;

Alle lyethe in him alon.   *depends/on*

But and it be so, I wolle do my labour   *if/make/effort*

5 In saving of my life to make it secour;

To Gawen wolle I make my mone."   *complaint*

"Welle," said she, "nowe go home again

And faire wordes speke to Sir Gawen,

For thy lif I may save.

o Thoughe I be foulle, yet am I gaye;   *lusty*

Thourghe me thy life save he maye

Or sewer thy dethe to have."

"Alas!" he said, "nowe wo is me

That I shold cause Gawen to wed thee,

5 For he woll be lothe to saye naye.   *unwilling*

So foulle a lady as ye ar nowe one

Sawe I nevere in my life on ground gone,   *walk*

I not whate I do may."   *know not*

"No force, Sir King, thoughe I be foulle;   *matter*

o Choise for a make hathe an owlle.

Thou getest of me no more.

When thou comist again to thine answere,   *for*

Righte in this place I shalle mete thee here

Or elles I wot thou art lore."   *know/lost*

5 "Now farewelle," said the King, "Lady."

277–278   "Tell me and I shall grant everything you ask for."

292   "To give guarantee that Sir Gawain will wed you."

295   "In the [process of] saving my life to make it [the wedding] a certainty."

302   "Or [be] certain to suffer death."

310   "[Even] an owl has the choice of a mate."

"Ye Sir," she said, "ther is a bird men calle an owle . . .
And yet a lady I am."
"Whate is your name, I pray you telle me?"
"Sir King, I highte Dame Ragnelle, truly,   *am called*
320 That nevere yet begilid man."
"Dame Ragnelle, now have good daye."
"Sir King, God spede thee on thy way!
Righte here I shalle thee mete."
Thus they departid faire and welle
325 The king fulle sone com to Carlylle,
And his hart hevy and great.   *heart/sad*
The first man he met was Sir Gawen,
That unto the king thus gan sain,   *did/say*
"Sir, howe have ye sped?"
330 "Forsothe," said the King, "nevere so ille!
Alas, I am in point myself to spille,
For nedely I most be ded."   *by necessity*
"Nay," said Gawen, "that may not be!
I had lever myself be dead, so mot I thee.   *rather/indeed*
335 This is ille tidand."   *bad/news*
"Gawen, I met today withe the foulist lady
That evere I sawe sertenly.   *certainly*
She said to me my life she wold save . . .
But first she wold thee to husbond have.
340 Wherfor I am wo begon–
Thus in my hart I make my mone."
"Is this alle?" then said Gawen;
"I shalle wed her and wed her again,
Thoughe she were a fend,   *fiend*
345 Thoughe she were as foulle as Belsabub,
Her shalle I wed, by the rood,   *cross*
Or elles were not I your frende;
For ye ar my king withe honour
And have worshipt me in many a stoure.
350 Therfor shalle I not let.   *hesitate*
To save your life, lorde, it were my parte,   *duty*
Or were I false and a great coward;
And my worship is the bet."
"Y-wis, Gawen, I met her in Ingliswood.   *indeed*
355 She told me her name, by the rode,   *cross*
That it was Dame Ragnelle.
She told me but I had of her answere,

---

316   The lady's remark breaks off, but her implication is that even an ugly bird like
        an owl has its day and so must she.
331   "Alas, I am on the verge of killing myself."
349   "And have done me honor in many an encounter."
353   "And [because I shall save your life] my honor is the greater."

Elles alle my laboure is nevere the nere;
Thus she gan me telle. *did*
And but if her answere help me welle,
Elles let her have her desire no dele: *part*
This was her covenaunt;
And if her answere help me, and none other,
Then wold she have you, here is alle togeder,
That made she warraunt." *guarantee*
"As for this," said Gawen, "it shalle not let: *hinder*
I wolle wed her at whate time ye wolle set;
I pray you make no care. *have/worry*
For and she were the most foulist wighte *if/being*
That evere men mighte see withe sighte,
For your love I wolle not spare."
"Gramercy, Gawen," then said King Arthor; *many thanks*
"Of alle knightes thou berest the flowre
That evere yet I fond.
My worship and my lif thou savist forevere;
Therfore my love shalle not frome thee dissevir, *be severed*
As I am king in lond."
Then within five or six days
The King must nedis go his ways *set out*
To bere his answere.
The King and Sir Gawen rode oute of toun . . .
No man withe them, but they alone,
Neder ferre ne nere. *neither/far/near*
When the King was withein the forest:
"Sir Gawen, farewelle, I must go west,
Thou shalt no furder go." *further*
"My lord, God spede you on your jorney,
I wold I shold nowe ride your way,
For to departe I am right wo."
The king had ridden but a while,
Litelle more then the space of a mile
Or he met Dame Ragnelle. *before*
"A, Sir King, ye are nowe welcum here,
I wot ye ride to bere your answere;
That wolle availle you no dele." *help/not at all*
"Nowe," said the King, "sithe it wolle none other be, *otherwise*
Telle me your answere nowe, and my life save me;
Gawen shalle you wed.
So he hathe promised me my lif to save
And your desire nowe shalle ye have,

357–358   "She said to me unless I got the answer from her, all my effort would be no
      nearer [a solution]."
364   The inserted phrase probably amounts to our "this is the sum and substance of it."

Bothe in bowre and in bed.   *chamber*
Therfor telle me nowe alle in hast.   *haste*
Whate wolle help now at last;
Have done, I may not tarry."
405 "Sir," quod Dame Ragnelle, "nowe shalt thou knowe
Whate wemen desiren moste of highe and lowe;
From this I wolle not varaye.   *deviate*
Summe men sayn we desire to be faire;
Also we desire to have repaire   *resort*
410 Of diverse straunge men;
Also we love to have lust in bed
And often we desire to wed,
Thus ye men not ken.
Yet we desire anoder manner thing,   *kind of*
415 To be holden not old, but freshe and yong,
Withe flattring and glosing and quaint gin,
So ye men may us wemen evere win
Of whate ye wolle crave.
Ye go fulle nise, I wolle not lye;
420 But there is one thing is alle oure fantasye,   *desire*
And that nowe shalle ye knowe.
We desiren of men above alle manner thing   *kind of*
To have the sovereinté, withoute lesing,   *in truth*
Of alle, bothe highe and lowe.
425 For where we have sovereinté alle is ouris,
Thoughe a knighte be nevere so feris,   *fierce*
And evere the mastry winne;
Of the moste manliest is oure desire:
To have the sovereinté of suche a sire;
430 Suche is oure crafte and ginne.   *art/skill*
Therfore wend, Sir King, on thy way,
And telle that knighte, as I thee saye,
That it is as we desiren moste;
He woll be wrothe and unsoughte   *angry/bitter*
435 And curse her fast that it thee taughte,   *much*
For his laboure is lost.
Go forthe, Sir King, and hold promise,
For thy life is sure nowe in alle wise;
That dare I well undertake."   *assert*
440 The king rode forthe a great shake,   *distance*
As fast as he mighte gate   *ride*
Thorowe mire, more, and fenne   *moor/bog*

---

406 "What women desire most of [men] of high and low [rank]."
413 "Thus [or: these things] you men do not perceive."
416 "With flattery and cajoling and artful attention."
419 *Nice* probably still has the sense of "foolish" and hence Ragnell's remark may
    imply "You act quite foolishly, I won't lie [about that]."

Wheras the place was signid and set then.   *designated*
        /appointed

Evin there withe Sir Gromer he met.   *right*
5 And stern wordes to the King he spak withe that,
"Com of, Sir King, nowe let see   *on*
Of thine answere whate it shall be,
For I am redy grathid."
The King pullid oute bokes twaine;   *books*
0 "Sir, ther is mine answer, I dare sayn,   *say*
For somme wolle help at nede."
Sir Gromer lookid on theim everychon;
"Nay, nay, Sir King, thou art but a dead man,
Therfor nowe shalt thou blede."   *bleed*
5 "Abide, Sir Gromer," said King Arthoure,
"I have one answere shalle make alle sure."
"Let see," then said Sir Gromer,
"Or els, so God me help, as I thee say,
Thy dethe thou shalt have with large paye,
0 I telle thee nowe ensure."   *surely*
"Now," said the King, "I see, as I gesse,   *guess*
In thee is but a litelle gentilnesse,
By God that ay is helpand.   *ever/helping*
Here is oure answere, and that is alle,
5 That wemen desiren moste specialle,   *to that which*
        /especially

Bothe of free and bond.
I saye no more, but above all thing
Wemen desire sovereinté, for that is their liking;   *pleasure*
And that is ther moste desire;
0 To have the rewlle of the manliest men,   *rule*
And then ar they welle, thus they me did ken,   *make aware*
To rule thee, Gromer Sire."
"And she that told thee nowe, Sir Arthoure,
I pray to God, I maye see her bren on a fire,   *burn/in*
5 For that was my suster, Dame Ragnelle.
That old scott, God geve her shame,   *trollop*
Elles had I made thee fulle tame;   *else*
Nowe have I lost moche travaille.   *effort*
Go where thou wolt, King Arthoure,
0 For of me thou maist be evere sure.
Alas, that I evere see this day!

---

448   "For I am indeed prepared."
451   Probably "For some [of the answers in the two books] will help in [my] need."
456   "I have one answer [which] shall make all sure."
459   *With large paye*, an intensive phrase, can mean "to [my] great satisfaction" or
      "in good measure."
481   "Alas, that I ever [lived to] see this day!"

Nowe, welle I wot, mine enime thou wolt be.   *enemy/know*
And at suche a prick shalle I nevere get thee;
My song may be welle-awaye!"
485 "No," said the King, "that make I warraunt;   *guarantee*
Some harnis I wolle have to make me defendaunt,
That make I God avowe!
In suche a plighte shalt thou nevere me finde,
And if thou do, let me bete and binde,   *have/beaten*
                                                   /bound
490 As is for thy best prouf."
"Nowe have good day," said Sir Gromer;
"Farewell," said Sir Arthoure, "so mot I thee,   *as/may/prosper*
I am glad I have so sped."
King Arthoure turnid his hors into the plain,
495 And sone he met withe Dame Ragnelle again,
In the same place and stede.   *spot*
"Sir King, I am glad ye have sped welle,
I told howe it wold be every delle;   *part*
Nowe hold that he have highte.   *that which*
                                                 /promised
500 Sin I have savid your lif, and none other,   *since*
Gawen must me wed, Sir Arthoure,
That is a fulle gentille knighte."   *who*
"No, lady, that I you highte I shalle not faille;   *promised*
So ye woll be rulid by my councelle,
505 Your wille then shalle ye have."
"Nay, Sir King, nowe wolle I not so,
Openly I woll be weddid, or I parte thee fro.   *before/from*
Elles shame welle ye have.   *otherwise*
Ride before, and I wolle com after,
510 Unto thy courte, Sir King Arthoure;
Of no man I wolle shame;
Bethink you howe I have savid your lif.
Therfor withe me nowe shalle ye not strife,
For and ye do, ye be to blame."   *if*
515 The king of her had great shame;
But forthe she rood, thoughe he were grevid,   *grieved*
Tille they cam to Carlyle forthe they mevid.   *moved*
Into the courte she rode him by
For no man wold she spare, securly.   *surely*

483–484   "And on such a note I'll never overcome you; my song can [well] be one of
       lament." *Prick*, especially in view of the line which follows, may refer to the
       "note" of medieval musical notation.
486–487   "[Next time] some armor I'll have for defense, that I vow to God!"
490   "As [it would] be for your best advantage."
504   "As long as you will be ruled by my advice." Arthur, the lady suspects, wants
       the wedding to be a private one which no one can know about.
511   "I desire shame for no man" [that is, my intentions are good].

20 It liked the king fulle ille.   *pleased*
   Alle the contraye had wonder great,
   Fro whens she com, that foule unswete;   *from/unlovely*
                                      one

   They sawe nevere of so foulle a thing.
   Into the halle she went, in certen.   *indeed*
25 "Arthoure, King, let fetche me Sir Gaweyn,   *have/summoned*
   Before the knightes, alle in hying,   *quite/haste*
   That I may nowe be made sekir;   *certain*
   In welle and wo trowithe plighte un togeder
   Before alle thy chivalry.   *knights*
30 This is your graunt, let see, have done.
   Set forthe Sir Gawen, my love, anon,   *bring*
   For lenger tarrying kepe not I."   *longer/coun-*
                                        /tenance

   Then cam forthe Sir Gawen the knighte,
   "Sir, I am redy of that I you highte,   *for/that which*
                                        /promised
35 Alle forwardes to fulfille."   *agreements*
   "Godhavemercy," said Dame Ragnelle then,
   "For thy sake I wold I were a faire woman,
   For thou art of so good wille."
   Ther Sir Gawen to her his trouthe plighte   *troth*
40 In welle and in wo, as he was a true knighte;   *weal/woe*
   Then was Dame Ragnelle fain.   *pleased*
   "Alas!" then said Dame Gaynor;   *Guenevere*
   So said alle the ladies in her bower   *chamber*
   And wept for Sir Gawen.
45 "Alas!" then said bothe king and knight,
   That evere he shold wed suche a wighte,   *person*
   She was so foulle and horrible.
   She had two teethe on every side   *each*
   As boris tuskes, I wolle not hide,   *like/boar's*
50 Of lengthe a large handfulle;
   The one tusk went up and the other doun;
   A mouthe fulle wide and foulle y-grown.   *foully/developed*
   With grey heris many on.   *hairs/one*
   Her lippes laye lumprid on her chin;   *lumped*
55 Neck forsothe on her was none y-seen—
   She was a lothly on!
   She wold not be weddid in no maner
   But there were made a crye in all the shire,   *unless/procla-*
                                        mation
   Bothe in town and in borrowe.   *borough*
60 Alle the ladies nowe of the lond,

---

528   "Plight our troth [that is, wed us] for weal or woe."
530   See Gromer's similar remark on line 100.

She let cry to com to hand
To kepe that bridalle thorowe.   *make/complete*
So it befille after on a daye
That married shold be that foulle lady
565 Unto Sir Gawen.
The daye was comin the daye shold be;
Therof the ladies had gr ~t pitey.
"Allas!" then gan they say...   *did/say*
The queen prayd Dame Ragnelle sekerly   *earnestly*
570 To be married in the morning erly . . .
"As privaly as we may."
"Nay," she sayd, "by Hevin King,
That wolle I nevere for no thing,
For oughte that ye can saye.   *anything*
575 I woll be weddid alle openly,   *quite/publicly*
For withe the king such covenaunt made 1.
I put you oute of doute,
I wolle not to churche tille highe masse time
And in the open halle I wolle dine,
580 In middis of alle the route."   *amidst/assem-*
                                                          blage

"I am greed," said Dame Gaynour,   *agreed/Guenevere*
"But me wold think more honour
And your worship moste."
"Ye, as for that, lady, God you save,
585 This daye my worship wolle I have,
I telle you withoute boste."   *boast*
She made her redy to churche to fare
And alle the states that there ware,   *people of rank*
Sirs, withoute lesing.   *denial*
590 She was arrayd in the richest maner,
More fresher than Dame Gaynour;
Her arrayment was worthe three thousand mark
Of good red nobles stiff and stark,   *gold coins*
So richely she was begon.   *decked out*
595 For alle her rayment she bare the belle   *despite/took*
                                                          /prize

Of foulnesse that evere I hard telle–
So foulle a sowe saw nevere man.   *sow*
For to make a short conclusion,
When she was weddid, they hyed theim home;   *hastened*
600 To mete alle they went.   *dinner*

---

561 "She had summoned to come into [her] presence."
566 "The day arrived [that] was to be the day."
577 "I put you out of fear" with the sense here of "I assure you."
582–583 "But [if you were wed privately it] would seem to me more honorable and
          to your best advantage."

This foulle lady began the highe dese;
She was fulle foulle and not curteis,   *well mannered*
So said they alle verament.   *indeed*
When the service cam her before,
605 She ete as moche as six that ther wore;
That mervailid many a man.   *astonished*
Her nailes were long inchis three;
Therwithe she breke her mete ungoodly;   *ate/food/indeli-*
                                                                       cately

Therfore she ete alone.
610 She ette three capons and also curlues three,   *curlews*
And great bake metes she ete up, perdé.   *baked/foods*
                                                                       /indeed

All men therof had mervaille.
Ther was no mete cam her before,
But she ete it up lesse and more,   *completely*
615 That praty foulle dameselle.   *vile*
Alle men then that evere her sawe
Bad the deville her bonis gnawe,   *prayed/bones*
Bothe knighte and squire.
So she ete tille mete was done,
620 Tille they drewe clothes and had washen
As is the gise and manner.   *custom*
Meny men wold speke of diverse service,
I trowe ye may wete y-noughe ther was,   *trust/know*
Bothe of tame and wilde;   *domestic*
625 In King Arthours courte ther was no wont   *lack*
That mighte be gotten withe mannis hond,   *of that which*
Noder in forest ne in feld.   *neither*
Ther were minstralles of diverse contrey.

                    *   *   *

"A, Sir Gawen, sin I have you wed,   *since*
630 Shewe me your cortesy in bed;
Withe righte it may not be denied.   *by/rights*
Y-wise, Sir Gawen," that lady said,   *certainly*
"And I were faire ye wold do anoder braid,   *if/take/another*
                                                                       /course

---

601   "This foul lady took the place of honor at the table" [literally, sat first at the
      dais].
620   "Till they took towels and washed [their hands]." *Cloth* in ME usually means
      "table cloth" in such a context, but here, followed by the verb *washen*, it may
      have the sense (not attested elsewhere) of 'towel.'
622   Probably "[Even though] men may discuss [and weigh the virtues of] various
      kinds of meals."
628   Here a leaf is lacking in the MS and hence possibly some 70 lines. The missing
      context probably noted how the wedded couple left Arthur's hall and retired
      to the bridal chamber.

But of wedlock ye take no heed.   *except*
635 Yet of Arthours sake kisse me at the leste;   *least*
    I pray you do this at my request,
    Let see howe ye can spede."   *succeed*
    Sir Gawen said, "I wolle do more
    Then for to kisse, and God before!"
640 He turnid him her untille.
    He sawe her the fairest creature
    That evere he sawe withoute mesure.
    She said, "What is your wille?"
    "A, Jhesu!" he said, "whate are ye?"
645 "Sir, I am your wif, securly;   *indeed*
    Why ar ye so unkinde?"
    "A, lady, I am to blame;
    I cry you mercy, my faire madame–
    It was not in my minde.
650 A lady ye ar faire in my sighte
    And today ye were the foulist wighte   *person*
    That evere I sawe withe mine ie.   *eye*
    Wele is me, my lady, I have you thus";   *well*
    And brasid her in his armis and gan her kisse   *embraced/did*
655 And made great joye sicurly.   *surely*
    "Sir," she said, "thus shalle ye me have;
    Chese of the one, so God me save,
    My beauty wolle not hold: *remain constant*
    Wheder ye wolle have me faire on nightes   *whether*
660 And as foulle on days to alle men sightes
    Or els to have me faire on days
    And on nightes on the foulist wife,   *one of/women*
    The one ye must nedes have.   *necessarily*
    Chese the one or the oder.   *other*
665 Chese on, Sir Knighte, whiche you is levere,
    Your worship for to save."   *honor*
    "Alas!" said Gawen, "the choise is hard.
    To chese the best it is froward.   *hard*
    Wheder choise that I chese,
670 To have you faire on nightes and no more,
    That wold greve my hart righte sore
    And my worship shold I lese.   *lose*
    And if I desire on days to have you faire,
    Then on nightes I shold have a simple repaire.
675 Now fain wold I chose the best,   *gladly*
    I ne wot in this world what I shall saye,   *know*

---

649   A vague line as to sense; perhaps the exclamation "I had no idea" would do, at least in this context.
665   "Choose [the] one, Sir Knight, which is more desirable to you."
674   *Simple repaire*, whatever the exact ME idiom may be, here means 'bleak prospects.'

But do as ye list nowe, my lady gaye.   *please*
The choise I put in your fist.   *hand*
Evin as ye wolle, I put it in your hand,   *just/desire*
80 Lose me when ye list, for I am bond.   *relieve/please*
I put the choise in you.
Bothe body and goodes, hart, and every dele,   *heart/part*
Is alle your own, for to by and selle–   *buy*
That make I God avowe!"
85 "Gramercy, corteis knighte," said the lady;   *many thanks*
"Of alle erthly knightes blissid mot thou be,   *may*
For now am I worshippid.   *honored*
Thou shalle have me faire bothe day and nighte
And evere while I live as faire and brighte;
90 Therfore be not grevid.   *grieved*
For I was shapen by nigramancy,   *transformed*
        /necromancy

Withe my stepdame, God have on her mercy,   *by*
And by enchauntement,
And shold have bene oderwise understond,
95 Evin tille the best of Englond
Had weddid me verament.   *indeed*
And also he shold geve me the sovereinté
Of alle his body and goodes, sicurly;
Thus was I disformid;   *in such wise*
        /misshapen

00 And thou, Sir Knighte, curteis Gawen,
Has gevin me the sovereinté sertein,
That wolle not wrothe thee erly ne late.
Kisse me, Sir Knighte, evin now here,
I pray thee, be glad and make good chere,
05 For welle is me begon."
Ther they made joye oute of minde,
So was it reason and cours of kinde,
They two theimself alone.
She thankid God and Mary milde
10 She was recovered of that that she was defoilid;
So did Sir Gawen.
He made mirthe alle in her boure   *chamber*
And thankid of alle oure Savioure,   *for/everything*
I telle you, in certain.
15 With joye and mirthe they wakid tille daye
And than wold rise that faire maye.   *maid*

---

694   "And should have been taken as different [from what I actually am]."
695   "Just until such time as the best [knight] in England."
702   "Who will not anger you at any time."
705   "For [it] has turned out well for me."
707   "As it was right and the usage of nature."
710   "[That] she had recovered from that which had defiled her."

"Ye shalle not," Sir Gawen said;
"We wolle lie and slepe tille prime
And then let the king calle us to dine."
720 "I am greed," then said the maid.   *agreed*
Thus it passid forth till middaye.
"Sirs," quod the king, "let us go and assaye   *find out*
If Sir Gawen be on live.   *alive*
I am fulle ferd of Sir Gawen,   *anxious/about*
725 Nowe lest the fende have him slain;   *fiend*
Nowe wold I fain preve.   *gladly/discover*
Go we nowe," said Arthoure the king.
"We wolle go see their uprising,
Howe welle that he hathe sped."
730 They cam to the chambre alle in certain.   *indeed*
"Arise," said the king to Sir Gawen;
"Why slepist thou so long in bed?"
"Mary," quod Gawen, "Sir King, sicurly,   *surely*
I wold be glad, and ye wold let me be,   *if/alone*
735 For I am fulle welle at eas.
Abide, ye shalle see the dore undone!
I trowe that ye wolle say I am welle gon;   *believe/favored*
I am fulle lothe to rise."   *reluctant*
Sir Gawen rose and in his hand he toke
740 His fair lady and to the dore he shoke   *hastened*
And opinid the dore fulle faire.
She stood in her smock alle by that fire;
Her her was to her knees as red as gold wire.   *hair*
"Lo, this is my repaire!   *pleasure*
745 Lo!" said Gawen Arthoure untille,
"Sir, this is my wife, Dame Ragnelle,
That savid onis your life."   *once*
He told the king and the queen hem beforn
Howe sodenly from her shap she did torne,   *suddenly/shape /turn*

750 "My lord, nowe by your leve."
And whate was the cause she forshapen was   *misshapen*
Sir Gawen told the king both more and lesse.
"I thank God," said the queen,
"I wenid, Sir Gawen, she wold thee have miscaried;   *thought/harmed*
755 Therfore in my hart I was sore agrevid;   *heart*
But the contrary is here seen."
There was game, revelle, and playe
And every man to other gan saye,   *did*
"She is faire wighte."   *person*

---

718 *Prime,* although able to indicate the hours between six and nine, here means "late morning."
752 *More and lesse* "in every detail."

760	Than the king them alle gan telle	*did*
	How did held him at nede Dame Ragnelle,	*preserve*
	"Or my dethe had bene dighte."	*prepared*
	Ther the king told the queen, by the rood,	*cross*
	How he was bestad in Ingleswood	*beset*
765	Withe Sir Gromer Somer Joure	
	And whate othe the knighte made him swere	*oath*
	"Or elles he had slain me righte there	
	Withoute mercy or mesure.	
	This same lady, Dame Ragnelle,	
770	From my dethe she did help me right welle	
	Alle for the love of Gawen."	
	Then Gawen told the king alle togeder	
	Howe forshapen she was withe her stepmoder	*deformed/by*
	Tille a knighte had holpen her again;	
775	Ther she told the king faire and welle	
	Howe Gawen gave her the sovereinté every delle	*part*
	And whate choise she gave to him.	
	"God thank him of his curtesie;	
	He savid me from chaunce and vilony	
780	That was fulle foulle and grim.	
	Therfore, curteis knighte and hend Gawen,	*gracious*
	Shalle I nevere wrathe thee sertain,	*anger/surely*
	That promise nowe here I make;	
	Whiles that I live I shall be obaisaunt;	*obedient*
785	To God above I shalle it warraunt,	
	And nevere with you to debate."	*argue*
	"Garamercy, lady," then said Gawen,	*many thanks*
	"With you I hold me fulle welle content,	
	And that I trust to finde."	
790	He said, "My love shalle she have;	
	Therafter nede she nevere more crave,	*at all*
	For she hathe bene to me so kinde."	
	The queen said (and the ladies alle),	
	"She is the fairest nowe in this halle,	
795	I swere by Saint John!	
	My love, lady, ye shalle have evere,	
	For that ye savid my lord Arthoure,	
	As I am a gentilwoman."	
	Sir Gawen gat on her Gyngolyn,	*begot/Guinglain*
800	That was a good knighte of strengthe and kin	
	And of the Table Round.	
	At every great fest that lady shold be.	
	Of fairnesse she bare away the bewtye,	
	Wher she yed on the ground.	*wherever/went*
805	Gawen lovid that lady Dame Ragnelle;	

---

803   "In appearance she took the prize for beauty."

In alle his life he lovid none so welle,
I telle you withoute lesing. *denial*
As a coward he lay by her bothe day and night. *submissively*
/stayed

Nevere wold he haunt justing arighte; *jousting/as usual*
810 Therat mervailed Arthoure the king.
She praid the king for his gentilnes,
"To be good lord to Sir Gromer, y-wisse, *indeed*
Of that to you he hathe offendid."
"Yes, lady, that shalle I nowe for your sake,
815 For I wot welle he may not amendes make; *know*
He did to me fulle unhend."
Nowe for to make you a short conclusion,
I cast me for to make an end fulle sone *intend*
Of this gentille lady.
820 She livid withe Sir Gawen but yeris five; *years*
That grevid Gawen alle his life, *saddened*
I telle you securly. *surely*
In her life she grevid him nevere; *grieved*
Therfor was nevere woman to him lever. *dearer*
825 Thus leves my talking. *ends/tale*
She was the fairest lady of alle Englond,
When she was on live, I understand; *alive*
So said Arthoure the king.
Thus endithe the adventure of King Arthoure,
830 That oft in his days was grevid sore,
And of the wedding of Gawen.
Gawen was weddid oft in his days;
But so welle he nevere lovid woman always,
As I have hard men sayn. *say*
835 This adventure befelle in Ingleswood,
As good King Arthoure on hunting yod; *went*
Thus have I hard men telle.
Nowe God as thou were in Bethleme boren
Suffer nevere her soules be forlorne *their/lost*
840 In the brinning fire of helle! *burning*
And, Jhesu, as thou were borne of a virgin,
Help him oute of sorrowe that this tale did devine, *devise*
And that nowe in alle hast,
For he is beset withe gailours many, *jailors*
845 That kepen him fulle sewerly, *securely*
With wiles wrong and wraste. *powerful*
Nowe God, as thou art veray king royalle, *true*
Help him oute of daunger that made this tale,
For therin he hathe bene long.

---

816 "He acted toward me [so] very ungraciously."
843 "And [I pray you do] that now in all haste."

850 And of great pety help thy servaunt,   *out of/pity*
For body and soulle I yeld into thine hand,
For paines he hathe strong.

Here endithe the wedding of
Sir Gawen and Dame Ragnelle
855 For helping of King Arthoure.

Sir Gawain and the Carl of Carlisle

HERE are two versions of this romance. One was written in the late fifteenth century, the other in the mid-seventeenth century. The former is printed here. It exists in but one copy, in MS Porkington 10, presently in the National Library of Wales, Aberystwyth. The later version is in the Bishop Percy Folio, now in the British Museum. Both were first printed by Sir Frederic Madden in his *Syr Gawayne* (London, Bannatyne Club, 1839) and the earlier version given the name *Syre Gawene and the Carle of Carelyle*, apparently by Madden himself, since no title for the poem appears in the manuscript. There is a manuscript title, however, for the Percy version, *Carle off Carlile*; the poem and its title were printed by F. J. Child in *English and Scottish Ballads* (Boston 1857) and by J. W. Hales and F. J. Furnivall in *Bishop Percy's Folio Manuscript* (London 1867–1868) with the result that until recently the Percy version has been better known than the Porkington, a regrettable fact since the former is, however primitive some of its features may be, more of a long narrative poem than a romance. Now, fortunately, two excellent editions of the earlier poem exist, by R. W. Ackerman (1947) and by Auvo Kurvinen (1951), and these should give students opportunity to look upon *Sir Gawain and the Carl of Carlisle* as a genuine product of the late fifteenth-century romance and not merely as a hard-to-come-by literary curiosity.

Gawain and the Carl suffers much because it contains several motifs (a temptation scene, a hunting scene, a variation of a beheading scene) strongly reminiscent of the great West Midland poem *Sir Gawain and the Green Knight*, to which, perhaps, it stands in the scale of literary excellence much as *Titus Andronicus* does to *Hamlet* or *Lear*. The late fifteenth-century minstrel may indeed have known the greater romance; but judging by his finished product he did not, as did his contemporary who wrote the South Midland poem *The Grene Knight* (528 lines), attempt to retell it. His product is less ambitious, his narrative purpose chiefly to let Gawain emerge from a series of courtesy tests victorious. *Gawain and the Carl* also suffers because it is so easy to read into and behind it and thereby ignore its actual performance. The Carl himself may indeed suggest a giant of Norse mythology; the tests to which the hero is put do resemble those undergone by Thor; the Carl's castle can have its ultimate prototype in dwellings of other-world kings in ancient Celtic, Norse, and classical tales. Yet the Porkington minstrel did rework his material into a coherent structure, and it is unfair to ignore it and regret he did not utilize older mythological motifs correctly and thoroughly.

The minstrel begins with the usual call to his audience for attention— in short, "Listen to a tale about the paragon of knighthood, Sir Gawain!" We are then told that once upon a time King Arthur and his knights were sojourning (by Carlisle presumably) on lands set aside for hunting. Here, what may seem to us a narrative interruption occurs: from, roughly, line 25 to line 114, the minstrel rattles off a list of Arthurian personages who take part in the hunt. One day, by mid-morning, when five hundred deer lie in a row under the forest branches, Sir Gawain, Sir Kay (who is his usual irritable self), and Bishop Baldwin follow a reindeer into the mist-covered moorland. (The animal can be interpreted as a fey creature designed to lead them astray and into a world where things strange to ordinary mortals can and do happen.) By evening, the three admit themselves lost and, despite the Bishop's warning, take shelter in the castle belonging to the Carl of Carlisle. (*Carl*, from Old Norse *karl* 'man,' never attained the status of a recognized title like *baron* or *earl*; it meant, during Middle English times, basically 'churl' or 'oaf,' although in some texts, chiefly Northern, it does substitute for 'warrior' or 'knight' or 'retainer'; in early Scots it could also mean 'strong man' or 'big fellow' and such a connotation, plus a supernatural one, fits well into the present context.) Once in the great hall of the castle, the three are confronted with a monstrous, shaggy creature, the Carl, and his four *whelpus*—a bull, a boar, a lion, and a bear. The Carl is both hospitable and threatening; only Gawain greets him civilly. After presupper wine, the Bishop goes out to the stable to check his steed. He finds a *lyttyll folle* (here simply a small, perhaps inferior horse) eating alongside his own mount. He roughly turns the *folle* aside; the Carl suddenly appears and knocks him down for his discourtesy. The same fate awaits Kay. Gawain, however, finds the *folle* in the rain, feeds it, covers it with his green mantle, and is complemented by the Carl for his courtesy. The first test (it can be called an echo of an initiation rite) is passed. At table, the Carl's beautiful wife appears and Sir Kay is reproved for thinking more than he dare say out loud. A second test (the one corresponding to the beheading scene in *Sir Gawain and the Green Knight*) occurs when the Carl has Gawain throw a spear directly at him; he misses, but the Carl complements him on his audacity—and his courtesy in obeying the behests of a host. The third and final test occurs when the Carl dares Gawain to get in bed with his wife and kiss her; he obeys and, at the command of the Carl, desists. (Here, of course, is the temptation scene of *Sir Gawain and the Green Knight*.) Satisfied with Gawain as the one true model of courtesy, the Carl rewards him by letting him spend the night with his fair daughter, whom Gawain, we are told, ultimately marries.

Once familiar with *Gawain and the Carl*, one is hard put to say much against it if it is kept in mind that the minstrel's artistic intent was modest. True, the screed of Arthurian personages (lines 25 to 114) is disturbing, particularly when one realizes from the research that Ackerman and Kurvinen have done on it that the minstrel frequently did not know his Arthurian names and material very well. The tail-rhyme stanzas, rhyming *aabccbddbeeb*, are no more and no less than adequate for the matter on hand. They are sometimes irregular and stanza breaks occasionally are disputable. (The stanza numeration of Kurvinen is here followed, although Ackerman's could have been used just as well.) The language, not the orthography, is more Northern than Midland, although it is not predominantly either one or the other. Old English *ā*, for example, appears often as *a*, but also as *o*, a Northern feature beside a Midland; some infinitives lack *-n* (Northern) and some retain *-n* (non-Northern). Other dialect considerations are equally as ambiguous and it is predominantly on the localization of the story and not on a linguistic basis that Kurvinen concludes that the poem was composed in Cumberland or Westmorland. Orthography is another matter. In the printing which follows the original spelling has been kept except that modern graphemes have been substituted for yogh and thorn. The distinctive, and inconsistent, doubling of consonants by the "J scribe" (lines 1–515) and the "K scribe" (lines 515–660) has been retained. Whether such was intended to indicate vocalic length or rhetorical emphasis is debatable. At any event, the lexical, syntactic, and idiomatic features of the poem are simple enough to allow such spellings to stand. They offer no real difficulty and provide a basis for the individual reader to make up his own mind as to their significance —if indeed they have significance.

REFERENCES: Brown and Robbins. No. 1888; Billings, pp. 215–217; *CBEL*, I:138; Kane, p. 53; Wells, pp. 59–60. The two modern editions: Robert W. Ackerman, *Syre Gawene and the Carle of Carelyle* (University of Michigan Press, 1947, No. 8 in the University of Michigan Contributions in Modern Philology); Auvo Kurvinen, *Sir Gawain and the Carl of Carlisle in Two Versions* (Helsinki, 1951, Tom 71,2 in the Annales academiae scientiarum fennicae). The latter edition prints the *The Carl of Carlisle* (500 lines) from the mid-seventeenth-century Percy Folio. John Speirs in his *Medieval English Poetry: The Non-Chaucerian Tradition* (New York, Macmillan, 1957), pp. 206–211, discusses the Percy Folio poem briefly and well, although unfortunately he omits mention of the earlier Porkington version. B. J. Whiting in his "Gawain: His Reputation, His Courtesy, and His Appearance in Chaucer's *Squire's Tale*," *Mediaeval Studies*, IX (1947), 189–234, creates a literary biography of Gawain drawn from the whole corpus of Arthurian legend.

1.

Lystonnyth, lordyngus, a lyttyll stonde	*space*
Of on that was sekor and sounde	*one/true*
And doughty in his dede.	
He was as meke as mayde in bour	*gentle*
5 And therto styfe in euery stour,	*bold/fight*
Was non so doughtty in dede.	
Dedus of armus wyttout lese	*deeds/denial*
Seche he wolde in war and pees	*go questing*
	/peace
In mony a stronge lede.	*foreign/country*
10 Sertaynly, wyttoutyn fabull,	*falsehood*
He was wytt Artter at the Rounde Tabull,	
In romans as we reede.	*romance/read*

2.

His name was Syr Gawene;	
Moche worschepe in Bretten he wan,	*Britain/won*
15 And hardy he was and wyghte.	*valiant*
The yle of Brettayn icleppyde ys	
Betwyn Skotlond and Ynglonde iwys,	
In storry iwryte aryghte.	*written/properly*
Wallys ys an angull of that yle;	*Wales/corner*
20 At Cardyfe soiornde the kynge a whylle	*Cardiff/tarried*
Wytt mony a gentyll knyghte	
That wolde to Ynglonde to honte,	*wanted/in/hunt*
As grete lordys dothe and be wonte,	*accustomed*
Wytt hardy lordys and wyghte.	

3.

25 Kinge Arttor to his lordis gan saye	*did*
As a lorde ryall that well maye,	*royal*

16–17 "Both Scotland and England are indeed called the Isle of Britain."
20 *Cardyfe* is probably an error for *Carlisle* since the romance later indicates that Arthur was staying no more than a few hours' ride from the Carl's castle.

"Do vs to have a masse;
Byschope Bawdewyn schall hit don;   *Baldwin/do*
Then to the forrest woll we gon,   *shall/go*
30   All that evyr her ys,   *here/is*
For nowe ys grece-tyme of the yeer
That baruns bolde schulde hont the der,   *when/hunt/deer*
And reyse hem of her reste."
Wondor glad was Syr Mewreke,   *exceedingly*
                                                     /Marrok

35 So was the knyght Sir Key Caratocke,   *Kay/Caradoc*
And other mor and lase.

4.

Glad was Launccelet de Lacke,   *Lancelot/Lake*
So was Syr Percivall, I vndortake,   *Perceval*
And Lanfalle, I wene,   *Lanval*
40 So was Syr Eweyn the Vyttryan   *Ywain/son of*
                                                     Urien
And Syr Lot of Laudyan,   *Lothian*
That hardy was and kene,
Syr Gaytefer and Syr Galerowne,   *Gadiffer/Galeran*
Syr Costantyn and Syr Raynbrown,   *Constantine*
                                                     /Reinbrun
45   The knyght of armus grene.   *green*
Syr Gawen was stwarde of the halle;   *steward*
He was master of hem all
And buskyde hem bedenne.

5.

The kyngus vncull Syr Mordrete   *king's/uncle*
                                                     /Modred
50 Nobull knyghtus wytt hym gan lede,   *did/lead*
In romans as men rede.   *romance/read*
Syr Yngeles, that genttyle knyghte,
Wytt hym he lede houndys wyght
That well coude do her dede.
55 Syr Lebys Dyskoniis was thare   *Le Bel Inconnu*

---

27 "Let us hear mass."
31 *Grece-tyme* 'grease time,' the season when deer are fat, namely in August and early
    September.
33 "And flush them [the deer] from their cover."
36 "And others of high and low rank."
48 "And got them [the hunting party] prepared at once."
52–53 Kurvinen suggests *Yngeles* is a scribal error for *Yngleswode* and hence the lines
    would mean "To Inglewood that gentle knight [Modred] led with him swift
    hounds." Ackerman identifies *Yngeles* with Sir Engely in the romance *Merlin*
    by Henry Lovelich.

Wytt proude men les and mare
   To make the donne der blede;   *dun/deer/bleed*
Syr Petty Pas of Wynchylse,   *Petipace*
                                                /Winchelsea

A nobull knyght of cheualré,   *chivalry*
60   And stout was on a stede.   *valiant/steed*

6.

Syr Grandon and Syr Ferr Vnkowthe,   *Grandon*
                                          /Fair Unknown

Meryly they sewyde wytt mouthe,
   Wytt houndys that wer wyght;   *swift*
Syr Blancheles and Ironsyde,   *Brandelys*
                                          /Ironside
65 Monny a doughty that day con ryde   *many/bold man*
                                          /did

   On hors fayr and lyghte.   *swift*
Irounsyde, as I wene,   *believe*
Gat the knyght of armus grene   *begot/green*
   On a lady bryght,
70 Sertenly, as I wnderstonde,   *certainly/am told*
   The fayr may of Blanche Lonnde,   *maid/Blanchland*
   In bour that louely wighte.   *chamber/person*

7.

Ironsyde, as I wene,   *believe*
I-armyd he wolde ryde full clene,   *armed/quite*
                                          /properly
75   Wer the sonn nevyr so hoot;
In wyntter he wolde armus bere,   *bear*
Gyanttus and he wer euer at were   *giants/war*
   And allway at the debate.   *always/strife*

8.

Fabele Honde hyght ys stede,   *was called/steed*
80 His armys and his odir wede   *clothing*
   Full fayr and goode hit was.
Of asur for sothe he bare   *azure/sooth/bore*
A gryffyn of golde full feyr   *griffin/fair*
Iset full of golde flourrus.   *adorned*
                                          /fleurs-de-lis

---

62   "Merrily they followed [the hounds] with shouts" [literally, with mouth].
75   "Were the sun ever so hot."
79   Ackerman suggests *Fabele* is an error for *Favele* 'tawny'; *hond* is recorded by the
      OED in the sense 'forefoot.' Kurvinen suggests *hond* is an error for *hewed*
      'colored.' Either suggestion makes a better reading than that in the MS.

9.

85 He coude mor of venery and of wer   *knew/hunting*
                                                  /war
   Then all the kyngus that wer ther;   *than*
   Full oft asay hem he wolde.
   Brennynge dragons hade he slayn   *burning*
   And wylde bullus mony won   *bulls/many a/one*
90   That gresely wer iholde.   *horrible*
                                                  /considered

   Byge barrons he hade ibonde,   *strong/captured*
   A hardyer knyght myght not be fonde, *found*
   Full herdy he was and bolde.   *courageous*
   Therfor ha was callyd, as I hard say,   *heard*
95 The kyngus fellowe by his day,   *king's/companion*
                                                  /lifetime
   Wytt worthy knyghttus itolde.   *among/accounted*

10.

   A lyon of golde was his creste;
   He spake reyson out of reste;
   Lystynn and ye may her.
100 Whereuer he went, be est or weste,   *east/west*
   He nold forsake man nor best   *abandon/beast*
   To fyght fer or ner.   *far/near*

11.

   Knyghttus kene fast they rane;   *ran*
   The kynge followyd wytt mony a man,
105   V C and moo, I wene.   *five hundred*
                                                more/believe
   Folke followyd wytt fedyrt flonus,   *feathered/arrows*
   Nobull archarrus for the nons,   *archers/occasion*
   To fell the fallow-der so cleyn.   *fair*

12.

   Barrons gan her hornnus blowe,   *did/horns*
110 The der cam reykynge on a rowe,   *running/one after*
                                                  another

---

87   "Quite often he would put them [the kings] to the test."
98   "He spoke wisdom" is clear, but the translation of *out of reste* is not. Ackerman suggests "without hesitation," basing his translation on the *OED's without but rest* "without delay" (see *rest* sb.[1] 3c), which Kurvinen rejects and then proposes that *out of* is an error for the Northern *out-over* "above." Even this Kurvinen rejects—on historical grounds—and ultimately concludes that the original meaning is lost for good.

Bothe hert and eke heynde.   *also/hind*
Be that tyme was pryme of the day   *mid-morning*
V C der dede on a lond lay   *deer/dead*
Alonge vndur a lynde.   *in a row/linden*

13.

115 Then Syr Gawen and Syr Key
    And Beschope Bavdewyn, as I yow say,
        After a raynder they rode.   *reindeer*
    Frowe that tym was prym of the day   *from*
    Tyl myde-vndur-non, as i yow saye,
120   Neuer styll hit abode.   *stopped*
    A myst gan ryse in a mor,   *did/moor*
    Barrons blowe her hornis store;   *loudly*
        Meche mon Syr Key made,   *much/complaint*
    The reyneder wolde not dwelle.   *tarry*
125 Herkon what aventer hem befelle;   *listen/adventure*
    Herbrow they wolde fayn haue hade.   *shelter/gladly*

14.

Then sayde the gentyll knyght Syr Gawen,
"All this labur ys in wayne,   *effort/vain*
    For certen trowe hit me.
130 The dere ys passyde out of our syght;   *gone/beyond*
    We mete no mor wytt hym to-nyght,   *shall meet/with*
        Hende herkon to me.   *kindly/harken*
    I reede that we of our hors alyght   *advise*
    And byde in this woode all nyght   *abide*
135   And loge vndur this tree."   *camp*
    "Ryde we hens," quod Keye anon,
    "We schall haue harbrowe or we gon;   *lodging/before*
    Dar no man wern hit me."

15.

Then sayd the Beschope, "I knowe hit well,
140 A Carle her in a castell
    A lyttyll her ner honde.   *here/nearby*
    The Karl of Carllyll ys his nam,   *name*
    He may vs herborow, be Sent Iame,   *put up/James*
    As I vndurstonde.   *have heard say*

118–119 "From the time of nine in the morning till late afternoon, as I say to you."
129   "Indeed take my word for it."
136   " 'Let us ride hence,' said Kay immediately."
138   "Let no man deny it me."

145 Was ther nevyr barnn so bolde   *fellow*
   That euer myght gaystyn in his holde   *lodge/castle*
     But evyll harbrowe he fonde.   *evil/welcome*
   He schall be bette, as I harde say,   *beaten*
   And yefe he go wytt lyfe away   *if/alive*
150   Hit wer but Goddus sonde.

16.

Nowe ryde we thedyr all thre."
Therto sayd Key, "I grant hit the,
   Also mot I well far;
And as thou seyst, hit schall be holde.   *say/done*
155 Be the Carle neuer so bolde,
   I count hym not worthe an har   *hair*
And yeyf he be neuer so stovte,   *if/strong*
We woll hym bette all abowt   *beat/thoroughly*
   And make his beggynge bar.   *dwelling/desolate*
160 Suche as he brewythe, seche schall he drenke,   *brews/such*
He schall be bette that he schall stynke   *beaten*
   And ayenst his wyll be thar."

17.

Syr Gawen sayd, "So hav I blyse,   *as/bliss*
I woll not geystyn ther magré ys,
165   Thow I myght neuer so well,
Yefe anny fayr wordus may vs gayn   *if/fair/help*
To make the larde of vs full fayn   *lord/glad*
   In his oun castell.
Key, let be thy bostfull fare;   *conduct*
170 Thow gost about to warke care,
   I say, so haue I helle.
I woll pray the good lorde, as I yow saye,
Of herborow tyll to-morrow daye   *for/lodging*
   And of met and melle."   *food/meals*

18.

175 On her way fast they rode;   *their*
   At the castell yat they abode;   *gate/stopped*
     The portter call they schulde.   *were obliged to*

---

148   "He [a stray guest] is supposed to be beaten [by the Carl], as I have heard tell."
150   "It would be through God's dispensation."
153   "As I may fare well"—an asseveration.
162   "And remain there unwillingly [in his own castle]."
164–165   "I shall not lodge there against his will though I could [do so] very well."
170–171   "You are setting out to stir up trouble, I say, as I may have my health."

Ther hynge a hommyr by a cheyn;

To knocke therat Syr Key toke dayn,
80   The hommyr away he wold have pold.
The portter come wytt a prewey fare

And hem fonde he ther;
He axid what they wolde.
Then sayd Gawen curttesly,
85 "We beseche the lorde of herbory,
The good lorde of this holde."

hung/hammer
/chain

pulled
with/sneaky
/mien

asked/wanted

for/lodging
castle

19.

The portter answerd hem agayn,
"Your message wold I do full fayn;
And ye have harme, thanke hyt not me.
90 Ye be so fayr, lyme and lythe,
And therto comly, glad therwytt,
That cemmely hyt ys to see.
My lorde can no corttessye;
Ye schappyth notte wyttout a wellony,
95   Truly trow ye mee.
Me rewyth sor ye came this waye;
And ar ye go, so woll ye say,
But yefe mor grace be."

in turn
deliver/gladly
if/suffer

handsome/also

knows/courtesy
escape/indignity
believe

20.

"Portter," sayde Key, "let be thy care;
00 Thow sest we mey no forther fare;

Thow iappyst, as I wene.
But thou wolt on our message gon,
The kyngus keyis woll we tane
And draw hem doun cleyn."
05 The portter sayde, "So mot I thryfe,
Ther be not thre knyghttus alyve
That dorst do hit, I wene.

worry
see/may/further
/go

jeer/suspect
unless/errand

may/thrive

dare/know

179 "Sir Kay felt disinclined to knock there [with it]."
190 "You are so sound in life and limb" (literally, limb and limb).
192 "That it is pleasant to look upon."
196 "I am sorry you came this way."
197–198 "And before you go, you will say likewise, unless there be more good fortune [than usual]."
203–204 Kurvinen would interpret "We shall take the crowbars [provided by the King to break into houses] and draw them [the gates] down completely." See OED *key* sb.[1] 1b.

Wyst my lorde your wordys grete,   *knew/boastful*
Some your lyvys ye schold forlete   *some of you/lose*
210   Or ellus full fast to flen."   *otherwise/flee*

21.

The portter went into the hall,
Wytt his lord he mett wyttall,
    That hardy was and bolde.
"Carl of Carllhyll, God loke the,
215 At the yatt be barnnus thre,   *gate/men*
    Semley armus to welde,   *fit/use*
To knyghttus of Arterys in,   *two/house*
A beschope, and no mor men,
    Sertayn, as they me tolde."
220 Then sayd the Carle, "Be Sent Myghell,   *by/Michael*
That tythingus lykyth me ryght well,   *news/pleases*
    Seyth thei this way wolde."

22.

When they came befor that syr,
They fond iiij whelpus lay about his fyer,   *creatures*
225   That gresly was for to see: *horrible*
A wyld bole and a fellon boor,   *bull/fierce/boar*
A lyon that wold bytte sor–   *bite/savagely*
    Therof they had grete ferly.   *wonder*
A bege ber lay louse vnbounde,   *huge/bear/loose*
230 Seche iiij whelpus ther they founde
    About the carllus kne.
They rose and came the knyghttus agayn,   *towards*
And soun thei wold hem haue slayn;   *quickly*
    The Carle bade hem let bee.   *stop*

23.

235 "Ly doun," he sayd, "my whelpys four."
Then the lyon began to lour
    And glowyd as a glede,   *ember*
The ber to ramy, the boole to groun,   *growl/roar*
The bor he whett his toskos soun   *tusks*
                                                    /immediately
240   Fast and that good spede.

---

214 *God loke the* "may God save you."
222 "Since they would wish [to come] this way."
230 "Four such creatures they found there."

Then sayd the Carle, "Ly style, hard yn!"
They fell adoun for fer of hyme,   *out of/fear*
  So sor they gan hyme drede.   *did/dread*
For a word the Carle gan say   *just by one/did*
45 Vnder the tabull they crepyd away;   *crept*
  Therof Syr Key toke hede.   *heed*

24.

The Carle the knyghttus can beholde,   *did*
Wytt a stout vesage and a bolde;
  He semyd a dredfull man:
50 Wytt chekus longe and vesage brade,   *broad*
Cambur nose and all full made,
  Betwyne his browus a large spane,
Hys moghth moche, his berd graye,   *mouth/large*
Ouer his brest his lockus lay
55   As brod as anny fane;   *winnowing basket*
Betwen his schuldors, whos ryght can rede,
He was ij tayllors yardus a brede.   *yardsticks/broad*
  Syr Key merweld gretly than.   *marveled*

25.

IX taylloris yerdus he was hyghtht,   *tall*
60 And therto leggus longe and wyghtht,   *powerful*
  Or ellus wondor hit wer.
Ther was no post in that hall,
Grettyst growand of hem all,
  But his theys wer thycker.
65 His armus wer gret wyttoutyn lese,   *denial*
His fyngeris also, iwys,   *indeed*
  As anny lege that we ber.   *bear*
Whos stoud a stroke of his honde,   *whosoever*
          /withstood

He was not wecke, I vndurstond,   *weak/heard tell*
70   That dar I safly swer.   *dare/safely/swear*

---

241 *Ly style* is "lie quiet," but *hard yn* (in the MS *hardyn*) is a puzzle: it could be
     "herd, down!" and it could be a scribal corruption of several commands reserved
     for use with animals.
248 "[Who had] a strong and arrogant face."
251 "Aquiline nose and very foully formed"; *full*, of course, may be 'fully' and, if so,
     the phrase is "generously proportioned."
256 "Between his shoulders, whoso can judge properly."
261 "Or else it were strange [if his legs were not powerful]."
263 "[The] largest grown of them all." Kurvinen believes *growand*, a present participle,
     an error for *growan*, a past participle.
264 "[Compared with which] his thighs were thicker."

26.

Then Syr Gawen began to cnele.	*did/kneel*
The Carle sayd he myght be knyght wylle	*well*
And bad hyme stond vpe anon.	
"Lett be thy knellynge, gentyll knyght;	*kneeling*
275 Thow logost wytt a Carll to-nyght,	*lodge/with*
I swer, by Sennt Iohnn.	*saint/John*
For her no corttessy thou schalt have,	
But carllus cortessy, so God me save,	
For serttus I can non."	*know*
280 He bad brynge wyn in gold so der;	*precious*
Anon hit cam in coppus cler,	*cups*
As anny sonn hit schon.	*sun*

27.

IIII gallons held a cop and more;	*cup*
He bad brynge forthe a grettor:	*larger*
285 "What schall this lyttyll cope doun?	*do*
This to lyttyll a cope for me	*too/little*
When I sytt by the fyr onn hy	*on/the dais*
By myself aloun.	
Brynge vs a gretter bolle of wynn;	*bowl/wine*
290 Let vs drenke and play sethyn	*afterwards*
Tyll we to sopper goun."	*go*
The butteler brought a cope of golde	
(IX gallons hit gane holde)	*did*
And toke hit the Carle anon.	*gave/at once*

28.

295 IX gallons he hyld and mare;	*it/held/more*
He was not weke that hit bare	*weak*
In his won honde.	*one*
The knyghttus dronkon fast about	
And sethe arose and went hem out	*then*
300 To se her hors stond.	
Corne and hey thei had reydy;	*hay/they/within reach*
A lyttyll folle stod hem bye	*horse*
Wytt her hors fast ettand.	*their/horses /eating*
The besschope put the fole away:	*aside*
305 "Thow schalt not be fello wytt my palfray	
Whyll I am beschope in londe."	

---

300 "To see [how] their horses were."

29.

The Carll then cam wytt a gret spede   *with*
And askyde, "Who hathe doun this dede?"   *done*
   The beschope seyd, "That was I."
310 "Therfor a bofett thou schalt have,   *buffet*
I swer, so God me sawe,   *as/may save*
   And hit schall be sett wytterly."   *dealt/truly*
"I ame a clarke of ordors hyghe."   *cleric/high*
"Yett cannyst thou noght of corttessyghe,   *know/courtesy*
315   I swer, so mott I trye."
He yafe the besschope a boffett tho   *then*
That to the ground he gan goo;   *did/go*
   I sonynge he gann lyghe.   *a/swoon/did/lie*

30.

Syr Key came in the same cas   *Kay*
320 To se his stede ther he was;   *look at/steed*
                                    /there where
   The foll fond he hym by.   *horse*
Out att the dor he drof hym out   *door*
And on the backe yafe hym a clovt.   *gave/clout*
   The Carle se that wytt hys yghe.   *saw/eye*
325 The Carll yafe hym seche a boffett
That smertly onn the grond hym sett;   *which*
   In sonynge gan he lyghe.   *a/swoon/did/lie*
"Euyll-tavght knyghttus," the Carl gan sey;   *ill-taught/did say*
"I schall teche the or thou wend away   *before/go*
330   Sum of my corttessye."

31.

Then they arose and went to hall,
The beschope and Syr Key wyttall,   *together*
   That worthy was iwroght.
Syr Gawen axyd wer they had byne.   *asked/where*
                                    /been
335 They seyd, "Our horssys we have sene   *seen*
   And vs sor forthoght."
Then ansswerd Gawen full curttesly,
"Syr, wytt your leyf then wyll I."
   The Carll knewe his thought.   *perceived*
                                    /intention

---

315   "I swear, as I may thrive."
333   "Who was handsomely proportioned."
336   "And we sorely repent [it]."
338   "Sir, now, by your leave, I shall [go out]."

340 Hett reynnyd and blewe stormus felle   *rained/cruel*
    That well was hym, be bocke and belle,   *book*
       That herborow had cavght.   *who/lodging/got*

32.

    Wyttout the stabull dor the foll gan stond;   *did/horse*
    Gawen put hyme in agayn wytt his hond;   *back in*
345   He was all wett, I wene,   *suspect*
    As the foll had stond in rayne.   *since/stood*
    Then keueryd he hym, Sir Gawene,   *covered*
      Wytt his manttell of grene.   *green*
    "Stond vpe, fooll, and ectte thy mette;   *eat/fodder*
350 We spend her that thy master dothe gett,
      Whyll that we her byne."
    The Carle stode hym fast by
    And thankyd hym full curtteslye   *very/graciously*
    Manny sythis, I wene.   *times/suspect*

33.

355 Be that tyme her soper was redy dyght,   *by/their/supper*
                                      /made

    The tabullus wer havfe vpe an hyght;
    Icowert they were full tyte.   *spread/indeed*
                                      /promptly

    Forthwytt, thei wolde not blynne:
    The besschope gan the tabull begynne
360   Wytt a gret delytte.   *delight*
    Syr Key was sett on the tother syde   *other*
    Ayenst the Carllus wyfe so full of pryde,   *opposite/well*
                                        adorned

    That was so feyr and whytte: *fair/white*
    Her armus small, her mydyll gent,   *waist/slender*
365 Her yghen grey, her browus bente;   *eyes/brows*
                                      /arched
    Of curttessy sche was perfette.   *complete*

350–351   Literally, "We spend here that which your master earns, during the time we are here." Gawain is being courteous, in contrast to Baldwin and Kay, and his words may imply "Since we aren't bearing the cost, it's our duty to show appreciation."

356   "The [trestle-]tables were erected" [literally, lifted up on high].

358   "At once, they would not delay."

359   "The bishop took the seat of honor" [literally, began the board]; Kurvinen notes that the seat would be on the right of the host at the table elevated above the rest of the hall on a dais.

34.

Her roode was reede, her chekus rounde,	*complexion/full*
A feyrror myght not goo on grounde,	*fairer one/walk*
Ne lowelyur of syghte.	*lovelier/in*
	/appearance
370 Sche was so gloryis and soo gay	
I can not rekon her araye;	*describe/clothing*
Sche was so gayly dyghte.	*decked out*
"Alas," thought Key, "thou lady fre,	*noble*
That thou schuldyst this ipereschde be	*thus/wasted*
375 Uytt seche a foulle weghtht!"	*on/such/fellow*
"Sytt styll," quod the Carl, "and eete thy mette;	*food*
Thow thinkost mor then thou darst speke;	
Sertten I the hyght."	

35.

I do yow all well to wette	
380 Ther was noo man bade Gawen sitte,	*asked*
But in the halle flor gann he stonde.	*on/did*
The Carle sayde, "Fellowe, anoun,	
Loke my byddynge be well idoun!	
Go take a sper in thy honde	*spear*
385 And at the bottre-dor goo take thy passe	*buttery-door/way*
And hitt me evyn in the face;	*right*
Do as I the commande.	
And yeyfe thou ber me ayenst the wall,	*if/bear/against*
Thow schalt not hort me wyttalle,	*hurt/at all*
390 Whyll I am gyaunt in londe."	

36.

Syr Gawenn was a glade mann wytt that;	
At the bottre-dor a sper he gatte	*got*
And in his honde hit hente.	*seated*
Syr Gawen came wytt a gret ire.	*went/passion*
395 Doun he helde his hede, that syre,	*head*
Tyll he hade geue his dentte.	*given/blow*
He yafe the ston wall seche a rappe	*gave/rap*
That the goode sper all tobrake;	*broke to pieces*
The fver flewe out of the flente.	*fire/flint*
400 The Carl sayde to hym ful soune,	*at once*

378   "Of that I assure you."
379   "I shall have you all know well."
383   "See [that] my bidding is well carried out."
390   "While I am the strong man here."

"Gentyll knyght, thou hast well doune."
And be the honde hyme hente.   *by/took*

37·

A cher was fette for Syr Gawene,   *chair/fetched*
That worthy knyght of Bryttayne;   *Britain*
405   Befor the Carllus wyfe was he sett.
So moche his love was on her lyght   *settled*
Of all the soper he ne myght   *supper*
    Nodyr drynke nor ette.   *neither/eat*
The Carle sayde, "Gawen, comfort the,
410 For synn ys swete, and that I se,   *sin*
    Serten I the hete.   *certainly/assure*
Sche ys myn thou woldyst wer thynn.
Leve seche thoghttus and drenke the wynne,   *leave/such/wine*
    For her thou schalt nott geytt."   *get*

38.

415 Syr Gawen was aschemmyde in his thowght;   *ashamed/of*
The Carllus dovghtter forthe was brovght,   *daughter*
    That was so feyr and bryght.
As gold wyre schynyde her here.   *wire/shone/hair*
Hit cost a M li and mar,
420   Her aparrell pertly pyghte.
Wytt ryche stonnus her clothus wer sett,   *jewels*
Uytt ryche perllus about her frete,   *with/scattered*
    So semly was that syghte.   *beautiful*
Ouyr all the hall gann sche leme   *throughout/did*
                                                           /shine

425 As hit were a sonbeme–   *as if/sunbeam*
    That stonnus schone so bryght.

39·

Then seyde the Carle to that bryght of ble,
"Uher ys thi harpe thou schuldist have broght wytt the– *where*
    Uhy hast thou hit forgette?"   *why/forgotten*
430 Anon hit was fett into the hall   *brought*
And a feyr cher wyttall   *fine/chair/also*
    Befor her fador was sett.   *father*
The harpe was of maser fyne;   *maple wood*
The pynnys wer of golde, I wene,   *pins/suspect*

---

412   "She is mine [whom] you would wish were yours."
419–420   "Her attire [so] skillfully adorned, it cost a thousand pounds and more."
427   "Then said the Carl to the [girl] bright of complexion."

35   Serten wyttout lett
      Furst sche harpyd and sethe songe   *then/sang*
      Of love and of Artorrus armus amonge,
        How they togeydor mett.

                              40.

      Uhen they hade sovpyde and mad hem glade,   *when/dined*
                                                            /themselves
40   The Beschope into his chambur was lade,   *led*
        Uytt hym Syr Key the kene.   *with/bold*
      They toke Syr Gawen wyttout lessynge   *denial*
      To the Carlus chamber thei gan hym brynge,   *did*
        That was so bryght and schene.   *radiant*

                              41.

45   They bade Syr Gawen go to bede,
      Uytt clothe of golde so feyr sprede,   *with/fairly*
        That was so feyr and bryght.
      Uhen the bede was made wytt wynne,   *when/joy*
      The Carl bade his oun lady go in,   *wife/get*
50   That loufesom was of syghte.   *delightful/sight*
      A squyer came wytt a prewey far
      And he vnarmyde Gawen then;
        Schaply he was vndyght.
      The Carle seyde, "Syr Gawene,   *said*
55   Go take my wyfe in thi armus tweyne   *twain*
        And kys her in my syghte."   *kiss*

                              42.

      Syr Gawen ansswerde hyme anon,
      "Syr, thi byddynge schall be doune,   *done*
        Sertaynly in dede,   *certainly/indeed*
60   Kyll or sley or laye adoune."
      To the bede he went full sone,   *bed/quickly*
        Fast and that good spede.
      For softnis of that ladys syde   *body*
      Made Gawen do his wyll that tyde;   *time*
65   Therof toke the Carle goode hede.   *heed*

---

435   "Certainly without doubt" (literally, without hindrance).
437–438 "Of love and Arthur's feats of arms [and] how they came together"—prob-
         ably an allusion to an idea that the two are inseparable at Arthur's court.
451–453 "A squier came discreetly [literally, with privy behavior] and [helped] dis-
         arm Gawain then; fittingly he was [helped to] undress."
460   "[Even if you] strike or kill or throw [me] down."

Uhen Gawen wolde haue doun the prevey far,
Then seyd the Carle, "Whoo ther.
   That game I the forbede.   *forbid*

43.

But, Gawen, sethe thou hast do my byddynge,   *since/done*
470 Som kyndnis I most schewe the in anny thinge,   *something*
   As fer forthe as I maye.
Thow schalt have wonn to so bryght
Schall play wytt the all this nyghte
   Tyll to-morrowe daye."
475 To his doughtter chambur he went full ryght   *straightway*
And bade her aryse and go to the knyght
   And wern hym nott to playe.
Sche dorst not ayenst his byddynge doun,   *contrary to/do*
But to Gawen sche cam full sone   *went/quickly*
480   And style doun be hyme laye.   *quietly/by*

44.

"Now, Gawen," quod the Carle, "holst the well payde?" *hold/yourself*
                                                  /satisfied
"Ye, for Gode, lorde," he sayde,   *before*
   "Ryght well as I myghte!"
"Nowe," quod the Carle, "I woll to chambur go;
485 My blessynge I geyfe yow bouthe to,   *both/two*
   And play togeydor all this nyght."
A glad man was Syr Gawen
Sertenly, as I yowe sayne,   *say*
   Of this lady bryght.   *about*
490 Serten, sothely for to say,
So, I hope, was that feyr maye
   Of that genttyll knyght.

45.

"Mary, mercy," thought that lady bryghte,
"Her come neuer suche a knyght
495   Of all that her hathe benne."   *been*
Syr Key arose vppon the morrown   *Kay/morrow*

---

466   *Prevey far*, in contrast to its use in line 451, here means 'intercourse.'
471   "In so far as I am able."
472–473   "You also shall have one [a lady] as radiant [who] will disport with you
       throughout this night.
477   "And not reject his attentions [literally, deny him not to play]."
483   "[And] right well I might!"
491   "Likewise, I think, that fair girl was [glad]."

And toke his hors and wolde a goune *have/left*
   Homwarde, as I wenne. *suspect*
"Nay, Syr Key," the Beschope gann seye, *did/say*
oo "Ue woll not so wende our waye *we/go*
   Tyll we Syr Gawen have sene." *seen*
The Carll arose on morrow anon
And fond his byddynge reddy doune: *already/done*
   His dyner idyght full cleyne. *meal/prepared*
                                         /fittingly

46.

o5 To a mas they lett knelle;
Syr Gawen arose and went thertyll *thereto*
   And kyst that lady bryght and cler. *kissed*
"Maré, marcé," seyde that lady bryght,
"Uher I schall se enny mor this knyght *where/any*
o   That hathe ley my body so ner?" *lain/near*
Uhen the mese was doune to ende, *when/mass*
Syr Gawen toke his leve to wende *go*
   And thonkyde hym of his cher. *for/hospitality*
"Furst," sayde the Carle, "ye schall dynn *dine*
15 And on my blessynge wende home syne, *with/go/then*
   Homward al yn fere." *all/together*

47.

"Hit is xx wynter gon," sayde the Karle, "nowe
That God I maked a vowe, *to God*
   Therfore I was fulle sad: *for which*
2o Ther schulde neuer man logge in my wonys *lodge/dwelling*
But he scholde be slayne, iwys, *unless/indeed*
   But he did as I hym bad. *except*
But he wolde do my byddynge bowne, *unless/quickly*
He schulde be slayne and layde adowne, *low*
25   Whedir he were lorde or lad. *whether/servant*
Fonde I neuer, Gawen, none but the.
Nowe Gode of heuyn yelde hit the;
   Therfore I am fulle glade."

48.

"He yelde the," sayde the Carle, "that the dere boughte,
3o For al my bale to blysse is broughte *misery*

---

505   "They had bells rung for mass."
526   "I never found, Gawain, any one except you [who would do my bidding at once]."
527   "Now may God of heaven reward you for it."
529   " 'May He who redeemed you at [so] great cost reward you,' said the Carl."

Throughe helpe of Mary quene."
He lade Gawen ynto a wilsome wonys — led/lonely /dwelling

There as lay x fodir of dede menn bonys — wherein/cart-loads/bones

Al yn blode, as I wene. — blood/suspect
535 Ther hynge many a blody serke, — shirt
And eche of heme a dyuers marke;
Grete doole hit was to sene. — pity/see

49.

"This slowe I, Gawen, and my helpis, — these/slew /helpers

I and also my foure whelpis,
540 For sothe, as I the say
Nowe wulle I forsake my wyckyd lawys; — customs
Ther schall no mo men her be slawe, iwys, — more/slain /indeed

As ferth forthe as I may.
Gawen, for the love of the
545 Al schal be welcome to me — everyone
That comythe here by this way. — along
And for alle these sowlys, I vndirtake, — souls/promise
A chauntery here wul I lete make,
X prestis syngynge til domysday."

50.

550 Be that tyme her dyner was redy dyghte, — by/made
Tables wer hovyn vp an hyghte,
Ikeuerid thei were fulle clene. — covered
Syr Gawen and this lady clere,
They were iseruyd bothe i fere; — served/together
555 Myche myrthe was theme bytwene. — much
Therfore the Carle was full glade.
The Byschop and Syr Kay he bad — asked
Mery that thei scholde bene. — be
He yafe the bischop to his blessynge — gave/in return for

560 A cros, a myter, and a rynge, — mitre
A clothe of golde, I wene. — suspect

536 Kurvinen suggests "And each of them had a different mark [of ownership]."
539 The *whelpis* are the bull, boar, lion, and bear of lines 224ff.
543 See line 471.
548–549 "I shall have made a chapel here [so provided for it will have] ten priests singing till doomsday."
551 See line 356.

He yaf Syr Kay, the angery knyght,   *gave/difficult*
A blode-rede stede and a whight;   *blood-red/swift*
 Suche on had he neuer sene.   *such a/one/seen*

51.

65 He yaf Syr Gawen, sothe to say,   *truth*
His doughter and a whighte palfray,   *white*
 A somer ichargid wyth golde.   *pack horse/laden*
Sche was so gloryous and so gay
I kowde not rekyn here aray,   *reckon*
70 So bryghte was alle here molde.
"Nowe ryde forthe, Gawen, on my blessynge, *with*
And grete wel Artyr, that is your kynge, *greet*
 And pray hym that he wolde,
For his loue that yn Bedlem was borne, *Bethlehem*
75 That he wulle dyne wyth me to-morne."
 Gawen seyde he scholde.

52.

Then thei rode syngynge away
Wyth this yonge lady on here palfray,
 That was so fayre and bryghte.
80 They tolde Kynge Artir wher thei had bene, *been*
And what wondirs thei had sene   *strange things*
               /seen
 Serteynly in here syght.
"Nowe thonkyd be God, cosyn Gawyn,
That thou scapist alyve vnslayne,   *escaped/alive*
85 Serteyne wyth alle my myght."
"And I, Syr Kynge," sayd Syr Kay agayne, *in turn*
"That euer I scapid away vnslayne
 My hert was neuyr so lyght.
The Carle prayde you for his love that yn Bedlem was borne
90 That ye wolde dyne wyth hym to-morne."
 Kynge Artur sone hym hyght.
In the dawnynge forthe thy rade;   *forth/rode*
A ryalle metynge ther was imade
 Of many a ientylle knyght.   *gentle*

---

570 Kurvinen suggests the line originally read *So bryghte was non on molde* "So radiant was none on earth," although *molde* might mean '(top of the) head,' a sense which would fit, however awkwardly.
583 ME *cosyn* 'cousin,' often used as an equivalent of 'friend.'
591 "King Arthur quickly promised him [to do so]."

53.

595 Trompettis mette hem at the gate,   *met*
Clarions of siluer redy thcrate,
   Sertcyne wythoutyn lette;   *denial*
Harpe, fedylle, and sawtry,   *fiddle/psaltery*
Lute, geteron, and menstracy   *gittern/minstrelsy*
600   Into the halle hem fett.   *brought*

54.

The Carle knelyd downe on his kne
And welcomyd the kynge wurthyly
   Wyth wordis ware and wyse.   *well-chosen*
When the Kynge to the halle was brought,
605 Nothynge ther ne wantyd nought   *lacked/at all*
   That any man kowde deuyse.   *think of*
The wallys glemyd as any glasse,
Wyth dyapir colour wroughte hit was   *in/figured*
    pattern

55.

   Of golde, asure, and byse,   *azure/gray*
610 Wyth tabernacles the halle aboughte,   *canopies*
Wyth pynnacles of golde sterne and stoute;   *sturdy*
   Ther cowde no man hem preyse.   *evaluate*
Trompettys trompid vp in grete hete;   *heat*
The kynge lete sey grace and wente to mete
615   And was iseruyde wythoute lette.   *delay*
Swannys, fesauntys, and cranys,
Partrigis, plouers, and curlewys
   Before the Kynge was sette.

56.

The Carle seyde to the Kynge, "Dothe gladly.
620 Here get ye no nothir curtesy,
   As I vndirstonde."
Wyth that come yn bollys of golde, so grete   *bowls*
Ther was no knyght sat at the mete   *table*
   Myght lyfte hem wyth his on honde.
625 The Kynge swore, "By Seynte Myghelle,   *Michael*
This dyner lykythe me as welle   *pleases*
   As any that euyr Y fonde."
A dubbyd hym knyght on the morne;   *he*
The contré of Carelyle he yafe hym sone   *gave/at once*
630   To be lorde of that londe.

619   Kurvinen explains the Carl's expression as one used in ME in wishing a guest a good appetite.

57.

"Here I make the yn this stownde   *at/moment*
A knyght of the Table Rownde,
  Karlyle thi name schalle be."
On the morne when hit was daylyght
635 Syr Gawen weddyid that lady bryght,
  That semely was to se.   *beautiful*

58.

Than the Carle was glade and blythe
And thonkyd the Kynge fele sythe,   *many a/time*
  For sothe, as I you say.
640 A ryche fest had he idyght   *feast/prepared*
That lastyd holy a fortenyght
  Wyth game, myrthe, and playe.
The mynstrellis had yeftys fre   *gifts/liberal*
That they myght the better be,
645   To spende many a day.
And when the feste was broughte to ende,
Lordis toke here leve to wende
  Homwarde on here way.

59.

A ryche abbey the Carle gan make   *did/found*
650 To synge and rede for Goddis sake
  In wurschip of oure Lady.
In the towne of mery Carelyle
He lete hit bylde stronge and wele;   *had/built/well*
  Hit is a byschoppis see.
655 And theryn monkys gray   *monks*
To rede and synge tille domysday,
  As men tolde hit me,
For the men that he had slayne, iwis.   *because of*
                            /indeed

Iesu Cryste, brynge vs to thy blis
660   Aboue in heuyn, yn thy see. Amen.   *abode*

644–645 Kurvinen suggests the sense "That they might be more inclined to spend many a day."

Glossary

Glossary

—————— ◆◄►◆ ——————

THIS glossary is selective, although two groups of words are covered rather fully: first, high frequency Middle English words that look like Modern English words but have different meanings and, second, high frequency Middle English words that have no obvious Modern English counterparts. Line references are numerous, but far from inclusive. As a possible aid to pronunciation, "open o" [ɔ] has been given its characteristic hook, as has also "open e" [ɛ:]. Presumably, the former was pronounced like the first syllable in *awful* and the latter like the *e* in *bet* only of longer duration. Double vowels are not present in head words. The macron over a long vowel indicates length; hence, the Middle English *free* is to be looked for under *frē*. The prefix *y-* has been omitted unless a permanent part of an entry, as in *y-nough*; such forms as *y-gon* and *y-fere* should be looked up under *gon* and *fere*. For convenience, the graphemic combinations *cch* and *thth* have been listed in the Middle English head words as *ch* and *th*; hence, *siththen* and *fecchen* appear as *sithen* and *fechen*.

ABBREVIATIONS

Ath—Athelston, Flr—Floris and Blancheflour, Frn—Lai le Fresne, Gml— Gamelyn, Gwn—Sir Gawain and the Carl of Carlyle, Hrn—King Horn, Hvl—Havelok the Dane, Lnf—Sir Lanfall, Orf—Sir Orfeo, Rgn—The Wedding of Sir Gawain and Dame Ragnell, Sqr—The Squire of Low Degree, Trn—The Tournament of Tottenham.

AF—Anglo-French, F—French, Lat—Latin, ME—Middle English, ModE —Modern English, OE—Old English, OF—Old French, OI—Old Icelandic, ON—Old Norse.

Acc. accusative, *adj.* adjective, *adv.* adverb, *art.* article, *aux,* auxiliary, *c.* circa, *comp.* comparative, *conj.* conjunction, *contr.* contraction, *coord.* coordinating, *correl.* correlative, *cp.* compare, *dat.* dative, *def.* definite. *dem.* demonstrative, *fem.* feminine, *fr.* from, *fut.* future, *gen.* genitive, *ger.* gerund, *imp.* imperative, *impers.* impersonal, *interj.* interjection, *indef.* indefinite, *indic.* indicative, *infin.* infinitive/infinitival, *intr.* intransitive, *interrog.* interrogative, *masc.* masculine, *n.* noun, *neut.* neuter, *obj.* object, *p.* past, *pass.* passive, *pers.* person/personal, *phr.* phrase/phrasal, *pl.* plural, *ppl.* participle/participial, *prep.* preposition,

375

pres. present, *pret*, preterite, *pron.* pronoun, *reflex.* reflexive, *rel.* relative, *sg.* singular, *subj.* subject, *subjunc.* subjunctive, *subord.* subordinating, *superl.* superlative, *tr.* transitive, *usu.* usually, *v.* verb/verbal, *vr.* variant.

An asterisk placed before a word indicates a hypothetical form.

A

a *art.* Before vowels **an.** (OE *ān*): a, *Hvl* 7; an, *Hvl* 114; a single *Hvl* 2010, *Orf* 198.

ā *interj.* (OE): oh, ah, *Orf* 89.

abeġgen *v.* Vr of **abȳen;** *Gml* 816.

abīden *v.* P. **abǫd.** (OE *abīdan.*): await, *Hvl* 1797.

abǫd *v.* P. of **abīden;** *Frn* 163.

aboughte *v.* P. of **abȳen;** *Gml* 76.

aboute *adv.* Also **abūte/abouten.** (OE *ābūtan.*): about, around; *faste aboute*, all over, *Crl* 158; *faste aboute*, intent on, *Gml* 240.

abȳen *v.* Also **abeġgen.** P. **aboughte.** (OE *abycgan.*): pay for; atone for.

ac *conj.* (OE): but, *Hrn* 527, *Orf* 32.

adighten *v.* (OE): treat, *Gml* 731.

adoun *adv.* (OE *ādūne.*): down, *Gml* 149.

adręden *v.* Forms at **dręden.** (OE *ofdrǣdan.*): fear greatly, *Gml* 562.

adrenchen *v.* (OE *ādrenċan.*): drown, *Hrn* 109.

after *adv.* (OE *aefter.*): afterwards; thereafter, in turn, *Orf* 354.

again *adv.* Also **ayen/agen/oyain.** (OE *on gēn*, fr. *on gegn.*): again; back, *Gml* 528; in turn, *Lnf* 982.

again *prep.*: against, *Hvl* 569.

againes *prep.* Also **agēnes/ayēnes.** (Fr. ME *again* plus adv. *-es.*): toward; in comparison with, *Lnf* 296.

agast *adj.* (P. ppl. of ME *agasten* "frighten," fr. OE *ā* and *gǣstan* "terrify."): frightened, terrified, *Gml* 526; respectful, *Gml* 7.

ais *n.* (OF *aise.*): comfort, *Orf* 215.

algāte *adv.* (ON; cp. OI *alla gǫtu.*):at any event, *Gml* 115; indeed, *Gml* 449.

alighten *v.* P. **alighte.** (OE *alihtan.*): descend, get down, dismount, *Hrn* 51.

all *n.* (OE *eall.*): all, everything, *Ath* 660.

all *adv.* (OE): completely, utterly, *Orf* 82.

aller *pron.* Also **alther.** (OE *ealra*, gen. pl. of *eall* "all."): of all; *oure aller*, of us all, *Gml* 321.

almight *adj.* (OE *aelmiht.*): almighty, *Frn* 37.

alonged *adj.* (OE *oflangod*, p. ppl. of *oflangian.*): eager, craving, *Gml* 636.

als *adv.* Vr. of **alsǫ;** *Orf* 507.

alsǫ *adv.* Also **als.** (OE *alswā.*): also, *Frn* 217, *Orf* 4; in adv. phr.'s with such words as *blive, prest, swithes*: very, *Hrn* 475.

alsǫ *conj.* (OE *alswā.*): just as, *Hvl* 815, *Sqr* 673; as, *Hrn* 32.

alther *pron.* Vr. of **aller,** *Gml* 256.

amidde *prep.* Also **amiddes.** (OE *onmiddan.*): in the middle of, *Orf* 167, 331.

amonges *prep.* (OE *on gemong.*): amongst, *Gml* 836.

amorwe *adv.* (OE *on morgene.*): on the next day, *Orf* 157.

an *prep.* Vr. of **on;** *Frn* 38.

and *conj.* (OE): and, *Gml* 1; if, *Gml* 819.

anǫn *adv.* (OE *on ān.*): at once, immediately; *anon-right*, immediately, *Gml* 734; *anon rightes*, immediately, *Lnf* 127; *right anon*, immediately, *Hrn* 289.

any *adj.* Also **ǫny.** (OE *ǣnig.*): any, *Crl* 606.

ār *prep.* Vr. of **ęr** *prep.*; *Gml* 605.

aright *adv.* (Fr. ME phr. *on right.*): rightly, *Gml* 29; closely, *Gml* 1.

arọwe *adv.* (OE *on rāwe.*): in a row, *Hrn* 1501.

arsoun *n.* (OF *arson.*): the front (pommel) or back (cantle) of a saddle; the saddle itself, *Lnf* 370.

ārst *adv.* (OE *ǣrest.*): formerly, *Gml* 538.

as *conj.* (ME, ultimately fr. OE *ealswā* "just as."): as, *Orf* 7; as fast as, *Orf* 117; *anon as*, as soon as, *Gml* 731; as if, *Gml* 502, *Orf* 84.

as *prep.* (Fr. conj.): like, *Gml* 560.

asoilen *v.* Vr. of assoilen; *Ath* 677.

assoilen *v.* Also **asoilen**. (OF *assoiler.*): absolve, *Gml* 516.

atte *prep.* and *def. art.* (Contr. of OE *aet* and *the*, the latter a late form of *sē* "that."): at the, *Gml* 136.

atwinne *adv.* (Fr. ME phr. *on twinne.*): asunder, *Gml* 317.

aunter *n.* Also **auntre**. (OF *aventure.*): adventure.

auntren *v.* (OF *aventurer.*): risk, take the risk, *Gml* 666; with reflex.: venture oneself, *Gml* 217.

auter *n.* (OF): altar, *Hvl* 389.

aventer *n.* Vr. of aventour; *Crl* 125.

aventour *n.* Also **aventure/aventer**. (OF *aventure.*): adventure, experience, *Orf* 8.

aventure *n.* Vr. of aventour; *Gml* 777.

awayward *adv.* (OE *onweg* and *weard.*): away, *Lnf* 121.

awrẹken *v.* Forms at **wrẹken**. (OE *āwrecan.*): avenge, *Gml* 723.

axen *v.* P. axede. (OE *āxian.*): ask, *Hrn* 43, 1482.

ay *adv.* (ON; cp. OI *ei.*): ever, *Hvl* 1248.

ayen *adv.* Vr. of again.

B

bacheler *n.* (OF): a young noble; a young knight; a youth serving under the banner of a noble and awaiting knighthood.

bāld *adj.* Vr. of bọld.

bāle *n.* (OE *bealu.*): evil, *Gml* 32; misery, hardship, *Ath* 665.

bāret *n.* (OF *barat.*): trouble, contention, *Hvl* 1932, *Ath* 294.

barm *n.* (OE *bearm.*): bosom, *Frn* 207.

be *prep.* Vr. of bȳ; *Gwn* 402.

be- *prefix.* See also entries in **bi-**.

bēden *v.* P. bẹd. (OE *bēodan.*): command, urge, *Hrn* 508, *Hvl* 2392; make known, tell, *Hrn* 466.

beginnen *v.* P. sg. began/begon; p. pl. begunnen/begonnen; ppl. begunnen. (OE *beginnan.*): begin—often a meaningless v. aux. that can be rendered with "do" or "did"; *Lnf* 1015.

bench *n.* (OE *benċ.*): bench, esp. one before the meal-table, *Hrn* 373.

bēn *v.* Pres. sg. am/art, bēth/is, bēo; p. was. (OE *bēon.*): be.

bēnde *n.* (OE *bend.*): bond, bondage, *Gml* 837; in pl.: fetters, *Gml* 457.

benesōn *n.* Also **beneisūn**. (OE *beneisun.*): blessing, *Hvl* 1723, *Ath* 502.

bēo *v.* Pres. sg. of bēn; *Hrn* 10.

berken *v.* (OE *bercan.*): bark, *Frn* 154.

bet *adv.* (OE): better, *Gml* 112, *Lnf* 979.

bẹten *v.* P. bēt; ppl. bẹten. (OE *bēatan.*): beat, *Gml* 115.

bidden *v.* P. sg. bad; p. pl. beden; ppl. beden. (OE *biddan* "ask, request."): pray (for), *Hrn* 84; ask, implore, *Lnf* 998.

bihest *n.* (ME fr. OE *behǣs.*): promise, *Frn* 289.

bihọtan *v.* Forms at **họten**. (OE *behātan.*): promise, *Gml* 789.

bileman *n.* (ME *bȳ* and *lemman.*): paramour, *Frn* 105.

bilẹven *v.* P. bilefte/bilafte; ppl. bilẹved. (OE *belǣfan.*): remain, *Hrn* 367; leave, relinquish, *Gml* 98.

bilēven v. (OE gelȳfan.): believe, Hrn
2333.

bilinnen v. (OE blinnan.): tarry, Gml
557.

binne adv. (OE binnan.): within,
Hvl 584.

biquęthan v. P. biquath. (OE be-
cwethan.): bequeath, Gml 99.

biręven v. P. birafte/birefte. (OE
berēafian.): take away, steal, Gml
85.

bisēchen v. Also bisēken. P. bi-
soughte/besoghte. (OE besēcan.):
beseech, implore, Gwn 185.

bisēken v. Vr. of bisēchen; Gml 35,
Hvl 2994.

bisetten v. Forms at setten. (OE beset-
tan.): surround, Rgn 844; adorn,
beset, Rgn 246.

bispęken v. Forms at spęken. (OE
*bespēcan fr. besprēcan.): say, Gml
101.

bistad p. pl. adj. (Fr. ME stad ppl. fr.
ON staddr ppl. of stethja "to set-
tle."): beset, Gml 676.

bistanden v. Forms at standen. (OE
bestandan.): stand by, Hvl 507.

bistōd v. P. form of bistanden; Hvl
507.

biswīken v. P. biswǫc; ppl. biswiken.
(OE biswīcan.): deceive, Hrn 294.

bitāken v. Forms at tāken. (ME fr.
bi- and tāken.): give into the charge
of, commit, Hvl 1226.

bitęchen v. Forms at tęchen. (OE
betāecan.): give into the charge of,
commit, Hvl 203.

bithenken v. Also bithenchen. P. bi-
thoughte. (OE bethencan.): reflex.:
take thought, Hrn 268, Ath 85.

biwreyen v. Also biwrayen. P. bi-
wreyed. (ME, fr. OE wrēgan.): reveal, betray, Hrn 366, Ath 152, Rgn
146.

blinnen v. (OE blinnan.): cease, Hvl
329.

blīve adv. (OE *be līfe.): quickly, im-
mediatelv.

bǫ adv. (OE bā.): both, as well, Orf
3.

bǫdy n. (OE bodig.): body, Orf
30.

bokeler n. (OF bocler.): buckler, a
small oval or round shield; playen
atte bokeler, to fence, Gml 136.

bǫld adj. Also bāld. (OE beald.): bold,
arrogant, courageous, Hrn 94.

bǫn n. (OE bān.): bone, Gml 489.

bōn n. (ON; cp. OI bōn.): prayer,
boon, Gml 153.

bōrd n. (OE): table, dining table,
Hrn 257.

borrwe n. (OE borg.): pledge, bail,
Gml 795; ben under borwe, be under pledge, be on bail, Gml 795.

borrwen v. (OE borgian.): give bail
to, Gml 441; save, rescue, Gml 204.

bǫst n. (Orig. obscure.): boast, Lnf
362.

bǫt n. (OE bāt.): boat, Hrn 206.

bōt n. (OE): remedy, help, Gml 32.

bot prep. Vr. of but; Frn 160.

bǫthe adj. (ON; cp. OI bāthir.):
both—in such phr.'s as bothe they,
both of them, Lnf 83; bothe two,
both of them, Lnf 149.

bǫthe correlative conj.: both—as in
bothe yong and olde.

bour n. (OE būr.): bedchamber.

bourde n. (OF): jest, Gml 858.

bręd n. (OE brēad.): bread, Hvl 825,
Gml 532.

brēme adj. (OE brēme.): bright, radiant, Orf 37.

brennen v. (ON; cp. OI brenna.):
burn, Ath 84, Rgn 474.

brēr n. (OE): briar, Ath 72.

bręth n. (OE brāeth.): breath, Lnf
1007.

bretheren n. Pl. of brōther; Gml 736.

bright adj. (OE bryht.): bright, Ath
72; of a woman: radiant, Frn 288.

brōther n. Pl. brothers/bretheren.
(OE brōthor.): brother, Hvl 1396.

brouken v. (OE brūcen.): use, enjoy,
Hrn 210, Trn 45; often in assevera-

tions: *so brouke I my swere*, as I may use my neck, *Gml* 273.

but *conj*. (OE *būtan*.) : but, *Lnf* 44; unless, *Hvl* 1159, *Lnf* 56; *but if, but yif*, unless, *Hvl* 2546, 2972; *but that*, unless, *Lnf* 679.

but *prep*. Also **bot**. (OE *būtan*.) : except; *do hem but good*, do them (nothing) but good, *Gml* 521.

bȳ *prep*. Also **be**. (OE *bī*.) : by, *Gml* 231; during, *Gml* 65.

bȳen *v*. P. **boughte/boghte**. (OE *bycgan*.) : buy; atone for; redeem.

bysīden *adv*. (OE *bi sīdan*.) : close by, *Gml* 171.

C

can *v*. Pres. sg. of **cunnen**.

cāre *n*. (OE *cearu*.) : anxiety, sorrow, *Gml* 200.

cāren *v*. (OE *carian*.) : worry, *Gml* 11.

cark *n*. (AF vr. of OF *charge*.) : responsibility, *Gml* 760.

carl *n*. (ON; cp. OI *karl*.) : churl, *Hvl* 1789.

cas *n*. (OF) : incident, event, *Orf* 151.

casten *v*. Also **kesten**. P. **cast**. (ON; cp. OI *kasta*.) : cast, throw, *Gml* 726.

chanoun *n*. (OF) : canon, *Gml* 509.

chēp *n*. (OE *cēap*.) : market; bargain, *Lnf* 336; *in to good cheep*, at too low a price, *Gml* 278.

chēre *n*. (OF) : countenance, *Gml* 534; manner, demeanor, *Lnf* 66; good cheer, hospitality.

cherche *n*. (OE *cirice*.) : church, *Gml* 508.

chēsen *v*. P. sg. **chēs**; p. pl. **chōsen**; ppl. **chōsen**. (OE *cēosan*.) : choose, *Hrn* 668, *Hvl* 372, *Orf* 193.

chēst *n*. (OE *cēast*.) : strife, *Gml* 328.

child *n*. Pl. **children**. (OE *cild*.) : child, youth—often used as a quasi-title, either before or after a name, to indicate an aspirant to knighthood; cp *Hrn* 27.

chivalrie *n*. (OF *chevalerie*.) : knightly conduct or deeds, *Lnf* 1041.

citē *n*. (OF *citē*.) : city, *Orf* 24.

clēpen *v*. Also **clipen/clupen**. P. **clepede**; ppl. **clēped**. (OE *cleopian, clypian*.) : call, summon, *Hrn* 229.

clerk *n*. (OF *clerc*.) : a person in religious life, *Hvl* 33; priest, *Hvl* 1177; literate person, scholar, *Frn* 2.

clipen *v*. Vr. of **clepen**.

clupen *v*. Vr. of **clepen**.

cōld *n*. (OE *ceald*.) : cold, *Hvl* 416.

cōld *adj*. (OE *ceald*.) : cold, *Ath* 610; *cold red*, evil advice, grievous counsel, *Gml* 531.

comen *v*. Pres. **cometh**; p. **cōm**; ppl. **comen**. (OE *cuman*.) : come.

con *v*. Pres. sg. form of **cunnen**.

connen *v*. Vr. of **cunnen**.

contek *n*. (OF *contek*.) : strife, *Gml* 132.

coppe *n*. Vr. of **cuppe**.

cors *n*. Vr. of **curs**; *Gml* 779.

corūne *n*. (OF *corūne*.) : crown (of a king), *Hvl* 1319.

coude *v*. P. form of **cunnen**.

couthe *v*. P. form of **cunnen**; *Hvl* 93, *Gml* 164.

crachen *v*. (Orig. obsc.) : scratch, *Orf* 56.

croune *n*. (OF *corūne*.) : crown of the head, *Hvl* 568; clerical tonsure, *Gml* 523.

crȳen *v*. (OF *crier*.) : cry, *Ath* 244; proclaim, *Gml* 171.

cunnen *pret. pres. v*. Also **connen**. Pres. sg. 2nd pers. **can**; 1st and 3rd pers. **can/con**; pres. pl. **cunnen/connen**; p. **coude/couthe/cūthe**. (OE *cunnan*.) : can, be able, *Hrn* 357, *Lnf* 359; know how, *Gml* 164; with the forms *can/con* and a p. ppl.: did—so used through confusion with *gan/gon* fr. *ginnen* (q.v.).

cuppe *n*. Also **coppe**. (OE *cuppa*.) : cup.

curs *n*. Also **cors**. (OE *curs*.) : curse, *Gml* 8.

curteis *adj.* (OF *courteis*.): well-bred, *Hvl* 2916, *Orf* 4.
cūthe *v.* P. form of **cunnen.**
cȳthen *v.* (OE (*cȳthan*.): make known, show, *Lnf* 69, 359.

D

dāle *n.* (OE *dael*.): valley, *Hrn* 158.
dar *v.* Pres. sg. of **durren;** *Orf* 312.
datheit *interj.* (OF *dahait*.): a curse on, cursed be, *Hvl* 296.
dawen *v.* (OE *dagian*.): dawn, *Frn* 180.
dawes *n.* Pl. vr. of **day;** *Hvl* 27, 2344.
day *n.* Pl. **dayes/dawes.** (OE *daeg*, pl. *dagas*.): day, *Hvl* 143, 355; *dages*, gen. sg., by day, *Hvl* 2353.
dęd *adj.* (OE *dēad*.): dead, *Hvl* 232.
dęl *n.* (OE *dǣl*.): part, portion, share, *Hvl* 208, *Gml* 635.
dęled *v.* P. ppl. form of **dęlen;** *Gml* 49.
dęlen *v.* P. **dalte/delte;** ppl. **dęled.** (OE *dǣlan*.): apportion out, *Gml* 18, 45.
dēmen *v.* (OE *dēman*.): judge, *Hvl* 2467; condemn, *Gml* 863.
dent *n.* Vr. of **dint;** *Hrn* 156.
dēr *n.* (OE *dēor*.) deer, *Gml* 97.
dēre *adj.* (OE *dēore*.): dear, beloved, *Sqr* 5; costly, precious, *Sqr* 317.
dęren *v.* (OE *derian*.): harm, injure, *Hvl* 490.
dērling *n.* (OE *dēorling*.): darling, *Sqr* 981.
derne *adj.* (OE *derne, dierne*.): secret, private, *Lnf* 354.
dęth *n.* Also **dīth.** (OE *dēath*.): death, *Lnf* 77.
devīsen *v.* (OF *deviser*.) perceive, see, *Frn* 267.
deyen *v.* Also **dȳen.** P. **deyde.** (ON; cp. OI *deyja*.): die, *Hvl* 169, *Gml* 68.
dight *v.* P. ppl. form of **dighten;** *Sqr* 493.
dighten *v.* P. **dighte/ppl. dight.** (OE

dihtan.): treat, handle, *Gml* 344; make up, draw up, *Gml* 847; prepare, make certain, *Ath* 463; adorned, decked, *Sqr* 222; *evil dight*, poorly clothed, *Lnf* 141.
dint *n.* Also **dent/dunt.** (OE *dynt*.): blow, stroke; power, *Hrn* 156.
diol *n.* Vr. of **dōl;** *Orf* 174.
dīth *n.* Vr. of **dęth;** *Hrn* 62.
dol *n.* Also **diol.** (OF *duel*.): grief, pain, *Ath* 367; lamentation, *Ath* 287.
dōm *n.* (OE *dōm*.): judgment, judicial sentence, *Gml* 847.
dōn *v.* Pres. sg. **dōst, dōth;** p. **dide;** p. ppl. **diden.** (OE *dōn*.): do, *Hvl* 117; put, place, *Hvl* 535; of clothes: take (off), put (on), *Lnf* 979; bring about (for), cause, *Hvl* 611; act, live, *Hvl* 17; carry out, perform, *Orf* 9, *Sqr* 173; *don after*, act according to, *Gml* 819; reflex.: set out, *Orf* 208; as a substitute for another verb: do, *Sqr* 331; with a following infinitive: a causal auxiliary: *doth him fetten*, cause him to be fetched, have him fetched, *Hvl* 2037; as a verbal auxiliary to form periphrastic tenses: do, *Sqr* 684.
dōre *n.* (OE *duru*.): door, *Gml* 127.
dorste *v.* P. sg. of **durren;** *Hrn* 1416.
doughty *adj.* (OE *dohtig*.): brave, valiant, *Crl* 3.
doun *n.* Also **dūn.** Pl. **dounes.** (OE *dūn*.): hill, *Hrn* 214—often in the phr. *by dales and by dune* "in valleys and hills."
dout *n.* (OF *doute*.): fear, *Gml* 630.
douten *v.* Also **dūten.** (OF *douter*.): fear, be afraid of, *Gml* 517.
dręde *n.* (Fr. ME *drȩden*.): fear, *Hrn* 262.
drȩden *v.* P. **dredde/dradde.** (OE *drǣdan*.): fear, dread, *Hrn* 124.
drępen *v.* P. **drȍp.** (OE *drepan*.): kill, *Hvl* 506.
dressen *v.* (OF *dresser*.): divide evenly, *Gml* 18; put in order, *Gml*

848; with reflex. pron.: act, conduct (oneself), *Frn* 307.

driven *v.* P. sg. drǫf; p. pl. **driven**; ppl. **driven**. (OE *drīfan*.): drive, push, force; move quickly, rush, *Hrn* 123.

drǫp *v.* P. sg. of **drępen**; *Hvl* 2229.

drurie *n.* (OF *druerie*.): love, love-making, *Lnf* 995.

dubben *v.* (OE *dubbian*.): dub; *dubben to knighte*, confer knighthood on, *Hrn* 462.

dūn *n.* Vr. of **doun**.

dūren *v.* (OF *durer*.): endure, *Gml* 831.

durren *pret. pres. v.* Pres. sg. **dar**; p. **durste/dorste**. (OE *durran*.): dare; in confusion of meaning with *thurfen*: need, *Lnf* 1030.

durste *v.* P. sg. of **durren**; *Hvl* 272.

dūte *v.* Pres. sg. vr. of **douten**; *Hrn* 348.

dwellen *v.* (OE *dwellan*.): tarry, linger, *Hvl* 1185.

dȳen *v.* Vr. of **deyen**; *Orf* 165.

E

ęch *pron.* (OE *ǣlc*.): each, *Crl* 536.

ęch *adj.* Also **īch**. (OE *ǣlc*.): each, *Lnf* 446.

eft *adv.* (OE): again, *Lnf* 1008.

eir *n.* (OF): heir, *Hvl* 110.

ęk *adv.* (OE *ēac*, non-WS *ēc*.): also, *Hvl* 1025.

ēlde *n.* (OE *yldu*.): age, *Gml* 649.

elles *adv.* Also **els**. (OE *elles*.): else, otherwise, *Lnf* 162; elsewhere, *Hrn* 250.

els *adv.* Vr. of **elles**; *Rgn* 148.

enough *adv.* Vr. of **y-nough**.

ęr *adv.* (OE *ǣer*.): before, formerly, *Lnf* 1019, *Frn* 184.

ęr *conj.* (OE *ǣer*.): before, *Hvl* 15; *er thane*, before the time that, *Hrn* 1450.

ęr *prep.* (OE *ǣer*.): before; *er that*, prior to that.

eritage *n.* (OF): heritage, *Hvl* 2836.

ērl *n.* (OE *eorl*.): earl, *Ath* 61.

ęrly *adv.* (ME fr. ME *ēr* adv.): early, *Rgn* 570.

ernan *v.* P. urn. (OE *eornan*.): run, *Orf* 61.

ęrthe *n.* (OE *eorthe*.): earth, *Hvl* 248.

ęst *n.* (OE *ēast*.): East, *Gml* 891.

ęten *v.* P. ēt; ppl. **eten**. (OE *etan*, p. *āēt*.): eat, *Hvl* 657.

ęthe *adv.* (OE *ēathe*.): easily, *Hrn* 841.

evere-mār *adv.* Vr. of **evermǫre**; *Hvl* 1971.

everich *adj.* Vr. of **every**; *Hvl* 137.

everichǫn *pron.* (ME fr. *every* and *ǫn*.): every one, *Orf* 165.

evermǫre *adv.* Also **evere-mār**. (ME fr. OE *āēfre* and *māre*.): evermore, *Orf* 189.

every *adj.* Also **everich**. (ME fr. OE *āēfre* and *āēlc*.): every, *Hvl* 8.

eye *n.* Pl. **eyen/eyne/eyghen**. (OE *ēge*.): eye, *Hvl* 1152.

eye *n.* (OE *ege*.): awe, *Gml* 129, 253.

eyghen *n.* Pl. vr. of **eye**; *Orf* 87.

eyne *n.* Pl. vr. of **eye**; *Hvl* 1273.

F

fable *n.* (OF): fable, tale; *withouten fable*, without doubt, indeed.

fader *n.* (OE *faeder*.): father, *Hvl* 1224, *Ath* 2, *Gml* 7.

fadme *n.* (OE *faedme*, vr. of *faethme*.): fathom, *Gml* 306.

fadmen *v.* P. **fadmede**. (OE *faedmian*.): embrace, *Hvl* 1295.

faire *adv.* (OE *faegre*.): fairly, well, *Lnf* 982.

fairie *n.* Also **fairy**. (AN *feierie*.): land of enchantment, *Lnf* 1035; enchantment, *Orf* 380.

fāle *adj.* Vr. of **fęle**; *Lnf* 496.

fallen *v.* P. **fell**; ppl. **fallen**. (OE *feallan*.): fall, *Hvl* 1303; befall, *Lnf* 3; befit, *Hrn* 424.

fāre *n.* (OE *faru*.): demeanor, *Gml* 199.

fāren *v.* P. **fōr**; ppl. **fāren**. (OE *faran*.): go, journey, *Hvl* 51; fare, get on, Gml 616, Hrn 472; faren with, treat, handle, Hvl 2705.

faste adv. (OE faeste.): firmly, Hvl 1894; securely, Hvl 82; closely, Hvl 2148; faste by, close by, Sqr 284.

fasten v. Also festen. P. feste; ppl. fest. (OE faestan): secure, hold, Hvl 144.

fay n. Vr. of fey; Gml 555.

fē n. (OE feh.): goods, property, Hvl 44.

fechen v. P. feched. (OE feċċan.): fetch, bring, Hrn 354—in the p. and p. ppl. forms of fetten appear.

fēld n. (OE feld.): field, Orf 36.

fẹle adj. Also fāle. (OE fela.): many, Hvl 778, Frn 157.

fẹle adv. (Fr. ME fēle adj.): very, exceedingly, Hvl 2442.

fell n. (OE fel.): skin, hide, Gml 76.

fell adj. (OF fel.): cruel, Gml 151; malicious, spiteful, Lnf 157; fierce, savage, Rgn 46; violent, Crl 340.

fellawe n. Also fellowe. (ON; cp. OI felagi "share-holder, partner."): comrade, Hrn 1004, Gwn 305; companion, equal, Gwn 95; fellow—a familiar term of address, Ath 726; lad—a term of contempt, Gml 276.

fer adv. (OE feor.): far, Lnf 1022; afar, Hvl 1863.

fēr n. Vr. of fir; Frn 205.

fēre n. (OE gefēra.): comrade, Hrn 21; often in the phr. in fere "together."

fere adj. Also ferre. (OE feorren.): far, Lnf 54.

fēren v. P. ferde. (OE fēran.): go, proceed, Hvl 447; fare, get on, Gml 780, Hvl 287; act, behave, Ath 250; feren with, treat, Hvl 2411.

feste n. (OF feste.): festival, feast, Hvl 2344.

festen v. Infin. vr. of fasten; Hvl 144.

fetten v. P. fette; p. ppl. fett. (OE gefetian, fatian.): fetch.

fẹwe adj. (OE fēawe.): few, Hrn 54.

fey n. Also fay. (OF fei.): faith, Hvl 255.

fin n. (OF fin.): end, Hvl 22.

fin adv. (OF): well, Gml 427; very, Orf 70.

finden v. P. fānd/fǫnd; ppl. founden. (OE findan.): find, Hvl 42.

finen v. (OF finer.): end, Hrn 266.

fint v. Pres. sg. of finden; Orf 215.

fir n. Also fēr. (OE fȳr.): fire, Rgn 474.

flet n. (OE flett.): floor, Lnf 979.

flour n. (OF flour.): flower, Orf 43.

fǫ n. (OE gefā/fāh.): foe, Hvl 67, Gml 541.

fōl n. (OF): fool, Hvl 298.

for conj. (ME fr. OE for tham.): because, for, Hvl 2222.

for prep. (OE for.): because of, Orf 8; out of, Gml 698; for all, despite all, Gml 750.

fōr v. P. of fāren; Hvl 2382.

fordōn v. (OE): kill, Frn 116.

fōren v. P. pl. of fāren; Hvl 2380.

forlẹten v. P. forlēt; ppl. forlẹten. (OE forlǣtan.): abandon, part with, Hrn 222.

forsāken v. P. forsōk. (OE forsacan.): forsake, relinquish, Hvl 2778.

forsōke v. P. sg. of forsaken; Orf 203.

forsworn p. ppl. adj. (OE forsworen, p. ppl. of forswerian.): perjured, Hvl 1423, Gml 376.

forthē adv. (OE forthē.): therefore, Frn 233.

forthward n. Vr. of forward; Gml 747.

forward n. Also forthward. (OE foreweard.): agreement, Hvl 554.

foryaf v. P. sg. of foryeven; Gml 893.

foryat v. P. sg. of foryeten; Gml 800.

foryeten v. P. foryat. (OE forgietan.): forget.

foryeven v. Also forgiven. Forms at yeven and given. (OE forgiefan.): forgive, Hrn 353.

foul n. (OE fugol.): bird, Orf 44.

foul adj. Also fūl. (OE fūl.): foul, filthy, Hvl 555; ugly, Gml 534.

foule *adv.* Also **fūle.** (OE *fūle.*): foully, evilly, *Gml* 485.

foy *n.* (F): faith, *Gml* 367.

fram *prep.* Vr. of **from;** *Hrn* 207, *Orf* 166.

frankelein *n.* (AF *fraunclein.*): a landowner ranking just below the gentry, franklin, *Gml* 275.

frē *adj.* (OE *frēo.*): free; noble; generous—often a meaningless rhyme word; cp. *Lnf* 142.

frein *n.* (OF *fresne.*): ash tree, *Frn* 231.

frēly *adj.* (OE *frēolic.*): lovely, *Sqr* 545.

frēman *n.* (OE *frēomann.*): freeman, *Hvl* 628.

fremde *adj.* (OE *fremede.*): foreign; as n.: stranger, foreigner, *Hrn* 68, *Hvl* 2277.

frēnd *n.* (OE *frēond.*): friend, *Lnf* 858, *Ath* 253.

frēnde *n.* (ON *fráendi.*): relative, ?*Hvl* 375; cp. *Rgn* 96.

frēre *n.* (OF *frere.*): friar, *Gml* 529.

frith *n.* (OE *fyrhth.*): woodland, *Orf* 136.

frō *prep.* (ON *frā.*): from, *Lnf* 80.

from *prep.* Also **fram.** (OE): from.

fūl *adj.* Vr. of **foul;** *Hvl* 506.

fūle *adv.* Vr. of **foule;** *Hrn* 326.

full *adv.* (OE *full.*): quite, altogether, *Hvl* 6.

fūnden *v.* (OE *fundian.*): hasten, *Hrn* 107.

G

gadeling *n.* (OE *gaedeling.*): fellow —a term of contempt, *Hvl* 1121, *Gml* 102.

gāme *n.* (OE *gamen.*): sport, pleasure, amusement, *Hrn* 202.

gat *n.* Also **yat.** Dat. **gāte.** (OE *geat,* pl. *gatu.*): gate, *Hrn* 1081.

gat *v.* P. sg. of **geten;** *Hvl* 495.

gāte *n.* (ON *gata.*): road, street, *Hvl* 846.

gāten *v.* (Fr. ME *gate* n.): go, *Rgn* 441.

gāten *v.* P. pl. of **geten;** *Hvl* 2934.

gent *adj.* (OF *gent.*): slender, *Crl* 364.

gentrīse *n.* (OF *genterise.*): good manners, breeding, *Frn* 268.

gēren *v.* P. **garte.** (ON; cp. OI *gøra.*): cause to, *Hvl* 189.

geten *v.* P. sg. **gat;** p. pl. **geten/gaten;** ppl. **geten/gotten.** (ON; cp. OI *geta.*): get, obtain, *Hvl* 147; beget, *Frn* 316.

geten *v.* P. ppl. of **geten;** *Rgn* 204.

geten *v.* P. pl. of **geten;** *Hvl* 2893.

gēth *v.* Pres. sg. of **gōn;** *Lnf* 1006, *Frn* 148.

gīle *n.* (OF *guile.*): guile, *Frn* 7.

gin *n.* Also **ginne.** (OF *gin.*): device, *Sqr* 97; cunning, *Rgn* 430; *queint of gin,* clever of invention, *Lnf* 536; trickery, *Ath* 771.

ginne *n.* Vr. of **gin;** *Sqr* 692.

ginnen *v.* P. sg. **gan/gon;** p. pl. **gunnen/gonnen;** ppl. **gunnen.** (OE *ginnan.*): begin—often a meaningless v. aux. that can be rendered with "do" or "did"; *he gan him sayn,* he did say to him; cp. *Lnf* 111.

given *v.* P. **gaf;** ppl. **given.** (ON *gefa.*): give.

glē *n.* (OE *glēo.*): revelry, minstrelsy, *Orf* 9.

glēd *n.* (OE): burning coal, *Ath* 572.

gleowing *n.* (OE *glēowung.*): merriment, minstrelsy, *Hrn* 1480.

glōsen *v.* (OF *gloser.*): flatter, *Frn* 290.

god *n.* (OE): God, *Ath* 180.

gōd *n.* (OE *gōd* adj.): good thing, *Hvl* 797; *alle gode,* all (sorts of) good things, *Hvl* 1221; *hit nas for none gode,* it was not for any good, *Hrn* 286.

gōd *adj.* (OE *gōd.*): good, *Hvl* 1.

gōme *n.* Also **gume.** (OE *guma.*): man, *Hvl* 7.

gōn *v.* Pres. **gōth/gēth;** p. ppl. **gōn.**

(OE *gān.*): go, walk, *Hvl* 848—for þ forms see **wenden** and **yēde**.

gǭstly *adj.* (ME fr. OE *gāstlic.*): spiritual, *Ath* 394.

gotten *v.* P. ppl. of **geten**; *Rgn* 626.

grāce *n.* Also *grās.* (OF): (divine) grace, *Ath* 614; good luck, fortune, *Gml* 268; *hard grace*, ill luck, misfortune, *Orf* 523.

gramercy *interj.* (OF *grand merci.*): many thinks, *Lnf* 335.

grās *n.* Vr. of **grāce**; *Ath* 58.

grāten *v.* Also **grǫten**. Ppl. **grāten/grǫ-ten**. (ON; cp. OI *grāta.*): weep, *Hvl* 329.

graunt *n.* (OF *graant.*): favor, concession, *Sqr* 584, *Rgn* 530.

graunten *v.* P. **grauntede**. (OF *graanter.*): grant, concede to, *Hvl* 1154; agree, *Lnf* 259.

grāven *v.* (OE *grafan.*): bury, *Gml* 900.

grēden *v.* P. **gredde**. (OE *grēdan.*): cry, exclaim, *Hvl* 96.

gredde *v.* P. sg. of **grēden**; *Hvl* 2417.

gręt *adj.* (OE *grēat.*): great, *Frn* 34.

grēten *v.* (1) P. **grette**. (OE *grētan.*): greet, salute, *Hvl* 452, *Lnf* 982; assail, attack, *Hvl* 1811.

grēten *v.* (2) (OE *grēotan.*): weep, *Hvl* 454.

grette *v.* P. sg. of **grētan** (1); *Hvl* 2625.

grēven *v.* (OF *grever.*): grieve, hurt, *Lnf* 72.

grīpen *v.* P. **grǭp**; ppl. **gripen**. (OE *grīpan.*): grip, seize, snatch, *Hvl* 1776.

grīs *n.* (OF): grey fur, *Orf* 217.

grith *n.* (ON; cp. OI *grith.*): peace, *Hvl* 61.

grōm *n.* (ME; prob. akin to OE *grōwan* v. "grow."): man, fellow, *Rgn* 50.

grǭp *v.* P. sg. form of **grīpen**.

grǭten *v.* P. ppl. of **grāten**; *Hvl* 285.

ground *n.* Also **grūnd**. (OE *grund.*): ground; *to grunde*, on land, *Hrn*

138; bottom (of the sea), *Hrn* 108.

gruchen *v.* (OF *groucier.*): grumble, make a fuss, *Gml* 319.

gruching *ger.*: grumbling, *Gml* 322.

gume *n.* Vr. of **gōme**; *Hrn* 165.

gunne *v.* P. pl. form of **ginnen**; *Hrn* 55.

H

hadde *v.* P. sg. of **hāven**; *Orf* 27.

halp *v.* P. sg. of **helpen**; *Gml* 60.

hals *n.* (OE *heals.*): neck, *Gml* 391.

hānd *n.* Also **hǫnd**. (OE *hand.*): hand.

hap *n.* (ON; cp. OI *happ.*): chance, (ill-) fortune, *Frn* 89.

hatte *v.* Pres. sg. form of **hǭten**; *Lnf* 5.

hāven *v.* P. **had/hadde**. (OE *habban.*): have.

hē *pron.* Vr. of **hēo**; *Hrn* 296.

hē *pron.* Vr. of **hīe**; *Hvl* 54, *Orf* 161.

hēd *n.* (ME fr. OE *hēdan* "to heed."): heed, *Rgn* 634.

hęd *n.* Also **hęved**. (OE *hēafod.*): head, *Gml* 430.

hēden *v.* (OE *hēdan.*): take heed, *Hvl* 2389.

hegh *adj.* Vr. of **hey**; *Lnf* 472.

heighe *adj.* Vr. of **hey**; *Frn* 158.

hęle *n.* (OE *hǣlu.*): good health, *Gml* 41.

helm *n.* (OE): helmit, *Hvl* 379.

helpen *v.* P. **halp**; ppl. **holpen**. (OE *helpan.*): help, *Hvl* 166.

hem *pron.* (OE): them, *Hvl* 376, *Orf* 166, *Crl* 33.

hem *reflex. pron.* (OE *heom.*): themselves, *Crl* 299, 439.

hēnde *adj.* (OE *gehende.*): gracious, well-bred, *Lnf* 42; courteous, hospitable, *Gml* 663; kindly, helpful, *Lnf* 368, *Gml* 838; skillful, adroit, *Hvl* 2628.

henne *adv.* (OE *heonan.*): hence, away, *Hrn* 50.

henten *v.* P. **hente**. (OE *hentan.*): seize, grasp, *Gml* 590.

hēo *pron.* Also **hīe/hē.** (OE): she, *Hrn* 73, 656.

hēr *n.* (OE *hǣr.*): hair, *Hvl* 1924.

her *poss. adj.* Vr. of **here**; *Gml* 688.

hēr *adv.* Also **hire.** (OE *hēr.*): here, *Hvl* 689.

here *pron. adj.* (OE *heora.*): their, *Hvl* 52, *Gml* 7, 543.

herte *n.* (OE *heorte.*): heart, *Hrn* 279.

hęte *n.* (OE *hǣtu.*): ardor, fervor, *Gml* 117, *Crl* 613.

hęth *n.* (OE *hǣeth.*): heath, moor, *Orf* 213, *Frn* 147.

hęved *n.* Vr. of **hęd**; *Hvl* 1906.

hēw *n.* (OE *hēow.*): hue, color, *Sqr* 226.

hey *adj.* Also **hegh/heigh/highe/hȳ/ hye.** (OE *hēah.*): high, *Hvl* 1289; *on hey*, on high, above, *Lnf* 262; tall, *Hvl* 1071; *hey and lowe*, everyone, *Hvl* 2431.

hider *adv.* (OE): hither, *Lnf* 992.

hīe *pron.* Also **hē.** (OE): they, *Orf* 67.

hīe *pron.* Vr. of **hēo**; *Frn* 148.

highe *adj.* Vr. of **hey**; *Crl* 313.

hight *v.* P. sg. form of **hǫten**; *Lnf* 5.

him *dat. and acc. pron.* (OE *him* dat.): him, *Rgn* 170; to him, *Rgn* 2, 15.

him *reflex. pron.* (OE *him.*): himself, *Frn* 47.

himself *reflex. pron.* (ME): himself, *Lnf* 402.

himself *intensive pron.* (ME): himself—sometimes used without an antecedent, *Orf* 13.

hīne *n. pl.* (OE *hīna,* gen. of *hīwan* n. pl. "household."): servants, *Hvl* 620.

hīre *n.* Also **hure.** (OE *hȳr.*): hire, pay, *Hvl* 908.

hire *pron.* (OE *hire.*): her, *Hvl* 333; to her, *Hvl* 130.

hire *pron. adj.* Also **hure.** (OE *hire.*): her, *Hvl* 127.

hire *adv.* Vr. of **hēr**; *Gml* 222.

hīren *v.* (OE *hȳran.*): bribe, *Gml* 786.

hit *nom. and acc. pers. pron.* Also **it.** (OE): it, *Lnf* 6.

hǫl *adj.* (OE *hāl.*): sound, safe, healthy, *Hrn* 153.

hǫlden *v.* P. sg. **hēld**; p. pl. **hēlden**; ppl. **hǫlden.** (OE *healdan.*): hold, *Hrn* 380; reflex.: consider oneself, *Gml* 553.

holpen *v.* P. ppl. of **helpen**; *Hvl* 901.

holt *n.* (OE *holt.*): wood, forest, *Lnf* 171.

hǫly *adj.* (OE *hālig.*): holy, *Hvl* 36.

hǫm *n.* (OE *hām.*): home, *Gml* 528.

hǫnd *n.* Vr. of **hānd**; cp. *Hrn* 64.

hǫr *adj.* (OE *hār.*): grey, *Gml* 817; *holtes hore*, ancient woods, *Orf* 190, *Lnf* 231.

hǫse *n.* Pl. **hǫsen.** (OE *hose.*): hose (the garment covering feet and legs), *Lnf* 200.

hǫten *v.* Pres. sg. **hatte**; p. **highte**; ppl. **hǫten.** (OE *hātan.*): be called, be named, *Gml* 727, *Lnf* 27; promise, *Crl* 591; assure, *Crl* 378.

hound *n.* (OE *hund.*): dog, *Frn* 154.

housbond *n.* (ON; cp. OI *hūsbōndi.*): farm worker, *Gml* 713.

how *adv.* (OE *hū.*): interrog.: how, *Ath* 8.

how *conj.* Also **hū.** (OE *hū.*): how, to what extent, *Hvl* 288.

hū *adv.* Vr. of **how**; *Hvl* 120.

hure *n.* Vr. of **hire**; *Gml* 832.

hūre *pron. adj.* Vr. of **hīre**; *Hrn* 281.

hȳ *adj.* Vr. of **hey**; *Crl* 287.

hye *adj.* Vr. of **hey**; *Gml* 879.

hȳen *v.* P. **hȳed.** (OE *higian.*): hie, hasten, *Rgn* 599.

hȳing *ger.*: *in hying, on hying*, in haste, immediately, *Rgn* 290.

I

Ī *pron.* Vr. of **ich**; *Lnf* 33.

i- *prefix.* Vr. of **y-.**

ich *pron.* Also **Ī.** (OE *ič.*): I, *Hvl* 3.

ich *adj.* Vr. of **ēch**; *Orf* 134, *Frn* 63.

ichave *v. phr.* (ME *ich* and *have.*): I have, *Frn* 274.

ichil v. phr. (ME ich and will.): I will, Frn 22.

if conj. Vr. of yif; Lnf 58.

ilkān pron. Vr. of ilkǫn; Hvl 2357.

ilke adj. (OE ilca.): each, Ath 20; same, very, Lnf 465.

ilkǫn pron. Also ilkān. (OE ilc ān.): each one, Ath 25.

in n. (OE inn.): lodging, Lnf 112.

insāme adv. (ME in and samen.): together, Frn 370.

intill prep. (OE in and ON til.): to, up to, Hvl 1926.

it pron. Vr. of hit; Hvl 2686.

ithe adv. Vr. of ethe; cp. Hrn 61.

K

kēnd n. Vr. of kīnd; Frn 144.

kēne adj. (OE cēne.): bold, daring, Hrn 42.

kenne n. Vr. of kin; Lnf 153.

kēp n. (ME fr. kēpen v.): care, heed; nimen god kepe, take good heed, Lnf 997.

kēpen v. (OE cēpan.): watch for, Hvl 879; look after, care for, Frn 201; stand guard by, Gml 515.

kesten v. Vr. of casten; Hvl 81.

kin n. (OE cynn.): kin, family, Rgn 800.

kīnd n. Also kēnd. (OE gecynde.): nature; cours of kind, manner of nature, Rgn 707; manner, way, Rgn 168.

kīnde adj. (ME fr. OE gecynde.): kind, generous, Rgn 792.

kirke n. (ON; cp. OI kirkja.): church, Hvl 36, Ath 5.

knāve n. (OE cnafa.): boy, Hvl 409; servant, Hvl 1123.

knitten v. P. knitt. (OE cnyttan.): fasten, Frn 141.

L

lachen v. P. laughte/laghte; ppl. laught. (OE gelǣcċan.): seize, catch, grasp, Hrn 247.

ladde v. P. sg. of lęden; Hrn 1512.

lādy n. Also lęfdy/lęvedy. (OE hlǣfdige.): lady, Ath 621.

laide v. P. sg. form of leyen; Orf 14.

lainen v. (OE legnian.): conceal, hide, Ath 159.

lānd n. Also lǫnd. (OE land.): land.

lappen v. (ME fr. OE laeppa "fold of a garment."): wrap, Frn 139.

large adj. (OF): generous, Lnf 35.

largesse n. (OF): generosity, Lnf 31.

last n. (OE laetest, superl. of laet "late."): atte last, at last, finally, Orf 93.

lāten v. Inf. vr. of lęten; Frn 293.

lawe n. (OE lagu fr. ON lög.): law, Hvl 28; religion, religious practice, Hrn 69; custom, practice, Gml 544.

lay n. (OF lai.): song, Hrn 1489.

lęche n. (OE lǣce.): doctor, Gml 614.

lęden v. P. ledde/ladde; ppl. led/lad. (OE lǣdan.): lead, conduct, Hrn 293.

lęf n. Pl. lęves. (OE lēaf.): leaf, Orf 220.

lēf n. (Fr. adj.): dear one, Hvl 2606; lef and loth, friend and foe, Hvl 261.

lēf adj. Oblique lēve. (OE lēof.): dear, precious, Orf 78.

lęfdy n. Vr. of lādy; Hrn 335.

leman n. Vr. of lemman; Hvl 1191.

lēmen v. P. lēmede. (OE lēomian.): shine, sparkle, Lnf 288.

lemman n. Also leman. (ME fr. OE lēof "dear" and mann "being."): darling, sweetheart, Lnf 301; paramour, lover (of either sex), Lnf 47.

lengere adv. Also lengore. (ME fr. OE leng adv. "longer."): longer, Lnf 1011.

lengore adv. Vr. of lengere; Frn 163.

lępen v. P. lēp; ppl. lępen. (OE hlēapan.): leap, Lnf 1009.

lęren v. (OE lǣran.): learn, Hvl 12; teach, Hrn 229.

lęs n. (ME; cp. lēsing n.): withouten

les, without falsehood, truly, *Ath* 109.

lēsen v. Ppl. **lǫren.** (OE *lēosan*.) : lose, *Orf* 154.

lęsing n. (OE *lēasing*.) : lie, *Gml* 385; *without lesing*, in truth, indeed, *Gml* 659.

let n. (Fr. *letten* v.) : hindrance; *without lette*, without delay, *Lnf* 340.

lēt v. P. sg. of **lęten;** *Frn* 228.

lęten v. Also **lāten.** P. lęt. (OE *lǣtan*; also *lāten*; cp. OI *lata*.) : let, allow, *Rgn* 40; with inf.: have, cause to; *let clepen*, caused to be called, had called, *Frn* 227; stop, *Frn* 156.

letten v. P. **let.** (OE *lettan*.) : hinder, *Hvl* 1164, *Sqr* 668.

lęve n. (OE *lēaf*.) : leave, permission, *Hvl* 1626; *leve taken*, take leave to depart, *Sqr* 271.

lēve adj. Oblique form of **lēf;** *Hvl* 431.

lęvedy n. Vr. of **lādy;** *Hvl* 171.

lęven v. P. **lafte;** ppl. **laft.** (OE *lēaf: an*.) : leave; permit, allow.

lēver adj. (Comp. of *lēf*.) : dearer; *him were lever*, he would rather, *Hvl* 1193.

lęwed adj. (OE *lǣwede*.) : common, ignorant, *Gml* 505.

leyn v. P. **leyd.** (OE *lecgan*.) : lay, put, *Hvl* 50, *Orf* 14.

libben v. Vr. of **liven;** *Hrn* 63.

lif n. Pl. **līves.** (OE *lif*.) : life, *Hvl* 349; *lives* gen. sg.: alive, *Hvl* 509; *to live*, alive, *Hrn* 97.

liggen v. Vr. of **lȳen;** *Orf* 50, *Frn* 191.

light adj. (OE *liht*.) : light, bright, *Hvl* 593; light-hearted, gay, *Gml* 732.

lighten v. P. **lighte.** (OE *lihtan*.) : alight, come down, *Lnf* 135.

lingen v. (ON; cp. OI *lengja*.) : linger, *Ath* 535.

linnen v. (OE *linnan*.) : cease, stop, *Hrn* 354.

list n. (OE) : cunning, guile, *Hrn* 1471.

listen v. Also **lesten/lusten.** P. **liste.**

(OE *lystan*.) : please—usu. impers. *so well so hir luste* "as much as (it) was pleasing (to) her," *Hrn* 410.

listen v. Also **lesten.** (OE *hlystan*.) : listen, *Hrn* 337, 477.

lith v. Pres. sg. of **lyen;** *Orf* 219.

lithen v. (ON; cp. OI *hlȳtha*.) : harken, listen, *Lnf* 63.

liven v. Also **libben.** (OE *libban*.) : live, *Hvl* 199.

lives n. Pl. and gen. sg. of **lif;** *Hvl* 509.

lōken v. (OE *lōcian*.) : look, behold, *Hvl* 2726; see, find out, *Gml* 757; care for, look after, *Hvl* 376.

lǫnd n. Vr. of **lānd;** *Hrn* 59.

lǫrd n. Also **lōverd.** (OE *hlāford*.) : lord, *Gml* 26.

lǫrding n. (OE *hlāfording*.) : nobleman, lord, *Orf* 2; in calls for attention, pl.: people, ladies and gentlemen, *Ath* 7.

lǫren v. P. ppl. of **lēsen;** *Orf* 185, *Sqr* 582.

lōs n. (OF) : praise, *Lnf* 20.

lǫthly adj. (OE *lāthlīc*.) : horrible, *Orf* 54.

loud adj. Also **lūd.** (OE *hlūd*.) : loud, *Hrn* 209.

loude adv. (OE *hlūde*.) : loud, loudly, *Ath* 244; *loude and stille*, in every circumstance, *Frn* 292.

lǫven v. P **lovede;** ppl. **loved.** (OE *lufian*.) : love, *Hrn* 251.

lǫverd n. Vr. of **lǫrd;** *Hvl* 1954.

lovesum adj. (OE *lufsum*.) : lovely, *Frn* 269.

lust v. Imp. sg. form of **listen.**

lȳen v. Also **liggen.** P. **lay.** (OE *licgen*.) : lie, *Hvl* 673.

M

māde v. P. of **māken.**

maine n. Also **meine.** (OF *mainee*.) : household, *Sqr* 911; followers, *Lnf* 93, *Sqr* 185.

māke n. (OE *gemaca*.) : mate, *Hrn* 1421.

māken v. P. mākede/māde. (OE macian.): make, Hrn 352, Trn 11.

mālais n. (OF malaise.): distress, Orf 216.

may n. (OE maeg.): maiden.

may pret. pres. v. Pres. 2nd sg. mayst, 1st and 3rd sg. may; pres. pl. mōwen/māwen; p. mighte. (OE magan.): may, Hvl 11.

me indef. pron. (OE man.): one, a person, Lnf 1025.

mēd n. (OE mēd.): reward, Lnf 363.

meine n. Vr. of maine; Hvl 827.

mēk adj. (ON; cp. OI mjukr.): meek, humble, Hvl 945.

mēlen v. (OE melan.): speak, Hvl 2059.

mēnd n. Vr. of mīnd; Frn 143.

merry adj. Also miry/merye. (OE myrge.): merry, Sqr. 52.

merye adj. Vr. of merry; Ath 635.

męst superl. adv. (OE māēst.): most, in the greatest degree, Hrn 252.

mesaventur n. (OF mesaventur.): ill-luck, Hrn 330.

mester n. (OF): occupation, skill, Hrn 233.

męte n. (OE mete.): food, Lnf 197; meal, Crl 614.

mēten v. P. mette. (OE mētan.): meet, Hvl 2624.

męten v. P. ppl. met. (OE māētan.): dream—impers.: me haveth met, I have dreamed, Hvl 1285.

mette v. P. sg. of mētan; Hvl 1810.

mich adj. Vr. of much; Orf 254.

michel adj. Also mikel/muchel. (OE micel.): great, Frn 175.

mide prep. (ME fr. OE mid.): with; hir mide, with her, Frn 145.

mikel adj. Vr. of michel; Hvl 2342.

mīnd n. Also mēnd. (OE gemynd.): mind, thought, Rgn 649; out of mind, exceedingly, Rgn 206.

miry adj. Vr. of merry; Orf 34.

mǫ adj. (OE mā.): more, Sqr 59.

mǫ adv. (OE mā.): more, Orf 66;

nevere mo, never at any time, Hvl 511.

moch adj. Vr. of much; Orf 12.

moch adv. Vr. of much; Lnf 305.

mōd n. (OE mōd.): thought, mind, Hrn 285.

mōder n. (OE mōdor.): mother, Hvl 974, Orf 6.

mōlde n. (OE molde.): earth; under molde, under the earth, dead, buried, Hrn 321.

mǫn n. (Prob. OE; cp. OE māēnan v. "lament."): lamentation, moan, Orf 174.

mōne n. (OE mōna.): moon, Gml 235, Lnf 989.

mōr n. (OE mōr.): moor, waste land.

mǫre n. (Fr. adj.): more, Ath 306.

mǫre comp. adj. (OE māra.): taller, Hvl 981.

mǫst superl. adj. (OE māst, also māēst.): greatest, Ath 1.

mot v. (OE, fr. motan "may."): may, Gml 227; must, Gml 756.

much adj. Also moch/mich. (ME fr. OE mycel.): much, Rgn 478; great, Gml 6.

much adv. Also moch. (Fr. adj.): much, to such an extent, Crl 406.

muchel adj. Vr. of michel; Hrn 336.

N

naght pron. Vr. of nought; Lnf 57.

nāked adj. (OE nacod.): naked, Hvl 1949; ill-clothed, Hvl 6.

nas v. P. sg. of nis; Gml 29, Frn 159.

naught adv. Vr. of nought; Lnf 296.

nay n. (ON; cp. OI nei.): nay; withoute nay, without denial, Gml 26.

ne adv. (OE): not, Lnf 52.

ne conj. (OE): nor, Lnf 45.

nēdes adv. (OE): by necessity, Gml 672.

negh adv. Also nȳ/nighe/neh/neigh. OE nēah.): almost, nearly, Hrn 256, Frn 204.

nēr adv. Also nir. (OE nēar, comp. of nēah "near."): nearer, Sqr 18; ner

and ner, closer and closer, *Frn* 156;
I *not* nere, I know nothing further,
Frn 218.

nēr *prep.* (Fr. adv.): close to, *Hrn*
368, *Hvl* 990.

nēre *v.* P. subjunc. of nis; *Hrn* 91.

neste *v.* P. sg. vr. of niten.

nēt *n.* (OE *nēat.*): ox, *Hvl* 1891; cattle, *Hvl* 700.

nevermore *adv.*: never—with preceding neg.: anymore, *Lnf* 105.

nil *v.* P. nolde. (OE **nyllan.*): will
not, *Orf* 187; in p.: would not, *Orf*
116.

nimen *v.* P. nam/nom; ppl. numen/
nomen. (OE *niman.*): take, *Lnf* 77.

nis *v.* P. nas. (OE *nis*, p. *naes.*): is
not, *Lnf* 12.

niten *v.* neg. v. Pres. sg. not, nost, not;
pres. pl. niten; p. niste/neste/nuste.
(ME contr. of *ne* and *witen.*):
know not, *Hrn* 280.

nǫ *adj.* Before vowels nǫn. (OE *nān.*):
no, *Hvl* 864, 518, *Orf* 32; as
quasi-n.: *withouten no*, without denial, *Orf* 26.

nǫ *adv.* (OE *nā.*): no, *Orf* 60.

nǫ *conj.* (ME for OE *ne.*): nor, *Orf*
116.

noght *adv.* Vr. of nought; *Lnf* 44.

nold *v.* P. sg. of nil; *Frn* 203.

nomen *v.* P. ppl. of nimen; *Gml* 584.

nǫn *adj.* Vr. of nǫ; *Hvl* 685.

nǫnes *pron.* (ME from *for then ones*,
fr. (presumed) OE *for thǣm
ānum*, the ME *-es* being an adverbial suffix.): to be sure, indeed,
Orf 29.

not *adv.* Vr. of nought; *Rgn* 74.

nǫt, nǫst. *v.* Pres. sg. forms of niten.

nǫthing *adv.* (ME fr. OE *nān* and
thing.): not, not at all, *Hrn* 278,
Orf 15.

nought *n.* (OE *naht.*): nothing, *Ath*
492.

nought *adv.* Also naght/naught/noght
/not. (OE *naht, nawiht.*): not, not
at all, *Ath* 35.

now *adv.* Also nū. (OE *nū.*): now,
Frn 19.

nū *adv.* Vr. of now; *Hvl* 2421.

numen *v.* P. ppl. of nimen; *Hvl* 2265.

nuste *v.* P. sg. vr. of niten.

ny *adv.* Vr. of negh; *Gml* 559.

O

ǫ *adj.* Vr. of ǫn; *Gml* 150, *Orf* 71.

of *prep.* (OE): of; from, *Gml* 522,
Orf 12; by, *Frn* 111.

oftensīthe *adv.* (ME fr. OE *on
oftsīthas.*): often, *Ath* 76.

ōk *adv.* (ON; cp. OI *auk.*): also, *Hvl*
187.

ǫn *pron.* (OE *ān.*): one (thing), *Frn*
281; a single person, *Hvl* 2263; *ben
at on*, be agreed, *Gml* 156, *Frn*
285.

ǫn *adj.* Also ō. (OE *ān.*): one, *Hvl*
425.

on *prep.* Also an. (OE): on, *Frn* 47.

ǫne *adj.* (OE *ana.*): alone, *Hvl* 1153;
him one, by himself, *Hvl* 815.

ǫny *adj.* Vr. of any; *Orf* 9.

ǫr *adv.* (ON; cp. OI *ār.*): before, before that, *Hvl* 728.

ǫr *conj.* (ON; cp. OI *ār.*): ere, before,
Hvl 417.

ōrd *n.* (OE): (sword) point, *Hrn*
1498.

ǫre *n.* (OE *ār.*): mercy, grace, *Hvl*
153.

ǫth *n.* (OE *āth.*): oath, *Ath* 456; *withouten othe*, without denial, indeed,
Lnf 456.

ǫther *pron.* (OE): other, *Hvl* 2349.

ōther *adj.* (OE *other.*): other; next,
Hvl 879.

ǫther *conj.* (OE *other.*): or, *Gml* 104;
either, *Gml* 320.

ought *pron.* (OE *āht*, fr. *āwiht.*): anything, *Frn* 241.

ought *adv.* (OE, fr. pron.): at all, *Ath*
97.

oute *adv.* Also ūte. (OE *ūte.*): outside, without, *Hrn* 249.

overall *adv.* (OE *ofer eall.*): everywhere, *Orf* 38.

oyain *adv.* Vr. of again; *Orf* 138.

P

palefrey *n.* Also **palfrey.** (OF *palefrei.*): saddle-horse—usu. in distinction to a steed.

pall *n.* Also **pell.** (OE *paell,* also *pell.*): robe; mantle, *Frn* 226.

panier *n.* (OF): basket, *Hvl* 760.

paramour *adv.* (OF *par amour.*): passionately, fervently, *Lnf* 106.

paynim *n.* Also **payn.** (OF *paienime.*): heathen—used loosely for any foreign enemy, *Hrn* 45.

pell *n.* Vr. of **pall;** *Frn* 178.

pēr *n.* (OF): equal, peer, *Hvl* 989, *Ath* 69.

peradventure *adv.* (OF *par aventure.*): perhaps.

pēs *n.* (OF *pais.*): peace, *Gml* 689; *his pees was imade,* his pardon was granted, *Gml* 689.

pīne *n.* (OE *pīn.*): torment, pain, *Hrn* 265.

plāce *n.* Vr. of **plas;** *Gml* 195.

plās *n.* Also **plāce.** (OF *place.*): place, *Orf* 16; a place for public wrestling, *Gml* 203.

plawen *v.* Vr. of **playen;** *Hvl* 950.

playen *v.* Also **plawen.** (OE *plegan.*): sport, take one's ease, *Orf* 42.

playing *n.* (Fr. vb.): sport, amusement; *on his playing,* for his amusement; cp. *Hrn* 34.

plighten *v.* P. **plighte.** (OE *plihtan.*): promise, pledge, *Hrn* 309; *I you plight,* I assure you.

prēst *n.* (OE *prēost.*): priest, *Frn* 227.

prest *adj.* (OF): ready, *Ath* 745.

prest *adv.* (OF): quickly, *Lnf* 1012.

prīde *n.* (OE *prȳte.*): pride; splendor, magnificence; power, distinction, *Lnf* 51.

proud *adj.* Also **prūd.** (OE *prūd* fr. O.F.): proud, *Frn* 60; valiant, *Crl* 56.

prīs *n.* (OF *pris.*): value, worth, *Hvl* 283, *Orf* 27.

prūd *adj.* Vr. of **proud;** *Hvl* 302.

Q

quaint *adj.* Also **queint.** (OF *cointe.*): skillful, clever, *Sqr* 692.

quath *v.* P. sg. of **quęthen;** *Hvl* 606.

queint *adj.* Vr. of **quaint;** *Lnf* 536.

quellen *v.* P. **quelde;** ppl. **quelled.** (OE *cwellan.*): kill, *Hrn* 65.

quēn *n.* (OE *cwēn.*): queen, *Hrn* 1531, *Orf* 39.

quęthen *v.* P. quath/quoth/quod. (OE *cwethan*—cwaeth, cwǣdon.): say, speak—used in the p.; *Hrn* 131, *Hvl* 1951.

quick *adj.* (OE *cwic.*): alive, *Hrn* 90.

quiten *v.* (OF *quiter.*): pay, repay, *Gml* 512.

quod *v.* P. sg. of **quęthen;** *Hvl* 1800.

R

rāpe *n.* (ON; cp. OI *hrapa* v. "hurry."): (need for) haste, *Hrn* 1430.

rāpe *adj.* (ON; cp. n. and adv.): hasty, *Gml* 101.

rāpely *adv.* (ON; cp. OI *hrapal-liga* "hurriedly."): quickly, *Gml* 219, 424.

raughte *v.* P. sg. of **rechen;** *Ath* 154.

rechen *v.* P. **raughte.** (OE *raeccan.*): reach, *Ath* 154.

rechen *v.* Also **recken.** P. **roughte.** (OE *reccen.*): care, heed, *Hrn* 356, *Gml* 881.

rẹd *n.* (OE *rǣd.*): advice, *Hvl* 518; remedy, *Hvl* 148; counsel, *Hvl* 180.

rẹd *adj.* (OE *rēad.*): red, *Hvl* 1262, red-haired, *Hvl* 1686.

rẹden *v.* P. redde/radde; p. ppl. rẹd/rād. (OE *raedan.*): advise, counsel, *Hrn* 187, *Lnf* 39.

rēfe *n.* (ME fr. OE *gerēfa.*): official, magistrate, *Hvl* 1627.

refte *v.* P. sg. of **ręven;** *Hvl* 94.

rent *n.* (OF *rente.*): income, *Frn* 282.

rēs n. (OE rǣes.) : anger, Gml 101; attack, sudden swoop, Gml 547.

reuthe n. Also rewthe. (OE hrēowe.) : pity, ruth, Lnf 99.

rēven v. P. refte. (OE rēafian.) : rob, deprive, Hvl 480—often impers. me reweth "I am sorry"; him hit reweth "he was sorry."

rēwen v. (OE hrēowan) : grieve, Lnf 102.

rīche adj. (OE rīce.) : powerful; rich.

rīden v. P. sg. rǫd; p. pl. riden; ppl. riden. (OE rīdan.) : ride, Hrn 36.

right n. (OE riht.) : justice, Hvl 36; in all rightes, in every respect, Frn 30.

right adv. (OE rihte.) : right, directly, Orf 142; exactly, Hvl 872; properly, Hvl 420; full right, straightway, immediately, Orf 61.

rīke n. (ON; cp. OI rīki.) : kingdom, Hvl 290.

rīve adj. (ON; cp. OI rīfr.) : aplently, much, Gml 783.

rōd n. (OE rōd.) : cross, Hrn 332.

rōde n. (OE rudu.) : complexion, Orf 83.

rout n. (OF route.) : press, throng, Trn 173.

S

sāmen adv. (ON; cp. OI saman.) : together, Hvl 467.

sat v. P. sg. form of sitten; Hvl 399.

satte v. P. pl. of sitten; Gml 629.

saugh v. P. of sēn; Gml 628.

sclāvin n. (OF esclavine.) : pilgrim's mantle, Orf 204.

sę n. (OE sǣ.) : sea, Hrn 121.

sēchen v. Also sēken. P. soghte/ soughte; ppl. soght/sought. (OE sēcan.) : seek, Hrn 173.

seck n. (ON; cp. OI sekkr.) : sack, Hvl 2019.

sēde v. P. sg. of seyen; Hrn 313.

seighe v. P. of sēn; Orf 123, Frn 157.

selve adj. (OE selfa.) : same, very, Frn 94.

sęly adj. (OE sǣlig.) : blessed, Frn 170; innocent, Hvl 477.

sēn v. Pres. sg. sē/sēst/sēth; pres. pl. sēn; p. sg. saw/say/seigh/sigh/ saugh/sagh; p. pl. sawen/sayen; p. ppl. sayen/sayn/sēn. (OE sēon.) : see—often in asseverations: God you see, may God look after you.

sergaunz n. pl. (OF sergant.) : men-at-arms, Hvl 1929.

seten v. P. pl. and ppl. of sitten; Hvl 1738.

sęthe adv. Vr. of sithen; Lnf 1036; Gwn 298.

sęthen adv. Vr. of sithen; Orf 563.

setten v. Pres. sg. set; p. sette; ppl. set. (OE settan.) : set, place, Hvl 2612; appoint, set up, Hvl 266; compose, Lnf 4.

seyen v. Pres. say/sey; p. sēde/seide. (OE secgan.) : say, Frn 105.

shall v. (OE sceol, fr. sculan.) : will, shall—indicating futurity, Hvl 21.

shāme n. (OE scamu.) : shame, disgrace, Hvl 799.

shaw n. (OE sceaga.) : thicket, grove, Gml 788.

shē pron. Also sho. (Orig. obsc.) : she, Hvl 174.

shenchen v. (OE scencan.) : pour (out), serve, Hrn 374.

shenden v. P. shende/shente; ppl. shended/shent. (OE scendan.) : revile, Hrn 326.

shērrēf n. (OE scīrgerēfa.) : sheriff, Gml 613.

shilden v. (OE scildan.) : shield, ward off, Frn 101.

shīr adj. (OE scīr.) : bright, Hvl 588, Lnf 247.

shō n. Pl. shōn. (OE scēoh.) : shoe, Hvl 860.

sho pron. Vr. of shē; Hvl 112.

shod v. P. of shoen; Hvl 971.

shoen v. P. shod. (OE scoian.) : shoe, Hvl 1138.

sholde v. Also **shulde**. (OE *sceolde*, fr. *sculan*.): should, would, would be obliged to, *Orf* 20.

shrēwe n. (?Fr. OE *scrēawa* "shrew-mouse."): rogue, miscreant, *Hrn* 60.

shrīden v. Ppl. **shrid**. (OE *scrÿdan*.): wear, *Hvl* 963; clothe, *Hvl* 978.

shrūden v. P. **shrudde**. (OE *scrÿdan*.): clothe; disguise, *Hrn* 1476.

shulde v. Vr. of **sholde**; *Hvl* 245.

sibbe n. (OE *sibb.*): relation, kin, *Hrn* 68.

sīde n. (OE): side, *Orf* 132; with preceding *by* plus object: beside; *by a forest side*, beside a forest, *Frn* 151.

sīken v. (OE *sīcan.*): sigh, *Hrn* 430, *Hvl* 291.

siker adj. (OE *sicor.*): sure, *Orf* 11.

sikerly adv. (OE *sicerlīce.*): certainly, *Frn* 97.

sister n. Also **suster/soster**. (ON; cp. OI *systir*; vr. fr. OE *sweoster.*): sister, *Hvl* 911.

sith adv. Vr. of **sithen**; *Sqr* 1112.

sithen adv. Also **sith/sethen/sethe**. (OE *siththen.*): afterwards, *Hvl* 399.

sithen conj. (OE *siththen.*): after, *Hvl* 1888.

sitten v. P. sg. **sat**; p. pl. **satten/seten**; ppl. **seten**. (OE *sittan.*): sit, *Hvl* 1316.

skāpen v. (ME fr. OF *eschaper.*): escape, *Gml* 576.

skāthe n. (ON; cp. OI *skathi.*): harm, *Gml* 488.

skēt adv. (ON; cp OI *skjōtt.*): quickly, *Hvl* 1926.

slēn v. Also **slōn**. Pres. sg. **slow/slough**; pres. pl. **slōwen**; ppl. **slain/slawen**. (OE *slēan.*): slay, kill.

slēp n. (OE): sleep, *Frn* 208.

slōn v. Inf. vr. of **slēn**; *Hrn* 47.

small adj. (OE *smael.*): small; slender, *Orf* 85.

smīten v. P. **smǫt**. (OE *smītan.*): smite, *Hvl* 1854.

smǫt v. P. sg. of **smītan**; *Hvl* 1676.

snell adj. (OE): active, bold, *Hrn* 1475.

sǫ adj. (OE *swā.*): thus, *Hrn* 215; to such an extent, *Orf* 15.

sǫ conj. (OE *swā.*): as, *Hvl* 279—often used to introduce asseverations; *so Christ me mote rede*, as Christ may counsel me; *so as*, whereas, even though, *Hvl* 337; *so . . . so . . .*, as . . . as . . . , *Hrn* 314.

softe adv. (OE): softly, easily, *Hvl* 305; steadily, *Hvl* 2618.

sǫlās n. (OF *solas.*): comfort; merriment, amusement; pleasure, *Lnf* 9.

som pron. Also **sum**. (OE *sum.*): some, *Lnf* 379.

som adj. Also **sum**. (OE *sum.*): some, *Lnf* 448; *som time*, at one time, *Orf* 7.

sǫnde n. (OE *sand.*): messenger, *Hrn* 275.

sone n. Pl. **sones**. (OE *sunu.*): son, *Hrn* 23.

sōne adv. (OE *sōna.*): quickly, straightway, *Hvl* 78; *sone so*, as soon as, *Hrn* 204.

sǫng v. P. sg. of **singen**; *Frn* 181.

sonne n. (OE *sunne.*): sun, *Lnf* 989.

sǫr n. (OE *sār.*): pain, *Hvl* 1985; sorrow, *Hvl* 234.

sǫre adv. (OE *sāre.*): bitterly, greatly, *Frn* 73.

sorrwe n. Also **sorr(e)ghe**. (OE *sorg.*): sorrow, anxiety, *Hrn* 265.

sǫrry adj. (OE *sārig.*): sad, *Hvl* 151; wretched, mean, *Hvl* 2229; deplorable, grievous, *Gml* 547.

soster n. Vr. of **sister**; *Frn* 244.

sōthe n. (OE *soth.*): truth, *Lnf* 1004 —often in asseverations and rhyme phr.'s, as *in soth*, *for soth*.

sōthlike adv. (OE *sōthlīce.*): truly, indeed, *Hvl* 276.

souchen v. (OF *souchier.*): suspect, *Frn* 275.

sought v. P. of **sēken**; *Gml* 764.

soul n. (OE *sāwol.*): soul, *Ath* **485**

soun *n.* Also **sūn.** (OF *soun.*) : sound, *Orf* 248.

sounde *n.* (ME fr. OE *sund adj.* "healthy.") : health; *with sounde*, safely, *Frn* 51.

spēden *v.* (OE *spēdan.*) : make succeed, *Gml* 827.

spēken *v.* P. sg. **spak;** p. pl. **spēken/spāken;** ppl. **spōken.** (OE *specan,* fr. *sprecan.*) : speak, *Hrn* 93.

spell *n.* (OE *spell.*) : story, *Hvl* 338.

spēre *n.* (OE *spere.*) : spear, *Hvl* 380.

spillen *v.* P. **spil(le)de;** ppl. **spild/spilt.** (OE *spillan.*) : perish, *Hrn* 198.

sprēden *v.* P. **sprad.** (OE *sprǣdan.*) : spread, *Hvl* 2920; grow, *Orf* 43.

sprengen *v.* (OE) : sprinkle, *Gml* 503.

spūse *n.* (OF) : wife, *Hrn* 426.

staf *n.* Pl. **stāves.** (OE *staef.*) : staff, cudgel, *Gml* 536.

stalworthe *adj.* Also **stalworth.** (OE *staelwyrthe.*) : stalwart, *Orf* 3.

standen *v.* Also **stōnden.** Pres. sg. **stant/stont;** p. **stōd;** ppl. **standen/stōnden.** (OE *standan.*) : stand.

stant *v.* Pres. sg. of **standen;** *Gml* 812.

stark *adj.* (OE *stearc.*) : strong, *Hvl* 341.

stēde *n.* (OE *stēda.*) : steed, *Hvl* 10.

stēde *n.* (OE *stede.*) : place, location, *Hvl* 142.

stēm *n.* (OE *stēam.*) : ray of light, *Hvl* 591.

stēpel *n.* (OE) : steeple, *Frn* 158.

stert *n.* (OE *steort.*) : tail, *Hvl* 2823.

steven *n.* (OE *stefn.*) : voice, *Hvl* 1275.

steward *n.* Also **stiward.** (OE *stīweard.*) : steward—usu. used for the chief official of a manorial household.

stille *adv.* (OE *stille.*) : secretly, privately, *Hrn* 291.

stōn *n.* (OE *stān.*) : stone, *Hvl* 569; precious stone, *Hvl* 1633.

stound *n.* (OE *stund.*) : while, time,

Gml 349; hour, *Frn* 213; *in a stounde*, at once, *Hrn* 337.

stoute *adj.* (OF *estout.*) : hardy, bold; stately, *Lnf* 985.

strōnde *n.* (OE *strand.*) : shore, *Hrn* 115.

strōnge *adv.* (OE *strange.*) : strongly, bitterly, *Ath* 636.

stȳ *n.* (OE *stīg.*) : road, way, *Hvl* 2618.

sum *pron.* Vr. of som; *Orf* 376.

sum *adj.* Vr. of som; *Hvl* 1092.

sūn *n.* Vr. of soun; *Hrn* 213.

suster *n.* Vr. of sister; *Lnf* 82.

sūthe *adv.* Vr. of swithe.

swain *n.* (ON; cp. OI *sveinn.*) : servant, *Gml* 527.

swank *v.* P. sg. of swinken; *Hvl* 788.

swēre *n.* (OE *sweora.*) : neck, *Hrn* 408.

swēte *adj.* (OE *swēte.*) : sweet; dear—often used in phr.'s of endearment.

swich *adj.* (OE *swylc.*) : such, *Gml* 747, *Lnf* 1007, *Frn* 295; *swiche on,* such a one, *Frn* 317.

swīke *n.* (OE *swica.*) : traitor, *Hvl* 423.

swikel *adj.* (OE *swicol.*) : treacherous, *Hvl* 1108.

swingen *v.* Ppl. **swungen.** (OE *swingan.*) : beat, *Hvl* 214.

swinken *v.* P. **swank.** (OE *swincan.*) : toil, *Hvl* 798.

swīthe *adv.* Also **sūthe.** (OE *swithe.*) : very, exceedingly, *Hvl* 111; quickly, immediately, *Hvl* 140; *as swithe as,* as soon as, *Gml* 541.

swōnen *v.* (OE *geswōgan.*) : swoon, *Orf* 173.

swungen *v.* P. ppl. of **swingen;** *Hvl* 226.

T

tabour *n.* (OF) : tabor, small drum, *Hvl* 2329.

tāken *v.* P. **tōk;** ppl. **tāken.** (ON; cp. OI *taka.*) : take, *Gml* 96; give, commit, *Frn* 200.

tęchen v. P. taughte. (OE tǣcan.): teach, Hrn 244; entrust, Hvl 2214.

tēl n. (OE): withouten tel, without reproach, Hvl 191.

telde v P. ppl. form of tellen; Lnf 576.

tellen v. P. tǫlde/telde. (OE tellan.): tell, relate, Hvl 3; add up, reckon, Hvl 2615; account, Hvl 1036; litel man of him tolde, people thought little of him, Lnf 189.

tēn v. (OE tēon.): go, Frn 49.

tēne n. (OE tēona.): vexation, anger, Hrn 353.

than adv. Also thanne. (OE): then, Lnf 988.

than conj. (OE): than, Hrn 320, Lnf 1002; than if, Hvl 944.

thanne adv. Vr. of than; Hvl 51.

thare adv. Vr. of thēr; Frn 194.

that dem. pron. (OE thaet.): that, Hvl 565; with that, thereupon, then, Lnf 1012.

that rel. pron. (OE): that, Hvl 726; who, Hvl 2361; often with superfluous pron. following: that . . . he, who, Hvl 2392; that . . . his, whose, Hvl 28; that . . . hem, whom, Hvl 2966; that it, which, Hvl 2686; that which, Hvl 668.

that dem. adj. (OE): that, Hvl 166.

that conj. (OE): that, Hvl 571; so that, Hvl 548; in order that, Hvl 18; until, Hvl 576; because, Hvl 161; by that, by the time that, Frn 238.

thē n. (OE thēh.): thigh, Hvl 1983.

thēd n. (OE thēod.): land, country, Orf 511.

theder adv. Vr. of thider; Ath 547, Sqr 524.

thēf n. (OE thēof.): thief, Hrn 327.

thegh conj. Vr. of they; Hrn 321.

thēn v. (OE thēon "thrive."): so mot I well the, as I may prosper, Gml 833.

thenchen v. Vr. of thenken; Orf 349.

thenken v. Also thenchen. (OE thencan.): think, Hvl 306.

thenne adv. Also thennes. (OE thanon; also with ME adverbial -s.): thence, Hvl 777, Gml 545.

thēr adv. Also thare/thore. (OE thǣr.): there, at that place, Hrn 302.

thēr subord. conj. (OE thǣr.): there where, Lnf 228.

thēw adj. (OE thēow.): bound, serf, Hvl 2205.

they pron. (ON; cp. OI their, pl. of sā "this, that."): they, Gml 625.

they conj. Also thegh. (OE thēh, also thēah.): although, Orf 149.

thider adv. Also theder. (OE): thither, Frn 218.

thīn pron. adj. (OE): your (thine), Hrn 1466.

thing n. (OE): thing, Hvl 66; pl.: affairs, Orf 194: for no thing, on no account, Hvl 1936.

thinken v. P. thoughte. (OE thyncan, p. thūhte.): me thinketh, it seems to me, Gml 632.

this dem. adj. (OE this, neut. of thēs; pl. form fr. the sg.): this, Hvl 260; these, Hvl 1145.

thǫ dem. pron. (OE thā.): these, Lnf 156.

thǫ adv. (OE thā.): then, Orf 25.

thǫ conj. (OE thā.): when, Gml 191.

thou pron. Also thū. (OE thū.): you (thou), Hvl 388.

thraw n. Vr. of throw; Hvl 1215.

thridde adj. (OE thridda.): third, Gml 687.

thrīven v. P. thrīved. (ON; cp. OI thrifask reflex. v.): thrive, Ath 692, Frn 235; often in asseverations: so mot I thrive, as I may prosper, Crl 205; evel mot I thrive, may I prosper ill, Gml 586.

throw n. Also thraw. (OE thrāg.): time, short space, Hrn 340.

thrǫwen v. (OE thrāwan.): throw, Hrn 1502.

thū pron. Vr. of thou; Hvl 662.

thurch prep. Vr. of thurgh; Frn 148.

thurfen *pret. pres. v.* Pres. sg. thar/
tharf; p. thurfte. (OE *thurfan.*):
need, *Lnf* 103; in preterite: might,
Hvl 10.

thurgh *prep.* Also thurch/thurth. (OE
thurh.): through, *Gml* 28.

thurth *prep.* Vr. of thurgh; *Orf* 213.

thȳ *poss. adj.* (OE *thīn.*): thine
(your), *Frn* 66.

tīden *v.* (OE *tīdan.*): betide, befall;
well mote thee tide, may (things)
fall out well for you, *Hrn* 208.

tīdinge *n.* Also tīthinge. (ON; cp. OI
tīthindi.): news, tidings, *Hrn* 132.

tō *adv.* (OE): too, *Hvl* 689.

tō *prep.* (OE): as; *to his leman,* for
his paramour, *Frn* 272.

tō- *v. prefix.* (OE): utterly, to pieces;
tohewen, cut to pieces, *Hvl* 2001,
toshattered, completely shattered,
Trn 161.

tōdrawen *v.* Forms at drawen. (ME):
draw to pieces (as punishment or
form of execution), *Hrn* 185.

tōfǫre *conj.* (OE *tōforan.*): before,
Hrn 1448.

tōgider *adv.* (OE *tōgaedre.*): together,
Orf 97.

tōk *v.* P. sg. of tāken; *Hvl* 114.

tonge *n.* Vr. of tunge; *Frn* 112.

toun *n.* Also tūn. (OE *tun.*): town;
gon to toune, set out; *Hrn* 157.

tour *n.* Also tūr. (OF): tower, *Orf*
335.

tōyēnes *prep.* (OE *tōgēanes.*): against,
Hrn 60.

trēwe *adj.* (OE *trēowe.*): true, faithful, loyal, *Hrn* 381.

trēwe *adv.* (Fr. adj.): faithfully, truly,
Hrn 1534.

trewthe *n.* Also throwthe. (OE
thrēowth.) truth, pledged word,
Hrn 676.

trome *n.* (OE *truma.*): troop, *Hvl* 8.

-tū *pron.* (OE): you—postclitic 2nd
per. sg., as in *wenestu* "do you
think"; *Hvl* 1787.

tūn *n.* Vr. of toun.

tunge *n.* Also tonge. (OE *tunge.*):
tongue, *Hvl* 369.

tūr *n.* Vr. of tour; *Hrn* 1449.

tweie *num. adj.* Also tweien/twain/
twaien. (OE *twegen.*): two, twain,
Hrn 350.

U

uncouth *adj.* (OE *uncūth.*): foreign,
strange, *Orf* 511, *Sqr* 136.

under *prep.* (OE): close by, *Lnf* 222.

undren *n.* (OE): the time between six
and nine in the morning; nine
o'clock in the morning; noon; mid-
afternoon—a designation shifting
from context to context.

undrentīde *n.* (OE *underntīde.*): the
time of undren (q.v.); *Orf* 41, *Lnf*
210.

unnēthe *adv.* (OE *unēathe.*): with
difficulty, *Orf* 197.

urn *v.* P. sg. of ernan; *Orf* 61.

W

wāden *v.* (OE *wadan.*): go, *Hvl* 2645.

wain *n.* (OE *waegn.*): cart, wagon,
Gml 528.

wālāway *interj.* Also weilawei. (OE
wā lā wā. Also *wei lā wei.*): alas,
Hvl 462; *walaway maken,* make
lamentation, *Hrn* 1490.

wan *adj.* (OE *wann.*): pale, *Orf* 84.

wantede *v.* P. sg. of wanten; *Hvl* 1243.

wanten *v.* P. wantede. (ON; cp. OI
vanta.): be lacking, *Hvl* 712.

war *adj.* (OE *waer.*): conscious,
aware, *Gml* 497.

warien *v.* (OE *waergan.*): curse, *Hvl*
433.

wāwe *n.* Vr. of wǫwe; *Hvl* 474.

wax *v.* P. sg. of wexen; *Frn* 152.

wēd *n.* (OE *wāēd.*): clothing, *Hvl* 94,
Orf 122.

weder *n.* (OE): weather, *Frn* 150.

weilawei *interj.* Vr. of wālāway; *Hvl*
570.

wēle *n.* (OE *wela* n. "prosperity."):
in wele and wo, in good and bad

fortune, *Sqr* 113; *for wele ne wo*, for weal or woe, on any account, *Hvl* 2777.

wele *adv.* Vr. of well; *Frn* 161.

well *adv.* Also **wele**. (OE): well, *Hvl* 29; very, *Orf* 47.

wēnden *v.* P. **wēnde;** ppl. **went.** (OE *wendan*.): go, depart, *Lnf* 80; turn, *Gml* 703.

wēnen *v.* P. **wēnde;** ppl. **wǫnde/went.** (OE *wēnan*.): think, suppose, assume, *Hrn* 301.

wēpe *n.* (ME fr. *wēpen*.): lamentation, *Orf* 210.

wēpen *v.* P. pl. **wēpen.** (OE *wēpan*.): weep, *Hvl* 152.

wer *n.* (OE *werre* fr. OF.): war, *Frn* 5.

werchen *v.* Vr. of **wirchen;** *Gml* 507.

werd *n.* (OE *weorold*.): world, *Hvl* 1290.

weren *v.* (OE *werian*.): defend, *Hvl* 2152.

werk *n.* (OE *werc*.): work, *Hvl* 866; pl.: deeds, *Hvl* 34.

wernen *v.* (OE *wiernan*.): deny, *Gml* 662.

wers *adj.* (OE *wyrsa*.): worse, *Frn* 82.

werst *superl. adj.* Vr. of **worst.**

wet *adj.* (OE): wet, *Orf* 56.

wexen *v.* Also **waxen.** P. **wēx/wāx/wǫx;** ppl. **waxen/woxen.** (OE *weaxan*.): grow, *Hrn* 99, *Orf* 38.

whan *conj.* Vr. of **when;** *Lnf* 990.

whanne *conj.* Vr. of **when;** *Ath* 567.

when *conj.* Also **whenne/whanne.** (OE *hwaenne*, also *hwanne*.): when, *Ath* 624.

whenne *conj.* Vr. of **when;** *Ath* 78.

whēr *subord. adv. conj.* (OE *hwāēr*.): wherever, *Hrn* 322.

whider *adv.* (OE *hwider*.): whither, *Orf* 104.

whīl *n.* (OE *hwīl*.): space, time, *Gml* 546, *Sqr* 878; *other whil*, on another occasion, *Orf* 273; *som while*, at one time, *Lnf* 7.

wicke *adj.* (ME fr. (?) OE *wicca* n. "wizard."): wicked, evil, *Hvl* 66; wretched, *Hvl* 2825.

wīde *adv.* (OE *wīde*.): far and wide, *Hvl* 959.

widwe *n.* (OE): widow, *Hvl* 33.

wīf *n.* Pl. **wīves.** (OE *wīf*.): woman, *Hvl* 1; wife, *Trn* 200.

wight *adj.* (ON: cp. OI *vigt*.): courageous, bold, *Hvl* 9.

wīke *n.* (OE *wicu*.): week, *Gml* 687.

wiket *n.* (OF *guichet*.): wicket (small door within a gate), *Gml* 563.

wille *n.* (OE *willa*.): will, desire, *Frn* 291.

wiltow *v.* (ME *wilt* and *thou*.): will you (thou), *Orf* 104.

winter *n.* Pl. **winters/winter.** (OE): winter, *Orf* 235; in pl.: years, *Frn* 238.

wirchen *v.* Also **werchen/worchen.** P. **wroughte.** (OE *wyrcan*.): work, *Hvl* 510.

wīsen *v.* Vr. of **wissen.**

wissen *v.* Also **wīsen.** P. **wissede;** ppl. **wissed.** (OE *wissian* and *wisian*.): instruct, *Hrn* 241.

wit *n.* (OE *witt*.): wit, intelligence, *Hrn* 178.

witen *v.* (OE *witian*.): govern, *Orf* 182.

wīten *pret. pres. v.* Pres. sg. **wǫst, wǫt;** pres. pl. **witen;** p. **wiste;** ppl. **wist.** (OE *witan*.): know; know about, learn, *Hrn* 292—often used vaguely in the phr. *I wot* "I know, I suspect, I suppose," esp. as a rhyme tag.

witterly *adv.* (ON; cp. OI *viturliga* adv. "wisely."): certainly, indeed, *Ath* 80.

wǫ *n.* (OE *wā*.): sorrow, sadness, *Hrn* 267.

wǫ *adj.* (Fr. n.): distressed; *wo him was*, he was in distress, *Frn* 88.

wōd *adj.* (OE): angry, enraged; insane, *Ath* 250, *Gml* 472.

wōde *n.* Also **wude.** (OE *wudu*.): wood, *Hrn* 234.

wolves-hęd n. (OE): cryen (maken) wolves-hed, declare outlawed, Gml 700.

wǫn n. (ON; cp. OI vān.): opinion; by mine wone, in my opinion, Hvl 1711; quantity; ful god won, very large number, Hvl 1024, Lnf 360.

wonder n. Also wunder. (OE wundor.): wonder, miraculous thing, Hrn 282; I have wonder, I wonder, Frn 65.

wonder adv. Also wunder. (Fr. OE wundor n. as used in cpd.'s.): very, extremely, Gml 732.

wone adj. (OE wuna.): accustomed, Hvl 2151.

wonen v. (OE wunian.): dwell, Hvl 105; to be accustomed to—sometimes followed by an infinitive without to; cp. Hrn 36.

wǫng n. (OE wang.): field, Hvl 397.

worchen v. Vr. of wirchen; Gml 500.

wōrd n. Also wurd. (OE): word, Hvl 959.

wors adj. Also wurs/wers. (OE wyrs.): worse, Hrn 120.

worst superl. adj. Also wurst/werst. (OE wyrst.): worst, Hrn 72.

worthen v. Also wurthen. (OE woerthan.): be, Gml 491; fut. aux.: will be, Hrn 688; often in exclamations: ever worthe him wo, may evil ever be his lot, Hvl 2221.

wōwe n. Also wāwe. (OE wāg.): wall, Hvl 2078.

wręken v. P. wrak; ppl. wrēken/ wrǫken. (OE wrecan.): avenge, Hvl 1884.

wreyen v. (OE wregan.): betray; reveal, Lnf 146.

wreyere n. (OE wregere.): traitor, Hvl 39.

wrǫken v. P. ppl. of wręken; Gml 541.

wroughte v. P. of wirchen; Gml 525.

wurd n. Vr. of word; Ath 87.

wurthe v. Pres. subj. sg. vr. of worthen; Hvl 434.

Y

yaf v. P. sg. of yeven; Gml 500, Lnf 67.

yāre adv. (OE gearwe.): well, quickly, readily, Hrn 471.

yat n. Vr. of gat; Gml 293.

y-coren adj. (OE gecoren, p. ppl. of cēosan "to choose."): exquisite, Orf 81.

yē nom. pl. pron. (OE gē.): you, Hvl 11.

yē adv. (OE gēa.): yes, yea, Crl 482.

yēd v. Vr. of yēde; Rgn 804.

yēde v. Also yēd/yēode/yōd/yōde. (OE ēode.): went, walked, Hvl 6— the p. form of gon.

yef conj. Vr. of yif; Lnf 972.

yēmen v. P. yēmede; ppl. yēmed. (OE gīeman.): control, have charge of, Hvl 2276; govern, rule, Hvl 975; supervise, Gml 267; take care of, Hvl 1753.

yēode v. Vr. of yēde; Hrn 384.

yēr n. (OE gēar.): year, Lnf 1024.

yęrd n. (1) (OE geard.): yard, enclosure, Hvl 702.

yęrd n. (2) (OE gierd.): stick, rod, Ath 274.

yērne adv. (OE georne.): eagerly, earnestly, Hvl 153.

yērnen v. (OE geornian.): desire, Hvl 299.

yeven v. Also yiven. P. yaf: ppl. yeven/yoven. (OE giefan.): give, Hvl 22.

yif subord. conj. Also yef/if. (OE gif.): if, Hrn 111, Frn 81; yif that, provided, Gml 663—but if, see but conj.

yiven v. Vr. of yeven; Orf 430.

y-nough adv. Also y-nowe. (OE genog.): enough.

yōd v. Vr. of yēde; Rgn 836.

yōde *v.* Vr. of **yēde;** *Ath* 647.

yong *adj.* Also **young.** (OE *geong.*):
young, *Hrn* 283.

yǫre *adv.* (OE *geara.*): long ago, some
time ago, *Lnf* 108.

yoven *v.* P. ppl. of **yeven;** *Hvl* 224.

y-wis *adv.* Also **y-wisse.** (OE
gewisse.): certainly, indeed—often
a meaningless rhyme word.